Servants and Friends does not get c
world principles of leadership, bu
exploration of biblical foundations _____ _____y contexts. This book should be read widely by those engaged in the on-
the-ground work of spiritual leadership: leadership that cultivates
the transformation of people and their world.

Kurt N. Fredrickson
Associate Dean for Doctor of Ministry and Continuing Education
Assistant Professor of Pastoral Ministry
Fuller Theological Seminary

Servants and Friends is an outstanding anthology on a biblical
theology of leadership. The impressive collection of contributing
authors not only balances both Old and New Testament leadership examples and definitions, but also skillfully integrates current
leadership theory. The third section of the book is an exceptionally
rich look at some biblical narratives including women in leadership,
contextualization, and empowerment. As the church continues to
be confronted with new leadership paradigms, *Servants and Friends*
is a valuable resource to help the church recalibrate its perspective
of leadership with solid theological truth.

Larry Lindquist
Associate Professor and Director of Leadership Development
Denver Seminary

This is a rich and thoroughly researched book. The breadth and
depth of this powerful book will make it an excellent guide for
Christian leaders, especially for framing and fulfilling their calling
from a biblical point of view. It will be a valued resource for me, and
I'm sure many others, for years to come.

Nick Howard
Christian leadership consultant, coach, and trainer
www.drnickhoward.com

This splendid compilation of biblical insight and guidance should prove to be one of the most valuable treasures of spiritual and professional wisdom available to leaders of this era in any context. It achieves the noble goal of "teaching" universal truths for leadership that "both transcends human experience and transforms human relationships."

Ella Smith Simmons
General Vice President
General Conference of Seventh-day Adventists

Servants and Friends is a well-conceived book describing and analyzing a biblical perspective of leadership. Regardless of religious persuasion, the accounts and historical profiles are instructive for understanding leadership.... For those seeking guidelines for Christian leadership aptly described by Dr. Bell as "for some, as for us, scripture is normative for the way leadership is understood and practiced," the book is surely a must.

Daniel W. Wheeler
Professor Emeritus of Leadership Studies
University of Nebraska-Lincoln

Skip Bell has assembled a group of skilled leaders and biblical scholars who share their research in a compelling and theologically sound basis. The principles of leadership discussed here are vitally important to every area of our lives—including business, education, family, and church.

James W. Gilley
President & CEO
Three Angels Broadcasting Network

SERVANTS
&FRIENDS

A BIBLICAL THEOLOGY OF LEADERSHIP

Skip Bell, Editor

Andrews University Press

Berrien Springs, Michigan

Andrews University Press
Sutherland House
8360 W. Campus Circle Dr.
Berrien Springs, MI 49104–1700
Telephone: 269-471-6134
Fax: 269-471-6224
Email: aupo@andrews.edu
Website: http://universitypress.andrews.edu

ISBN 978-1-883925-90-1 (paperback)
ISBN 978-1-883925-95-6 (e-book)

Printed in the United States of America
21 20 19 18 17   3 4 5 6 7

Library of Congress Cataloging-in-Publication Data

Servants and friends : a biblical theology of leadership / edited by Skip Bell.
    pages cm
    ISBN 978-1-883925-90-1 (pbk.)
    1. Leadership in the Bible. 2. Leadership—Biblical teaching. I. Bell, Skip,
editor of compilation.
    BS680.L4S47 2014
    262'.1--dc23
                        2013048649

Project Director	Ronald Alan Knott
Project Editor	Deborah L. Everhart
Line Editor	Ronald Alan Knott
Copy Editors	Rose Decaen, Paul State
Editorial Assistant	Nathan Berglund
Indexer	Carol J. Schoun
Cover Designer	Robert N. Mason
Text Designer	Arielle Pickett
Proofreader	Rose Decaen

Typeset: 12/14 Adobe Garamond Pro

To those who joined in this effort,
my colleagues who form the relational community
from which we serve,
and, more personally,
to Joni, the love of my life,
who has led me to joy.

Contents

SECTION TWO:
THE NEW TESTAMENT

SECTION THREE:
SELECTED BIBLICAL NARRATIVES

Permission Statements for Bible Translations

Foreword

The title of this book brings to center stage both the promise and the dangers faced by such a work. By choosing to write *A Biblical Theology of Leadership,* the editor and contributors face a number of challenges that lie embedded in these significant words. A *biblical theology* requires the navigation of a series of critical decisions that will guide and influence the entire process. Any thorough treatment of *leadership* will demand definitions and the acknowledgment of presuppositions upon which the entire work is based. Taken together, the writing of a biblical theology of leadership is a daunting task.

The editor and contributors are to be commended both for their courage in attempting such a challenging piece of work and for the quality and clarity with which they have accomplished it. In your reading of this text, I would encourage you to pay special attention to the writers' adept handling of five critical tensions that will naturally emerge in a work of this nature.

The first tension is stated up-front. The writers acknowledge that a true biblical theology of leadership will both transcend and transform people and cultures. This is no easy task. Yet the book gives adequate and careful treatment to both sides of this tension. The writers acknowledge that a study of leadership must understand and draw from the culture in which it is practiced, lest it become a detached theory of little practical use. On the other hand, they develop the argument that effective leadership must also transcend culture if it is to speak critically into it and serve as an agent of transformation. The theology they develop successfully navigates this important tension and provides us with an understanding that has the potential to inform and instruct leaders who can be used by God to lead and serve faithfully wherever they are called.

A second tension they navigate successfully is the balance in their understanding of leadership as either a replication of characteristics of historic successful leaders or a process of inner transformation that produces right decisions and actions contributing to effective leadership. Far too many leadership studies throw us back upon ourselves to mimic the attitudes and actions of successful leaders. When we are told that there are "12 marks of a successful leader," or "21 habits of effective leadership," our role as leaders is reduced to impersonation rather than transformation. This book does an excellent job of drawing on the experience and characteristics of biblical leaders without falling prey to this temptation. They see these practices as the fruit of the inner transformation that is taking place in the hearts of God's people and, as such, allow us to embrace these attitudes and actions without being required to simply mimic them in order to be effective. The writers also acknowledge the flawed, human side of the biblical figures who illustrate leadership relationships. We are all beneficiaries of this critical balance which has been achieved in this book.

The third tension is endemic in biblical theologies. It is the balance the authors choose to strike between an emphasis on quality biblical exegesis and the extent to which they draw out what that exegesis means for life and praxis. It is clear that this book is not meant to be a scholarly work of biblical exegesis for its own sake. It is also not a how-to leadership book that features scattered Bible verses and the occasional Hebrew and Greek root words and called itself a biblical theology. The authors have done a commendable job of providing us with solid, biblical exegetical work while continually drawing out the clear implications they have seen emerge from Scripture. This balance of scholarly biblical work and the unambiguous conclusions drawn from that work will serve the church and all Christian leaders.

The fourth tension is the pull of a work of this nature between being descriptive and prescriptive. There is a temptation in scholarly works to present the data and leave it solely to the reader to draw the conclusions. There is a similar temptation in more practical writings to state conclusions in such a way as to be heavy-handed and prescriptive. The authors have provided us with a fine balance between these two errors. The examination of the biblical narratives yields clear descriptions of how God's people have led through the ages. The description of these leadership styles is worth the read alone. The authors are careful to recognize humanity in these narratives while extracting from the descriptions what they believe are unmistakable qualities inherent in authentic biblical leadership. Even here they are not presented as a "take it or leave it" list of absolutes. For this reason every reader will be able to discern for themselves how they will engage with these qualities as they are being transformed to the power of the Holy Spirit into the disciples and leaders God called them to be.

Finally, the authors give us an unequivocal understanding of the direction of this work. That is, they clearly name Scripture as their starting point for their inquiry and conclude by focusing on the nature of God as our source of all of the qualities of authentic leadership. By maintaining a unilateral theological methodology, they avoid the temptation of letting experience shape the biblical message. They also steer clear of reading secular leadership traits back into the biblical revelation of the character and work of God. Their focus on the nature of God as revealed to us in the biblical witness gives this entire work the foundation and credibility to guide the church and her leaders in a reliable and authoritative manner. The authors' insistence on the centrality of Scripture for their work gives us confidence that their conclusions and recommendations align with the highest form of biblical scholarship. And by holding consistently to these two commitments, they have produced a work that does indeed transcend culture while also being able to be used by God to help leaders transform culture as they are being transformed as leaders and followers of Jesus Christ.

For these reasons I am deeply grateful to the team of contributors for writing this book, and I am confident of the substantial impact it will have on the study and practice of faithful, Christ-centered leadership for the sake of God's kingdom and to His glory.

R. Scott Rodin, President
Rodin Consulting

Preface

None of the forty or more seminarians peering at me over their laptops and textbooks dared to respond to the question. The challenges of dealing with a new professor, launching an academic year, and preparing for a career in ministry were daunting enough to silence even the most courageous soul. They also sensed the aim of my query posed on that first day of their church leadership course was deceptively simple. I had asked them, "What is leadership?"

Gathering strength from one another, answers eventually began to flow. Some offered opinion, voiced with conviction or humble uncertainty. Others, hoping to hit the mark, quoted the views of current popular leadership gurus. "Leadership is influence" a student from the southeastern United States confidently proclaimed. A Korean student described leadership as making the right decisions and leading as God intends; a Californian envisioned helping the congregation gain consensus; a South American student eloquently described inspirational leadership; a Kenyan espoused keeping the congregation focused on mission. All spoke from their particular experience and formed their response with the nuances of their culture.

Students inspire us. Their questions, passionate comments, testimonies, and stories of sacrifice combine to remind us why we do what we do. These young men and women define our purpose. They move us to learn as they learn, to study, reflect, research, examine our experience, and write. As they serve God, His world, and His church, we find meaning by contributing to their journey.

This volume is the work of twenty colleagues in theological education who explore a scriptural basis for understanding leadership. The effort reflects our belief that understanding leadership draws us beyond our own situation and experience. As will be explained in the introduction, we approach the shared work with the conviction that truth regarding God is revealed in the Old Testament and New Testament Scripture. Further, as you read this text, you must bear in mind our belief that God intends humankind to reflect His character and will in human interaction. So we offer that knowing God, seeing a revelation of His character in relationship to creation, especially in Jesus, is the key to unlocking universal truths about leadership. How do we go about understanding leadership? We believe the starting point for leadership understanding is theological learning, and the center of that learning process is Scripture. Our understanding of leadership is rooted in what we know of God, and the way humanity approaches the practical challenge of leading should be shaped by truths about God.

Some who pick up this text may not share our convictions about God or Scripture. This text will still offer valuable insights. We invite everyone, regardless of faith position, to consider the light that Scripture can bring to leadership understanding. Certainly the weight of scriptural interpretation is proportionate to the faith one has in God, or what one believes about God. For some, as for us, Scripture is normative for the way leadership is understood and practiced. For others the biblical record may simply be one more resource for understanding leadership.

We offer this work in the hope every reader will recognize common threads of understanding and principles surrounding the nature of leadership that are consistent through the centuries of time, true in differing cultures, and applicable in varying environments, not only the church. We believe these principles reveal and affirm God and His will in our relationships. We are confident that every reader, even if unmoved by the character of God, will recognize that leadership practices that are formed and guided by these emerging principles will contribute joy to their experience!

We share a passion for the church and God's Word. We have undertaken the work knowing that leadership is everyone's opportunity. We believe a biblical foundation for leadership will be blessed by God to transform our personal lives and our life in the public square and in the church.

Various chapters represent the work of biblical, systematic, and applied theologians writing in their own styles. The reader will hear differing personalities and approaches. Still, there is a common voice to our manuscripts. The editing has respected the contribution to theological work each has provided. This book is meant for serious readers who wish to explore a biblical theology of leadership, students who are committed to Scripture and theology. The writing is generally analytical in nature, though there are some moments when the investigation has moved us to more eloquent tones or inspirational application.

When I first considered this book, I consulted a handful of colleagues in theological education regarding the need for such a work. From that time on, my seminary friends have encouraged me to go forward. Their support and encouragement have been essential. It is an incredible blessing to be a part of an empowering community!

As editor, I am indebted, and deeply grateful, to the colleagues who accepted my invitation to join me in writing. By each writing a chapter, they have demonstrated their passion for a biblical theology of leadership. They shared the vision and helped make the book a collaborative effort. I not only respect the scholarship of these colleagues, but also, in the process of our conversations and reflections, I have been blessed to develop new friendships. My thanks goes to each of those women and men for contributing their time, expertise, experience, knowledge, and heart. The administration of the Seventh-day Adventist Theological Seminary of Andrews University has joined the chorus of voices encouraging me in this project.

My friends at Andrews University Press, whose names are listed on the copyright page, have been supportive and encouraging partners. They also have shared a passion for the contribution this volume can make to those who serve. They are professionals in publishing, and they patiently labor to assure the highest standard.

My wife, Joni, has so often listened to my worries regarding this book, skillfully returning my focus to the contribution such a work can make for years to come. She is a true friend, companion, and servant in the most honorable sense of the word. I love Joni deeply, more than words could express, and pray that this book might help raise up other leaders like her.

This effort is for nothing if it does not bring glory to God and advance His purposes for us. Everything good is from God. If this volume makes any difference, it is because of Him and the guidance His Spirit provides in our human endeavors. My colleagues and I prayerfully offer this work as servants and friends. May it be used by Him to bless your service.

Skip Bell, Editor

Introduction

Skip Bell

I s there truth about leadership that both transcends human experience and transforms human relationships? If such truth exists, where do we look for it? We generally develop our understanding of leadership from our culture. Academicians, business leaders, students, and religious leaders alike are commonly shaped, formed, and even led by the culture in which they move, think, and act. In this context, culture refers to the underlying developed habits and styles of a community emerging from a particular and shared worldview. So a Puerto Rican in Queens develops leadership in one cultural perspective, a Sudanese Christian in another.

The question is obvious: Is there actually a basis for leadership understanding more universal than our cultural habits? Is there a need for such universal understanding?

The purpose of this book is to provide a biblical theology as the foundation and starting point for understanding Christian leadership. Such an understanding transcends our various cultures. Questions about leadership require such a foundation. Many theorists and practitioners agree that *leadership* is hard to define. Perhaps it is so because we are looking in the wrong places, or at least not centering our search in the right place. We typically observe leadership in action and seek from that reality clues to improving the human condition through better leadership.

However, for the Christian, leadership understanding must begin with theological inquiry. The challenge is to understand leadership and, through that understanding, to contribute to human life as our Creator wishes. That challenge requires a theological foundation and starting point.

Biblical leadership principles are universal to the leadership challenges experienced in all areas of life—business, education, community, family—and not just the church. In this book, application is most frequently made in the context of the church because our mission is primarily to inform religious leadership.

Four sections form the structure of this book. The first two consist of an examination of the Old Testament and New Testament for the purpose of identifying leadership principles embedded in the scripture. Each testament section begins with selected word studies, then proceeds to exegetical portions. These two sections constitute the largest portion and more scholarly contribution of *Servants and Friends*.

The third section contains studies of selected characters. These chapters are not offered as traditional scholarly work but as narratives for application within the scriptural context. Thus, no synthesis is provided. The contributors were asked to select narratives that most interested them in applying the principles.

The fourth and last section of the book is a summary offering of reflections on biblical principles of leadership and then a biblical theology of leadership. It is meant to provide a scholarly application of biblical principles to our actions as leaders in our communities, families, organizations, schools, and churches. This section is not intended to serve as an exhaustive prescription for administrative procedures; rather, it presents leadership principles broad enough for the reader to apply to the context of their leadership challenges.

THE THEOLOGICAL FOUNDATION
OF LEADERSHIP

Theology lies at the heart of Christian leadership. If a starting point for understanding and defining leadership is imagined, this is it. Theology, however, is many things to many people. In the most expansive sense, *theology* is seeking God and meaning through life experience. To do theology, or to think theologically, in this broadest sense helps us understand God and His ways by reflecting on liturgy and experience, history and ethics, teaching and pastoral care, literature and story, as well as inspired text. The idea of theologically centered leadership suggests the integration of several disciplines, some academic and some personal. Among the contributions of expansive theological reflection to understanding leadership are: (1) it seeks understanding in universal experience, (2) it provides grounds for defining leadership beyond cultural context, and (3) it reveals a capacity within leadership to both transcend and transform people and culture.

This book confronts the idea that leadership is a culturally defined phenomenon, and this is perhaps its most controversial position. Yes, leadership in religious and nonprofit organizations, as in business and secular environments, is shaped by cultural influences. From one perspective, cultural vulnerability and influence are essential to leadership—without that awareness we are at best insensitive and ineffective.

It is vital that we think critically about culture. On the surface culture may appear neutral in relationship to theology. However, culture emerges out of our worldview, the way we think and form beliefs. People of faith think and form beliefs out of reflection on a divine pattern in submission to the teaching and leading of God. In short, theology changes our worldview and ultimately the way we go about living. It follows that theologically centered leadership will inevitably be distinct in some ways from secular culture.

The thoughtful reader will note that a challenge to theological reflection itself emerges at this point. Can theological reflection that transcends culture be experienced in the context of ordinary living by people busily engaged in public life? Can theological reflection be trusted in the realities of life as people go about leadership? Max Stackhouse takes the position that any people can have some prospect of knowing something reliable about God, truth, and justice in a sufficient enough degree to recognize those tenets in views and practices. In fact, we are constantly judging what is and what is not divine, true, and just. Stackhouse argues that sacred text and spiritual thought provide basic authority for that work in any culture when theological reflection is properly approached.[1]

Applying theological reflection to leadership understanding offers the opportunity for persons of faith to extricate themselves from the dominance of time and culture as they approach their vocation. Such theological reflection draws them beyond the barriers of their own experience. Herein lies the rationale for the distinct focus of our theological work. The opportunity is especially true in the case of a biblical theology approached with confidence in the inspiration of the text. Authority that transcends our reflection on liturgy and experience, history and ethics, teaching and pastoral care, literature and story, is needed. Sacred text and spiritual thought provide that basic authority.

At the same time, God is able to guide our broad theological reflection. He is not limited to the revelation of sacred Scripture. However, with the conviction that Scripture is the inspired revelation of God, and the correct starting point, we have chosen to limit our pursuit to a biblical theology of leadership. This book sets out with an assumption that the Bible exists as revelation from God and provides the clearest, most objective starting point and the best hope to preserve a church's leadership from being formed by a particular personality, the peculiarities of a specific culture, or the bent of a specific faith tradition.

Writing a biblical theology of leadership is ambitious. Objectivity is both a worthy goal and a significant challenge. In this work, the Scriptures have been allowed to speak for themselves and to reveal broad principles. This assumes a conservative position in regard to the inspiration of Scripture. It is not necessary to defend that position, nor are we so naïve as to believe every reader shares that view. Biblically formed leadership principles transcend such arguments.

This book is not a missiological work. It is not a book that sets out to define culture or the interaction of faith with culture. Biblical leadership principles are applied in diverse places and times. While we acknowledge the implications of freeing oneself from the confinement of culture when understanding leadership, it is not our intention here to develop an argument about culture. This is a biblical theology of leadership.

A SCRIPTURE-CENTERED THEOLOGY

The revelation of God must be allowed to emerge from Scripture unbiased by personal cultural filters. The art and learning of theological scholarship must be practiced so carefully that we hear the will of God through interaction with ancient cultures. This is done with a humble recognition of the humanness of our work. Some may wish to identify the voice of this work as theologically conservative. This study reveals confidence in Scripture as inspired, that through the thoughts and narratives of the biblical writers inspiration has functioned to communicate God's will. Of course, the realities of culture operated in scriptural times, and thus the exegetical work here is done carefully. It deliberately does not address a theology of revelation and inspiration, as that is not the purpose of this volume.

Such a Scripture-centered theology preserves Christ's headship of the church by acknowledging His will as the source of understanding. A Scripture-centered theology provides perceptions of leadership within universal truths that transform people and culture and inform the definition of leadership. The grounds for a theology of leadership in Christian scripture are extensive. While we do not presume to have discovered all such material, this is the most complete biblical theology of leadership available. For the purpose of this introduction, a few of the aspects characterizing the richness that a biblical theology of leadership provides will follow. The reader will be introduced to the contribution of Scripture for universal leadership understanding.

The first part of this work is devoted to Old Testament and New Testament scripture. We approach this study aware that it is common ground for three of the world's major religions. In the

Hebrew scriptures we examine the Creation narrative, then the broader Pentateuch, the historical books, Hymnic and Wisdom Literature, and finally the Prophets. We begin with a focus on leadership language and conclude the section with a synthesis of principles found. We seek patterns of God's engagement that provide a basis for understanding leadership. We also explore the experience of His people, especially His servants, for understanding. In the process, some significant word studies contribute to the inquiry. We do not presume to treat every narrative or passage in each division of Scripture; rather, we explore portions from each.

The New Testament completes the first half of our work. In the New Testament we examine the Gospels, the book of Acts, Pauline writings, the General Epistles, and the Apocalypse. The New Testament expresses a theology of leadership through the life and words of Jesus. Jesus came to this world to demonstrate the character of God. In doing so, He demonstrated the highest form of leadership, the leadership provided by a servant. The Epistle to the Philippians reveals that Jesus took on the role of servant precisely because He was God, that being His essential nature. Jesus explored a relational theology of leadership by His application of the term "friends" to those He personally mentored for mission leadership.

Biblical characters themselves provide case studies for leadership understanding in the third section of our work. Perhaps unfortunately, the Bible stories that have inspired us from childhood have directed our perspective to the heroic nature of such giants in time. We hope to discover the deeper interaction of God with His people through the life experiences of these figures, whose stories themselves are intended to reveal the nature of God, His relationship with His people, and our relationships in a transforming community. Thus these biblical narratives become leadership case studies involving selected biblical characters whose stories reveal the interaction of God with His people. In doing so, we do not seek to tell the heroic stories of such personalities in new or creative ways; rather, we are searching for deeper leadership understanding through their experiences.

The final part of the book both summarizes the work and provides a concise biblical theology of leadership. Biblical principles that provide a theological foundation for leadership practices are reviewed. Christian leadership is defined. An applied theology of leadership is provided. The result is a view of leadership that both serves as a starting point for broader theological reflection and centers leadership practice.

ENDNOTE

1. M. Stackhouse, *Apologia: Contextualization, Globalization, and Mission in Theological Education* (Grand Rapids, MI: Eerdmans, 1998), 9–26.

Section One:
The Old Testament

1

Leadership Language in the Old Testament

Richard M. Davidson

The language of leadership in the Old Testament is rich and varied. At least eight different Hebrew verbs have as one of their meanings "to lead," with reference to the leadership of human beings.[1] The vast majority of the references utilizing these terms refer to God as the One who leads—almost two hundred occurrences.[2] Repeatedly Scripture mentions that God led Israel out of Egypt and through the wilderness (e.g., Exod. 15:13; Deut. 8:2; Isa. 48:21; Neh. 9:12). The psalmists frequently petition or thank God for His leading (e.g., Pss. 23:3; 27:11). The prophets also speak often of God's leading Israel during the time of the Divided Monarchy and His promise to lead His people in the eschatological future (e.g., Isa. 40:11; 42:16; 57:18; Jer. 31:9).

In contrast with the many references to God's leadership using verbs meaning "lead," these terms are used only a few times with regard to human leaders. Jacob speaks regarding his leadership of his family as he returns to his homeland: "I will proceed [*nāhal* Piel, 'lead' in NKJV, ESV, NRSV] at my leisure, according to the pace of the cattle that are before me and according to the pace of the children" (Gen. 33:14).[3] God tells Moses: "But go now, lead [*nāḥah*] the people where I told you" (Exod. 32:34). Moses, as he nears the time of his death, speaks of the need of one to take his place, one "who will lead them out [*yāṣa'* hif.] and bring them in, so that the congregation of the LORD will not be like sheep without a shepherd" (Num. 27:17); God tells Moses to appoint Joshua for this purpose (vv. 18–23). The inspired psalmist speaks of David as one who led Israel: "So he shepherded them [Jacob, God's people] according to the integrity of his heart; and guided [*nāḥah* Hif., 'led' in NIV, NLT] them with skillful hands" (Ps. 78:72). Several passages refer to the leading of an army, using various Hebrew words: Ehud (Judg. 3:27, *hālak* Hif.); the "long-haired leaders" in the time of the judges (Judg. 5:2, *pāra'* Qal infin. const.); Joab (1 Chron. 20:1, *nāhag*); and Amaziah (2 Chron. 25:11, *nāhag*). Finally, Isaiah speaks of the ones who lead ('*āšar* Piel) Israel, but lead them astray (Isa. 3:12; 9:16 [Heb. 15]).

A number of occurrences in the Old Testament of verbs for "lead" appear in close connection with the concept or terminology of shepherding. God is described as a Shepherd of His people,[4] and the coming Messiah is envisioned as a Shepherd.[5] As for human leaders in Old Testament times, the judges were described as shepherds of Israel (2 Sam. 7:7; 1 Chron. 17:6). David, in particular, is portrayed as coming from his youthful occupation as a shepherd of sheep to shepherd the people of Israel (2 Sam. 5:2; 1 Chron. 11:2; Ps. 78:11–12). God speaks of Cyrus as His shepherd (Isa. 44:28); Jeremiah refers to himself as a shepherd who has faithfully followed God (Jer. 17:16). And Ezekiel calls the leaders of Israel shepherds—unfaithful shepherds (Ezek. 34:5, 8).

Beyond the specific use of terms meaning "lead," and the context of leading as a shepherd, the Old Testament refers to numerous positions of authority, utilizing a wide variety of terminology. These include some thirty different Hebrew terms, which may be translated by such expressions as "lord/master," "ruler," "tribal chief," "noble," "princess," "prince/ruler/leader," "judge," "king," "priest," "prophet," "court official," "leader," "commander," and "captain," to name a few.[6] Verbs used to describe the function of the various Old Testament leaders include various Hebrew words which may be translated by such expressions as rule, rule over, judge, govern, supervise, direct, superintend, subdue, have power [over], and so forth.[7]

The terms surveyed above are primarily used to *identify* various kinds of leadership or to indicate the general *function* of such leadership. But one additional concept (involving a number of specific Hebrew or Aramaic terms) specifically goes beyond mere identification and function and serves to *characterize* the nature of leadership articulated in the Old Testament, whether civil (such as the judge or king), cultic (such as the priest), military (such as the commander), or religious (such as the prophet). This concept is that of servant. The term and the concept are not universal in the Old Testament. Rather it appears in the context of God, His nature, and the nature of godly leadership. It is to this fundamental terminological characterization of Old Testament leadership that we now turn our attention.

THE CONCEPT OF SERVANT(HOOD) IN THE OLD TESTAMENT

Specific Terminology for Servant(hood)

The language of servanthood is pervasive throughout the Hebrew Bible. Some sixteen different Hebrew/Aramaic terms for "servanthood" are found in the Hebrew Bible. Eight terms and the majority of occurrences are from the Hebrew root *'bd*: (1) *'ābad* "to serve" (289 occurrences [hereafter "x"]); (2) *'ebed* "servant, slave" (805x); (3) *'ăbōdâ* "service, servile (customary, ordinary, heavy, laborious) work, worship" (145x); (4) *'ăbēd* (Aram.) "servant, slave, subordinate" (7x); (5) *'ăbūdâ* "service (of household servants as a body), workforce" (3x); (6) *'abdût* "servitude, forced labor" (3x); (7) *ma 'ĕbād* "deed, act" (2x); and (8) *'ăbād* "work, labor" (1x).

Other terms denoting some kind of servanthood include the following: (9) *'āmâ* "female servant/slave, maidservant" (56x); (10) *nĕtînîm* "temple servants" (16x); (11) *nĕtînîn* (Aram.) "temple servants" (1x); (12) *pĕlaḥ* (Aram.) "to pay reverence to, serve (deity)" (10x); (13) *ṣābā'* "to wage war, be on duty, serve (at the tabernacle)" (4x); (14) *šipḥâ* "handmaid, female servant/slave" (63x); (15) *šārat* "to wait on, be an attendant, serve, minister (unforced)" (97x); and (16) *šārēt* "minister, attendant" (2x). These sixteen terms for service involve more than 1,500 occurrences in the Hebrew Bible. This astonishing number of occurrences reveals the pervasiveness of the concept of servanthood in the Old Testament, and, as the discussion below indicates, the concept of servanthood embraces the whole range of Old Testament leaders, thus comprising what may be regarded as a universal term depicting leadership in the Hebrew Bible.

Paradoxical Ambiguity of Meaning

Several paradoxical semantic ambiguities are important to recognize before examining the association of terms meaning "servant" with leadership in the Old Testament.

No Semantic Distinction Between Slave and Servant. The primary Hebrew word for "slave/servant" (*'ebed*) can imply a relationship of subordination to another person that is permanent or temporary, voluntary or involuntary, and literal or figurative. It can describe both the very lowest social status—abject slavery—and the highest title of honor and privilege afforded a person—being God's servant. The Hebrew term itself simply does not distinguish among slave, servant, subject, vassal, official, or "servant" of deity. Only the immediate context makes the precise relationship plain.[8]

Paradox of Israel's "Slavery" and "Service/Worship." The same Hebrew words are used for Israelites serving (*'ābad*) as slaves (*'ebed*) to Pharaoh in Egypt and their serving (*'ābad*) as servants (*'ebed*) of God after being delivered from Egyptian bondage (e.g., Exod. 1:13–14; 3:12; 4:23; Lev. 25:42; Deut. 32:36). In the first case it was servitude (slavery), and in the second instance it was voluntary service (which many English translations translate as "worship"). This is expressed in Exodus 7:16: "Let My people go, that they may serve [*'ābad*, 'worship' in NIV, NRSV, and NJPS[9]] Me in the wilderness."[10]

Paradox of Joshua's Roles as Minister/Servant. It is instructive to note that when Joshua is first introduced in the narrative of the Pentateuch, he functions as Moses's "minister" (*mĕšārēt*), a term that denotes the elevated status of those who are disciples of elect men of God.[11] In Joshua 1:1, after the death of Moses, Moses is referred to as "[menial] servant [*'ebed*] of the LORD," while Joshua is still referred to as Moses's "[prime] minister" (*mĕšārēt*). However, by the time of Joshua's death, Joshua is also called the Lord's "[menial] servant" (*'ebed*).

Literal References to Slaves and Household Servants

More than one-fifth of the Old Testament terms for "servant" designate a literal slave or household servant held by Israelites or foreign nations. The permanent slaves of Israelites were not native Israelites (Lev. 25:42; 2 Chron. 8:9) but prisoners of war (Josh. 9:23) or purchases from neighboring nations (Gen. 39:17; Lev. 25:44–45) or descendants of these (Gen. 14:14–15). Hebrew debt slaves were only temporarily (and voluntarily) in slavery, and they were released after six years of service (Exod. 21:2–4) and amply supplied with goods to avoid debt slavery in the future (Deut. 15:12–18). These "debt slaves" were to be treated like hired workers, not as slaves (Lev. 25:39). No slaves were to be physically abused by their masters, and those who ran away were not to be returned but protected (Deut. 23:15–17). Yahweh was the Great Liberator from forced bondage, as with His people at the Exodus (Exod. 13:3, 14; 20:2; Lev. 26:13; Deut. 5:6; 6:12, 21; 7:8; 8:14; 10; 13:5; Josh. 24:17; Judg. 6:8; Jer. 34:13; Mic. 6:4). Israelite attitudes toward, and treatment of, slaves were unique in the ancient Near East because they remembered that they themselves had been slaves and had been redeemed by the Lord (Deut. 5:15; 15:15). Principles were in place in the Torah that, if followed, would have eventually eliminated all slavery.[12]

Figurative/Theological Use of Terminology: Old Testament "Servants"

As noted in the introduction of this chapter, the concept of "servant" (including the sixteen terms that express this concept) is applied as one descriptor characterizing God's leaders—be they prophets, priests, kings, or any number of other kinds of leaders in the Old Testament. In the following discussion one can see the ubiquity of the concept of servanthood for Old Testament leaders.

Two Old Testament individuals were most frequently called God's servant: Moses and David. Moses is called "My servant" (e.g., Num. 12:7–8) and "the servant of the LORD" (e.g., Deut. 34:5; Josh. 1:1). The language of servanthood is used to describe him more than thirty times in the Old Testament. David is referred to repeatedly by God as "My servant" (e.g., 2 Sam. 3:18; 1 Kings 11:13) and by the inspired biblical writer as "servant of the LORD" (Ps. 18:1). The language of servanthood is used with regard to David nearly sixty times in the Old Testament.

Other Old Testament figures were also called God's servant ("My [God's] Servant" or "His/Your [God's] Servant").[13] Still other Old Testament individuals (figuratively) described themselves as "servant" or as ones who "served."[14] Individuals and groups "served" or "ministered" at the sanctuary/temple, beginning with Adam and Eve at the Eden sanctuary.[15] Other groups are metaphorically called "servants" or in situations portrayed as "serving."[16]

Finally, a number of biblical verses speak of the coming Messiah as God's Servant, the Messianic Servant as Branch (Zech. 3:8), and the Messiah as the Suffering Servant (Isa. 42:1, 19; 49:5–7; 50:10; 52:13; 53:11). About the Messianic Suffering Servant we will have more to say in a later section of this chapter.

The language of "servant[hood]" is used to describe some thirty-five named individual leaders and a total of more than sixty different individuals or groups of people in the Old Testament, spanning the entire scope of biblical history and including the full range of leaders in Old Testament times: patriarchs (Abraham, Isaac, Jacob, Joseph and his brothers, Job); prophets (Isaiah, Elijah, Elisha, Ahijah, Jonah, Daniel); priests (Adam and Eve, plus all the Aaronic priests and Levites who were to "serve"); judges (Samuel); kings (David, Solomon, Hezekiah, Nebuchadnezzar); various civil leaders (Ziba, Eliakim, Shadrach, Meshach, Abednego, Zerubbabel, Nehemiah); military figures (Caleb and Joshua, Uriah the Hittite); and many unnamed individuals who filled various offices and occupations and situations of service.

It is noteworthy how many women are noted as providing leadership, using explicit language of servanthood. They included Eve, Ruth, Hannah, Abigail, Bathsheba, the wise woman of Tekoa, and the wise woman of the city of Abel, in addition to those numerous unnamed women who served at the sanctuary or in other capacities. When females such as the wise woman of Tekoa and of the city of Abel spoke, they spoke with a voice of authority, and men listened.

Perhaps the most remarkable and greatest concentration of servant language in a single passage is used of Abigail in 1 Samuel 25 (see citation on p. 19). Though most of these Old Testament women who are referred to by "servant" terminology apparently did not hold an official office in ancient Israel, their leadership was nonetheless influential and far-reaching.[17]

The Hebrew/Aramaic terms for "serving/service" are also used as a general reference to worship and covenant loyalty to God. Israelites were to serve Yahweh, i.e., worship at the sanctuary and in their covenant faithfulness and be His servants (Deut. 6:13; Josh. 22:27; 1 Kings 8:23; 2 Chron. 29:35; Neh. 1:6; Isa. 41:8 plus about fifty more occurrences). The people of Israel were warned against rejecting Yahweh and serving other gods (2 Kings 10:23 plus more than forty more occurrences). Foreign nations who would accept Yahweh were to serve Him (Ps. 2:11; Isa. 19:23). "Service" is a term referring to the observance (rite) of the Passover (Exod. 12:25–26; 13:5). Ultimately, "service" refers to all that happens in the cultic activity of the sanctuary (Exod. 30:16; 1 Chron. 31:10; 35:16).

SOME BASIC THEOLOGICAL INSIGHTS INTO LEADERSHIP

Based on the usage and context of servant terminology in the Old Testament, fundamental insights regarding leadership have emerged from my study, which may be summarized in the following points.

1. Scripture contrasts two different forms of leadership: power leadership and servant-oriented leadership. The contrast between power leadership and servant-oriented leadership is dramatically illustrated in the counsel of elder and younger statesmen to the young king Rehoboam as he takes office. The elder statesmen counsel the king to adopt leadership characterized by the attitude of service (1 Kings 12:7): "If you will be a servant to this people today, and will serve them and grant them their petition, and speak good words to them, then they will be your servants forever." But the theory of the younger counselors "is that servant leadership will not work."[18] They counsel the king to exercise power leadership: "Thus you shall say to this people who spoke to you, saying, 'Your father

made our yoke heavy, now you make *it* lighter for us'—But you shall speak to them: 'My little *finger* is thicker than my father's loins! Whereas my father loaded you with a heavy yoke, I will add to your yoke; my father disciplined you with whips, but I will discipline you with scorpions!'" (1 Kings 12:10–11, emphasis added).

Unfortunately, King Rehoboam chose power leadership over servant leadership, as is evidenced by his response to the people, following the advice of the young men: "The king answered the people harshly…saying, 'My father made your yoke heavy, but I will add to your yoke; my father disciplined you with whips, but I will discipline you with scorpions'" (1 Kings 12:13–14). The results of this choice of power leadership are all too evident in the consequent breakup of the United Monarchy (1 Kings 12:16–20) and may have been a significant factor leading to the rebellious and idolatrous acts of the king against God (1 Kings 12:21–33).

The contrast between two forms of leadership finds its ultimate basis in two contrasting root attitudes, as set forth in the book of Proverbs. Underlying servant-oriented leadership (servant leadership) is the root attitude of a "servant's heart," whereas power leadership imbibes the root attitude of pride and a haughty spirit (Prov. 11:2; 16:18; 29:23). It should be noted that those called of God, who were functioning as servants of the Lord and who provided leadership in the Old Testament community, did not always or necessarily evidence this characteristic servant-oriented leadership.

2. A servant leader is someone whose nature is characterized by service to God and to others, possessing a servant's heart, and such an individual need not be in a position or office of responsibility to exercise leadership. Witness, for example, the servant leadership of Abigail, wife of Nabal, as she spoke words of tact and wisdom to David (note the repeated use of various terms for "servant" in this narrative/dialogue):

> She fell at his feet and said, "On me alone, my lord, be the blame; And please let your maidservant [*'āmâ*] speak to you, and listen to the words of your maidservant [*'āmâ*].… Now let this gift which your maidservant [*šipḥâ*] has brought to my lord be given to the young men who accompany my lord. Please forgive the transgression of your maidservant [*'āmâ*]; for the LORD will

certainly make for my lord an enduring house, because my lord is fighting the battles of the Lord; and evil will not be found in you all your days.…When the Lord deals well with my lord, then remember your maidservant [*'āmâ*].…" Then David said to Abigail, "Blessed be the Lord God of Israel, who sent you this day to meet me."…Then David sent a proposal to Abigail, to take her as his wife. When the servants of David came to Abigail at Carmel, they spoke to her, "David has sent us to you to take you as his wife." She arose and bowed with her face to the ground and said, "Behold, your maidservant [*'āmâ*] is a maid [*šipḥâ*] to wash the feet of my lord's servants [*'ebed*]" (1 Sam. 25:24, 27–28, 31–32, 39–41).[19]

Abigail influenced David. She exercised influence through her relationship. She did not merely direct or order; instead, she exercised persuasion, exerting influence, and thus provided servant leadership.

3. There is a stark contrast between the (forced) service of the world and the (voluntary) service of God. We have already noted above how in the context of Israel's exodus from Egypt, the same Hebrew root *'bd* is used for Israelites serving (*'ābad*) as slaves (*'ebed*) to Pharaoh in Egypt and their serving (*'ābad*) as servants (*'ebed*) of God after being delivered from Egyptian bondage. In the first case it was servitude (slavery) and in the second instance it was voluntary service. Later in Israel's history, God teaches this same lesson to His people, by allowing them to be attacked and subjugated by Egypt under Pharaoh Shishak and his army. God explicitly spells out the point He wants Israel to learn: "But they [the Israelites] will become his [Pharaoh Shishak's] slaves, so that they may learn the difference between My service and the service of the kingdoms of the countries" (2 Chron. 12:8). The way of service to God is one of liberty, while the way of service to the kingdoms of foreign nations is bondage.

4. Service is ultimately done to the Lord, but it necessarily also involves serving the covenant community. On one hand we find clear indication in Scripture that the full-time workers for God were ultimately serving Him. Regarding the Levites, Moses writes: "At that time the Lord set apart the tribe of Levi to carry the ark of the covenant of the Lord, to stand before the Lord, to serve [*sharat*] Him, and to bless in His name until this day" (Deut. 10:8; cf. 17:2;

18:5, 7; 1 Chron. 15:2; 23:13; 2 Chron. 13:10; 29:11). On the other hand, Moses makes very clear to the Levites that they are serving the congregation: "the God of Israel has separated you from the rest of the congregation of Israel, to bring you near to Himself, to do the service [*ăbōdâ*] of the tabernacle of the LORD, and to stand before the congregation to minister to [*šārat*, 'serve' NKJV, NRSV, NJPS] them" (Num. 16:9).

In later Israelite history, King Josiah summarizes this two-directional focus of service, as he addresses the Levites: "Now serve [*ʿābad*] the LORD your God and his people Israel" (2 Chron. 35:3). Ezekiel juxtaposes this same duo-directional service: "Yet they [the Levites] shall be ministers [*šārat*, 'serve' NIV, 'servants' NJB] in My sanctuary, having oversight at the gates of the house and ministering [*šārat*, 'serving' NIV] in the house; they shall slaughter the burnt offering and the sacrifice for the people, and they shall stand before them to minister to [*šārat*, 'serve' NIV, NRSV, NJPS] them" (Ezek. 44:11).

5. Service is a gift from God. God instructs Aaron the high priest and the other priests: "But you and your sons with you shall attend to your priesthood for everything concerning the altar and inside the veil; and you are to perform service. I am giving you the priesthood as a bestowed service [*ăbōdat mattānāh*, lit. 'service of gift']" (Num. 18:7). Several modern versions emphasize this point by translating this latter clause: "I give your priesthood as a gift" (ESV, NIV, NRSV, etc.). The ministry of servant leadership is a precious gift from God Himself.

6. Servant leadership calls for a wholehearted, willing-spirited personal relationship with God. God evaluates the service of His servant Caleb: "But my servant Caleb, because he has had a different spirit and has followed Me fully, I will bring into the land which he entered, and his descendants shall take possession of it" (Num. 14:24). David was called "a man after God's own heart" (1 Sam. 13:14) because of his wholehearted commitment to divine service, despite his times of failure to live up to the divine ideal. David gave wise advice to his son Solomon about the kind of servanthood God desires: "As for you, my son Solomon, know the God of your father, and serve him with a whole heart and a willing mind; for the LORD

searches all hearts, and understands every intent of the thoughts. If you seek Him, He will let you find Him; but if you forsake Him, He will reject you forever" (1 Chron. 28:9).

7. The call and career of the servant leader is marked by humility and total dependence upon God, not self. Hear the self-appraisal of Moses, the servant of God: "Please, LORD, I have never been eloquent, neither recently nor in time past, nor since You have spoken to Your servant; for I am slow of speech and slow of tongue" (Exod. 4:10). God's own evaluation of Moses coincides with His servant's self-testimony: "Now the man Moses was very humble, more than any man who was on the face of the earth" (Num. 12:3). Solomon displayed this quality of humility as he took up the task of leadership over the people of Israel, as evidenced in his prayer: "Now, O LORD my God, You have made Your servant king in place of my father David, yet I am but a little child; I do not how to go out or come in. Your servant is in the midst of Your people which You have chosen, a great people who are too many to be numbered or counted. So give Your servant an understanding heart to judge Your people, to discern between good and evil. For who is able to judge this great people of Yours?" (1 Kings 3:7–9).

8. Servant leaders exhibit other character qualities and life habits that lead to successful leadership. Qualities and life habits associated with successful "servant" leaders in the Old Testament that have emerged from this terminological survey include: (a) integrity: Job (Job 2:3, 9); (b) undaunted, optimistic, courage: Joshua (Josh. 1:5–9); Jonathan (1 Sam. 14); (c) implicit trust in God's ability to deliver: Jonathan (1 Sam. 14:6: "for the LORD is not restrained to save by many or by few"); (d) perseverance in claiming God's blessing: Jacob (Gen. 32:26: "I will not let you go unless you bless me"), Nehemiah (see the many prayers in his book); (e) empowering by the Holy Spirit: Joseph (Gen. 41:38), Bezaleel (Exod. 35:31), Joshua (Deut. 34:9), and Zerubbabel (Zech. 4:6); (f) ability to cast a vision from God and motivate others to follow: Nehemiah (Neh. 2:17; 4:6: "Come, let us rebuild the wall of Jerusalem so that we will no longer be a reproach.... So we built the wall...for the people had a mind to work"); and (g) focus upon the Word: Joshua (Josh. 1:8: "This book of the Law shall not

depart from your mouth, but you shall meditate on it day and night…and then you will have success"). These character qualities and life habits will be elaborated upon in succeeding chapters of this book.

THE MESSIANIC SERVANT MODEL IN THE SERVANT SONGS OF ISAIAH 42–53

Nowhere else in Scripture is the terminology of "servant" (*'ebed*) so concentrated in a large section of scripture as in the repeated references to "servant" in Isaiah 41–66 (a total of thirty-one references to "servant"). The individual Suffering Servant in Isaiah 42–53 is the Representative Israelite, the promised Messiah, who embodies servant leadership. The context and content of the four individual Servant Songs (42:1–9; 49:1–13; 50:4–11; and 52:13–53:12) clearly show the Servant to be the coming Messiah: the various "Servant" passages of Isaiah 42–53 alternate between the corporate servant (Israel) and the individual Servant (the Messiah) who represents the nation, and the characterization of both servants is very similar, except that the individual (Messiah) will bring salvation and atonement for the corporate sinful nation (and for the Gentiles as well).[20] The New Testament witnesses clearly see these individual Songs fulfilled in Jesus (Matt. 8:17; 12:18–21; Mark 10:45; Luke 2:32; 4:16–30; 22:37). Strikingly, the New Testament also recognizes that the life of the Messianic Servant provides a model of servant leadership for Christian leaders (see citations in Acts 13:47; 26:18; Rom. 15:21; 2 Cor. 6:2; Gal. 2:2; Phil. 2:16).[21] A detailed exegesis of the Servant Songs is not attempted in this chapter,[22] but a survey of the four Messianic Servant Songs will highlight some of the attributes, attitudes, and actions of the Messianic Servant—predicted by the inspired Old Testament prophet Isaiah and lived out by the Messiah in New Testament times—that are relevant for those who wish to construct a biblical model of servant leadership. Profound principles for today's leaders emerge from Scripture's unparalleled concentration of servant language in the Servant Songs.

The Call of the Servant (Isa. 42:1–9)

The first Servant Song sets forth the following details regarding the Messianic Servant that are particularly relevant for servant leadership today: He is chosen and called by God (v. 1); he is empowered by the Spirit (v. 1); He is meek and humble, not seeking publicity (v. 2); He deals gently with the oppressed, the "bruised reed" and "smoking flax" (v. 3); He does not get discouraged and does not fail, but endures and perseveres (v. 4); He receives divine empowerment, sustenance, and support (vv. 5–7); God's glory will be upheld in the Servant's work.

The Commission of the Servant (Isa. 49:1–13)

The second Servant Song describes numerous aspects of the commissioning of the Messianic servant that are applicable to modern servant leaders: He is called from the womb (v. 1); God gives Him ability to speak, with piercing and far-ranging effect (v. 2); He is commissioned (v. 3); He will experience apparent failure but holds on with absolute confidence and trust and does not despair (v. 4); He has a mission to bring God's people back to Him and to bring light to the ends of the earth (vv. 5–6); Yahweh assures the servant of help, support, and ultimate success, although He may be despised and even rejected by His people (vv. 7–12); God will comfort His people through His Servant (v. 13).

The Commitment of the Servant (Isa. 50:4–11)

The third Servant Song highlights many components of the Messianic Servant's commitment that constitute principles appropriate to servant leaders today: God gives Him the tongue of the learned, He knows how to speak a word in season to the one who is weary, and He awakens early at God's beckoning to hear as the learned and obey (v. 4); He does not shun persecution, even extreme physical and psychological abuse (vv. 5–6); He knows that God will help Him and therefore He refuses to be discouraged or afraid or ashamed (v. 7); He is confident that God will vindicate Him and His enemies will be defeated (vv. 8–9); the Servant's disciples walk by faith in the darkness, but some walk in the sparks of their own kindling (vv. 10–11).

The Career of the Servant (Isa. 52:13—53:12)

The fourth Servant Song describes the career of the Messianic Servant, concentrating on His vicarious suffering on behalf of sinners, and many of the descriptions have a derived application for servant leaders today who are called to suffer on behalf of those to whom they minister: There is the assurance that God will ultimate glorify and vindicate His Servant, although He may have been despised by his peers (Isa. 52:13–15); He is often superficially misjudged and rejected, in His vicarious suffering (53:1–3); He bears the guilt and punishment upon Himself that others deserved, that by His suffering others may find healing and peace (vv. 4–6); He is willing to submit to unjust condemnation, and even to die for His people (vv. 7–9); His suffering is according to God's will, and God promises to ultimately exalt His Servant (v. 10); the Servant sees the travail of His soul and is satisfied that the suffering was worth it for the salvation of others (v. 11); and His life is one of vicarious suffering and intercession for others (v. 12).

CONCLUSION

The Old Testament features an array of leadership roles and numerous terms to identify such leaders. While the Old Testament actually uses the term *lead* a few times to depict humans, it is usually God who is described as leading. The shepherd imagery is sometimes used to depict leaders, whether divine or human. From an examination of the more than 1,500 occurrences of the sixteen different Hebrew/Aramaic terms for "service/servant/ serve," referring to some thirty-five named leaders and many other unnamed individuals and categories of leaders, a profound theology of servant-oriented leadership emerges, culminating in the example of servant leadership par excellence—the Messianic Servant. The pervasive leadership language of the Old Testament, viewed in context, offers incalculably rich insights into the nature of servant leadership.

FOR REFLECTION

Personal:

1. How does the language of leadership in the Old Testament inform and perhaps alter your own concept of leadership?
2. What principles of servant-oriented leadership emerging from Old Testament passages do you see most lacking in your own practice of leadership, and what steps can you take to facilitate the adoption of these principles?

Organizational:

1. How does the Old Testament contrast between power leadership and servant-oriented leadership provide principles that apply to organizational leadership structures and practices of church organizations?
2. How may we systematically and practically implement the principles of servant leadership embodied in the Servant Songs of Isaiah 42–53 (and lived out in the life of the Messiah), as we train and equip servant leaders for the church?

ENDNOTES

1. The Hebrew verbs are the following: (1) *nāḥah* (qal and hif.) "to lead"; (2) *nāhag* (qal and piel) "to lead, guide"; (3) *nāhal* (piel) "to lead or escort with care"; (4) *yāṣa'* (hif.) "to lead out, cause to go out"; (5) *dārak* (hif.) "to cause to tread [upon], lead"; (6) *hālak* (hif.) "to cause to walk, lead"; (7) *'āšar* (piel) "to lead, stride"; and (8) *pāra'* "to take the lead [as a 'long-haired leader']" (qal infin. const., with this meaning only in Judg. 5:2). Definitions of Hebrew and Aramaic words in this chapter are taken from Ludwig Kohler and Walter Baumgartner, *The Hebrew and Aramaic Lexicon of the Old Testament* (Leiden: Brill, 2001) (hereafter *HALOT*); Willem A. Van Gemeren, ed., *New International Dictionary of Old Testament Theology and Exegesis*, 5 vols. (Grand Rapids, MI: Zondervan, 1997) (hereafter *NIDOTTE*); and G. Johannes Botterweck and Helmer Ringren, eds., *Theological Dictionary of the Old Testament*, 15 vols. to date, trans. John T. Willis (Grand Rapids, MI: Eerdmans, 1974–) (hereafter *TDOT*).

2. The Hebrew word *nāḥah* occurs some 25 times referring to God; *nāhag* is used at least 5 times with reference to God; *nāhal* appears at least 6 times with God as the referent; *yāṣa'* (hif.) has God as the subject at least 125 times; and *dārak* (hif.) is used of God at least 3 times with the meaning of "lead." This totals about 190 references to God as leader.

3. Unless otherwise noted, scripture quotations in this chapter are taken from the New King James Version.

4. Genesis 49:24; Psalms 23:1; 28:9; 80:1; Ecclesiastes 12:11; Isaiah 40:11; Jeremiah 31:10; Ezekiel 34:12.

5. Ezekiel 34:23; 37:24; Zechariah 13:7.

6. The full range of nouns includes the following (with Hebrew expressions and number of occurrences in the Hebrew Bible in parentheses): "lord/master" (*'adôn*, 334 times [hereafter "x"]); "[ram], ruler/mighty one" (*'ayil* I, 7x with this meaning); "tribal chief" (*'allûp*, 60x); "noble" (*'aṣil* II, only in Exod. 24:11); "mistress, queen mother" (*gĕbîrâ/gĕberet*, 15x); "elder" (*zāqēn*, ca. 127x with the meaning of an office of leadership); "free, noble one" who exercises some kind of authority and leadership (*ḥōr*, 13x); "prince, ruler, leader" (*nāgîd*, 44x); "leader, chief, prince" (*nāsîk*, ca. 131x); "judge" (both the verb *šapaṭ* and the substantivized participle *šōpēṭ*, ca. 228x); "king/reign" (noun *melek* "king" and verb *mālak* "reign," ca. 2891x); priest (noun *kōhēn* "priest" and denominative piel verb *kihēn* "to act as priest," ca. 773x); prophet/prophesy (*nābî'* "prophet," ca. 317x, *nābā'* "prophesy," ca. 115x); "eunuch, court official" (*sārîs*, 45x); "(Philistine) prince, ruler" (*seren* II, 18x); "[he-goat], leader" (*'attûd*, ca. 6x with reference to human leaders); "administrator, steward, overseer" (*sōkēn*, 3x); "provincial governor" (*peḥâ*, 38x); "appointed official [civil, military, or cultic]" (*pāqîd*, 13x; cf. *pĕquddâ* "oversight," 5x with this meaning); "[military] commander, leader [in general]" (*qāṣîn*, 12x); "head, leader, chief" (*rō'š*, ca. 37x with meaning of leader); "[non-Israelite] captain, chief, commander" (*rab* II, ca. 50x); "rule/ruler" (verb *rāzan* "ruler" 6x, subtantivized participle *rōzēn* II "ruler, dignitary" only in Prov. 14:28); "official, chieftain, leader, prince" (*šar*, ca. 421x; cf. *šārāh* I, "woman of rank, princess," 5x + the name "Sarah," 39x); "[high-ranking] noble" (*šôa'*, only in Job 34:19 and Isa. 32:5); and "ruler" (*šallîṭ*, 3x).

7. Examples of Hebrew verbs for leadership include the following: "[marry], rule over, [own]" (*bā'al* I, 16x); "[dispute, reason together, prove, reprove,] judge, rule" (*yākaḥ*, Isa. 2:4; Mic. 4:3); "make subservient, subdue" (*kābaš*, 15x); "rule, govern" (*māšal* II, ca. 69x); "supervise, direct" (*nāṣaḥ*, ca. 64x); "[repel,] subdue" (*rādad*, 3x); "rule, govern" (*râdâ* I, ca. 24 x); "rule, direct, superintend" (*šārar*, 6x); and "gain power, have power, lord it over" (*šālaṭ*, 6x).

8. For full discussion of the semantic range of this Hebrew term, see *TDOT* 10:376–405.

9. NJPS is a publication titled *Tanakh: A New Translation of The Holy Scriptures According to the Traditional Hebrew Text* (Philadelphia: The Jewish Publication Society of America, 1985).

10. For an insightful summary of the "richness of this vocabulary ambiguity," see especially, Douglas K. Stuart, *The New American Commentary*, vol. 2, *Exodus* (Nashville, TN: Broadman & Holman, 2006), 71–72.

11. *TDOT* 15:505.

12. These included, among other things, seventh-day rest for all slaves (Exod. 23:12); seventh-year release for Hebrew slaves (Lev. 25:39–43); provisions for slaves upon release (Deut. 15:12–18); admonitions against harshness to slaves (Exod. 21:20–21, 26–27); refuge and safety for foreign runaway slaves (Deut. 23:15); and denouncement of slave traders (Deut. 24:7). For further discussion, see, e.g., William J. Webb, *Slaves, Women and Homosexuals: Exploring the Hermeneutics of Cultural Analysis* (Downers Grove, IL: InterVarsity, 2001), 44 and passim; Willard M. Swartley, *Slavery, Sabbath, War and Women* (Scottdale, PA: Herald, 1983), passim; and *TDOT* 10:387–390.

13. Abraham: "My servant" (Gen. 26:24); Jacob: "My servant" (Ezek. 28:25); Abraham, Isaac, and Jacob: "Your servants" (Exod. 32:13); Job: "My servant" (Job 1:1; 2:3; 42:7–8); Caleb: "My servant (Num. 14:24); Joshua: "Moses's minister" (Josh. 1:1); "Servant of the LORD" (Josh. 24:29; Judg. 2:8); the prophets: "My servants" (2 Kings 17:13 plus sixteen times); Isaiah: "My servant" (Isa. 20:3); Elijah: "His servant" (2 Kings 9:36; 10:1); Jonah: "His servant" (2 Kings 14:25); Ahijah: "His servant" (1 Kings 14:18, 29); Eliakim: "My servant" (Isa. 22:20); Nebuchadnezzar: "My servant" (Jer. 25:9; 27:6; 43:10); Shadrach, Meshach, and Abednego: "Servants of the Most High God" (Dan. 3:26, 28); Daniel: "servant of the living God" (Dan. 6:20 [Heb. 21], Aram.); Zerubbabel: "My servant" (Hag. 2:23); the people of Israel: "My servants" (Lev. 25:42; Isa. 43:10; plus more than twenty more times).

14. Lot (servant to strangers-angels: Gen. 19:2); Joseph (served the prison officials: Gen. 39:4; 40:4); brothers of Joseph (servants of Joseph: Gen. 42:10); Ruth: "your [Boaz's] servant" (Ruth 3:9); Hannah: "your [Eli's] servant" (1 Sam. 1:16); Samuel: "Speak, LORD, for Your servant hears" (1 Sam. 3:9–10); Abigail: alternation of *'āmâ* and *šipḥâ* (1 Sam. 25:24–25, 27–28, 31, 41); Ziba (servant of the house of Saul: 2 Sam. 9:2); Mephibosheth (servant of David: 2 Sam. 9:6, 8); wise woman of Tekoah: *'āmâ* (2 Sam. 11:15–16), *šipḥâ* (2 Sam. 14:12, 15, 19); Uriah the Hittite (David's servant: 2 Sam. 11:21–24); wise woman of the city of Abel (Joab's [maid]servant: 2 Sam. 20:17); Bathsheba (David's [maid] servant: 1 Kings 1:13, 17); Solomon (God's servant: 1 Kings 8:28–30; 2 Chron. 6:19–21); Elisha (who served Elijah: 1 Kings 19:21; 2 Kings 4:43; 6:15); Hezekiah (began "service" in the house of the Lord: 2 Chron. 31:21); Nehemiah (Yahweh's servant: Neh. 1:11).

15. Genesis 2:15 uses the same paired Hebrew words— *'ābad* and *šāmar*—for the work of Adam and Eve as for the priests' and Levites' service in the Mosaic sanctuary (Num. 3:7–8; 18:3–7). For some seventeen lines of evidence that the Garden of Eden is to be regarded as the original sanctuary on earth, with additional bibliography, see Richard M. Davidson, "Cosmic Metanarrative for the Coming Millennium," *Journal of the Adventist Theological Society* 11, nos. 1–2

(Spring–Autumn 2000): 108–111; and idem, *Flame of Yahweh: Sexuality in the Old Testament* (Peabody, MA: Hendrickson, 2007), 47–48. Other individuals and groups serving in the sanctuary/temple include: priests (Num. 18:7; 1 Chron. 24:3, 19; Ezra 8:20; Ezek. 44:14; plus many more references); Levites (Num. 3:7–8 [and dozens of times in succeeding chapters]; 16:9; 1 Chron. 6:33; 9:13, 19, etc.; "to celebrate and to thank and praise the LORD God of Israel" [1 Chron. 16:4 NASB]); gatekeepers (1 Chron. 26:1; 35:15); musicians (1 Chron. 6:17, 32; 25:1, 6); other temple servants who assisted the Levites (1 Chron. 9:2; Ezra 2:38, 43, 70, 77; 8:20; Neh. 3:31; 7:46, 60, 72; 10:28–29; 11:3, 21).

16. Forced (*corvée*) labor by the people for the king (Solomon): 1 Kings 12:4; 2 Chronicles 10:4; political "servants" (=vassal nations): 2 Kings 24:1; 25:24; 1 Chronicles 18:2, 6, 13; 2 Chronicles 12:8; soldiers as "servants": 2 Kings 24:10–11; 25:8; 1 Chronicles 20:8; royal personal attendants: 2 Samuel 13:17–18; 1 Kings 1:4; 10:5; 2 Chronicles 22:8; Esther 1:10; 2:2; 6:3; Psalm 101:6; political officials: 1 Chronicles 27:1; 28:1; 2 Chronicles 17:19; Proverbs 29:12; agricultural workers in the service of the king: 1 Chronicles 27:26; foreign vassal nations who were to "serve" the king who was suzerain over them (1 Kings 4:21; Pss. 18:43; 72:11); captive Israelites who would serve their captors in Babylon: Jeremiah 25:11; 27:6–8; 40:9; Israelites after returning from captivity who were still virtual slaves of a foreign power (Persia): Nehemiah 9:36.

17. For discussion of women leaders in Scripture, including many whose names are not accompanied by explicit "servant" terminology, see the chapter on biblical women as leaders in this book. Cf. Davidson, *Flame of Yahweh*, 213–295.

18. Paul R. House, *The New American Commentary*, vol. 8, *1, 2 Kings* (Nashville, TN: Broadman & Holman, 1995), 182.

19. See the penetrating description of Abigail's servant leadership, as penned by Ellen White: "Abigail addressed David with as much reverence as though speaking to a crowned monarch.... With kind words she sought to soothe his irritated feelings, and she pleaded with him in behalf of her husband. With nothing of ostentation or pride, but full of the wisdom and love of God, Abigail revealed the strength of her devotion to her household; and she made it plain to David that the unkind course of her husband was in no wise premeditated against him as a personal affront, but was simply the outburst of an unhappy and selfish nature.... The piety of Abigail, like the fragrance of a flower, breathed out all unconsciously in face and word and action. The Spirit of the Son of God was abiding in her soul. Her speech, seasoned with grace, and full of kindness and peace, shed a heavenly influence.... Abigail was a wise reprover and counselor." Ellen G. White, *The Story of the Patriarchs and Prophets* (Mountain View, CA: Pacific Press Publishing Association, 1958), 667–668.

20. For evidence supporting the Messianic interpretation of these Servant Songs, see esp. C. Kaiser, "The Identity and Mission of the 'Servant of the Lord,'" in *The Gospel According to Isaiah 53: Encountering the Suffering Servant in Jewish and Christian Theology*, ed. Walter Darrell L. Bock and Mitch Glaser (Grand Rapids,

MI: Kregel, 2012), 87–107; J. Alec Motyer, *The Prophecy of Isaiah: An Introduction and Commentary* (Downers Grove, IL: InterVarsity Press, 1993), 289–458; and Edward J. Young, *New International Commentary on the Old Testament*, vol. 3, *The Book of Isaiah* (Grand Rapids, MI: Eerdmans, 1972), 108–359.

21. For analysis of the New Testament use of the Servant Songs, see esp. Walter Darrell Bock and Mitch Glaser, eds., *The Gospel According to Isaiah 53: Encountering the Suffering Servant in Jewish and Christian Theology* (Grand Rapids, MI: Kregel, 2012), chaps. 4–6.

22. For exegesis of the Servant Songs, see esp. Duane Lindsey, *The Servant Songs: A Study in Isaiah* (Chicago: Moody Press, 1985); I am following Lindsey's fourfold outline in my summary of insights from the successive Songs. Cf. Stephane A. Beaulieu, "The Identity and Role of the Servant in Isaiah 42:1–9: An Exegetical and Theological Study" (PhD diss., Andrews University, forthcoming); Kye Sang Ha, "Cultic Allusions in the Suffering Servant Poem (Isaiah 52:13–53:12)" (PhD diss., Andrews University, 2009); Steve Jeffery, Michael Ovey, and Andrew Sach, *Pierced for Our Transgressions: Rediscovering the Glory of Penal Substitution* (Wheaton, IL: Crossway, 2007), 52–67; James M. Kennedy, "Consider the Source: A Reading of the Servant's Identity and Task in Isaiah 42:1–9," in *The Desert Will Bloom: Poetic Visions in Isaiah*, ed. A. Joseph Everson and Hyun Chul Paul Kim (Atlanta: Society of Biblical Literature, 2009), 181–196; John N. Oswalt, *The Book of Isaiah: Chapters 40–66* (Grand Rapids, MI: Eerdmans, 1998), 96–410; Motyer, *The Prophecy of Isaiah*, 289–458; and Young, *Isaiah*, 3:108–359.

2 | The Creation Narrative

Jacques B. Doukhan

The first word of the Hebrew Bible, *bĕrēšît,* which is generally translated "in the beginning" (Gen. 1:1), encapsulates
the essence of leadership; it is derived from the word *rō᾽š,*
which literally means "head" and is the technical term normally
used to designate one who is leading in a given situation.[1] Thus
the creation event is described as an act of leadership. Creation is
leadership *par excellence.* The passage on creation covering the
first two chapters of Genesis (Gen. 1:1–2:4a and Gen. 2:4b–25)[2]
provides valuable insights regarding a biblical view of leadership.
In order to explore these lessons, the biblical text will be
approached inductively, but without conducting a comprehensive exegesis. The interrogation of the text and even the technical
discussions will be engaged only insofar as they serve this purpose: What does this biblical account of creation have to say
about leadership? A careful examination of the text requires
thoughtful theological inquiry but will yield rich biblical insight
into the concept of leadership.

GOD PRECEDES

The first premise of the Bible is an affirmation of God's leadership: "In the beginning, God" (Gen. 1:1).[3] It is certainly significant that the first word *bĕrēšît* ("in the beginning"), which connotes leadership, is both syntactically and liturgically attached to God as Creator. This connection is first of all indicated syntactically: not only does mention of the creating God follow immediately after the word *bĕrēšît* but also the three Hebrew words of the phrase "In the beginning God created" (Gen. 1:1) are intended to be uttered in one single breath. Indeed the phrase seems to be used in the construct form and could be rendered "In the beginning of the creation…God said" (my literal translation), a reading that has been attested to in early Jewish tradition and is reflected in John's statement, "In the beginning was the Word" (John 1:1).[4] The liturgical chanting of the text which follows the directions of the accents confirms this orientation, since we have a conjunctive accent under the verb "created" (*bārā᾽*), indicating that it has to be read in close connection with the following word, namely, "God" (*᾽ĕlōhîm*). More importantly, the use of the greatest disjunctive accent, the *Athnach* that is attached to the word *᾽ĕlōhîm* (God), suggests that the most important lesson in this story of leadership in creation is God. God is the subject of this work, not only the most important One, but indeed the only One. God is the only Leader, not simply because He is the Creator, because of His creating power, but more importantly because He is the One who preceded everything and everyone else. The Bible insists, indeed, that unlike the other ancient Near Eastern myths, there was no competitive power besides God in the genesis of the universe.[5]

The first lesson about leadership that the apprentice leader should hear in this distinct emphasis is a lesson of humility, and, at the same time, an implicit warning against assuming the prerogatives of God, against claiming power or prerogative that belongs to the Creator alone. Leadership opens one to the dangerous temptation to abuse power or to assume superiority over others. A desire for leadership should be closely examined, since it may be inspired by an ambition to dominate—to assume God's place. The Bible makes it clear from the very beginning that no one has a right to positional leadership. Only God, the Creator, the only One who came before, has the right and the power to lead.

TO LEAD IS TO RELATE

The biblical story of creation is the testimony of a relationship: the God of heaven, the God of the universe, took the initiative to come down and create the human realm. He did so for the particular purpose of having a loving relationship with humans. As humans appear on the scene of creation, this intention is immediately revealed through a number of specific observations, giving a unique character to God's relationship with humans.

The coming to be of humanity is the only creative act introduced by a preliminary statement of intent or divine deliberation. The expression "Let us make" (Gen. 1:26) replaces the seemingly impersonal words of divine fiat that characterize the other creation acts. Unlike the animals who come from the land (Gen. 1:24), humans are created by means of some other physical action besides the speaking of the divine Word. The human being is the only creature who is created in God's image: "Then God said, 'Let Us make man in Our image, according to Our likeness'.... So God created man in His own image" (Gen. 1:26–27). In the light of ancient Near Eastern and particularly Egyptian texts, this expression has been understood as a reference to the unique relationship between God and humans. It was believed that the image (as with the idol-image in the other cultures) contained the spirit of the represented deity, thereby ensuring a shared unity between the god and his or her image.[6] To say that humans were created in God's image means that they received the capacity to relate to God. This emphasis on relation has received a theological affirmation in the works of Karl Barth, who interprets the image as a capacity of relationship between God and humans. For Karl Barth, humankind's divine image means that God can enter into personal relationships with humans, speak to them, and make covenants with them, and that humans have the ability to relate with each other.[7]

As noted above, the human being is the only one whose creation implies an actual physical relation: "And the Lord God formed man of the dust of the ground, and breathed into his nostrils the breath of life; and man became a living being" (Gen. 2:7). The divine creation of humans involved the physical touch of God; God formed humans with His own hands, as a potter forms the vase of clay.

An intimate relationship is also clearly implied: God breathed in humankind His own life-spirit. Thus, in His act of creation, God is not indifferent or detached; He is personally, physically, and intimately involved in His act of creation. He gets His hands (and even His mouth) dirty in the process.

The human being is the only one with whom God shares the same holy time: "Then God blessed the seventh day and sanctified it, because in it He rested [*šābat*] from all His work which God created and made" (Gen. 2:3). God's blessing (*brk*) and His sanctification (*qdš*) of the Sabbath mean that God set apart this particular time, at the end of the creation week, for a manifestation of His special relationship with humanity.[8] Indeed the Sabbath day will be explained later in the Decalogue as the day of relationship *par excellence,* vertically between God and humans, horizontally between humans and humans, and again vertically, with humans in an *Imago Dei* application, between themselves and the creation over which they have been given dominion (Exod. 20:8–11).[9] The fact that the Sabbath—a day of relationship—was given as the commandment to help commemorate creation is another evidence of the connection between creation and relationship. Note also that Genesis 2:23–24, in the second creation story, refers to the relationship of the couple in a manner not used in reference to animals, thus confirming the relational dimension of the Sabbath.[10]

The human being is created as a social being in need of other human beings. God Himself recognizes this strong social dependence as He emphatically observes: "It is not good that man should be alone" (Gen. 2:18). It is also significant that this social dimension of the human being is expressed linguistically in the second creation story through the Hebrew word for "man," *'îš,* which has the connotation of "weakness" and "dependence."[11] It is also significant that the word *'îš* (man), which is specific to the second creation story (in contrast to the word *'ādām* in the first creation story), reappears only at the end of the chapter when its bearer fulfills his social vocation, in relation to the woman, the *'iššāh,* the other being who will ensure he will no longer be alone (Gen. 1:23–24).

The testimony of the biblical creation story affirming God's personal involvement and relationship with humankind and the human need for relationship contains a lesson about the nature of leadership. Instead of staying aloof, above his or her community, a leader should be part of a community, participating in their shared work, being spiritually one with them, devoting his or her prayers to the community, engaging with them, jointly initiating projects with them—in all things working together with them to fulfill their purposes.

TO LEAD IS TO COMMUNICATE

Because creation was meant to produce relationship, the biblical creation story presents itself fundamentally as a work of communication. "In the beginning...God said" (Gen. 1:1–3). Creation is bestowed through the Word of God: the phrase "God said" is repeated throughout the biblical account. This emphasis on God's Word is not just a message about the mechanism of creative activity. The emphasis itself is an act of communication. The message is designed to be heard. God did not create only with an intention to reveal Himself; He also wanted the story of this particular creation to be communicated.

God's first communication with humanity (Gen. 1:28–29) described both their similarity to and difference from the Creator. Verse 28 concerns what humans and God have in common, namely the capacity to create, while God's second address (v. 29) concerns what makes humans essentially different from, and dependent upon, divinity. God is the provider, the One who gives, while humans are those in need, those who must receive their existence from Him.

This structure of communication, based on similarity and difference, is confirmed later in the second creation story as it describes the relationship between the first human persons, Adam and Eve. After God's observation that "it is not good that man should be alone" (Gen. 2:18), He creates the woman as a helper who is *kĕnegdô,* translated variously as "suitable," "comparable," "just right," "fit," and so on. This expression is composed of two words, *kĕ,* "like," which implies similarity and *neged,* "against," "in front of," "opposite," which implies confrontation and difference. It is noteworthy that this root *ngd* refers also to verbal communication; it is associated with the expressions "open the lips" (Ps. 51:15), "in the ears of" (Jer. 36:20), or to the voice (Gen. 44:24). The verb is also used to describe nonverbal communication, when for instance "the heavens declare [*ngd*] the glory of God;...without speech or language" (Ps. 19:1, 3, my literal translation).

The fact that this relationship is built upon the reality of difference indicates the nature of this relationship. The recognition of difference and the respect for that difference are fundamental in the process of communication. There is no real communication if in the process the "other" is crushed and silenced. Unlike the ancient Near Eastern myths of a genesis that made humans out of the divine (either from his member, his spit, or his sperm), hence of the same nature,[12] the Bible dared to conceive the creation of humans out of *what God is not,* that is, essentially different from Him. It is this difference that paradoxically makes humans like God. They are unique like God is unique. The uniqueness of human individuals is another application of the *Imago Dei* principle. As McKeown comments, "Although it is difficult to ascertain the meaning of the 'image,' it is closely associated with the uniqueness and distinctiveness of humans."[13]

This sense of communication that defines the nature of relationship between Adam and Eve, the first human beings, sheds light on the leadership semantics implied in the creation story. Leadership, whether it occurs on the vertical level between God and humans or on the horizontal level between and among humans, should entail relationship and communication with the "other." The revelation that God not only set the tone and provided an example of communication in the exercise of His own leadership, but also implanted the necessity of communication through the manner in which He created humans reveals an important lesson for the exercise of leadership. Leaders collaborate, listen, and dialogue with mutual respect—a process that is crucial, especially considering the many leadership difficulties that emerge from poor communication.

TO LEAD IS TO SERVE

The leader's duty to communicate obliges him or her to take into consideration the other person and therefore to lead with respect for the other, in a spirit of service, rather than with a spirit of oppression. Unlike the ancient Near Eastern myths that describe the god who creates for his own benefit,[14] the biblical creation story depicts, by putting God not only at the beginning but also at the end of the process, a God who creates uniquely for the happiness of creation and, more importantly, for the happiness of humankind. Unlike the ancient Near East mythology which believed that man was only created by the gods to supply the gods with food,[15] Genesis 1 presents humans as the climax of creation; and instead of humankind providing the gods with food, God provides the plants as food for humans. The literary structure of the biblical text of creation accounts for this particular focus and divine interest in those He creates. In Genesis 1, the creation of humans comes at the end of the creation project, because everything has been created as a gift for their benefit: "I have given every herb that yields seed which is on the face of all the earth, and every tree whose fruit yields seed; to you it shall be for food" (Gen. 1:29). Humankind is here the climax of creation. Only at the end, after humans have been created, God says, "it is very good" (Gen. 1:31). God does not just provide what humans need to survive. His gifts are not just "good"; they are "*very* good"; they overflow (Ps. 23:5).

It is also significant that at the end of the creation week God shares the holy time of Sabbath with humans (Gen. 2:1–3). This rest is all the more a gift to humankind, as humans were not involved in the work of creation and did not require physical rest that first Sabbath. God's leadership is thus characterized by grace and generosity. Genesis 2 describes God placing humans in a garden He had prepared beforehand especially for them (Gen. 2:7, 15). God's first commandment to humans concerns His gift of "every tree of the garden," that they "may freely eat" (Gen. 2:16). God precedes humans not for His own benefit, to serve Himself first, as many corrupt leaders would have done, but, on the contrary, for the definite purpose to serve humankind. Creation thus is not an act of dominance but an act of service.

From the divine example of leadership humans should learn a lesson of service. The biblical text implies that Adam and Eve both learned and applied this lesson. The verb that describes the first human action, the first human duty in the Garden, as a direct response to God's blessing is *'bd,* "to till" (Gen. 2:5; 3:23), which means literally "to serve."[16] Service is, then, given as the primary lesson of humankind's role, indeed their vocation,[17] an idea that will be later recognized in Ecclesiastes' reading of that passage.[18]

TO LEAD IS TO SHARE

The biblical story of creation contains a paradoxical element: Although God was the only One who created, because He created in order to serve, He went so far as to share His creative power with others. The use of the plural form "Let us make" (Gen. 1:26) to refer to God's creation of humans in His image is particularly intriguing as it suggests that God shared His creative operation with one or several other beings. Although there is a diversity of opinions on how to read this passage, the majority of interpretations recognize that a real plurality is intended[19] and suggests some kind of cooperation with the divinity. Generally Jewish tradition held the plural to refer to God addressing His heavenly court, the angels,[20] as supported by Job: "when I [God] laid the foundations of the earth.... all the sons of God shouted for joy" (Job 38:4, 7). An important Jewish tradition reported by the great medieval commentator Rashi explains this text as a lesson of humility on the part of God: "The superior must take counsel and ask authorization from his inferior."[21] The text of the *Midrash Rabbah,* which is the source of Rashi's remark, is even more explicit; it reports that when Moses received this phrase by revelation he was disturbed and asked God to explain it. And God answered: "Since man will be the lord of creation, it is appropriate that I ask their agreement to the higher and lower spheres, before I create him. Humans will then learn from Me that the greatest should ask the agreement from the smallest before imposing on him a leader."[22]

From the time of the Church Fathers,[23] Christian theologians in general saw the plural as a reference to Christ or/and the Trinity.[24]

Certainly the traditional Christian interpretation would not exclude the traditional Jewish interpretation, insofar as the divine council (the heavenly host) is understood in a broad and larger sense, though with some nuances. In the former interpretation, the sharing operation involves beings other than God Himself. In the latter interpretation, it takes place within the Godhead and is here understood as an inherent quality of God Himself. Whatever interpretation one chooses, whether He shares with other heavenly beings or within Himself, the God of creation is presented as a God who shares.

The creation story goes further by suggesting that God also shares His creative initiative with humans. This human status of co-creator is already alluded to through the "image" that is tied to the human power of procreation through "male and female" (Gen. 1:27; cf. 5:1–2), as if human procreation alone contained a divine dimension—which would be absent in animal procreation.[25] To be sure, animals are also capable of procreation, yet only human procreation is retained in the creation story as directly connected to God. It is also significant that the creation story is qualified as a "genealogy" (*tôldôt*) at the conclusion of the creation account (Gen. 2:4a), just as the human genealogies that follow in the Pentateuch and in the whole Bible constitute human history (the word *tôldôt* also means "history"), thus suggesting that the human shaping of history was identified as a creation, just as in Genesis 1:1–2:4a. It seems clear that humans have received from God the capacity to create the humans of tomorrow and thus to create future history.

God, in the leadership expressed by His creative initiative, did not keep only for Himself the power to shape events. He entered into the risk of sharing His creative power of history with humans; hence the covenants that characterize God as walking side by side with Israel, and with every human individual. Further, God's sharing time with humans on the Sabbath day, the first day of human history, reveals God's intention to share His control over the course of history with humans.

The same status of co-creator reappears in Genesis 2 when humankind is granted the power to give names to animals, just as God gave names in the process of creation (see 1:5, 8, 10). Here also the human word is immediately followed by its fulfillment: "Whatever

Adam called each living creature, that was its name" (Gen. 2:19). This syntax reminds us of the description of the divine creation: "'Let there be light'; and there was light" (Gen. 1:3). The human power of co-creation concerns the other living beings of creation, thus suggesting that their existence, even their identity, was then dependent on humans.

The lesson of sharing is immediately applied horizontally on the human level. Since humans are created in God's image, they are then by implication also created as beings who by nature share. This social, relational, and sharing dimension of the human person, as we have already noted in the creation of "male and female" (Gen. 1:27), is in fact made explicit in Genesis 2 where the creation of the couple plays out. The woman is created out of the same flesh as the man. As a result, they share the same flesh, as Adam himself recognizes: "This is now bones of my bones, and flesh of my flesh; she shall be called woman, because she was taken out of man" (Gen. 2:23). This sharing is again emphasized and based on the original formula; further, it is still presented as an ideal to be reached in the future: "Therefore a man shall leave his father and mother and be joined to his wife, and they shall become one flesh" (Gen. 2:24). Because they were created one flesh, they will have to constantly strive to achieve that unity, that becoming one with each other. (It is interesting and perhaps significant that contrary to what some cultures might expect, it is the man who is supposed to "leave" in order to be joined to his wife.)

This movement that replicates God's movement toward humans contains the same lesson of humility that was discerned on God's level. The human sharing parallels and imitates the divine sharing and is therefore another expression of the *Imago Dei* principle. Now, in case one would be tempted to infer from this observation the equation that God is to humans as man is to woman—and ironically conclude the superiority of the man over the woman— one should remember that the same movement is attested reversely. Indeed in Genesis 2:18, the woman is identified as the "helper" (*'ēzer*), a qualification that usually refers to God as the Savior, that is, the one who assists and shares the burden (Exod. 18:4; Deut. 33:29; Pss. 20:2[3]; 121:1–2; 124:8). As the helper-savior, the woman replicates God's function. The downward sharing movement, mirroring God's sharing movement, exists, then, in both directions, and could be identified in both cases as an act of leadership of the same quality.

Immediately after this recognition of shared experience and nature, the biblical author concludes: "And they were both naked, the man and his wife, and were not ashamed" (Gen. 2:25). In addition, the two statements are connected through a chiastic structure AB B¹A¹ (the corresponding elements are indicated in bold):

A: be joined to **his wife** (*'ištô*)
　B: **and they shall be** (*wĕhāyû*) one (*'eḥād*)
　B¹: **and they were** (*waîyihyû*) **the two of them** (*šĕnêhem*) naked
A¹: and the man and **his wife** (*'ištô*), and were not ashamed (Gen. 2:24–25)

A is related to A¹ through the same word "his wife"; and B is related to B¹ through the same verb "to be" in the imperfect and the reference to a number ("one," "two").

If one takes the literary connection between the two statements as a clue to suggest some kind of thought connection between them, one is allowed to infer that their nakedness without shamefulness (v. 25) had something to do with the particular nature of their relationship (v. 24). In other words, the condition described in verse 25—feeling no shame though naked—was due to the state described in verse 24, the sharing of the same flesh. In the Bible "nakedness" (*'ārōm*) is in most occurrences associated with poverty and need[26] and is a sign of vulnerability and defenselessness (Job 1:21; 12:22; Ps. 139:8; Isa. 47:2–3; Hos. 2:3).[27] From our post-Fall perspective, the seeming risk they took in exposing themselves and being vulnerable (in a world where they actually knew no risk or vulnerability) was instead a natural, unclouded willingness derived from the complete trust they manifested in their sharing experience. "They were both naked" precisely because they had "become one flesh." This causal connection between the two attitudes suggests a lesson of leadership that deserves our reflection: to lead is to share, and to lead is to trust.

TO LEAD IS TO CREATE

The creation story not only provides us with lessons about how we should lead as sharing and relational servants, but also about the sense and the direction of this service. Just as God created as a manifestation of leadership, humans are now invited to create: to produce what has not yet existed. Leadership is not about maintaining the status quo. The leader is called to change the world, just as God has changed the world, from the state of nonexistence to a state of existence and potential. The first duty of the leader is to bring things into existence, to produce life. It is significant that Adam's first human assignment, as soon as he has been created in God's image, is an act of creation. Humans are urged to be fruitful and multiply (Gen. 1:28). It is also interesting and significant that this commandment of creation is directly associated with the commandment of stewardship: "Be fruitful and multiply; fill the earth and subdue it; have dominion over the fish of the sea, over the birds of the air and over every living thing that moves on the earth" (Gen. 1:28). It is even possible that the *wāw* in Hebrew that precedes the verbs expressing "subdue" and "have dominions"[28] functions as an epexegetical *wāw,* and serves "to clarify or specify the sense of the preceding clause."[29] In that case this syntactical construction would suggest that the act of creation should be understood more precisely as an act of leadership. Initiating something and working to construct order are implied.

The same ideas reappear in the parallel text of Genesis 2, the second creation story, where animals are brought to man that he may give them names (Gen. 2:19–20). Indeed both the ideas of creation and dominion are conveyed by this practice of giving names. In biblical civilization as well as in ancient Near Eastern culture the giving of the names was a part of the traditional covenant making between suzerain and vassal. By giving a name to his vassal, the suzerain would not only suggest creation, since the giving of a name gave new existence to the vassal, but he would also and consequently mark his dominion and lordship over him.[30] God named the humans of His creation, but He then designated to the humans the responsibility of naming the animal realm. That act implied a sharing of creative activity.

Humans are qualified for leadership insofar as the leadership they exert is intended to build up and create in the service of life. This testifies not only to the unselfish nature of the work of creation, which implies, as we indicated above, the responsibility of service and leadership, but it also clarifies and purifies the meaning of leadership. Instead of connoting the abuses of dominion and the brute power of destruction and death, the leadership that is inscribed in this perspective of creation will mean productivity and life.

CONCLUSION

An exegetical and theological analysis of the biblical creation story reveals the importance of servant leadership in the divine operation of creation. God's work of creation has been identified as the first act of leadership, to be followed as a model for human leadership. Thus this study should provide not only an understanding of the nature and quality of the biblical view of leadership, but also specific and practical lessons that are relevant in the delicate exercise of leadership.

God the Creator did not initiate His creative work simply because He wanted to create. He created with the definite purpose of relationship. Yet God did not just create for the pleasure of socializing—just to enjoy the company of humankind. Creation was to be approached not only *for* humankind, as a service for humankind but also *with* humankind, as a cooperative act. In order to accomplish this task, God submitted Himself to all the risks of the creative initiative and all the pains of humiliation. God moved away from His place and created humans, who were different from Himself. He shared with them His physical presence: He created them with a status that would allow them to confront Him, hence with the capacity to go a different way. God came down and communicated with them, using their own language, and respecting their differences and limitations. God went so far as to share His power and His time with humans. Thus the story of God's leadership is seen in the story of His incarnation.

The creation story does not confine itself to divine leadership; it applies the lessons to human leadership. From the perspective of the biblical story of creation, a human leader who unwittingly assumes the position of God and chooses to lead all by him- or herself, not relating, not serving, not sharing, not communicating, would be completely disqualified. For such leadership would not be like God's; instead, it would be a leadership of control, oppression, and death. Being created in God's image, humans are all called to lead by following God's model—leadership that initiates, relates, serves, communicates, shares, and creates; a leadership that is productive and creates life and a future.

FOR REFLECTION

Personal:

1. How has this biblical study changed your view of the relationships involved in leadership?
2. How has this biblical study influenced the way you communicate with people you work with?

Organizational:

1. How does your organization encourage and affirm creativity?
2. How does your organization value sharing leadership among positional leaders and others?

ENDNOTES

1. See Numbers 31:26; 32:28; 36:1; 2 Samuel 23:8; 1 Chronicles 9:34, 11:10; 23:8.

2. On the delimitations and structure of the two creation stories, see Jacques B. Doukhan, *The Genesis Creation Story, Its Literary Structure,* Andrews University Seminary Doctoral Dissertation Series 5 (Berrien Springs, MI: Andrews University Press, 1978), 78. For a discussion on Genesis 2:4a as the conclusion to the preceding creation account rather than the introduction to the text that follows, see P. J. Wiseman, *Clues to Creation in Genesis* (London: Marshall, Morgan and Scott, 1977), 34–45; cf. James McKeown, *Genesis* (Grand Rapids, MI: Eerdmans, 2008), 29.

3. Scripture quotations in this chapter are taken from the New King James Version.

4. For a discussion on this syntactical observation, see Jacques Doukhan, "The Genesis Creation Story: Text, Issues, and Truth," *Origins* 55 (2004): 12–33.

5. On the cosmogonic conflict as a means of creation in ancient myths from the Near East, see, for instance, the Mesopotamian epic of *Enuma Elish*, in E. A. Speiser, "The Creation Epic," *Ancient Near Eastern Texts Relating to the Old Testament*, ed. J. B. Pritchard, 3rd ed. (Princeton, NJ: Princeton University Press, 1969), 60–70; cf. M. K. Wakeman, *God's Battle with the Monster: A Study in Biblical Imagery* (Leiden: Brill, 1973), 38–39.

6. See D. J. A. Clines, "The Image of God in Man," *Tyndale Bulletin* 19 (1968): 81–83.

7. See *Church Dogmatics*, vol. 3, pt. 1 (Edinburg: T & T Clark; New York: Scribner's, 1958), 183–187.

8. For the blessing as implying "an intimate relationship," see Joseph Scharbert, "*brk*," in *Theological Dictionary of the Old Testament*, ed. G. Johannes Botterweck and Helmer Ringgren, trans. David E. Green, vol. 2 (Grand Rapids, MI: William B. Eerdmans Publishing Company, 1975), 285. For the concept of holiness as implying the idea of "a special relationship with Yahweh," see Helmer Ringgren, "*qdš*," in *Theological Dictionary of the Old Testament*, ed. G. Johannes Botterweck, Helmer Ringgren and Heinz-Josef Fabry, trans. Douglas W. Stott, vol. 12 (Grand Rapids, MI: William B. Eerdmans Publishing Company, 2003), 533. Cf. Niels-Erik A. Andreasen, *The Old Testament Sabbath: A Tradition-Historical Investigation*, Society of Biblical Literature Dissertation Series, no. 7 (Missoula, MT: Society of Biblical Literature, 1972), 208.

9. See Jacques Doukhan, "Loving the Sabbath as a Christian: A Seventh-day Perspective," in Tamara Eskenazi, Daniel J. Harrington, S.J., and William H. Shea, *The Sabbath in Jewish and Christian Traditions* (New York: Crossroad Publishing Company, 1991), 160.

10. See Doukhan, *The Genesis Creation Story,* 47–48. For the same association in Jewish tradition, see *Babylonian Talmud, Shabbat* 119a; cf. Abraham Heschel, *The Sabbath: Its Meaning for Modern Man* (New York: Raffar, Straus and Giroux, 1951), 54–55.

11. The root *'ānaš,* from which is probably derived the *'iš,* is also attested in Akkadian with the meaning of "weak"; see Edmond Jacob, *Theology of the Old Testament*, trans. Arthur W. Heathcote and Philip J. Allcock (New York: Harper, 1958), 156–157. See also the use of the word *'ĕnôš* for "man," especially in poetic texts which stress the weak character of the human person (Job 10:4–5; Ps. 8:5; Isa. 13:12).

12. See the Mesopotamian myths of *Atrahasis* and *Enuma Elish* where the blood of a god is used to create humanity, in Kenton L. Sparks, *Ancient Texts for the Study of the Hebrew Bible* (Peabody, MA: Hendrickson, 2005), 313, 315; cf. the Egyptian myths of "Atum Creation Stories" and "The Creations of Re" where creation is achieved through masturbation, sneezing, and spitting, in Sparks, *Ancient Texts,* 323, 326.

13. McKeown, *Genesis*, 27.

14. See the Mesopotamian myth that teaches that human beings are created "to carry the toil of the gods," in Sparks, *Ancient Texts*, 313.

15. See, for instance, the Babylonian stories of *Atrahasis Epic* 1.190–191 and *Enuma Elish* 6:35–37.

16. This connotation of *'bd* appears especially in association with *šāmar* ("to keep"); these two verbs occur together to apply to the cultic service (cf. Exod. 12:25; Num. 18:4–6). Umberto Cassuto, *Commentary on Genesis*, vol. 1 (Jerusalem: Magnes Press, 1967), 122; Luis Alonso-Schökel: "These verbs are technical terms used frequently for the service of God and observance of the commandments," in "Sapential and Covenant Themes in Gen 2–3," in James Crenshaw, ed., *Studies in Ancient Israelite Wisdom*, Library of Biblical Studies (New York: Ktav Publishing House, 1976), 474.

17. See William P. Brown, *The Ethos of the Cosmos* (Grand Rapids, MI: Eerdmans, 1999), 219. This lesson is also inferred in the book of Ecclesiastes 5:9.

18. See Jacques Doukhan, *Ecclesiastes: All Is Vanity* (Nampa, ID: Pacific Press, 2006), 63.

19. A minority of scholars has rejected the reference to plurality, yet their argumentation has not been convincing. The theory of "plural of majesty" (see S. R. Driver, *The Book of Genesis*, 3rd ed., Westminster Commentary [London: Methuen, 1904], 14) has been rejected on Joüon's observation (Paul Joüon, *A Grammar of Biblical Hebrew*, trans. and rev. T. Muraoka, vol. 2 [Roma: Editrice Pontificio Instituto Biblico, 1991], 114e) that the "we" as plural of majesty is not used with verbs. The view that this was a plural of self-deliberation, thus implying the singular of the subject (see Joüon, 114e), cannot be retained either since it is based on Genesis 11:7 and Psalm 2:3, where the context supports a plural intention. In Genesis 11, the "Let Us" of God echoes the "Let us" of the men of Babel; in Psalm 2:2, the subject of "let us" is clearly a plural, i.e., the kings of the earth and the rulers who take counsel.

20. This interpretation has also been supported by recent commentators such as John Skinner, Gerhard von Rad, Walther Zimmerli, and so on. See Gordon J. Wenham, *Genesis 1–15*, Word Bible Commentary (Waco, TX: Word Books, 1987), 27.

21. See *Miqraot Gdolot*, ad loc.

22. *Genesis Rabbah* VIII, 8.

23. See R. Wilson, "The Early History of the Exegesis of Gen 1:28," *Studia Patrisca* 1 (1957): 420–437.

24. Among more recent interpreters who advocated this view, see Clines, "Image of God in Man," 68–69; and G. F. Hasel, "The Meaning of 'Let Us' in Gen. 1:26," *Andrews University Seminary Studies* 13 (1975): 65–66.

25. See Kenneth A. Mathews, *Genesis 1–11:26*, The New American Commentary (Nashville, TN: Broadman and Holman Publishers, 1996), 174.

26. See H. Niehr, "*ārōm*" in *Theological Dictionary of the Old Testament*, ed. G. Johannes Botterweck, Helmer Ringgren and Heinz-Josef Fabry, trans. David

E. Green, vol. 11 (Grand Rapids, MI: William B. Eerdmans Publishing Company, 2001), 351.

27. Niehr, *Theological Dictionary of the Old Testament,* 11:353–354.

28. The term translated as "subdue" (*rādāh*) in Genesis 1:26, 28 is commonly used to define royal dominion (see, e.g., 1 Kings 4:24; Pss. 8:5–6; 72:8).

29. Bruce K. Waltke and M. O'Connor, *An Introduction to Biblical Hebrew Syntax* (Winona Lake, IN: Eisenbrauns, 1990), 652.

30. See Umberto Cassuto, *A Commentary on the Book of Genesis*, trans. Israel Abrahams, vol. 1 (Jerusalem: Magnes Press, 1961–1964), 130; cf. Claus Westermann, *Creation* (Philadelphia: Fortress Press, 1971), 85; and Doukhan, *The Genesis Creation Story,* 46–47.

3 | The Pentateuch

Roy E. Gane

The Lord demonstrated shared leadership when He created male and female in His image and assigned them the role of exercising dominion over Earth as His representatives and stewards (Gen. 1:26–28; 2:15). Their subsequent service to God through care for His creation is an expression of servant leadership.

After humankind fell into sin, God chose human leaders to shepherd His people through each stage of His redemptive covenant plan, most notably Noah, Abraham, Jacob, Moses, Aaron, and Joshua. He held these individuals accountable for properly representing Him. God personally ruled the nation of Israelites as their divine king (Num. 23:21) from His sanctuary at the center of their camp (Exod. 25:22; Num. 2–3). He was Israel's Legislator (e.g., Exod. 20–23), Supreme Court Chief Justice (Num. 5:11–31), and Commander-in-Chief (Num. 21:34; 31:1–2).

The enduring principles derived from God's instructions to ancient Israel can and should guide various aspects of modern Christian life, both individual and corporate. Following are eleven transcultural principles for human leadership that emerge from the Pentateuch; they guided God's people then and are just as valid for His people now.

DIVINE VISION AND GUIDANCE

The Pentateuch portrays Noah, Abraham, and Moses as individuals who received vision to see beyond immediate circumstances. Vision originating from the Lord and received by faith did not consist of fantasy or delusion. Rather, it was experienced as dependence on God's Word. From a human perspective, surviving a great flood and conquering the land of Canaan were impossible goals, but they were possible because the Lord made them so, according to His promises (Gen. 6–8, 12, 15; Exod. 3:8, 17; 13:5; cf. Heb. 11).

In the Pentateuch, human leadership proved effective to the extent that it submitted to God's superior perspective, wisdom, and power. When leaders failed to trust the Lord and did not seek His guidance, they and others suffered. Such suffering happened when Abraham repeatedly deceived monarchs by presenting Sarah as only his sister (Gen. 12, 20; cf. Isaac in Gen. 26); when Moses struck a rock rather than speaking to it so that it would yield water (Num. 20); when Aaron fashioned a golden calf and proclaimed an idolatrous festival to the Lord (Exod. 32); when ten scouts convinced the Israelites that conquest of Canaan was impossible (Num. 13–14); and when tribal chieftains led their people into idolatry and immorality at Baal Peor (Num. 25).

In the wilderness, Korah, Dathan, and Abiram rebelled against Moses and Aaron, the leaders whom God had appointed (Num. 16). Korah and his associates were impressive, and as a result, the Israelites considered them better leaders, but these men did not follow God's leading, nor did they look to God for vision beyond their present situation. Korah and his associates were popular because the people shared their myopic goal: to retreat from risk by returning to a known environment that they regarded as safer, namely slavery in Egypt.

The person whom God later singled out to replace Moses and lead the Israelites into the Promised Land was Joshua. The Lord chose Joshua because he was "a man in whom is the Spirit" (Num. 27:18),[1] that is, a man who allowed God to direct him. God did not chose Joshua because of his résumé as a tribal chieftain (Num. 13:8, 16), his experience as Moses's longtime assistant

(Exod. 33:11), or because he was general of the Israelite army (Exod. 17:8–13).

Without vision, a leader is simply a manager or bureaucrat. He or she may be highly competent and experienced, with an impressive command of details and strong political support. But God-given vision and submission to God's guidance are more essential qualifications. Without vision, the most impressive leader cannot help people reach the Promised Land.

LOVE

When Jesus was asked which is the greatest commandment (Matt. 22:36), He drew on two strategic Pentateuchal pronouncements: first, love for God in Deuteronomy 6:5, immediately following proclamation of the unity of Israel's deity; and second, love for one's fellow human beings in Leviticus 19:18, at the heart of legislation that teaches God's people how to emulate His holy character (v. 2). Jesus identified the divine moral, relational, interactional principle of unselfish, other-centered love as the basic principle of God's entire self-revelation in the Bible (Matt. 22:37–40).

In Exodus 34:6–7 the Lord declares to Moses His character of love (cf. 1 John 4:8), which includes justice, mercy, and patience. So the divine character is balanced (cf. Ps. 85:7–11), combining the necessity of boundaries and accountability with the need to take human weakness into account. God patiently waits and justly investigates before executing judgment (Gen. 11; 15:16; 18–19), both disciplines and encourages His failing people, and gives them victory when they trust Him (Num. 11–21).

God's people are to emulate His holy character in all of their dealings with Him and with others (Lev. 11:44–45; 19:2; 20:26). Since leadership relies on human interaction, in which there is always the potential for adversarial interpersonal dynamics, it follows that leaders have a special responsibility to show unselfish love (cf. Moses's attitude in Exod. 32:32). Though all humankind is imperfect, persistently dysfunctional individuals who lack love will inevitably fail in leadership relationships.

FALLIBILITY

Only God is omniscient (e.g., Gen. 20:6; Ps. 139). Humans rely on weighing evidence observed by themselves or witnesses (Deut. 19:15). However, the ultimate administration of justice, including the divine penalty of *kārēt*, "cutting off" (involving the denial of an afterlife), is reserved for God alone (e.g., Lev. 17:10, 14; 18:29).

Human leaders make decisions with limited knowledge, and they are of course subject to the weaknesses that have characterized all humanity since the Fall. Abraham thought he should heed his wife's urging to take Hagar as a surrogate and thus produce an heir to fulfill the divine promise. It became clear to Abraham that he had made a mistake, not only because of the negative consequences affecting his family dynamics, but more importantly, because he had not adequately trusted God's ability to fulfill His promise in His own way, even if it took a miracle (Gen. 16–18; 21).

Any leader is prone to making mistakes, including repeating the same error, as Abraham did when he twice attempted to protect himself from royal covetousness by introducing his wife as only his sister (Gen. 12; 20). Only full trust in God and close adherence to His will offer genuine assurance that one's actions are right. But trust and obedience grow through experience with the Lord over time, as the paradigmatic life of Abraham demonstrates.[2]

While leaders are responsible for emulating God in their interactions, they are well advised to recognize their human limitations. Leaders who believe they are infallible are experiencing delusions of grandeur (Exod. 5–15). Such arrogance is a fatal flaw. An effective leader's temptation to overconfidence is likely to grow after accumulated success and honor. It was toward the end of Moses's career that he lapsed into self-sufficiency by angrily striking a rock twice, rather than speaking to it as God had commanded (Num. 20:10–12).

All who engage with others in leadership should maintain proper perspective in relation to the King of kings and to his or her community, by regular assimilation of God's written word and careful adherence to it (Deut. 17:14–20).

SERVICE

The "Law of the King" (Deut. 17:14–20) indicates that a leader's role is to serve the community rather than his or her own self-interest. A leader is to be a member of the community (v. 15), which means that he or she understands the feelings and concerns of the group and has a vested interest in shared well-being. Leaders should not exalt themselves above other community members (v. 20), putting themselves in a unique, privileged class distinct from others and their interests. They should not hoard wealth (v. 17) or invest in expensive infrastructure for retaining power (v. 16). Instead, resources should be distributed to all according to their need.

Self-interest, including self-preservation, is a natural human instinct. It is the opposite of service to the community. When leaders are faced with the challenge of deciding between what is best for them and what is beneficial to the community, the tendency is to choose the former, even if the result is oppressive to the community. Selfish leaders often rationalize that their course is for the greater good because they, the leaders, are indispensable to corporate well-being. Thus a pharaoh justified infanticide by the need to protect himself and other Egyptians from the rising specter of revolt by the Israelites, who were multiplying in number (Exod. 1:8–10, 22).

Even Abraham was paralyzed by self-interest when he found himself vulnerable to those coveting his wife in a foreign country. He tried to save himself, even if it meant that his wife would become part of a royal harem (Gen. 12; 20). God intervened in each case to protect Sarah because the covenant promises were for her and Abraham as a couple. Together they would produce the heir through which their descendants would become a great nation, even though Sarah needed a miracle for this to happen (Gen. 17:15–21; 18:10–14). Through such experiences, Abraham learned a better model of leadership: He needed to do what was right for others and leave his own security to the Lord.[3]

Moses was remarkable for his subjugation of self-interest. His concerns were not for himself, but for God.[4] Moses courageously approached God to intercede for the people, and he linked his fate with theirs, even if they were going to be lost (Exod. 32). He had incredible courage and strength of will in defending both others and the honor of God, as when he stood against the pharaoh (Exod. 5–11) or against thousands of Israelites who had rebelled against the Lord (Exod. 32). He defended himself when God's authority was at stake (Num. 16:28–30), but he was speechless in defense of himself alone, even against his own brother and sister (Num. 12). According to Numbers 12:3, he was "very humble, more so than anyone else on the face of the earth."

Aaron and his sons were exclusively authorized to serve as priests by regularly approaching God in order to mediate for others through rituals (Exod. 28–30; Lev. 8–9) that foreshadowed the ministry of Christ (Heb. 7–10). Today Christian ministers serve God and their communities, but not in the same manner. An Israelite priest was an elite ritual functionary belonging to a dynasty descended from a single individual. There is no such elite human priesthood in the New Testament. The only priesthood through which Christians gain access to God is the priesthood of the divine Jesus Christ (Heb. 4:14–16; 5:1–10; 6:19–20; 7:1–28), the one Mediator between God and humanity (1 Tim. 2:5). Working with Christ is the egalitarian priesthood of all believers (1 Pet. 2:9, referring to Exod. 19:6), including males and females of all races (Gal. 3:28), who serve according to the gifts that God's Spirit grants to them (1 Cor. 12, 14).

Apart from Christ, our heavenly Priest, the Christian church does not *have* a priesthood; it *is* a priesthood.[5] So in a real sense it does not *have* a ministry; it *is* a ministry. This ecclesiology determines the paradigm of Christian ministry as service. In the church, disciples of Christ fill various leadership functions, some of which were within the job description of the Aaronic priests. These include, for example, coordinating worship, teaching God's Word, and administering resources dedicated to God (cf. Lev. 1–9; 10:11; Num. 18:8–32). People who do these things are ministers. But so are Christians who use any of the other gifts of the Spirit. Since ministry is service, and all are to serve, then all are ministers.

It is more than unfortunate that in Christian parlance the term *minister* is often descriptive of a religious professional, roughly equivalent to a *priest* in a sacramental church. This misunderstanding of what ministry is damages the Lord's work in several ways.

First, the community tends to see the minister in the same light that the Old Testament community saw a priest: as a member of the God-ordained elite. Second, the richly diverse, highly efficient power of Christian ministry by all believers is radically reduced to a relatively narrow set of activities performed by a few. Third, when a few are considered as leaders of the church, many are disenfranchised and unnecessary power struggles ensue over questions such as who can be ordained for ministry. If ordination were placed in the context of a New Testament ecclesiology as commission for varieties of service in a priesthood of all believers—rather than viewed as lifelong inauguration to an elite kind of priestly role above that of the lay community—all ministers called by God would be appropriately authorized by the community of faith to serve according to their spiritual gifts.

MUTUAL RESPECT

Israelite leaders were the Lord's servants, and members of their community were to treat them with respect. Thus the law, "You shall not revile God" is paralleled by "or curse a leader of your people" (Exod. 22:28). The Lord commanded the Israelites regarding their priests: "you shall treat them as holy" (Lev. 21:8), which implies that the people would not undermine the character or reputation of their priests.

God defended His appointed leaders against defamation of character and mutiny, holding disloyal individuals accountable, especially if they also held leadership positions. After Miriam, followed by Aaron, maligned Moses, the Lord punished her with scaly skin disease ("leprosy," Num. 12). After disgruntled Israelites threatened to stone Joshua and Caleb for encouraging them to trust God and take Canaan, the Lord's glory interrupted the lynching and He passed judgment on the rebels (Num. 14). After Korah and his associates attempted to usurp spiritual and civil leadership of Israel from Aaron and Moses, some of the ringleaders were swallowed alive by the earth, while others were incinerated by divine fire, and many of their sympathizers perished from a divine plague (Num. 16). Subsequently, God reaffirmed the priestly leadership of Aaron with a miraculous sign: Aaron's wooden staff budded, blossomed, and bore ripe almonds (Num. 17).

Respect describes the relationships that exist among God's people. Good leaders treat others with respect. The Pentateuch records a number of occasions when the Israelites brought concerns to Moses that he did not know how to address. He took the cases seriously by referring them to God, who demonstrated respect for the needs of individuals by providing solutions for their difficulties (Lev. 24:10–23; Num. 9:6–14; 27:1–11; 36:1–9).

When God's Spirit rested on Eldad and Medad, even though they had not responded to Moses's call for them to assemble at the sanctuary with the other elders, Joshua was alarmed and asked Moses to stop them from prophesying (Num. 11:26–28). But Moses calmly replied: "Are you jealous for my sake? Would that all the LORD's people were prophets, and that the LORD would put his spirit on them!" (v. 29). Thus, Moses treated them with respect as recipients of divine grace. Moses saw no need to exert his personal authority for the sake of his reputation as a leader, choosing rather to trust God in the situation.

PARTICIPATION

The Lord ruled the Israelite theocracy through leaders such as Moses. Aaron and Miriam, who possessed the prophetic gift, were also national leaders (Num. 12:2, 6; Mic. 6:4). There were also tribal leaders, with individual tribes represented by chieftains who reported to Moses (Exod. 16:22; 34:31). At the level of tribes, which were natural social units consisting of extended families, still others engaged in leadership.

The Christian church is not organized along tribal lines, but the church today still requires structure. Further, modern disciples still need leaders with whom they can identify, whom they can respect and trust (cf. Acts 6:3), and who share leadership. Whatever particular form church governance may take, it should be participatory, not merely in appearance, but in actual function. Making sure people within the church still maintain their individual voices requires ongoing effort and vigilance on the part of leadership.

RESPONSIBLE DELEGATION

The Pentateuch provides instructive examples of delegating responsibility to others along with the authority to carry it out. For example, Abraham commissioned his trusted servant to acquire a bride for his son, Isaac (Gen. 24). Moses had difficulty delegating at first. Thinking he needed to make sure everything was done perfectly, he attempted to personally resolve all disputes among his people. So his agenda was exhausting, crammed with judging cases from morning until evening. Moses's father-in-law wisely urged him to appoint judges to arbitrate minor cases, which he did (Exod. 18:13–26).

When Moses felt overwhelmed by the responsibility of leading his cantankerous community, God directed him to appoint seventy tribal elders, on whom the divine Spirit rested so that they prophesied (Num. 11:16–17, 24–25). The biblical text does not record the content of their speeches; the point was that the Lord validated them as His servants. Thus they were authorized to participate and to help Moses bear the burden of government. As representatives of their respective groups, they also bore the effects of any discontent.

As a wise leader, Moses learned to avoid mistakes that are common among leaders today. First, he did not assert authority out of a need to control, but rather for the sake of God and the well-being of others (cf. above regarding Eldad and Medad in Num. 11:26–29). Second, he did not micromanage. Rather, he treated his delegated leaders with trust that they would make proper choices within the framework of the instructions that he gave them, although he held them accountable if they did not (e.g., Lev. 9–10; Num. 31). "Although Moses was cautious about delegating some tasks, one of his greatest strengths was the fact that he believed in his people more than they believed in themselves."[6] Third, and related to the last point, Moses did not undermine the authority of those to whom he delegated by interfering in order to make sure they remained subservient to himself; rather, he treated them with due respect and let them do their jobs (e.g., Exod. 17:8–13).

GRACE

The Creator-God and theocratic King of Israel had the power to create an entirely new kind of society. But He generally chose to work within the constraints of the existing patriarchal society. Through Moses, He reformed and modified some aspects of life within Israel (e.g., Exod. 21; Lev. 25; Num. 27; 35; Deut. 15), but He did not overturn and replace the basic tribal and family structure (e.g., Num. 1; 26; 30; 36). Thus He graciously allowed people to thrive in their familiar social environment. God brought about change with grace, rather than imposing change more rapidly than they could handle.

In the Pentateuch, God addressed an ancient Near Eastern people in culturally conditioned language that they could understand. This explains why several aspects of biblical law and narratives, such as the respective roles of men and women (e.g., Num. 30); toleration of polygamy and debt slavery (e.g., Gen. 29–30; Exod. 21:1–11, 20–21, 26–27); and levirate marriage (Gen. 38; Deut. 25:5–10) are strange or offensive to modern readers. God was working with a culture that differs radically from ours. If He had abruptly abolished polygamy and debt slavery, the correction would have been ineffective and hurtful: barren women would have been divorced without opportunity for a respectable livelihood, and those whose crops failed would have starved. So the Lord regulated polygamy and debt slavery to prevent their worst effects, and the Bible undermines these institutions to the point that Christianity now rejects them.[7]

Patriarchal culture itself was not a timeless principle that is normative for modern Christians. As we study the Pentateuch, we can only uncover God's enduring principles when we understand they are encapsulated in the imperfect cultural garb of a particular time and place.[8]

The fact that God makes accommodation for human weakness (e.g., Matt. 19:3–8), sometimes choosing the better of two evils rather than forcing progress too rapid for a group to handle (cf. Gen. 33:12–14), is instructive for leadership. Good leaders are sensitive to the effects of radical change—effects for which people are not adequately prepared.

PERSUASION

When the Israelite nation was formed, God sought to encourage and mentor His people.[9] When God leads, He communicates, and He does so with persuasion which respects the free choice and the intelligence of others. It follows that human leaders who serve Him should do the same.

The Pentateuch contains striking examples of ways in which God's human instruments sought to persuade others. Joseph persuaded a pharaoh to make provision for a coming famine (Gen. 41). Jethro exercised persuasion in his reasoning with Moses regarding the burden of judging the controversies that arose among the people (Exod. 18). Caleb and Joshua employed strong logic in urging the Israelites to allow trust in God to overcome their fears of the inhabitants of Canaan (Num. 13:30; 14:6–9).

Moses, God's spokesman, was a master of persuasion. The book of Deuteronomy consists largely of Moses's remarkable homilies, through which he urged the second generation of Israelites to be loyal to God—unlike their recalcitrant parents. Deuteronomy is a model of powerful persuasion, connecting people to their just and merciful God, and encouraging them to loyally trust and follow Him.

Persuasion involves both motivational language and teaching that informs so that people can make sensible and educated choices. Much of the Pentateuch consists of instructions/laws regarding God's principles, which reflect and reveal His character. The positive effects of following them point to the wisdom and beneficence of their divine Source (Deut. 4:5–8). Leaders can learn much from the biblical model of persuasion.

MODELING

Noah, Abraham, Isaac, and Jacob taught worship of God by worshiping Him themselves (Gen. 8:20; 12:7–8; 26:25; 31:54; 35:6–7), not merely by commanding others to worship. Elderly Caleb demonstrated his advocacy of conquest with personal action by attacking Hebron, a stronghold of giants, to show that even the most powerful enemies could be overcome by God's strength (Josh. 14:6–15;

15:13–14). The Lord's priestly leaders were to model holiness in their own conduct, thereby showing the integral connection between faith and practice, holy worship and holy living (Lev. 21 in particular).

In the same way, God's leaders today are never above His law and are responsible for practicing what they preach. They are to model His way—the way. If they proclaim love while practicing selfishness, their net effect is to advocate hypocrisy. Leaders can delegate tasks, but not their core responsibility to lead by example. In reality, effective, godly leaders show the way by their own decisions and actions, rather than by simply commanding others.

ACCOUNTABILITY

In the Pentateuch, individuals and groups were accountable and received retribution for unlawful acts (Gen. 19; Exod. 14; Lev. 10; Num. 11–12; 14; 16; 21; 25). There were moments when God expected leaders to carry out retributive justice on those who rebelled against His law. He commanded Moses to have the community execute: a brawling blasphemer (Lev. 24:10–14, 23); one who rejected freedom from work on Sabbath (Num. 15:32–36); and idolatrous, immoral chieftains (Num. 25:4; cf. Exod. 32:25–28). Phinehas won divine approval by pointedly purging the Israelite camp of a rebellious chieftain's son who flaunted his Midianite girlfriend (Num. 25:6–8, 10–13).

Obviously, modern religious leaders who live in non-theocratic nations have no such authority to purge their religious communities. However, the removal of members by the community for serious violation of moral law is appropriate accountability (1 Cor. 5). The Israelite legal system instituted by God was designed to protect rights and responsibilities on an ongoing basis. Leaders who administered it were to be fair in holding members of the community accountable, not allowing themselves to be swayed by bribery, discrimination, or reverse discrimination (Exod. 23:3, 6–8; Lev. 19:15; Deut. 1:16–17).

The matter of accountability sharpens the administration of grace. Accountability for law breaking, which is better described as selfish disregard for the welfare of others, is not overlooked by grace. There is a substitution. Grace grants undeserved release from the retribution, or what is better understood as the consequence of selfish living. Grace substitutes freedom for retribution.

An important function of the Israelite judicial system was to resolve conflicts between members of the community (Exod. 18:13–26; Deut. 1:12–17; cf. Judg. 4:4–5). That function was an administration of accountability. The New Testament assumes that this service continues within the church through judicial leaders whom the church appoints (1 Cor. 6:1–6).

The Pentateuch mandated a distinctly higher level of accountability to God and the community from those who served as leaders. Thus, the high priest and a chieftain were required to offer more expensive purification offerings ("sin offerings") than others when they committed inadvertent violations of divine commands (Lev. 4:3, 22–23; compare vv. 27–28, 32). Their sins stood out because those committing them had a greater impact on others.

When Israelite leaders committed offenses, such as Aaron making an idol (Exod. 32), Nadab and Abihu offering unauthorized fire (Lev. 10), Miriam undermining Moses's leadership (Num. 12), Korah and his associates rebelling against Moses and Aaron (Num. 16), Moses striking rather than speaking to a rock (Num. 20), and chieftains leading their people into apostasy at Baal Peor (Num. 25), consequences were openly severe because of the negative impact on God's holy character (see Lev. 10:3 in particular; see also Num. 20:12).

As in ancient Israel, discipleship within the Christian community today is a responsibility that comes with a high level of accountability. Much is required from those to whom much is entrusted (Luke 12:48), especially now that Jesus has given us the ultimate demonstration of the way we are to serve with self-sacrificing love (e.g., Luke 22:24–27; John 13:1–18). Organizational leaders within communities of faith are distinctly accountable to their communities for consistent demonstration of obedience to God.

CONCLUSION: A PENTATEUCHAL PROFILE OF GOOD LEADERSHIP

The Pentateuch teaches that human leaders are subordinate to God, who provides vision and guidance for the community through

His presence. They are accountable for reflecting His love and His character in their lifestyle and interactions with others. Good leaders are humble, recognize their fallibility, are unselfish in service, are respectful of others, build participation, delegate responsibility when appropriate, change existing social structures to align with moral principle as much as possible, effectively communicate to persuade and encourage others, and lead by example. They practice accountability, and they themselves are accountable at a high level.

Self-exalting pride is a contradiction to these leadership principles. High-handed, autocratic, self-interested rule in the church should never be confused with genuinely strong leadership that humbly follows God in order to shepherd the community of believers and bring them closer to the heavenly Promised Land. Christian leaders serve by leading and lead by serving. We need leaders like Moses, who was notably humble (Num. 12:3), concerned only for God's honor, and interceded for God's people, caring about them to the extent that he was committed to sharing their fate (Exod. 32:32).

FOR REFLECTION

Personal:

1. How have leadership principles from the Pentateuch influenced your understanding of humility?
2. Are there ways you have sought self-interest in your leadership? What must happen in order for you to abandon that tendency?

Organizational:

1. To what extent does leadership within your organization empower others? What is the impact on the health and effectiveness of the organization?
2. In light of the concepts discussed in this chapter, what specific changes in leadership structure and practice could most benefit your organization?

ENDNOTES

1. Unless otherwise noted, scripture quotations in this chapter are taken from the New American Standard Bible.

2. Paul Borgman, *Genesis: The Story We Haven't Heard* (Downers Grove, IL: InterVarsity, 2001), 39–114.

3. See Borgman, *Genesis,* 38–114.

4. Stephen Dawes, "Numbers 12.3: What Was Special About Moses?" *The Bible Translator* 41 (1990): 338–39.

5. Russell Burrill, *Revolution in the Church* (Fallbrook, CA: Hart Research Center, 1979), 24.

6. Roy Gane, *Leviticus, Numbers*, NIV Application Commentary (Grand Rapids, MI: Zondervan, 2004), 790.

7. On slavery, see Gane, *Leviticus, Numbers,* 439–442. On polygamy, see Roy Gane, "Some Biblical Principles Relevant to Evangelism Among Polygamous Peoples," *Journal of Adventist Mission Studies* 2 (2006): 29–43.

8. Gane, *Leviticus, Numbers,* 308–9.

9. For strategies He employed in working with the Israelites, see Gane, *Leviticus, Numbers,* 683–86. For these and other aspects of divine leading relevant to Christians, see Roy Gane, "Sanctuary Principles for the Successful Church Community," *Journal of the Adventist Theological Society* 17/2 (2006): 110–121.

4 | The Historical Books

Jiří Moskala

The living God of the Bible, as Creator, reveals the nature of His leadership in relationship with creation by delegating leadership roles to humans (Gen. 1:28b).[1] The narratives of kings, prophets, priests, judges, elders, and others recorded in the Historical Books of the Bible must be approached with this understanding. These persons, entrusted as positional leaders within the community, were accountable for demonstrating spiritual leadership to the ultimate Leader, the highest Judge, who is the Creator and Redeemer (Gen. 1:1, 28; 3:15; 18:25; Pss. 82:1–8; 121:1–2; Isa. 43:1; 44:24; 45:11, 21; 46:9–10; 47:4; 49:26b). God set the tone, standard, and vision for leadership, and He gave these persons the opportunity through His revelation and their personal abilities to serve the people of God. Biblical narrators see leaders, their lives, accomplishments, and influence from this theocentric perspective. Thus kings were characterized by formulas reflecting their response to God: he (the name of a particular king) "did what was right in the eyes of the Lord" (e.g., 2 Kings 12:2; 18:3; 22:2) or he "did evil in the eyes of the Lord" (e.g., 2 Kings 13:2; 21:2; 24:19) and walked in the sinful path of his father or forefathers (e.g., 2 Kings 13:2; 23:37; 24:9).[2] King Jeroboam, the first king of the Northern Kingdom, was evaluated by God as someone who had "not been like my servant David who kept my commands and followed me with all his heart" (1 Kings 14:8), even though God through the prophet Ahijah called him to be faithful (1 Kings 11:38).[3] King Ahab is characterized as the one who "did more evil in the eyes of the LORD than any of those before him" (1 Kings 16:30). Adequate leadership is measured by God's ideals.

In the biblical context, God—His character, His plans, His mission, His will—provides the vision and imagination for leadership (Exod. 34:6–7; Ps. 16:8; Heb. 11:27). Faithful spiritual leadership actively lives, participates in, shares, and implements the vision and the mission of God to bless and save humans (Gen. 12:2–3; Isa. 45:22; Jer. 29:11; Mic. 6:8). Faithful leaders do not think about *God's place in their leadership role*, but they find *their place in God's leadership*. Thus, when James Kouzes and Barry Posner explain that "leadership begins with something that grabs hold of you and won't let go,"[4] their assertion is in harmony with the biblical record.

The modern word *leadership* does not occur in the Hebrew of the Historical Books of the Old Testament (Joshua–Esther).[5] The term *leader* (in singular or in plural) is associated with different positions: elders, tribe leaders, chiefs, army commanders (Josh. 8:10; 9:15, 18–19; 17:4 ; 22:30, 32; 23:2; 24:1; Judg. 7:25; 1 Sam. 7:6; 14:38; 1 Chron. 15:16).[6] Concepts of leadership are inherently present. These twelve historical books cover one thousand years, from the conquest of Canaan under Joshua starting around 1410 BC through the Assyrian captivity and the fall of Samaria (the Northern Kingdom) in 722 BC, the end of Judea with the fall of Jerusalem and destruction of the Solomonic Temple in 587/586 BC, the return from the Babylonian captivity in 537 BC to the rebuilding of the new House of God (known as the Zerubbabelian or the Second Temple) in 515 BC, and even beyond to the events occurring around 400 BC (see the Davidic genealogy of 1 Chron. 3:10–24).[7] The books record not only war and victory, but also defeat, treason, and murder: Tragedy and joy lived side by side. In those difficult times, people needed good, reliable leaders. It is impossible to do justice to all the outstanding personalities in these books and cover all their features, so this chapter will concentrate only on the lessons emerging from crucial turning points: the leadership of Joshua and the judges; transition to kingship (from the last judge Samuel to the first kings, Saul and David); schism (focusing on King Rehoboam and King Jeroboam); an overview of kings (stressing especially kings who were good and successful by God's standards), including the leading role of the prophet Elijah; and the return from the Babylonian captivity under the leadership activities of Zerubbabel, Joshua, Haggai, and Zechariah.[8]

LEADERSHIP TRANSITION FROM MOSES TO JOSHUA

The book of Joshua starts with the transfer of leadership from Moses to Joshua. Joshua, Moses's former assistant (Exod. 24:13; 33:11; Num. 11:28; Deut. 1:38), was assigned the new role of leading Israel into the Promised Land. Vision, mission, and strategies were identified for him in Joshua 1. There are ten important lessons we can learn from this leadership transition and Joshua's charge.

1. Leadership is *a gift* as well as *a commission* from God, who called Moses and Joshua to leadership positions (Exod. 3:10; Num. 27:18–23). Both stood under the direct command of God (Deut. 34:9; Josh. 1:2), and both were called to lead His people into the Promised Land. Robinson fittingly states: "My duty is a gift."[9]

2. Both leaders, Moses and Joshua, are called *servants.* The first time Moses is characterized with the title "the servant of the LORD" (Josh. 1:1) is at his death (Deut. 34:5). It is interesting to observe that Joshua is also named "the servant of the LORD" at his death (Josh. 24:29; Judg. 2:8). This obviously was intended as a summation of their life work. Servant leadership and integrity promote trust in leadership. "Servanthood is a way of life…, not so much a way of leading.… The key focus in biblical servanthood is on simply doing things for a great God, and not so much on doing great things for God."[10] The faithfulness of those who lead encourages others to

wholehearted obedience and faithful service to the Lord: "Israel served the LORD throughout the lifetime of Joshua and of the elders who outlived him and who had experienced everything the LORD had done for Israel" (Josh. 24:31).

3. Both Moses and Joshua experienced a *personal encounter* with God. Moses was met by the Angel of the Lord, who is identified as the Lord (Exod. 3:1–15), and Joshua was confronted by the Commander of the army of the Lord, who demanded from him the same reverence as was required of Moses: "Take off your sandals, for the place where you are standing is holy" (Josh. 5:13–15).

4. God assured Joshua that He would be with him as He was with Moses (1:5). Joshua is the new Moses (Deut. 18:15; 34:10), but the true New Moses, Jesus Christ, will come later in time and lead to the eschatological Promised Land (Acts 3:20–23; Heb. 3:18–4:11; Rev. 21:1–4).[11] Spiritual leaders need to be confident that God is with them, meaning that they need to seek His will and be sure that *they are with the Lord working according to His will.* As such, Abraham Lincoln aptly expressed: "My concern is not whether God is on our side; my great concern is to be on God's side, for God is always right."[12] This confidence does not overrule submission to the leading of God or humility.

5. Leaders are *dependent upon God's promises* (Josh. 1:3–5). The gift of land was finally given to Israel according to His promises to Abraham, Isaac, Jacob, and Moses (Gen. 12:7; 15:18; Exod. 3:16–17; Josh. 1:3). No enemies were able to stop their fulfillment and prevail against Joshua (Josh. 1:5). In return, Joshua needed to cultivate trust in the Lord and focus on God's promises (1:3–5, 9b).

6. Spiritual leadership is demonstrated. Both Moses and Joshua encouraged Israel to choose life and follow God (Deut. 31:19–20; 34:9–11). Joshua made a bold appeal: "Now fear the LORD and serve him with all faithfulness.… But if serving the LORD seems undesirable to you, then choose for yourselves this day whom you will serve,…but as for me and my household, we will serve the LORD" (Josh. 24:14–15). Leaders need to personify in their lives the qualities God wants to see reflected in His people. They need to be *models of God's* values and principles, reflect His character, and live in harmony with God's revealed law.

7. People want to know if *their leaders are with God,* as in the case of Joshua (1:17). This realization helps affirm their leadership role in the community and provides affirmation of the authority they must carry out in the community.

8. Leaders need to have a *clear vision* of their task and goal. Joshua 1:2–4 summarizes the literary structure of the whole book, as Richard Hess explains: "Verse 2 describes the crossing of the Jordan as found in 1:1–5:12. Verse 3 outlines the 'conquest' of 5:13–12:24. Verse 4 implies the distribution of the land in 13:1–22:34."[13] The first command invites action: "Get ready to cross the Jordan River into the land I am about to give" to you and the Israelites.

9. Leaders need to have *courage* to go forward and deal with difficult situations. They need to show firmness and boldness in order to fulfill their mission. Seven times the command "be strong and courageous" is mentioned in relationship to Joshua: four times it is given by God (Deut. 31:23; Josh. 1:6, 7, 9), once by Moses (Deut. 31:7), and once by the officers of the people to Joshua (Josh. 1:18). Finally Joshua himself commands his military officers to be strong and courageous, thus displaying that this phrase had become the motto for his life (Josh. 10:25).[14] Peter Koestenbaum recognizes that courage is crucial in the life of a leader and identifies this as an essential of leadership. He asserts that the heart and greatness of the leadership "results from the simultaneous activation of four fundamentally different styles of thinking or ways of greatness: *vision, reality, ethics,* and *courage.*"[15]

10. Faithful leaders constantly need to *meditate on the Torah* in order to know God's instructions and be able to make correct decisions: "Do not let this Book of the Law depart from your mouth; meditate on it day and night, so that you may be careful to do everything written in it" (Josh. 1:8). A leader's authority is rooted in the knowledge of, and conformity to, the Word of God as well as in the Presence of God. A leader must willingly obey God's will (Josh. 1:7–8) because this will determine his or her success. A leader's prosperity is closely associated with his or her respect for God, His values, will, and law (Josh. 1:8–9).[16] Walter Brueggemann rightly speaks about "Torah-based leadership"[17] for the kings in Israel (Deut. 17:18–20).

LEADERSHIP IN THE PERIOD
OF JUDGES/LIBERATORS

After Joshua's death, elders led Israel (Josh. 24:31; Judg. 2:7). Several times it is stated that "the Israelites did evil in the eyes of the LORD" because they forgot the Lord their God and served idols (2:11; 3:7, 12; 4:1; 6:1; 10:6; 13:1). "In those days Israel had no king; everyone did as he saw fit" (Judg. 21:25; also 17:6; 18:1; 19:1). The people departed from the standards of God's covenant, and their unethical behavior showed the worst debasement of morality and corruption (Judg. 17–21). There was no consistent, sustained action to stop idolatry and disobedience to God's law.

Israel was attacked and enslaved by their enemies. When they asked for God's intervention, He in His mercy sent judges (six major and six minor)[18] to help His people in those abusive and perilous circumstances: "Then the LORD raised up judges to save them out of the hands of these raiders" (2:16). Seven times it is stated that "the Spirit of the LORD came upon" or "clothed" the judges Othniel (3:10), Gideon (6:34), Jephthah (11:29), and Samson (13:25; 14:6, 19; 15:14). Leaders are called and guided by God's Spirit and enabled by Him to be capable leaders. In times of chaos, God's Spirit brings order, freedom, protection, and safety through leadership. The book of Judges demonstrates how crucial it is for leaders to cooperate with God, stay focused, and follow His instructions. Even judges considered good, such as Gideon, Jephthah, and Samson, marred their actions with wrong decisions and behavior (see, for example, Gideon's idolatry in 8:27, unwise Jephthah's promise and the fate of his daughter in 11:30–40, and the immoral and tragic life of Samson in 16:1–31).

The leadership challenge of the judges was obvious: deliver Israel from the oppression of its enemies, save people from bondage, bring freedom, and protect them so they might prosper. These judges were liberators. On the spiritual level, they warned people of idolatry and immorality, and they exhorted them to observe God's law.

LEADERSHIP TRANSITION FROM SAMUEL THROUGH SOLOMON

Samuel, the last judge, was an outstanding spiritual leader. He grew into greatness by obeying God and following His will. Thus, his ministry was highly valued and his word never failed. The biblical text underlines that God "let none of his words fall to the ground. And all Israel from Dan to Beersheba recognized that Samuel was attested as a prophet of the LORD" (1 Sam. 3:19–20). His character was exemplary. He played a key role in Israel's transition from an informal system of judges to a more formal monarchy even though he opposed making the change (1 Sam. 8:10–18; 10:1, 17–25; 12:17). Ironically, his ministry is closely associated with the kingship of Saul and David, the main figures of 1–2 Samuel.

When Samuel became old, the people demanded a king. He warned them of the dangers inherent in their request. Samuel felt rejected, but God reminded him: "It is not you they have rejected, but they have rejected Me as their King" (1 Sam. 8:7). God relented to the demands of the people and allowed them to have a king (1 Sam. 8:9; 10:24). Many narratives in the history of the kings illustrate the corruption that accompanies power when humans rule in their communities.

According to Deuteronomy 17, which is the first biblical statement about a kingship in Israel, God did not command Israel to have a king. He did not say: "And you shall or should say: 'We will set a king over us.'" But the Hebrew phrase *wě' āmartā 'asîmāh 'ālay melek*[19] described the people's wish for a king: "And you will say: 'Let us set a king over us'" (Deut. 17:14). God then commanded that such a potential future king must be an Israelite, should not seek military power or riches, nor have many wives (17:15–17). He should serve his people.[20] The king was to study the Torah every day in order to revere the Lord and follow carefully all of God's laws and instructions (17:18–20), which meant that this earthly king would be a vice-regent under the heavenly God-King, who must remain the Leader. The kings were to shape their leadership on the knowledge of the Torah.

Even though Samuel mentored Saul, it was the Spirit of the Lord who was working in his life preparing him for his service and guiding him. It is important to note that in the Historical Books the Spirit of the Lord is mentioned in reference to Saul more than to any other king including David or prophets like Elijah and Elisha. This frequency emphasizes that the focus is on the Spirit in Saul's narrative. Consequently, a Spirit-filled and Spirit-led ministry was to be a model for all subsequent kings. Unfortunately, Saul did not let God's Spirit change him; he did not cooperate fully with God (1 Sam. 13:13–14; 15:10–11, 19, 22–23, 26–29, 35). As a result, "the Spirit of the LORD departed from Saul" (1 Sam. 16:14a), and this verse describes a turning point in his life that led to his death (28:20; 31:3–6; 1 Chron. 10:13–14). Where there is no Spirit, there is no courage to face enemies or gain victory (1 Sam. 17:32; 28:5). On the other hand, David, filled with the Spirit, faced Goliath and victoriously overcame many other obstacles. The biblical text underlines that after Samuel anointed David to be king "from that day on the Spirit of the LORD came upon David in power" (1 Sam. 16:13). Even though David made mistakes, he always turned back in repentance to the Lord. The turning points in the lives of Saul and David are described in 1 Samuel 16:13–14 in regard to the role of the Spirit of the Lord in their lives.

David, the second king in Israel, was a dedicated and good leader, and he is characterized as a person "after God's heart," which means that he was willing to follow God's instructions and do His will. He was not always right, but he was humble and willing to be corrected. This upright behavior was prompted by his trusting in the Lord. Samuel said to Saul after his disobedience: "The LORD has sought out a man after his own heart and appointed him leader of his people, because you have not kept the LORD's command" (1 Sam. 13:14).

David misused his position and authority with regard to Bathsheba. Caroline Nolan speaks of David's "abuse of power,"[21] and Richard Davidson stresses that "Bathsheba was a victim of power rape on the part of David."[22] This abuse of power seriously damaged his credibility as a leader. From that time on, he encountered even greater problems in his family. David was a talented political leader, spiritual giant, literary genius, militarily strategist, and a national hero, but the biblical record honestly points out his failures as a leader of his own emotional life and his family (including sons Amnon and Absalom). Even with all David's failings, God's grace and forgiveness sustained him in his position. Those who receive grace should offer grace. Bill Robinson fittingly underscores: "Beneficiaries of grace should be benefactors of grace. Forgiven leaders should be gracious leaders."[23] However, this principle was not always honored in David's treatment of others (for example, 1 Kings 2:1, 5–9).

The third united king of Israel, Solomon, asked God for wisdom in order to be able "to govern" over Israel (1 Kings 3:9). Wisdom—the ability to discern between good and evil and to follow the right—is needed by every leader. Without it, the art of leadership will be hindered and true insight and knowledge necessary for mature decision making will be lacking.

It is noteworthy that the first king in Israel did not carefully follow God's instructions, consulted evil spirits, and committed suicide. The second king was acting according to God's will, but he misused his power and committed grievous sins. However, David repented, and God accepted him in such a way that Chronicles does not even mention his personal trespasses, and 1 Kings 14:8 stresses that David kept God's commands and followed Him "with all his heart doing only what was right." King Solomon was wise, but his imprudent decisions in marrying multiple foreign women led him from God and into the foolishness of idolatry (1 Kings 11:4; Eccles. 2:4–11). These life sketches of the three united kings demonstrate that when those who provide leadership from the office of kingship did so honorably the positive contribution to the community was lasting—and when they did not, the effect was devastating.

LEADERSHIP IN THE TIME OF SCHISM

The split of the United Kingdom after Solomon into two kingdoms presents an additional insight into leadership. The Northern (Israel) and Southern (Judah) Kingdoms were created by a leader's faux pas. Rehoboam, Solomon's son and successor, chose to follow the immature counsel of his friends instead of listening to the counsel of experienced advisors (1 Kings 12:3–15). After the ten tribes turned from him, he wanted to secure his leadership by force, which would have resulted in a civil war. God stopped that action through His faithful prophet Shemaiah (1 Kings 12:21–24). Rehoboam did not live to serve people. He used them to satisfy his selfish ambitions. Even though Rehoboam, for a time, repented (2 Chron. 12:6–12), his reign was characterized as "evil because he had not set his heart on seeking the LORD" (2 Chron. 12:14). The consequences of his immature leadership were irreversible. Discerning and accepting wise counsel and choosing collaboration with experienced people are strong features of a successful leader.

Jeroboam, the first king of the Northern Kingdom of Israel, completely separated from Rehoboam. In order to have an independent kingdom, he established a new worship center in Bethel as a counterpart to Solomon's Temple. He appointed his own non-levitical priests, and he made two golden calves, putting one in Bethel and the other one in the northern city of Dan. In this way, he wanted to secure his territory from north to south by a new system of worship. To discourage people from going to Jerusalem to celebrate festivals, he instituted a new feast (1 Kings 12:26–33). In this way, he led Israel away from God into idolatry. Jeroboam pursued his own evil way, which ultimately culminated in the destruction of the kingdom of Israel in 722 BC with the fall of Samaria and that resulted in Assyrian exile (1 Kings 13:34; 2 Kings 17:22–23). His political power was dearer to him than faithfulness to the Lord. He acted in direct opposition and disobedience to the Word of God, thus beginning "the tendency of kings to adopt forms of worship that suit[ed] their own interest."[24]

LEADERSHIP OF KINGS AFTER THE SCHISM

The history of the divided kingdoms is not encouraging from a leadership perspective. In both kingdoms, the triumph of godliness was rare, and apostasy was often present. Very few blessings can be seen among God's people due to the incompetent and wicked leadership of their kings. Most of them inherited the throne, while others usurped it. They were not prepared to rule. Almost all of them exemplify the thesis of Barbara Kellerman's book *Bad Leadership: What It Is, How It Happens*[25] because they did not know how to lead their community in a responsible way. Kellerman describes poor leadership behavior, and in the main chapters of her book, she demonstrates that bad leaders are incompetent, rigid, intemperate, callous, corrupt, insular, and evil. Unfortunately many Israelite kings embraced a majority or even all of these characteristics and so they fit into the category of bad leadership. John Kotter stresses that the leader needs to "walk the talk, or lead by example. Often the most powerful way to communicate a new direction is through behavior."[26] Almost all the kings in Judah and all in Israel would have failed this test.

After three united kings (Saul, David, and Solomon), there were twenty rulers in the Northern Kingdom of Israel (from Jeroboam to Hosea), and twenty kings in the Southern Kingdom of Judah (from Rehoboam to Zedekiah, including Queen Athaliah). Tragically, in Israel not one of the kings nor the queen was a godly leader; all of them did what was evil in the eyes of the Lord.[27] Seven of them were assassinated (Nadab, Elah, Joram, Zechariah, Shallum, Pekahiah, and Pekah); one committed suicide (Zimri); one died because of his war wound (Ahab); and one died as a result of God's prediction (Ahaziah). In Judah the situation was only slightly better because there were eight God-fearing rulers on the Davidic throne who did what was right: Asa, Jehoshaphat, Joash, Amaziah, Azariah, Jotham, Hezekiah, and Josiah. However, only Jotham is noted for demonstrating no wrong actions. Five kings were assassinated (Ahaziah, Athaliah, Joash, Amaziah, and Amon); three went into an exile (Jehoahaz taken by Necho to Egypt, and Jehoiakim and Jehoiakin taken by Nebuchadnezzar to Babylon); one died in a battle (Josiah); and two were "afflicted" by God (Jehoram and Azariah). The wickedness and incompetent leadership of these kings led to the Assyrian (722 BC) and Babylonian exiles (605, 597, 587/6 BC). Samuel was right when he warned the people not to choose a king because they would abuse power and only worsen the already terrible situation of God's people (1 Sam. 8:18; 10:19). Leadership on one level can be described as "about [the] behavior"[28] of the leaders.

Observing this gloomy overview of the history of the monarchies in Israel and Judah, one agrees with James Kouzes and Barry Posner that faithful "leadership is not about position or title. It's about relationships, credibility, and what you do."[29] Thomas Cronin well underscores that "learning about leadership means recognizing bad leadership as well as good."[30] Even though all kings were accountable to the King of kings, they miserably failed to live according to His high standards for ethical leadership.

Though almost nothing positive can be said about the Northern Kingdom, and the kings brought about only a little good in Judah, amazingly God did not abandon His people. He incessantly called them back to Himself because He loved them. He often intervened on their behalf, and in spite of their unfaithfulness, He worked with them and was faithful to His covenant. God's faithfulness is seen through the work of many prophets in calling kings to return to righteous leadership and the people to revival and reformation. Efrain Agosto aptly writes: "Perhaps the greatest leaders of the Hebrew Bible, the prophets, focus on their call as the impulse to respond to mission and leadership on behalf of their people. From the prophets we also learn the importance of leaders who understand their role in the context of history, events, and crisis, and who see these with spiritual, theological, and political eyes."[31] Prophets had the courage to face kings, stand against them, and proclaim unpopular truth. They stood against the status quo, and they reminded the people of their obligations and the consequences of the covenant relationship they had entered into with God. A good example of this endeavor is the ministry of the prophet Elijah.

LEADERSHIP OF THE PROPHET ELIJAH

There was great apostasy during the time of Elijah. Idolatry was rampant. It had been introduced by Solomon, "improved" by Jeroboam, and "perfected" by Ahab with his wife Jezebel with the worship of Baal and Asherah. This steady downward slide into idolatry brought devastating moral results to Israel and, in the end, brought the people to Assyrian and Babylonian exiles. God, therefore, called Elijah to stop the avalanche of evil. Under his leadership the people were called to return to the true worship of Yahweh, the God of Israel.

Prophet Elijah's main leadership task was to call the people back to the covenant relationship with their living God, Yahweh. In this time of deep religious, political, and social crisis, he affirmed their allegiance to the Lord. He stood alone on Mount Carmel against eight hundred and fifty Baal and Asherah priests. In the fierce battle between true and false worship, he powerfully appealed: "How long will you waver between two opinions? If the LORD is God, follow him; but if Baal is God, follow him" (1 Kings 18:21). Elijah helped the people in an extremely dramatic way to decide for the only true God. When God's fire fell upon Elijah's offering and not on Baal's, the people then correctly responded: "The LORD— he is God!" (1 Kings 18:39). Elijah impressed upon the minds of God's people the majesty and sovereignty of their covenant God, Yahweh: "O LORD, God of Abraham, Isaac and Israel, let it be known today that you are God in Israel and that I am your servant and have done all these things at your command" (1 Kings 18:36). Leadership in the matter of worship is crucial because on it everything else in life depends.[32] Whom we worship is who we emulate (Jer. 2:5; 2 Kings 17:15).

LEADERSHIP BY HAGGAI AND ZECHARIAH AFTER THE EXILE

In the period of the Temple restoration, leadership was characterized by close cooperation among governor, high priest, and people under the guidance of the prophets Haggai and Zechariah. Alec Motyer underscores that the prophets Haggai and Zechariah are "the two visionaries."[33] They were both called to their ministry and received God's message in the second year of Darius, king of Persia, in 520 BC, about seventeen years after the people returned home from Babylonian exile. They stirred up people from their stagnation and bitter disappointments to work on the House of God in Jerusalem (Hag. 1–2; Zech. 1–8). They successfully presented

God's vision for them and helped the people to work on the Lord's Temple in such an urgent and attractive way that the sanctuary was finished in five years. In March 515 BC, the Temple was dedicated to the Lord (Ezra 6:14–16).

Haggai and Zechariah were not simply managers. John Kotter explains that "leadership is different from management," but he stresses that "leadership and management are two distinctive and complementary systems of action."[34] He aptly adds: "The real challenge is to combine strong leadership and strong management and use each to balance the other.... Management is about coping with complexity.... Leadership, by contrast, is about coping with change."[35] The prophets Haggai and Zechariah brought about such change; they were true spiritual leaders (Ezra 5:1–2; 6:14). James Kouzes and Barry Posner rightly underscore that the best "leadership is a team effort."[36] Such team effort was demonstrated in the work on the Temple. This leadership created opportunity for people to contribute to the greater work according to their individual talents and gifts. It provided an experience of belonging, ownership, and participation in working together.

CONCLUSION

Several themes appearing throughout the Historical Books should have an impact on our leadership today.

1. God is our true Leader. At the heart of these historical narratives is God's tender but strong leadership. Every Christian, regardless of his or her role in the community, is always subject to God's authority and is ultimately accountable to Him.

2. At the core of the recorded sacred history is the covenant theme. God wants to maintain a true covenant relationship with His people. Our leadership should serve that purpose.

3. Contemporary Christian leaders should be future and hope oriented. The Historical Books start with great expectations as the people enter the Promised Land, and they end with the tragedy of the Assyrian and Babylonian exiles. However, the very last chapter points to a new hope because God's people received liberation from Cyrus's edict (2 Chron. 36:22–23). The new community of faith

appears as a sign of a new beginning, and Messianic expectations were strong (Ezek. 34:23–24; 37:24–26). The Second Advent is the ultimate hope (Isa. 25:9; Titus 2:11–14).

4. Worship plays a dominant role in shaping the nature of leadership. Our relationship to God and His dominion of our lives are crucial for morality and ethics.

5. Spiritual leaders must actually be Spirit-filled people, always oriented toward God and His Torah, meditating upon His Word day and night. Spirit-led and Spirit-filled leadership is the right way to accomplish God's given mission. It does not mean that such leaders will not make any mistakes; but if we stay in relationship with the Lord and trust Him, we will be secure because the Spirit will help us to repent and guide us into doing what is right.

6. In the Historical Books, the motivation of the main figures is often stressed. Faithful leaders follow God and His precepts with their whole heart.[37] One of the most tragic verses describes King Amaziah: "He did what was right in the eyes of the Lord, but not wholeheartedly" (2 Chron. 25:2). In striking contrast, Hezekiah "in everything that he undertook in the service of God's temple and in obedience to the law and the commands, he sought his God and worked wholeheartedly. And so he prospered" (2 Chron. 31:21). The greatest demand in our contemporary, consuming, and self-centered society is for leaders to serve others wholeheartedly and unselfishly. Our obedience to God should come from our willing and thankful hearts.

7. The Historical Books provide ample examples, in harmony with the theology of the book of Deuteronomy, that good leadership is accompanied by prosperity, safety, and abundant life, but bad leadership brings complications, disaster, defeat, and tragedy. Biblical wisdom literature nuances this "simplistic," white-black perspective by demonstrating that prosperity and success in life do not necessarily mean that people are righteous and cultivate godly lives or that misfortunes and calamities come only on the wicked (consider the book of Job and Psalm 73). Further, prosperity is affirmed when we distributed blessings broadly in a spirit of communion rather than hoard them in a spirit of selfishness.

8. Faithful leadership and ethics go hand in hand. How leaders treat other human beings—especially those who make a mistake or are underprivileged or without a defender—reveals their character. Spiritual leadership is characterized by respect, love, dignity, forgiveness, and restoration, and not superiority or arrogance. Only when we respect principles of life and establish proper boundaries will life flourish in abundance. Burns states, "the crisis of leadership today is the mediocrity or irresponsibility of so many of the men and women in power."[38]

9. Spiritual leadership is not about power or position but rather about positive relational influence.[39] Spiritual leaders influence others to pursue God's will through the exercise of moral power built on love, truth, justice, and freedom. Power is not in itself negative, though it may be. Moral power is used for others only through unselfish service.[40]

10. Leadership is relational. It is community oriented and shared. Biblical leadership is servant leadership. Robert Greenleaf rightly states that "the great leader is seen as servant first" and that he makes "sure that other people's highest priority needs are being served."[41]

11. A genuine spiritual leadership that is founded on trust in God and prayer (Josh. 1:1–9; and the prayer of Solomon in 1 Kings 8:14–61) must clearly communicate a vision and a goal that need to be accomplished (e.g., Josh. 1:10–15; 24:14–15; and 2 Chron. 20).[42] James Kouzes and Barry Posner underline that "turning possibility of thinking into an inspiring vision is the leader's challenge."[43]

12. Leadership is cultivated by the knowledge of God. To know God is one of the important themes in the Historical Books (Josh. 2:9; 4:24; Judg. 2:10; 14:4; 16:20; 17:13; 1 Sam. 3:7; 17:47; 1 Kings 8:60; 18:37; 20:13, 28; 2 Kings 19:19) and needs to be a part of a leader's daily experience.

Thus, faithful leadership, revealed in the Historical Books of the Old Testament, is and must be theocentric, focused on a God-given vision, oriented to service, courageous, team based, Spirit led, and Scripture driven. This kind of leadership will both praise the Lord and bring glory to Him.

FOR REFLECTION

Personal:

1. How is your leadership shaped by your personal relationship with God?
2. Have you experienced knowledge of God transforming the way you go about leading?

Organizational:

1. Are your position and authority helping or hindering your leadership in your organization? In what ways?
2. How do your organization members assure that what they do is within God's will and appropriate in terms of their relationship to others?

ENDNOTES

1. See Robert B. Sloan, "A Biblical Model of Leadership," in *Christian Leadership Essentials: A Handbook for Managing Christian Organizations*, ed. David S. Dockery (Nashville, TN: B & H Academic, 2011), 9. "A biblical view of leadership must begin with God. Human leadership, if it is good leadership, is analogous to the ways and motivations of God's ultimate acts of influence.... A biblical model of leadership that begins with God must therefore find its behavioral and convictional patterns in Christ the Lord," Sloan, *Christian Leadership*, 9–10.

2. Scripture quotations in this chapter are taken from the New International Version.

3. Even though David made some appalling mistakes, he repented and the Lord made him a model of leadership for following generations because of his servant-leadership style. David called himself and was perceived as the servant of Saul (1 Sam. 17:32, 34; 19:4); identified himself as the servant of the God of Israel (1 Sam. 23:10; 25:39; 2 Sam. 7:20, 26; 24:10); and was named by others as God's servant (2 Sam. 3:18; 7:5, 8; 1 Kings 3:6; 8:24–26, 66; 11:13; 1 Chron. 17:4; Pss. 18:1; 36:1; Isa. 37:35; Jer. 33:21–22; Acts 4:25). Because of that, he became a Messianic figure (Ezek. 34:23–24; 37:24–25; Luke 1:69).

4. James M. Kouzes and Barry Z. Posner, *The Leadership Challenge* (San Francisco: Jossey-Bass, 2002), 52. Dockery rightly states: "Leaders are marked by vision. Vision

makes the difference between leadership and misleadership....Leaders learn from the past, live in the present, and plan for the future," "Introduction," in *Christian Leadership Essentials: A Handbook for Managing Christian Organizations*, ed. David S. Dockery (Nashville, TN: B & H Academic, 2011), 2.

5. In our English Bibles, the Historical Books consist of the following twelve books: Joshua, Judges, Ruth, 1–2 Samuel, 1–2 Kings, 1–2 Chronicles, Ezra, Nehemiah, and Esther. The Hebrew Canon is divided into three parts: *Tôrah*, *Nĕbî'îm*, and *Kĕtûbîm* (Law, Prophets, and Writings), which means that there is no category designated as *Historical Books*. The Historical Books are distributed in the Hebrew Canon in this way: the section called *Former Prophets* (part of the prophetical section of the Old Testament) contains Joshua, Judges, 1–2 Samuel, and 1–2 Kings and to *Writings* belongs the other six historical books in the following sequence: Ruth, Esther, Ezra, Nehemiah, and 1–2 Chronicles (which closes the Hebrew Canon). It means that the history in the Historical Books is written from God's perspective (half of them are considered prophetical books because one of the crucial roles of biblical prophets was to remind God's followers how the Lord led them in the past). People need to understand their roots in order to make right decisions in present situations. One needs to see how God led His people in the past in order to face the future in a mature and balanced way.

6. For details, see Edward W. Goodrick and John R. Kohlenberger III, *The NIV Complete Concordance* (Grand Rapids, MI: Zondervan, 1981), 540–541.

7. William H. Shea, "Date of the Exodus," in *The International Standard Bible Encyclopedia*, vol. 2, ed. Geoffrey W. Bromiley (Grand Rapids, MI: Eerdmans, 1982), 234–235; John H. Walton, *Chronological and Background Charts of the Old Testament*, rev. and exp. ed. (Grand Rapids, MI: Zondervan, 1994), 12, 26; Gerhard F. Hasel, "Books of Chronicles," in *The International Standard Bible Encyclopedia*, vol. 1, ed. Geoffrey W. Bromiley (Grand Rapids, MI: Eerdmans, 1979), 670.

8. Space limitations of this study do not allow for the treatment of additional leadership personalities, e.g., priests—Abiathar (1 Sam. 22:20–23; 2 Sam. 15:24–36), Sadoch (1 Kings 1:32–40), Jehoiada (2 Kings 11:4–21), Hilkiah (2 Kings 22), and Azariah (2 Chron. 31:10); generals—Joab (2 Sam. 12:26–29) and Abner (1 Sam. 17:55; 2 Sam. 3:6–27); king's counselors—Ahithophel and Hushai (2 Sam. 16:15–17:23); prophets—Nathan (2 Sam. 12:1–15, 24–25), Elisha (1 Kings 19:19–21; 2 Kings 2:19–8:15; 9:1–3; 13:14–20), Micaiah (1 Kings 22:8–28); or reflect on the influence of mothers or parents on leaders' lives (1 Sam. 1:10–28; 2:18–21; 2 Kings 3:2, 13; 11:1–2; 23:29–38; 24:18; 1 Chron. 3:2; 4:9; 15:16; 22:3; compare 2 Chron. 25:1–2; 26:3–4; Ezek. 19:1–14).

9. Bill Robinson, *Incarnate Leadership: Five Leadership Lessons from the Life of Jesus* (Grand Rapids, MI: Zondervan, 2009), 65.

10. Siang-Yang Tan, "The Primacy of Servanthood," in *The Three Tasks of Leadership: Worldly Wisdom for Pastoral Leaders*, ed. Eric O. Jacobsen (Grand Rapids, MI: Eerdmans, 2009), 80–81.

11. There is a close connection between Christ and Joshua, who is a Messianic type.

12. See http://www.brainyquote.com/quotes/authors/a/abraham_lincoln_5. html.

13. Richard S. Hess, *Joshua: An Introduction & Commentary*, Tyndale Old Testament Commentaries (Downers Grove, IL: InterVarsity Press, 1996), 68.

14. The phrase "be strong and courageous" is also used on other occasions before enormous endeavors, e.g., David when encouraging Solomon (1 Chron. 22:13; 28:20) and King Hezekiah when speaking to his military commanders (2 Chron. 32:7).

15. Peter Koestenbaum, *Leadership: The Inner Side of Greatness (A Philosophy for Leaders)*, new and rev. ed. (San Francisco: Jossey-Bass, 2002), 17. See especially his whole chapter on courage from the business perspective, 136–166.

16. Here *success* means accomplishing things in harmony with God's vision and mission.

17. Walter Brueggemann, "Ancient Israel on Political Leadership: Between the Book Ends," in *Political Theology* 8, no. 4 (2007): 456.

18. Major judges are Othniel (Judg. 3:7–11), Ehud (3:12–30), Deborah (4–5), Gideon (6–8), Jephthah (10:6–12:7), and Samson (13–16). Among the minor judges belong Shamgar (3:31), Tola (10:1–2), Jair (10:3–5), Ibzan (12:8–10), Elon (12:11–12), and Abdon (12:13–15). The "anti-judge" Abimelech brought only terror (chap. 9).

19. Literal translation of this sentence is: "And you will say: 'I will set a king over me.'"

20. "Leaders are not normally described as servant kings. In fact the term servant king may seem at first glance to be an oxymoron. Kings do not seemingly serve; they are served by those in their kingdom," Don Page, *Servant Empowered Leadership: A Hands-On Guide to Transforming You and Your Organization* (Langley, Canada: Power to Change Ministries, 2009), 29. Page argues that only Jesus "was a serving king," 30.

21. Caroline J. Nolan, *A Critical Appraisal of the Origin and Nature of the Institution of the Monarchy in Israel in the Light of Eric Voegelin's Theory of Symbolic Forms* (Lewiston, NY: Edwin Mellen Press, 2003), 169.

22. Richard M. Davidson, *Flame of Yahweh: Sexuality in the Old Testament* (Peabody, MA: Hendrickson Publishers, 2007), 523; see also Moshe Garsiel, "The Story of David and Bathsheba: A Different Approach," *Catholic Biblical Quarterly* 55 (1993): 244–262.

23. Robinson, *Incarnate Leadership*, 81.

24. Peter E. Satterthwaite and J. Gordon McConville, *Exploring the Old Testament: A Guide to the Historical Books* (Downers Grove, IL: InterVarsity Press, 2007), 156. Ronald A. Heifetz stresses that there are no easy answers to the complex issues of leadership. He explains that "leadership arouses passion," because "leadership engages our values,…involves our self-image and moral codes," *Leadership without Easy Answers* (Cambridge, MA: Belknap Press of Harvard University Press, 1994), 13.

25. Barbara Kellerman, *Bad Leadership: What It Is, How It Happens, Why It Matters* (Boston: Harvard Business School Press, 2004). See also Ronald A.

Heifetz and Marty Linsky, *Leadership on the Line: Staying Alive through the Danger of Leadership* (Boston: Harvard Business School Press, 2002).

26. John P. Kotter, *Leading Change* (Boston: Harvard Business School Press, 1996), 95. See also Kouzes and Posner who speak about leaders who are credible: "They practice what they preach. They walk the talk. Their actions are consistent with their words. They put their money where their mouth is. They follow through on their promises. They do what they say they will do," *The Leadership Challenge*, 40.

27. A notable exception was King Jehu, who for some time did what was right; however, he mainly fulfilled the prophecy from a military point of view by executing the ungodly family of Ahab and Jezebel (yet with some exaggerations). Sadly, the biblical narrator states that he did not really follow the Lord with all his heart (2 Kings 10:31; also Hos. 1:4).

28. Kouzes and Posner, *The Leadership Challenge*, 15.

29. Kouzes and Posner, *The Leadership Challenge*, 383.

30. Thomas E. Cronin, "Thinking and Learning about Leadership," in *The Leader's Companion: Insights on Leadership through the Ages*, ed. J. Thomas Wren (New York: The Free Press, 1995), 31.

31. Efrain Agosto, *Servant Leadership: Jesus and Paul* (St. Louis, MO: Chalice Press, 2005), 7–8. See also Helen Doohan, *Leadership in Paul* (Wilmington, DE: Michael Glazier, 1984), 20–21.

32. See Revelation 13–14 where the final conflict between good and evil is described as a worship controversy. The battle of Armageddon of Revelation 16:16 points to the typological worship situation of Mount Carmel at the time of Elijah. See Jon Paulien, *Armageddon at the Door* (Hagerstown, MD: Review and Herald, 2008).

33. Alec Motyer, *Roots: Let the Old Testament Speak* (Kearn, Scotland: Christian Focus, 2009), 331.

34. John P. Kotter, "What Leaders Really Do," in *The Leader's Companion: Insights on Leadership through the Ages*, ed. J. Thomas Wren (New York: The Free Press, 1995), 114.

35. Kotter, "What Leaders Really Do," 115.

36. Kouzes and Posner, *The Leadership Challenge*, 18. They practically demonstrate how it works: "After reviewing thousands of personal-best cases, we developed a simple test to detect whether someone is on the road to becoming a leader. The test is frequency of the use of the word *we*.... Exemplary leaders *enable others to* act.... Leaders make it possible for others to do good work. They know that those who are expected to produce the results must feel a sense of personal power and ownership."

37. On many occasions the word *heart* occurs in relationship to behavior, emotions, or personality (Josh. 14:7–8; 22:5; Judg. 5:9, 15–16; 16:15–18; 18:20; 1 Sam. 1:8, 13; 2:1, 35; 4:13; 10:9; 13:14; 14:7; 16:7; 25:36–37; 2 Sam. 7:21; 13:20, 28, 33; 14:1; 17:10; 22:46; 24:10; 1 Kings 3:9, 12; 8:18, 23, 38–39, 66; 10:2, 24; 11:2–4, 9; 12:26–27, 33; 2 Kings 14:10; 1 Chron. 15:29; 16:10; 17:2,

19; 2 Chron. 29:10; 32:31; 34:27, 31; 36:13; Ezra 6:22; 7:10, 27; Neh. 2:2; Esther 1:10; 5:9); stresses change of life (1 Sam. 10:9; 1 Kings 18:37; 2 Kings 22:19); and motivations and thinking (1 Sam. 7:3; 12:20, 24; 2 Sam. 6:16; 1 Kings 2:4, 44; 3:6; 8:17, 48, 61; 9:4; 14:8; 15:3, 14; 2 Kings 10:15, 30–31; 12:4; 20:3; 23:3, 25; 1 Chron. 12:33, 38; 22:19; 28:9; 29:9, 17–19; 2 Chron. 6:8, 14, 18, 30, 38; 12:14; 15:12, 15, 17; 16:9; 19:3; 22:9; 26:16; 30:12, 19; 31:21; 32:25–26; Neh. 7:5; 9:8).

38. James MacGregor Burns, "The Crisis of Leadership," in *The Leader's Companion: Insights on Leadership through the Ages*, ed. J. Thomas Wren (New York: The Free Press, 1995), 9.

39. Stephen P. Robbins and Timothy A. Judge, *Organizational Behavior*, 12th ed. (Upper Saddle River, NJ: Pearson Education, 2007), 402: "Leadership is the ability to influence a group toward the achievement of a vision or a set of goals."

40. Robert Sloan defines leadership as "the art and practice of exerting an influence on the behavior and beliefs of others. Leaders shape and influence people, institutions, and events.… By definition leaders exert various kinds of power, or else they would have no influence on others or lack the ability to effect change in the world. Though the word *power* often has a negative connotation, the *stewardship* of power and influence—a softer form of power—marks the nature of leadership," 8–9. "Leadership is all about the exercise of power in order to make things happen through others. How that power is used will determine whether the led believe that good or bad leadership is being exercised.… In order to develop true servant-empowered leaders, we must change the way we think about power," Bill Hybels, *Courageous Leadership* (Grand Rapids, MI: Zondervan, 2002), 45. Gary Yukl defines leadership as "the process of influencing others to understand and agree about what needs to be done and how to do it, and the process of facilitating individual and collective efforts to accomplish shared objectives," *Leadership in Organizations*, 6th ed. (Upper Saddle River, NJ: Pearson-Prentice Hall, 2006), 8.

41. Robert K. Greenleaf, *Servant Leadership: A Journey into the Nature of Legitimate Power and Greatness* (New York: Paulist Press, 1999), 7.

42. Leadership involves (1) establishing a clear vision; (2) communicating that vision with others so that they will follow willingly; (3) providing the information, knowledge, and methods to realize that vision; and (4) coordinating and balancing the conflicting interests.

43. James M. Kouzes and Barry Z. Posner, *The Leadership Challenge*, 4th ed. (San Francisco: John Wiley & Sons, 2007), 106.

5 | Wisdom Literature and the Psalms

James R. Wibberding

B iblical wisdom literature offers few obvious correlations with standard leadership theory. The wisdom tradition, with the pathos and ethos, provides a different function for leaders. Its compass is spiritual inquiry, which distinguishes this literature from secular theories.

Although categorizing biblical wisdom books is somewhat problematic,[1] the Protestant canon includes three that are definitively classified as such[2]: Job, Proverbs, and Ecclesiastes (which scholars prefer to title Qohelet).[3] Some scholars include Song of Songs (also called Song of Solomon or Canticles), a view garnering enough support for Baker Academic to include it in its commentary series on wisdom literature.[4] Some likewise embrace Psalms, either in whole, or in part, because it contains wisdom psalms. Roland E. Murphy observes that "the Psalms have been analyzed for wisdom content" but without a resulting "list of 'wisdom psalms' on which everyone agrees."[5] The present study examines Job, Proverbs, and Ecclesiastes in detail, with a brief consideration of Psalms.

In pursuit of the contribution that wisdom literature makes to a theology of leadership, this chapter outlines (1) the impetus for spiritual leadership; (2) a definition of *wisdom* in Old Testament thought; (3) case studies of Job, Solomon, and Lady Wisdom; (4) an exploration of the psalms as devotional wisdom; and (5) a summary of the leadership principles derived.

IMPETUS FOR SPIRITUAL LEADERSHIP

Since the fall of humankind, the divine call to lead has always been a call to advance God's redemptive enterprise in the leader's sphere of influence; specifically, to help restore fallen humans to their pre-Fall state. One might object to this assertion on the basis that some leaders were called to destroy human life rather than redeem it but the assertion is defensible when such acts are perceived as part of God's larger redemptive strategy. Examples of the redemptive nature of leadership include Abram's call to bless all the nations of the earth with salvation (Gen. 12:1–3; Gal. 3:16), Moses's call to build a nation of priests to the world (Exod. 19:5–6), and David's call to build a messianic dynasty (2 Sam. 7:12–17).

Throughout Scripture the human agent is a mere participant in God's endeavor. This participation has two dimensions. First, God calls each leader to share in leading others to Him. Second, God calls each leader in order to redeem the leader. The first dimension is apparent in the commissioning and work of leaders throughout Scripture, but the second dimension needs explanation. It arises from the very nature of redemption.

The divine call to lead preceded the Fall. God instructed the first humans to "subdue and rule"[6] the earth (Gen. 1:26–28),[7] designating a lead role in the new creation. This holds two implications for leaders after the Fall.[8] First, when they aspire to restore humanity to its pre-Fall position, it is to that original position of leadership. Second, the practice of *godly* leadership is the behavior of a restored human; thus, the leader embodies the restoration. This second implication excludes contorted concepts of leadership involving the sin-induced dominance of other human beings (which resulted from sin—Gen. 3:16 and Gen. 9:24–25) and the usurping of God's role (which was the seed of sin—Gen. 3:5).

With a broad brush, biblical wisdom literature paints a picture of that restored human potential. The three primary wisdom books, along with Song of Songs, exhibit a fascination with creation. Yahweh answers Job's quandary with a detailed appeal to His creation act, starting with, "Where were you when I laid the foundation of the earth?" (Job 38:4). Proverbs presents ḥokmâ as the restored "tree of life to those who lay hold of her" (Prov. 3:18).[9] In Ecclesiastes, the first human family is an extended metaphor for a restored standing with Yahweh.[10] Finally, the lover's wisdom in Song of Songs manifests itself in imagery from Eden.[11] Wisdom literature is consumed with restoring human potential through a restored standing with Yahweh.

The impetus of biblical leadership is first theocentric and second anthropocentric;[12] it proceeds from the divine and works to align the human with the divine. This is the intended terminus for both the leader and those they lead. Thus the character of the leader is paramount, as both the beginning and the culmination of their work. Wisdom literature contributes to this bedrock of leadership: human character.

DEFINING *WISDOM*

What is wisdom literature? In the ancient Hebrew tradition, it is literature that advances a distinctly Hebrew brand of wisdom (ḥokmâ in Hebrew). A variety of literary features help identify it, but its emphasis on wisdom ultimately defines it.

Western thinkers are prone to misunderstand it because the authors of biblical wisdom literature worked from a different worldview. Western thought descends from Greek philosophers such as Plato, who conceived wisdom (*sophia* in Greek) as a largely intellectual pursuit.

Plato pictured human nature as a chariot pulled through the sky by two winged horses. One horse struggles to ascend and the other to descend. So he imagined a separation between the pure spirit and the sinful flesh.[13]

Perhaps because Plato's depiction resonates with our internal scrimmage between good and evil, platonic dualism took root in

Western thought and nudged it toward crisp distinctions between the various aspects of personhood. Plato distinguished between spirit and flesh but that idea has been transformed into a distinction between intellect and skill—the work of mind and the work of matter. René Descartes helped anchor this ontological division in Western thought by further development and articulation.[14]

Hebrew thought permits no such bisection of intellect and skill. In the Hebrew mind, the notion that a person could possess one without the other is implausible.[15] Although the language employs different words for these two traits, the word *ḥokmâ* (meaning "wisdom") encompasses both. Things such as God's creation (Ps. 104:24), Bezalel's craftsmanship (Exod. 31:1–5), and Solomon's administration of justice (1 Kings 3:28) are viewed as expressions of *ḥokmâ;* its ultimate expression is fear of Yahweh (Job 28:28).

With this practical wisdom concept, we might expect that biblical wisdom literature would have something to say about the conspicuous life dynamic of leadership. What it actually says is mostly indirect and focused on character formation. It emphasizes the interior life, or who the leader is, for which it expects to find natural expression in what the leader does. One might term this the *ḥokmâ* synthesis, or *ḥokmâ* integration.

CHARACTERS OF WISDOM

Job, Solomon, and Lady Wisdom are the central figures of biblical wisdom literature.[16] Job and Solomon are examples of leaders, and Lady Wisdom is a literary invention designed to shape leaders.[17] Leadership consumed Solomon's days, making it almost certain that the works linked to his life contain insights pertinent to leaders. Although we do not know Job's formal station in society, he is termed "the greatest [*gādôl* in Hebrew] of all the people of the east" (Job 1:3), and he showed himself to be a man of spiritual and intellectual leadership.

These characters present a strikingly different model of leadership from that of many behavior-based leadership writings today. Job and Solomon are recognizable as leaders by almost any definition of the term, but the records of their lives and lessons do not highlight their strategies as much as their character. Similarly, Lady Wisdom is the literary personification of fruitful character (*ḥokmâ*). They constitute a contrast to behavior-based leadership theories that accentuate formulas and methods.[18]

An examination of the three main characters of wisdom literature follows. Together, their lives and lessons lay the philosophical bedrock, but not the methodological contours, of the biblical leadership landscape. Their biographies illustrate the impetus for spiritual leadership described above. They are examples of how restoring the fear of Yahweh in fallen humanity helps restore pre-Fall leadership potential.

Case Study of Job

"A man there was in the land of Uz—Job, his name. And the man was blameless and upright and feared God and shunned evil" (Job 1:1).[19] His formal standing in the community is unknown, but Job exercised spiritual leadership in his family (1:4–5; 2:9–10) and among his friends (42:8) through known religious practices and philosophical enquiry into the unknown (31:35). He also managed an impressive estate, including "very many servants," making him "the greatest of all the people of the east" (1:2). He used his influence to instruct "many" (*rabîm* in Hebrew) and strengthen "the weak hands" (4:3).

As his biography unfolds, an unseen variable upsets the equilibrium of his life, challenging the mechanistic view of reality that Job's friends espouse. For them, the righteous prosper and the wicked suffer, without variation (4:7–8). Job and his friends are not aware of the debate between God and Job's accuser (*śāṭān* in Hebrew) but the reader is (1:6–22; 2:1–10). This background element, along with Job's ignorance of it, forcefully illustrates the limits of human capacity.

The Job story offers a solution to such limitations. It is not to abandon God's agenda, as Job's wife suggests (2:9–10). It is not to persist in formulas, as Job's friends suggest (4:7–8; 8:3; 11:3–6). It is, instead, to serve God with persevering trust while seeking comprehension. Job exemplifies this approach, expressing undying trust in Yahweh while he insists on understanding. For this, he is judged righteous (1:22; 2:10; 42:1–10). His cognizance of his own flawed understanding earns him Yahweh's approval while the strict wisdom formulas of his friends evoke Yahweh's anger (42:7).

For spiritual leaders, Job is a lucid reminder that human thinking is unequal to the clash between good and evil with which they contend. Mechanistic approaches to reality address only the scope of human perceptions, which may be a small part of reality. The solution is to keep serving and trusting God while acknowledging unknowns and pursuing knowledge. For Job, his disillusionment ended with broader understanding, deeper faith, and greater success (42:1–6, 10–17). The sage who narrates the Job saga hints that the same could be true for others. And while Job may not, during his trials, have been connecting his experience to any understanding of leadership, the reader readily makes the connection between Job's spirituality and his leadership.

Case Study of Solomon

Solomon's biography affords a similar picture of fertile disillusionment and enlightenment. It begins with the nervous young monarch's prayer. Yahweh offered to give the new king whatever he might ask (1 Kings 3:5). In reply, Solomon asked for "an understanding mind to govern" (v. 9), saying, "Give me now wisdom and knowledge to go out and come in before this people" (2 Chron. 1:10). He desired to embody the Hebrew concept of wisdom, namely, keen intellect with practical manifestation for the benefit of his people. He recognized that the wisdom to lead his people would come from his relationship with Yahweh.

God responded with pleasure (2 Chron. 1:11–12; 1 Kings 3:10–14) and Solomon's *hokmâ* was so marked that the world took notice. "God gave Solomon wisdom and understanding beyond measure, and breadth of mind like the sand on the seashore, so that Solomon's wisdom surpassed the wisdom of all the people of the east and all the wisdom of Egypt" (1 Kings 4:29–30). "All Israel… stood in awe of the king, because they perceived that the wisdom of God was in him to do justice" (1 Kings 3:28). "And people of all nations came to hear the wisdom of Solomon, and from all the kings of the earth, who had heard of his wisdom" (1 Kings 4:34).

The literary tradition that followed him bestows answers to life's quandaries. Although most scholars do not believe Solomon wrote the book of Proverbs,[20] its insights are attributed to him (Prov. 1:1).

It constitutes what William P. Brown calls "a powerfully compelling profile of normative character."[21] In the same tradition follows the Song of Songs, likewise attributed to Solomon (Song of Sol. 1:1). It offers practical wisdom for romance and sex. Its approach signals Solomon's restorative regard for his lover in a time when women were treated as property instead of equals. Thus, Solomon's thought and behavior comprise a practical expression of godly wisdom.

Solomon's early wisdom, as expressed in the books of Proverbs and Song of Songs, served him well. The formulas of Proverbs and the art of romance outlined in Song of Songs helped nurture the success that earned him renown. Nonetheless, in his later estimate, their contribution fell short.

The later Solomonic work of Ecclesiastes has prompted varied interpretations[22] but conveys an unambiguous message. After his years of stunning endeavors, the aged king concludes, "I have seen everything that is done under the sun, and behold, all is vanity and a striving after wind" (Eccles. 1:14). In recognition of the limits of human wisdom, he further observes,

> When I applied my heart to know wisdom, and to see the business that is done on earth, how neither day nor night do one's eyes see sleep, then I saw all the work of God, that man cannot find out the work that is done under the sun. However much man may toil in seeking, he will not find it out. Even though a wise man claims to know, he cannot find it out. (8:16–17)

Solomon's disillusionment with the best that human wisdom could achieve helped him perceive the true meaning of life and leadership. To this end, he writes, "Here is my final conclusion: Fear God and obey his commands, for this is the duty of every person" (12:13, NLT).[23] Once again, the corpus under study presents godly character as the solution for humanity's limited capacities. It follows, then, that godly character is the foundation of true greatness and the basis of genuine leadership.

Case Study of Lady Wisdom

Lady Wisdom personifies the core message of the biblical wisdom tradition, promoting a life of virtue through her presence and message.

Job 28 and Proverbs 8 present the most colorful portraits of her. In these passages, she stands as the ideal embodiment of *ḥokmâ*.

Job 28 shrouds her in mystery to such an extent that the literary device of personification is not immediately apparent. Murphy says,

> The poem in Job 28…claims that Wisdom belongs to God, who alone knows where she is. Because she is inaccessible to humans, the thrust of the poem is to underline the transcendence of this figure. However, although no human knows the "way" to her (28:13, LXX), God does know the "way" (28:23).… The theme of the way to Wisdom, and the mystery of her location…functions as an indicator of the futility of human probing into the divine mystery.[24]

By contrast to Job 28, Proverbs 8 portrays Lady Wisdom in full regalia. Here she is not only uniquely accessible to God (as in Job 28), but also something closer to God personified. In particular, the description of her in Proverbs 8:22–31 finds analogy with the depiction of Jesus in John 1:1–18. Murphy says:

> The very origins and the authority of Wisdom suggest more than a personified order of creation. Wisdom is somehow identified with the Lord. The call of Lady Wisdom is the voice of the Lord; she is the revelation of God, not merely the self-revelation of creation. She is the divine summons issued in and through creation, sounding through the vast realm of the created world, and heard on the level of human experience.[25]

Earlier in Proverbs, Lady Wisdom makes an appearance that elevates character above formulas: "You simpletons!" she cries. "How long will you go on being simpleminded? How long will you mockers relish your mocking? How long will you fools fight the facts? Come here and listen to me! I'll pour out the spirit of wisdom upon you and make you wise" (Prov. 1:22–23, NLT). She further describes the choice to reject this appeal as a failure to embrace fear (*yir'āh*) of Yahweh (v. 29).

Through the embodiment of *ḥokmâ*, these passages assert that wisdom is the solution for the challenges of human labors and then explain that human beings cannot wholly reach it because only God embodies it. This is a lucid reminder of the human need for God and godliness in all endeavors. Thus, Lady Wisdom's contribution to the message of the wisdom corpus is to reemphasize that being is a precondition of doing. Some reciprocity may also exist but wisdom literature presents the directionality of the relationship in terms of *being leading* to *doing leading* (e.g., Prov. 9:10).

WISDOM'S DEVOTIONAL FORM

The Psalms add devotional form to the gritty wisdom of Job, Solomon, and Lady Wisdom. Although the precise relationship between wisdom literature and the book of Psalms eludes scholarly consensus,[26] the psalter is replete with echoes of wisdom.

The first psalm reads like wisdom literature and exhibits a general parallel to the introduction of Proverbs, with both drawing a contrast between wisdom and wickedness (Prov. 1:1–7). Several psalms address *ḥokmâ* directly (Pss. 19:7; 37:30; 49:4, 10; 51:8; 90:12; 104:24; 105:22; 107:27, 43; 111:10), and others mirror wisdom form and content too closely to be ignored (e.g., Pss. 34; 78).

Superscriptions credit Solomon with two psalms, opening a narrow window into the devotional expressions of the wise king. Psalm 72 is a plea for wisdom to rule the nation, while Psalm 127 is an expression of Yahweh's sovereignty over success.

Job, Psalms, and Proverbs concur that "the fear of the LORD" is either "the beginning of wisdom" (Ps. 111:10; Prov. 9:10) or "is wisdom" itself (Job 28:28), highlighting the centrality of spiritual enquiry to wise leadership. As the spiritual expression of Israel's leaders, the psalter provides a devotional model for today's leaders. The present study includes only a cursory look at three prominent dimensions of that devotional model: candor, vision, and humility.

Devotional Dimension of Candor

Among the most striking features of the psalmist's devotional form is its candor. Contemporary practices tend to sanitize raw emotion for God's reception; not so with the Psalms.

King David intoned his profound depression regarding his sin, saying, "My bones wasted away through my groaning all day long...day and night your hand was heavy upon me; my strength was dried up as by the heat of summer" (Ps. 32:3–4). Later, while fleeing a coup attempt, David was heard composing the words, "Strike all my enemies on the jaw; break the teeth of the wicked" (Ps. 3:7).

The devotional model of Israel's leaders calls for candor among those who would become wise through the fear of Yahweh.

Devotional Dimension of Vision

In response to their candid portrayals of deficient realities, the psalmists continually looked beyond those realities to a desired future. Thus, the Psalms are visionary. As they cry out to a limitless God, they boldly ask for His intervention.

For instance, Solomon prayed that he might have "dominion from sea to sea, and from the River to the ends of the earth" (Ps. 72:8). This request would justly be termed a delusion of grandeur if not for the Being to whom he appealed.

The devotional model of Israel's leaders calls for faith-based vision that calculates its dreams by the measure of a measureless God.

Devotional Dimension of Humility

Amidst their grand visions, the psalmists repeatedly model humility as they submit to God's ultimate wisdom and sovereignty. In their candor and vision, they remember the supremacy of the One with whom they speak. To this end, Solomon writes, "Unless the LORD builds the house, those who build it labor in vain" (Ps. 127:1).

Thus the devotional model of Israel's leaders comes full circle, reminding leaders of today that the success of any great endeavor is best achieved through the humble wisdom that comes from knowing and trusting the Almighty.

LEADERSHIP PRINCIPLES DERIVED

From this cursory appraisal of Hebrew wisdom in connection with leadership, along with its role in the lives of Job and Solomon and its personification in Lady Wisdom, several principles emerge. These principles, if adopted, promise to nurture practical wisdom among leaders in their varied roles of engagement.

In keeping with the Hebrew concept of *ḥokmâ,* the principles group neatly as matters of *being* and the resultant matters of *doing.* Being—that is, the person's character—includes living in dynamic connection with God and loving others. Doing—that is, the tangible impact of the person's life—involves restoring others to a right standing with God and advancing God's broad salvation strategy.

Being a godly leader results from connecting with God, which allows the leader to pattern his or her life after God's character. The Solomonic sage expressed it this way: "Fear of the LORD teaches a person to be wise" (Prov. 15:33, NLT). Notably, the wisdom of both Job and Solomon arose from their encounters with God (Job 38:1–42:6; 1 Kings 3:1–15). It is partly because fallen humans cannot come to personify wisdom (Job 28:12–13) that they cannot lead wisely without God's active presence. Engaging with God includes the candor, vision, and humility modeled in the psalter. Because God's character is marked by love (Ps. 136), one result of His presence is a heart of love toward others. This is vital to biblical leadership. Love is a logical precondition of working to restore broken people (the impetus of leadership) because the ugliness of brokenness tempts one to discard instead of restore.

Doing is the consequence of being. Like Job, who led his family and his friends to God (Job 1:5; 42:8–9), a natural outgrowth of knowing God is leading others to Him. Leaders who successfully advance God's salvation enterprise do so as an expression of God's love. This is why leadership formulas, or methodologies, do not create spiritual leaders. The necessity of God's active presence for the effective doing of leadership also extends to God's larger mission strategy. Leaders can only lead individuals toward restoration in their narrow space and in their brief span of time. The ecosystem of God's larger strategy can hardly be understood from that narrow field, but its success depends on each person's connecting with God and living out his or her small part of God's larger plan. The humiliation of both Job and Solomon illustrate the profound limits of human perception. A leader can best make a successful contribution to the larger strategy by following God's dynamic guidance.

In summary, wise leaders will learn to (1) maintain a dynamic connection with God and (2) love others deeply; with the result of

(3) restoring others to a right standing with God and (4) advancing God's broad salvation strategy.

CONCLUSION

Leadership, as portrayed in biblical wisdom literature, is not oriented to the achievement of organizational goals, fundraising, or building projects. It is, instead, oriented toward restoring human beings to their proper standing with God. Neither is the primary means of that restoration the techniques used. It is, instead, the leader's standing with God.

Through a right standing with God, Solomon completed a stunning building project (2 Chron. 1–7) and Job's estate was a sparkling success (Job 1:2–3; 42:10–17). Everything these leaders accomplished was, in the end, an expression of who they had become by knowing God (2 Chron. 1:3–13; Job 42:1–6).

Practically, however, they did not withdraw to a cave or mountainside to achieve enlightenment and then expect their spectacular spirituality to exude success. Instead, in keeping with the integrated Hebrew concept of wisdom, their biographies show that they engaged with God throughout the daily grind of leadership. They kept God's redemptive agenda forefront in their decision making, and they thoughtfully adjusted to each circumstance. The spiritual focus of these leaders did not manifest itself in a lack of intentional practice, but their examples and teachings suggest that intentional practice fails or falls short apart from God, while it takes shape and thrives within His presence.

The exquisite leadership theory of wisdom literature is that leaders practice godliness—in both character and objectives. The practice of leadership is not only an expression of spirituality, but also a part of the spiritual pursuit; it is a means of knowing God. Wisdom begins and ends in the same place. Just as "the fear of the Lord is the beginning of wisdom" (Ps. 111:10), so also "the fear of the Lord is true wisdom" itself (Job 28:28, NLT).

Job 38 provides an apt source of contemplation for leaders to remind them that success begins and ends with God, and that this fact is good news. While contemplation of the entire chapter is helpful, these opening lines are appropriate to conclude this reflection on Scripture's wisdom literature:

> Then the LORD answered Job from the whirlwind:
> "Who is this that questions my wisdom
>   with such ignorant words?
> Brace yourself like a man,
>   because I have some questions for you,
>   and you must answer them.
>
> Where were you when I laid the foundations of the earth?
>   Tell me, if you know so much." (NLT)

FOR REFLECTION

Personal:

1. How can you, as a leader, prioritize character formation when you plan your schedule?
2. How does the priority of character formation impact how you think about your productivity?
3. How can you as a leader use wisdom literature in your own devotional and leadership development practices?

Organizational:

1. What can an organization do to nurture character formation in its team members?
2. What must an organization do to make sure that character formation is a source of success and not an excuse for inaction?
3. How can organizations use the pattern of wisdom literature to help their own organization shape core values that capture their shared wisdom?

ENDNOTES

1. Gerhard von Rad contended that the wisdom category is "by no means directly rooted in the [biblical] sources." See Gerhard von Rad, *Wisdom in Israel* (Nashville: Abingdon, 1972), 7. Nonetheless, most scholars agree that the literary features of Job, Proverbs, and Ecclesiastes align them with the wisdom tradition of the ancient Near East.

2. For decades, scholars have also identified wisdom elements and segments in other books of the Bible. One example of this discussion is J. L. Crenshaw, "Method in Determining Wisdom Influence upon 'Historical' Literature," *Journal of Biblical Literature* 88. 2 (1969): 129–142.

3. Robert Alter, *The Wisdom Literature: Job, Proverbs, and Ecclesiastes* (New York: W. W. Norton, 2010), xiii–xv; Roland E. Murphy, *The Tree of Life: An Exploration of Biblical Wisdom Literature* (New York: Eerdmans, 2002), 1.

4. Richard S. Hess, *Baker Commentary on the Old Testament Wisdom and Psalms: Song of Songs* (Grand Rapids, MI: Baker Academic, 2005).

5. Murphy, *The Tree of Life*, 98; Stuart Weeks, *An Introduction to the Study of Wisdom Literature* (London: T&T Clark, 2010), 86, confirms this lack of consensus.

6. The Hebrew terms are *kābaš* and *râdâ*. A survey of Old Testament usage reveals that *kābaš* denotes military conquest (e.g., Josh. 18:1) or bringing a person into bondage (e.g., Neh. 5:5). A similar survey shows that *râdâ* means civil rulership (e.g., 1 Kings 5:4).

7. Unless otherwise noted, Scripture quotations in this chapter are taken from *The English Standard Version.*

8. For an expanded discussion of this, see James R. Wibberding, "A Curriculum to Equip Lay Pastoral Candidates for Service in Pennsylvania Conference" (D.Min. diss., Andrews University, 2010), 20–22.

9. This is the point of departure for the interpretation of Proverbs found in Murphy, *The Tree of Life.*

10. Radisa Antic, "Cain, Abel, Seth, and the Meaning of Human Life as Portrayed in the Books of Genesis and Ecclesiastes," *Andrews University Seminary Studies* 44. 2 (2006): 203–211.

11. Richard M. Davidson, "Theology of Sexuality in the Song of Songs: Return to Eden," *Andrews University Seminary Studies* 27. 1 (1989): 1–19.

12. Scholars have alternatively posed an anthropocentric and a theocentric orientation for biblical wisdom literature as recorded in William P. Brown, *Character in Crisis: A Fresh Approach to the Wisdom Literature of the Old Testament* (Grand Rapids, MI: Eerdmans, 1996), 1–2.

13. Plato, *Dialogue with Phaedrus*, 246a–254e.

14. René Descartes, *Les passions de l'âme* (Paris: Henry Le Gras, 1649).

15. This changed with the Hellenistic influence of the first century CE, as noted in E. Elias Joseph Bickerman, *The Jews in the Greek Age* (Cambridge, MA: Harvard University Press, 1988), 166.

16. We might also include the Shulammite from Song of Songs but her origin and status are unknown, making it difficult to draw leadership insights from her biography.

17. For a discussion of those to whom wisdom literature was directed, see Murphy, *The Tree of Life,* 3–5. From his discussion, it seems clear that court leaders were among the recipients of its instruction.

18. A prime example of such methodological approaches is John C. Maxwell, *The 21 Irrefutable Laws of Leadership: Follow Them and People Will Follow You* (Nashville, TN: Thomas Nelson, 2007).

19. Translation from Alter, *Wisdom Books,* 11.

20. Murphy, *The Tree of Life,* 2.

21. Brown, *Character in Crisis,* 20.

22. Craig G. Bartholomew, *The Baker Commentary on the Old Testament Wisdom and Psalms: Ecclesiastes* (Grand Rapids, MI: Baker Academic, 2009), 21–22.

23. Scripture quotations marked (NLT) are taken from the Holy Bible, New Living Translation.

24. Murphy, *The Tree of Life,* 135.

25. Murphy, *The Tree of Life,* 138.

26. Weeks, *Study of Wisdom Literature,* 86.

6 | The Prophets

Paul B. Petersen

The ministry of the biblical prophets reached its climax during the reign of the kings of Judah in the south and Israel (Ephraim) in the north. Prophets were sent by God to proclaim His Word and to bring national leaders and the people back to lives that reflected the will of the Lord. Toward the end of this period, Jeremiah gave this description of the situation:

> The priests did not say, "Where is the LORD?" Those who handle the law did not know me; the shepherds transgressed against me; the prophets prophesied by Baal and went after things that do not profit. (Jer. 2:8)

The description was followed by this compassionate plea by God:

> "Go, and proclaim these words toward the north, and say, 'Return, faithless Israel', declares the LORD. 'I will not look on you in anger, for I am merciful', declares the LORD; 'I will not be angry forever. Only acknowledge your guilt, that you rebelled against the LORD your God.'" (Jer. 3:12–13)

What leadership principles can one deduce from the message and ministries of biblical prophets such as Jeremiah? This chapter examines the testimony of the prophets as we have received it through the books they left us. In their dramatic encounters with the kings and through their staunch criticism, prophets such as Elijah and Elisha also provide material relevant for the topic. Their preaching, however, was never written down, and their general teaching can only in part be deduced via the narratives about them found in the book of Kings.

The literary corpus of the Old Testament prophetic books covers a vast array of significant leadership issues, so many that it is impossible in a single chapter to do full justice to their teaching. For the sake of keeping a sharp focus, the book of Isaiah will be the primary source for a theology of leadership from the perspective of the canonical prophets.

The book of Isaiah is the longest of the prophetic books. It is the richest in terms of literary style, and there are few poetic metaphors or theological perspectives found in the prophetic books which are not also touched upon in the work of Isaiah. References to Isaiah, consequently, dominate the observations in this chapter.

Prophets spoke the "Word of the LORD" to kings and all other people. Their prophetic authority and their relationship to and description of leaders will provide the groundwork from which timeless principles for leaders will emerge.

THE PROPHETIC AUTHORITY: THE WORD OF GOD

The authority of the biblical prophets rests in the "Word of the LORD" (*dĕbar YHWH* in the Hebrew). This word was never inherent within the prophets; rather, it came to them externally, from outside, from God Himself (Jer. 18:5; Joel 1:1; Zeph. 1:1; et al.). For Isaiah this divine word, as the following texts exemplify, parallels the teaching of God or the law, the *tôrāh*[1]:

> Hear the word of the LORD, you rulers of Sodom! Give ear to the teaching of our God, you people of Gomorrah! (Isa. 1:10)[2]....

many peoples shall come, and say: "Come, let us go up to the mountain of the LORD, to the house of the God of Jacob, that he may teach us his ways and that we may walk in his paths." For out of Zion shall go *the law* [*tôrāh*] and *the word of the* LORD [*dĕbar YHWH*] from Jerusalem. (Isa. 2:3, emphasis added)

This word comes directly from God, since it is "the word of his mouth" (Jer. 9:20), but it is more than just words. *Dĕbar YHWH* can denote the specific prophetic utterance directed to people groups or persons (Isa. 16:23, addressed to Moab; and Isa. 39:5, addressed to king Hezekiah), but it is also used concerning the wider instruction by God to His prophets about what they are to do as His messengers (Isa. 38:4; Jer. 2:1; Ezek. 1:3).

The word (*dābār*) of God is the very content, the matter, of God's revelation; it is the reality of His intervening presence.[3] It includes what prophets see in visions (cf. Amos 1:1 and Obad. 1:1); it may be the "branch of an almond tree" seen by Jeremiah (1:11). Thus it can be said that "the word of the LORD came by the hand of Haggai the prophet" (Hag. 1:3), implying that both the verbal messages Haggai received and his ministry as a whole communicated the divine revelation. The *dābār* may be equated to an oracle, a *massā*', meaning "burden," making clear that the revealed message from God weighs heavily on the prophet who is to carry it to people.

The presence of the Word of God is thus the activity of a divine reality which otherwise would be absent. It comes with the power of the Creator. God ensures through the messages and ministry of the prophets that His purposes are fulfilled, as attested to by the prophets Isaiah and Jeremiah:

So shall my word be that goes out from my mouth; it shall not return to me empty, but it shall accomplish that which I purpose, and shall succeed in the thing for which I sent it. (Isa. 55:11)

Then the LORD said to me, "You have seen well, for I am watching over my word to perform it." (Jer. 1:12)

The Word of God transmitted through prophets to kings and other leaders of the time often contained harsh criticism. The revelations from God are not always encouraging reading. But before the reader is overtaken with gloom, it must be pointed out that the very revelation itself is an expression of the mercy of God. Moreover, it exemplifies God's own leadership qualities. He is a God who communicates. He calls, He informs, He explains, and He appeals. Speaking before events happen, God provides hope through His Word.

PROPHETS AS LEADERS

It is a consequence of the nature of the divine word that generally the prophets who were to carry this word to the people did not themselves occupy formal leadership positions within the people of God. Just as the Word of God is independent of what it creates (cf. Gen. 1), the *dĕbar YHWH* through the prophets was to be independent of the power structure or hierarchy of the time. However, during the period of the biblical prophets, a number of prophets did not maintain such independence. Kings and rulers employed prophets whose function was to legitimize the actions of the kings and rulers. Confrontations between these prophets and the prophets sent by God took place continuously.

Speaking about leaders in Judah, Isaiah lists "the mighty man and the soldier, the judge and the prophet, the diviner and the elder" (Isa. 3:2), and he complains that "the priest and the prophet reel with strong drink, they are swallowed by wine, they stagger with strong drink, they reel in vision, they stumble in giving judgment" (Isa. 28:7), perhaps implying the usage of alcoholic drinks to further ecstasy.

Jeremiah denounces the priests and prophets who teach and speak for profit, "for from the least to the greatest of them, everyone is greedy for unjust gain; and from prophet to priest, everyone deals falsely" (Jer. 6:13; cf. Jer. 8:10).

Jeremiah 28 tells the story of the confrontation between Jeremiah and the prophet Hananiah whose positive messages of peace and prosperity satisfied the king and the crowd, but did not come true because the Word of God was not with Hananiah. "Let him who has my word speak my word faithfully," God says through Jeremiah (Jer.

23:28). "The prophets are prophesying lies in my name. I did not send them, nor did I command them or speak to them. They are prophesying to you a lying vision, worthless divination, and the deceit of their own minds" (Jer. 14:14).

God's prophets in general faced the challenge of encounters with persons pretending to speak in the name of Yahweh, whether directly in the employ of kings, or simply uttering their message for personal gain and profit, proclaiming what people wanted to hear, not what God had revealed to them (cf. Lam. 2:14; Ezek. 13:9; et al.).

The independence of God's prophets is theologically linked to the theme of God's sovereignty. Yahweh is beyond measure and control, and the surprising actions of some of God's prophets, clearly outside the cultural norms of the day, may in part be related to this emphasis on the sovereignty of the God for whom they speak. Ezekiel's bizarre cooking (Ezek. 4:9 ff.) and Hosea's dysfunctional family life clearly illustrate that God was willing to transgress cultural norms in order to make His message clear.

The decisive point is that the authority of the prophetic Word of God was to stay independent of any human power structure or hierarchy. This independence was based on the sovereignty of God. As God is independent of the world, His creative Word is beyond any human structure or leadership role, even though God uses both.

LEADERS DURING THE TIME OF THE PROPHETS

Many different words are used to denote the various leadership positions in ancient Israel during the time of the prophets, and today it may be less certain what specific functions the various designations for these positions precisely covered.

Jeremiah includes all of Israel in the following four categories: kings, who of course possessed absolute royal authority; the various officials, who represented the king (Heb. *sar*, often translated "prince");[4] priests, with their ceremonial and ritual power; and the common people (Jer. 1:16). In chapter 26, verses 16–17, Jeremiah adds the hired court "prophets" to the list, and he also mentions "elders" as a separate group—most likely the traditional leaders of families in local communities.

Of these categories we repeatedly meet the term *sar* (meaning "prince") as a general term for those who are entrusted to exercise the authority of the king, as in Isaiah 1:23 and 3:14. Other words used in a general sense include *mōshēl* (Isa. 52:5, meaning "those who govern") and *'ōshēr* (Isa. 3:12; 9:16, meaning "those who guide/lead").

Even when the prophets speak in more exact terms about court officials, the detailed functions of these officials elude us, though we have a general sense of their responsibilities. In Isaiah 22:15 Shebna is mentioned as one who "is over the household" of the king. When we meet him again in Isaiah 36:3, he is "the secretary," and Eliakim has taken over the previously mentioned role as master "over the house," while Joah is labeled the "recorder."

The context makes it evident that these three are high-ranking court officials with direct access to the king, most likely belonging to what we today would call the president's cabinet. Precisely how authority was divided among them is not known.

This uncertainty helps to illustrate a significant point. Such positions were part of the leadership structure of the time, and there is no reason to understand this hierarchy as divinely instituted. We are presented with historical description, not divine prescription.

God spoke into this historical situation and was able, through the help of prophets who carried His Word, to provide guidance for leaders within that particular cultural context. The imperfectness of the situation did not prevent God from revealing His Word. From the messages He sent, it is possible, therefore, to deduce lasting principles for governance, which can then be applied to different circumstances and different cultural structures of power and authority.

ACCOUNTABILITY OF LEADERS

Leadership roles in Israel during the time of the prophets did not reflect a divinely instituted pattern, but leaders still ultimately received their power from God and were held accountable to Him.

Abuses of power were noted by God, and through the prophets He intervened, spoke into the culture, and called people in power to account. He did so by what was known as a *rîb*.[5]

The *rîb* was a lawsuit, an indictment, by which the prophets, on behalf of God, laid out in the open His case against kings, princes, priests, and prophets. Typical for such divine indictment were statements like these from Hosea and Micah:

> Hear the word of the Lord, O children of Israel, for the Lord has a controversy [*rîb*] with the inhabitants of the land. There is no faithfulness or steadfast love, and no knowledge of God in the land. (Hos. 4:1)

> Hear, you mountains, the indictment [*rîb*] of the Lord, and you enduring foundations of the earth, for the Lord has an indictment [*rîb*] against his people, and he will contend with Israel. (Mic. 6:2)

Though most often perceived as negative, the outcome of such a *rîb* could be deliverance or justification. God encourages leaders to "plead [from the related verb *rîb*, "to contend or dispute"] the widow's cause" (Isa. 1:17), and Micah describes how God will champion his "cause [*rîb*] and execute judgment." For Micah, this (*rîb*) was an expression of his trust in future divine forgiveness and subsequent vindication (7:9).

The *rîb* illustrates the grace of God. He is willing to listen, forgive, and change the fate of His people if they repent. But it also exemplifies another significant feature of ideal leadership, namely transparency. God openly invites people to His court of justice, "Come now, let us reason together" (Isa. 1:18). "Hear, O heavens, and give ear, O earth," the prophet Isaiah writes, as he introduces his message from God (cf. Mic. 1:2). The parallel reference to both "heaven" and "earth" signifies an address to everyone, a universal appeal. "Arise, plead your case before the mountains, and let the hills hear your voice," God appeals through Micah (6:1), and He passionately argues with Israel in the love parable about the vineyard, "What more was there to do for my vineyard, that I have not done in it?" (Isa. 5:4).

God's call to justice is comprehensive, even universal in scope: "The Lord has an indictment against the nations; He is entering into judgment with all flesh, and the wicked He will put to the sword, declares the LORD" (Jer. 25:31). Such a lawsuit against all peoples on earth implies the Lordship of God as the Creator of everyone. By nature this universal aspect includes an eschatological overtone, and the *rîb* equals the "Day of the LORD" so common in prophetic literature (Isa. 13:16; Joel 1:15; 2:11; Amos 5:18, 20; Zeph. 1:14; 2:3; et al.). What took place on a local scale in the course of the history of Israel followed a pattern which mirrored the universal end-time judgment. Further, the language of the prophets when speaking about the "Day of the LORD" often fluctuated between local and universal, present and eschatological, and between history and the temple ceremonies which cast light on the events from the perspective of the cult.

INDICTMENT OF LEADERS

When prophets present God's case against the leaders of the people, they address both the actions of the leaders against the people for whom they are to care, and the attitude of the leaders toward God. Like other prophets, Isaiah does little to hide the social injustice committed by the leaders of his day:

> Your princes [*sar*] are rebels and companions of thieves. Everyone loves a bribe and runs after gifts. They do not bring justice to the fatherless, and the widow's cause does not come to them. (Isa. 1:23)

> The LORD will enter into judgment with the elders and princes [*sar*] of his people: "It is you who have devoured the vineyard, the spoil of the poor is in your houses." (Isa. 3:14)

Selfishness toward other people is often accompanied by evident sin against God. Leaders are indicted and "will be cut off" for being "ruthless" toward fellow humans, but also for being arrogant "scoffers" against God (Isa. 29:20). The ungodly, foolish leader withholds from the hungry and thirsty what they need but also teaches "errors concerning God" (Isa. 32:6). There is, as attested to by Hosea, neither "faithfulness, steadfast love" nor any "knowledge of God in the land" (Hos. 4:1). Yet religious rituals are still performed, and the formal relationship to God seemingly is in order, while in reality the rituals cover blatant acts of exploitation and abuse of power. The Word of God through Isaiah challenges this sinfulness:

> Your new moons and your appointed feasts my soul hates; they have become a burden to me; I am weary of bearing them. When you spread out your hands, I will hide my eyes from you; even though you make many prayers, I will not listen; your hands are full of blood. (Isa. 1:14–15)

Yet, the prophet also opens the door for how the situation may be redeemed through repentance, forgiveness, and reform:

> Wash yourselves; make yourselves clean; remove the evil of your deeds from before my eyes; cease to do evil, learn to do good; seek justice, correct oppression; bring justice to the fatherless, plead the widow's cause. (Isa. 1:16–17)

Unfortunately, the leaders too rarely listened to the messages God sent through His servants the prophets (cf. Jer. 26:5). They led the people astray (Isa. 9:16); arrogance, haughtiness, and pride were their dominant attitudes (e.g., Isa. 28:14; 29:20) and sealed their fate. On the "Day of the LORD" those in high positions would be humiliated and thrown to the ground.

LEADERS IN TROUBLE: THE REVERSAL OF FORTUNE

The reversal of roles or fortune is a major theme in the book of Isaiah and illustrates some core characteristics of both good and bad leaders.

Isaiah presents God's lawsuit as an indictment, as "a day against all that is proud and lofty, against all that is lifted up—and it shall be brought low" (Isa. 2:12). Key terms in this *rîb* are the characteristics of the accused. While the word for "proud" or "haughty" (Heb. *gēʾeh*) is a rare Old Testament word, the words for "lofty" (*rûm*) and "lifted up" (*nāsāʾ*) are common and appear frequently in central passages throughout the book. The prophets in this context paralleled the social status of high rank with a spiritual and mental attitude of arrogance and self-exaltation.

Their fate because of such self-grandeur is repeated in verse 17: they will be "brought low" (Heb. *šapēl*), "and the LORD alone will be exalted in that day." The verb used for the exaltation of Yahweh is *nisgab,* once again a rarely used term, only found here in Isaiah. God's exalted status stands in sharp contrast to any temporary or pretended greatness on the part of earthly leaders.

In Isaiah's grand a vision of Yahweh in His temple, this contrast between God and humans is even further emphasized. Yahweh is on His throne, heavenly beings worship Him as holy, and in the presence of God the prophet must acknowledge the utter uncleanness of sinful creation and the need for divine forgiveness (Isa. 6:1–7). Yet in this vision God's exalted position is described with the terms similar to those used in chapter 2 about the fleeting nature of human grandeur. "In the year that King Uzziah died," Isaiah "saw the LORD sitting upon a throne, high [*rûm*] and lifted up [*nāsā'*]." The repeated use of the verbs *rûm* and *nāsā',* here both as participles describing God, emphasizes the difference between the eternal exaltation of the Creator, and the temporary high status of humans accountable to their Creator for their use (or abuse) of power.

One is able to follow this theme of the reversal of fortune of the high and lofty throughout the early part of the book of Isaiah:

Man is humbled, and each one is brought low, and the eyes of the haughty are brought low. (5:15)

The LORD of hosts has purposed it, to defile the pompous pride of all glory, to dishonor all the honored of the earth. (23:9)

The theme reaches a climax in the second part of the book. In Isaiah, God, through the prophet, provides self-characterization which speaks directly to the nature of leadership. Once again God is described as high (*rûm*) and lifted up (*nasa'*), but what is significant is that God as leader is not exalted as a selfish, distant ruler, looking down on those He governs. On the contrary, He is exalted exactly because He is willing to come close to fallen humankind, embracing the brokenhearted. The text speaks about the willingness of God to come down:

For thus says the One who is high [from *rûm*] and lifted up [from *nāsā'*], who inhabits eternity, whose name is Holy: "I dwell in the high and holy place, and also with him who is of a contrite and lowly spirit, to revive the spirit of the lowly, and to revive the heart of the contrite." (57:15)

As in Isaiah 2:17, the Hebrew word used for "lowly" is *šapēl*. The true leader, the one who is worthy of being exalted, is the one who is willing to come down—to be among the people in order to lift up those he or she serves. Only such a leader truly represents Yahweh, and just a few chapters earlier Isaiah prophesied about someone who fit the description:[6]

Behold, my servant shall act wisely; he shall be high [from *rûm*] and lifted up [from *nāsā'*], and shall be exalted. (52:13)

The servant of Yahweh described in chapter 53[7] has been the object of numerous studies throughout the years, but the following reflections will focus only on the significance of the leadership qualities of the servant of the Lord.

THE SUFFERING SERVANT

The word to describe the exaltation of the "Servant of the Lord" in Isaiah 52:13 (Heb. *gābahh*) can have negative connotations, as it may mean being haughty (cf. Isa. 3:16), but it also characterizes God Himself (Isa. 5:18). In contrast to the proud leaders of the time, the Servant is exalted because he is willing to lower himself to the level of the people to whom he ministers.[8]

How is the Servant of the book of Isaiah further characterized in chapter 53? It is wise to remember that the song in this chapter is only one of a number of servant songs found in chapter 40 and onward.[9] The difficulty in identifying the Suffering Servant in chapter 53 is in part due to the fact that the "Servant of the Lord" in these poems may refer to different entities.[10] It is, however, exactly this variety within the poems which provides us with further characteristics of the servant of the Lord as leader.

First we note that the Servant is a prophet. He represents Yahweh by sharing His Word, just as God's "servant Isaiah" had done (Isa. 20:3)—or like those prophets whose word God confirmed and whose councils He fulfilled (Isa. 44:26). In this prophetic ministry he is sent not only to Israel, but God will make him "a light for the nations" as well (Isa. 49:6). His task is universal.

In the context of the servant songs in the book of Isaiah, the suffering servant also represents the people of Israel, the "servant" in several of the poems:

> But you, Israel, my servant, Jacob, whom I have chosen, the offspring of Abraham, my friend; you whom I took from the ends of the earth, and called from its farthest corners, saying to you, "You are my servant, I have chosen you and not cast you off." (41:8–9)

> But now hear, O Jacob my servant, Israel whom I have chosen! (44:1)

> Remember these things, O Jacob, and Israel, for you are my servant; I formed you; you are my servant; O Israel, you will not be forgotten by me. (44:21)

The Servant in Isaiah 53 is in a sense the perfect representative of the people: the innocent who suffers on their behalf (cf. Isa. 53:5–8); and in identifying with the corporate body, he functions as an intercessor for "the transgressors," "justifying the many," that is, the people (Isa. 53:11–12). He is truly human, but, in contrast to the people, he is also an ideal human.

But he is more than just an oppressed sufferer (Isa. 53:10). He is a king. In the context of Isaiah, not only is David an anointed king of Yahweh (Isa. 37:35), but surprisingly so is Cyrus, the Persian king who let the people of Israel return to their land:

> Thus says the LORD to his anointed, to Cyrus, whose right hand I have grasped, to subdue nations before him and to loose the belts of kings, to open doors before him that gates may not be closed. (Isa. 45:1)

The Hebrew word *mišḥat* which describes the suffering servant in Isaiah 52:14 is found only here in the Old Testament. It is usually translated "marred" or "disfigured," and though its meaning may not be "anointed" (Heb. *mašîaḥ*), the phonetics certainly convey a rhetorical association to this adjective. The Suffering Servant has a royal function, and as a great king he will "divide the spoil" after his victory (Isa. 53:12).[11]

But more than anything, the Suffering Servant is the representative of God. He is high (from *rûm*) and lifted up (from *nāsā'*)—exactly what is said of God only a few chapters later (Isa. 57:15); He is the only one exalted when judgment arrives (Isa. 2:17). The servant represents God not as transcendent and distant, but as the divinely provided sacrifice who is brought near to sinners (Isa. 53:4–6).

MESSIAH AS THE IDEAL LEADER

The description of the Suffering Servant as an ideal leader naturally connects to the prophetic hope of a future perfect king on the Davidic throne. This hope dominates not only the book of Isaiah, but the whole of the prophetic corpus throughout the periods of kings, exile, and after the exile from Babylon (e.g., Isa. 9:6–7; 11:1–5; Jer. 23:5–6; Mic. 5:1–2; Zech. 9:9). The characteristics of this ideal ruler exemplify the leadership traits expected by God, and they are further underlined by their contrast not only to the ruling kings in Israel and Judah, but also to their enemies—kings and powers who attacked both the people and God Himself.

Given the generally corrupt rulers of the time, it is paradoxical that this notion of the ideal king developed in Israel. But it was precisely this reality which highlighted the need for, and strengthened the vision of, another type of leader. So the prophets made use of the Davidic king as a divinely established type of the ideal future king.

The traits of the Messianic leader fit into the two major categories of justice and wisdom. This leader is both righteous Judge and wise Teacher. In a time when there was no separation of the judicial and executive power, the king was also the supreme judge. This reality was more often than not a curse rather than a blessing for the people, and the prophets excelled in disclosing the widespread abuse of power. Justice was often bent, corruption rampant, and the cause of the poor was often hopeless.

In contrast, therefore, the Messianic king is characterized by His justice and by His compassion for those who are oppressed and easily exploited. He is to "establish" His government and "uphold it with justice and with righteousness" forever (Isa. 9:7). The term for righteousness, *ṣĕdāqāh,* is used again in Isaiah 11:4 as we are told that the Messiah "with righteousness...shall judge the poor." *Sĕdāqāh* is not to be read simply from a Western cultural tradition as the stern divine righteousness which tallies every sin and holds it against the sinner. Here, as in the Old Testament in general, it denotes the righteous acts of God by which He delivers and redeems those who are oppressed or held prisoners (Isa. 56:1; cf. Ps. 98:1–2, 9). "Righteousness shall be the belt" around the waist of the One who saves and protects the helpless (Isa. 11:5).

This righteousness implies that He will not evaluate people by appearance or hearsay; He "shall not judge by what his eyes see, or decide disputes by what his ears hear, but with righteousness he shall judge the poor, and decide with equity for the meek of the earth" (Isa. 11:3–4).

The word pair in Isaiah 9:7—justice (Heb. *mišpāṭ*) and righteousness (Heb. *ṣĕdāqāh*)—is found also in Jeremiah 23:5–6, once again with the sense of salvation, and the Messianic king is even titled "The Lord Our Righteousness."

But the future ideal king is only able to function as the righteous Judge because He is endowed with divine wisdom. The first title given to the future king in Isaiah 9:6 is "Wonderful Counselor,"[12] and Jeremiah introduces his short presentation of the ideal future king by a reference to His wisdom: He shall "deal wisely" (Jer. 23:5).

The description of the "shoot from the stump of Jesse" and of the sevenfold Spirit resting upon His shoulders underlines this aspect even more strongly. The characteristics almost read like a catalog of the major terms for divine wisdom in the Old Testament: a Spirit of wisdom (Heb. *ḥokmāh*) and understanding (Heb. *bînāh*), of counsel (Heb. *'ēṣāh*) and might (Heb. *gĕbûrāh*),[13] of knowledge (Heb. *dā'at*) and the fear of the Lord (Isa. 11:2).

For those who wish to emulate this ideal leader, they must possess the skills (Heb. *ḥokmāh*) of wisdom, and they also exercise the ability to discern (Heb. *bînāh*) between important and less important, appropriate and inappropriate, tasteful and unsavory, and good and evil. But the foundation for all their wisdom is summed up in the last expression, a Spirit of "fear of the LORD." The book of Proverbs highlights that "the fear of the LORD is the beginning of knowledge" (1:7). This characteristic of good leaders can be identified as humility. Wise leaders acknowledge that all wisdom comes from God, and they are open and willing to listen and learn, both in relation to God and those for whom they serve as leaders. Fools are unteachable because they think they already know; the wise are able constantly to learn because of their humility. In the face of the Creator-God, all humans must acknowledge their need for constant divine guidance.

ANOTHER WORLD

Leaders during the days of the prophets were admonished to exercise justice and compassion toward people, and they were also to humble themselves before God and lay aside human pride. For the prophets, leadership was never just a matter of a horizontal relationship. God was both the origin of their message and the focus of their worship and commitment.

The divine judgment preached by the prophets concerns not only the earthly regimes, but also the spiritual powers behind them, as expressed by Isaiah, "On that day the LORD will punish the host of heaven, in heaven, and the kings of the earth, on the earth" (24:21). Few texts highlight this parallel between the two worlds better than the famous dirge in Isaiah 14:

> How you are fallen from heaven, O Day Star, son of Dawn! How you are cut down to the ground, you who laid the nations low! You said in your heart, "I will ascend to heaven; above the stars of God I will set my throne on high; I will sit on the mount of assembly in the far reaches of the north; I will ascend above the heights of the clouds; I will make myself like the Most High." (14:12–14)

A superficial reading indicates that this elegy in Isaiah 14:4–21 is about the king of Babylon, yet the symbolic, mythical character of the language reveals that the prophet is also characterizing the heavenly representative of Babylon—its counterpart in the spiritual world whose attitudes the ruler of Babylon has imitated and exemplified. Isaiah 14 is thus in many ways a forerunner for the apocalyptic mood where this spatial dualism is a main feature,[14] yet it should be remembered that the belief in the parallel and close relation between this world and the heavenly realm is a characteristic feature of the Ancient Middle East cultures throughout their entire existence.

The essential attitude of both the king of Babylon and the Day Star of Isaiah 14:12–14 is pride. It is his ambition to be exalted and sit high. In the context of Isaiah's emphasis on the reversal of fate, this description is significant. The enemy of the king of God's people attempts to "lift up" (from Hebrew *rûm;* cf. Isa. 52:13 and 57:15) his throne above the stars of heaven, taking the very place of God Himself. This power grab is in sharp contrast to the work of the Suffering Servant and ideal King and Leader, who is exalted exactly because of His willingness to come down and in humility to serve the people, identifying with the people as an intercessor for their sins.

The dualism is not only spatial but also temporal. The future reign of Messiah envisioned by Isaiah moves beyond the present age to an age when "the wolf shall dwell with the lamb, and the leopard shall lie down with the young goat, and the calf and the lion and the fattened calf together; and a little child shall lead them" (Isa. 11:6–9), and that "of the increase of his government and of peace there will be no end," and that He will reign "from this time forth and forevermore" (Isa. 9:6).

The theological presupposition for this vision is once again the concept of creation. The Word of God spoke the world into existence; through the prophets this powerful *Děbar Yahweh* has transformed hearts and attitudes as well as political and social realities. One day this Word will re-create human environment and society and install a future ideal Leader whose reign shall last forever in a world like the one originally intended.

CONCLUSION

The prophets of Israel occupied no formal role in the hierarchy of authority in the kingdoms of Judah or Israel. They were representatives of a divine reality which was to be independent of any type of governance. They were sent by God with His revelation and His presence to confront human authority. The "Word of the LORD" through the prophets positioned the prophet outside of any ordinary human power structure.

Formal leadership roles depend on culture. The authoritative role of the prophet does not. The formal leaders in ancient Israel comprised kings, princes, officials, "masters of the royal house," and a number of other positions the exact definition of which may not be clear. This power structure during the reign of the kings is, however, not a universal, timeless divine invention, but reflects the historical reality of the day. It is a historical fact: descriptive, not prescriptive. The "Word of the LORD" through the prophets did not set out to revolutionize that system, but that does not mean it was the only system preferred by God. Rather, God's continuing interaction with His people's leadership demonstrates the ability of God to speak into any culture and to reveal His will to us in situations which are less than ideal.

The authority of the leaders in Israel was therefore, in spite of reflecting a less than ideal system of governance, nevertheless an authority delegated by God, and the leaders were held accountable for the way they exercised their divinely given power. The prophets were sent by God to make the formal leaders constantly aware of His expectations, the core of which were justice, fairness, mercy to the poor and the powerless, and the upholding of the Torah, the law and teaching of God.

It is one of the many functions of the prophetic books in the biblical canon that they serve to illustrate the way God addresses human leaders during a specific, culturally dependent type of human governance. Though the system of power itself was historically conditioned, the prophetic messages nevertheless provide fundamental and divinely revealed principles of leadership, applicable to all ages.

The theological basis found in the biblical prophets for this concept of leadership authority is the concept of creation. Creation

implies that all human power, whether the power of life or government, in the end is received from God, and that all individuals
and systems are to respond in obedience to God's Word. This delegation implies a certain amount of responsibility and freedom.
Leaders are therefore, as is everyone else, accountable to God.
Prophets were sent to remind leaders of that fact. There will be a
"Day of the LORD," and the final universal judgment will certainly
come. But that future day of reckoning is also already now reflected
in God's intervention of judgment in history, and the leaders of
Israel would not escape their fate if they opposed God through
pride, injustice, and lack of compassion. The eschatological judgment is thus anticipated and illustrated in God's actions in history.
Creation and eschatology go hand in hand and conceptually
belong together. The divine ideal for the future reaches beyond
just social restoration; it is a total re-creation of human existence.

God's call to go to court in a lawsuit (the *rîb*) illustrates the openness and transparency of His governance and thus exemplifies a central characteristic of good leadership. God willingly communicates
and invites people to dialogue.

During the period of the prophets, many human leaders were
targeted with a divine message because of their pride, injustice, and
lack of compassion. Of course the divinely expected leadership
qualities were at times reflected in human leaders, such as Eliakim
(Isa. 22:20–25), yet God Himself portrayed the ideal leader in the
Servant figure in Isaiah 53. The description of the Suffering Servant
in this chapter is the climax of a series of Messianic promises
throughout the book, and in a unique way it represents the ideal
leader in contrast to unfaithful leaders within the people of God,
enemy leaders from other nations, and even the spiritual powers
behind them (e.g., Isa. 14:12–14; 24:21).

The Suffering Servant is characterized by humility, in contrast
to all other human leaders whose pride results in continuous self-
exaltation, and who therefore on God's Day of Judgment will be cast
down. Part of this paradoxical reversal of fate described by Isaiah also
applies to the Servant. He is willing to lower Himself, minister to
and with the people, and is thus lifted up and exalted because His
humility reflects the character of God Himself (cf. Isa. 57:15).

FOR REFLECTION

Personal:

1. The judicial role of the Messianic King is qualified by His voluntary humility. Though seemingly counterintuitive, how advantageous would it be for a leader to adopt such a servant mentality?
2. *Binah,* a Hebrew term used for "wisdom," highlights the quality of discernment and denotes the capacity to distinguish among matters of varying degrees of importance. Ask yourself, *What specific things can I change or do in my personal life that will increase my level of leadership discernment?*

Organizational:

1. In light of God's sensitivity to the societal woes rampant during the prophetic career of Isaiah, what systems can leaders wisely adopt to curtail humanity's natural bent to employ oppressive means for desirous ends?
2. God's appraisal of the shallowness of Israel's spiritual devotion (which was used as a cloak to hide their blatant acts of exploitation and abuse) highlights the disparity between what they professed and how they lived. Is your leadership faithful to its organizational creed? In what areas might change be needed?

ENDNOTES

1. The basic sense of *tôrāh* is "instruction," not simply law, implying God's teaching to humanity; see G. Liedke and C. Petersen "tôrāh instruction" in *Theological Lexicon of the Old Testament,* ed. Ernst Jenni and Claus Westermann (Peabody, MA: Hendricksons, 1997), 3:1415.

2. Unless otherwise noted, Scripture quotations in this chapter are taken from the English Standard Version.

3. For this broad understanding of the Hebrew word *dābār,* see W. H. Schmidt, *"dābār"* in *Theological Dictionary of the Old Testament (TDOT),* ed. G. Johannes Botterweck and Helmer Ringgren (Grand Rapids, MI: Eerdmans, 1978), 3:111, and G. Gerleman, *"dābār* word" in *Theological Lexicon of the Old*

Testament (TLOT), ed. Ernst Jenni and Claus Westermann (Peabody, MA: Hendricksons, 1997), 1:330. In the grammatical construction "The Word of the Lord," *dābār* is changed to *děbar*. *Děbar Yhwh* is almost exclusively used as a technical term for the prophetic message.

4. *Sar* often refers to military commanders (e.g., Gen. 21:22; 26:26; 37:36; 1 Sam. 14:50). This is in no way, however, an exclusive usage (Gen. 39:21; 40:2; Exod. 2:14; 1 Chron. 15:22; Dan. 1:7). These passages speak in more general terms about officials exercising a certain amount of authority.

5. The *rîb* has been the focus of a large number of studies, e.g., G. Liedke, "rîb to quarrel" in *TLOT*, 3:1232–37.

6. A similar literary-thematic connection is made by the evangelist John in 12:27–41.

7. The poem about the servant of the Lord in Isaiah 53 contains five major sections and actually begins in chapter 52:13.

8. The very structure of the song underlines the movement from the highest to the lowest and back: (A) Exaltation: 52:13–15; (B) Humiliation: 53:1–3; (C) Atonement: 53:4–6; (B1) Humiliation: 53:7–9; (A1) Exaltation: 53:10–12; see J. Alec Motyer, *The Prophecy of Isaiah: An Introduction and Commentary* (Downers Grove, IL: InterVarsity Press, 1993), 423.

9. Scholars in general identify four such songs: Isaiah 42:1–9; 49:1–13; 52:13—53:12; and 61:1–3.

10. Traditional Christian interpretation follows the New Testament in identifying the servant as Jesus Christ (John 12:38; Acts 8:32–33; Rom. 10:16; 15:21; 1 Pet. 2:22). In critical scholarship, other suggestions include the prophet Isaiah himself, Israel (called a "servant" in Isa. 41:8), or the remnant of Israel. For an overview of the various positions, see Bryan E. Beyer, *Encountering the Book of Isaiah: A Historical and Theological Survey* (Grand Rapids: Baker, 2007), 209–213.

11. For further study regarding the royal connection to the Suffering Servant, see Roland de Vaux, *The Bible and the Ancient Near East* (Garden City, NY: Doubleday, 1971), 155, and expressions such as "seed" (Isa. 53:10).

12. The noun *yoets* is also used to refer to the wise man Ahithophel (2 Sam. 15:12)—and about the evil queen Athaliah, a counselor who brought about quite a negative effect (2 Kings 22:3).

13. The word *gěbûrāh*, meaning "might" or "power," is often used in connection with the power embedded in genuine wisdom (Dan. 2:23).

14. Succinctly expressed by J. Louis Martyn, "The dicta most basic to the apocalyptic thinker are these: God created both heaven and earth. There are dramas taking place both on the heavenly stage and on the earthly stage. Yet, these dramas are not really two, but rather one drama.… The developments in the drama on its heavenly stage determine the developments on the earthly stage.… Events seen on the earthly stage are entirely enigmatic to one who sees only the earthly stage," *History and Theology in the Fourth Gospel* (Nashville: Abingdon Press, 1979), 135–136.

Section Two:
The New Testament

7 | Leadership Language in the New Testament

Jon Paulien

The definitive source of leadership understanding is God, the author of creation. As Creator, God knows human beings and how they function as individuals and groups. Humankind does not have the privilege of seeing, hearing, or touching God. So direct knowledge of God, or of the leadership principles He manifests in governing the universe, is not available to us. In Scripture, however, God has chosen to reveal Himself in human language. While God's self-disclosure is limited by the human context of Scripture, the Bible offers the clearest revelation of God available to the human race. Christian leadership models must be built on a careful understanding of God's principles as revealed in the Scriptures.

The New Testament is centered on the life, death, resurrection, and intercession of Jesus Christ. Nearly every leadership title in the New Testament is applied to Jesus at one time or another.[1] He is called "servant" (Phil. 2:7); "apostle" (Heb. 3:1); "prophet" (John 4:44; Acts 3:22–23); "overseer" (1 Pet. 2:25); "deacon" (Rom. 15:8); "ruler" (Rev. 1:5); "captain" (Heb. 12:2); "shepherd" (John 10:1–7; Heb. 13:20; 1 Pet. 2:25); and "lord/master"

(Eph. 6:9; Phil. 2:11; Col. 4:1), among others. He models God's way of leadership in terms that human beings can understand. A study of Christian leadership must, therefore, center in Jesus Christ.

According to the biblical account, Jesus both modeled what God is like and mentored the apostles in divine principles of leadership. After His ascension He sent the Holy Spirit to inspire the Christian apostles and the Christian prophets to carry on the work that He had begun on this earth (John 14:16–17, 26; 16:12–13).[2] Those who were closest to Jesus during His earthly ministry absorbed His leadership skills directly. The apostles then passed on to followers of Christ what they had received from Jesus (1 Cor. 11:23; 15:3; 1 John 1:1–4). Jesus is, therefore, the clearest revelation of God, and His apostles passed on a clear understanding of Jesus Christ.

In the New Testament record, the role of apostle was particularly played by Paul (1 Cor. 11:23; 15:3). While not one of the twelve disciples, Paul frequently identified himself as an "apostle" (Rom. 11:13; 1 Cor. 9:1–2; 15:9). In Acts 20:17–35, Paul gathered the elders of the church of Ephesus at Miletus to pass on what he had learned from Jesus.[3] The heart of Christian leadership is to be like Jesus, doing and teaching what He taught.[4] Following in the leadership path of Jesus includes servanthood (Luke 22:24–27; John 12:26; Acts 20:19); self-sacrifice (Acts 20:19–23); a strong sense of accountability (20:26–28); vigilance in the face of spiritual and physical threats (20:29–32); and voluntary service, stemming from a strong sense of being commissioned by Jesus Himself (20:33–35).[5]

An examination of the specific New Testament words for "leadership" follows: first the words that describe leadership in general and then the words that act as titles for various leadership functions in the earliest church. The chapter concludes with a summary of what is known about the development of specific ministry roles in the first century. The New Testament language of leadership provides a foundation upon which other chapters in this section of the book will build.

GENERAL WORDS FOR "LEADERSHIP" IN THE NEW TESTAMENT

A number of words in ancient Greek expressed the idea of leadership in a general way. Understanding these words both in their context and in light of their application within the New Testament record helps us understand biblical leadership principles. Space considerations require selectivity, but the main issues will still emerge with clarity from this selection.

ἄγω *(agō)*, ἡγεμών *(hēgemōn)*

The root meaning of the verb *agō* is "to direct the movement of an object from one position to another."[6] By analogy the word meant "to lead" or "to take into custody, arrest."[7] The noun form *hēgemōn* was widely used in civic and military contexts, and is used in similar ways in the Gospels (e.g., Mark 13:11; Luke 22:54; John 8:3; Acts 17:15; 20:12).[8] It is also associated with spiritual leadership, encouraging people to move in the direction of God or of spiritual things.[9] The word is not used to describe human leadership in the church;[10] rather, it refers to the leadership of God, Christ, or the Holy Spirit in human lives (Rom. 2:4; 8:14; Gal. 5:18).

ἀρχή *(archē)*, ἄρχων *(archōn)*

Archē is a noun with a natural double meaning in Greek: "beginning" (first in time) or "ruler/authority" (first in power or position).[11] This corresponds to the verb form *archō*, which means "to rule" or "to begin."[12] The fundamental meaning of *archē* is primacy, either in time ("beginning") or in rank ("power" or "office").[13] For our purposes, the latter is more interesting, since it describes "an authority figure who initiates activity or process."[14] As such, the word is generally used in the New Testament for the authority of a governor or other secular ruler (Luke 12:11; 20:20; Titus 3:1) or for demonic powers (Rom. 8:38; 1 Cor. 15:24; Col. 2:10, 15). It is also used with reference to Christ (Col. 1:18; Rev. 3:14[15]). It is significant that it is never used in relation to leadership in the church.

The related word *archōn* means a "high official," someone in a prominent position who exercises authority. In the Greek Old Testament it is commonly used to refer to a "ruler" or "governor" or "commander."[16] It is combined there with the Greek words for "priest," "military officer," or "bureaucrat" to signify a top-level leader. It is also used in Daniel for celestial beings.[17] Although occurring in the New Testament, the word appears much less frequently than in the Old and usually is applied to leaders of the Jews (Matt. 9:18; Luke 8:41; John 3:1), the state (Rom. 13:3), or demonic powers (John 12:31; 16:11; 1 Cor. 2:6–8; Eph. 6:12), without specifying a particular office. There is also one reference each to Moses (Acts 7:35) and to Jesus Christ (Rev. 1:5).[18] As with *agō* this word group is not used for human leadership in the church.

ἀρχηγός *(archēgos)*

The meaning of the noun *archēgos* is related to that of *archē*. It can mean "one who has a prominent position" or "one who begins or originates something."[19] The original meaning of *archēgos* is the founder or "hero" of a city. It also came to mean something like "captain." In the Greek Old Testament, the *archēgos* is usually the political or military leader of a nation or of a tribe.[20] In the New Testament, Christ is the *archēgos,* the founder and hero of Christian faith (Heb. 12:2), salvation (Acts 5:31; Heb. 2:10), and life (Acts 3:15).[21] Though very prominent in secular Greek sources as a title of leadership, it is not used in this way with reference to leadership in the church or to those serving in formal leadership roles within the church.

κεφαλή *(kephalē)*

The root meaning of *kephalē* refers to a person's physical head, the part of the body that contains the brain.[22] By extension it is used metaphorically to refer to a person of high status or superior rank in a hierarchy.[23] In the Hebrew Old Testament, "head" (*rō'š*) is frequently applied to human leaders, such as the patriarch of a family (Exod. 6:14, 25), the leader of a tribe (Num. 7:2; 2 Chron. 5:2), or simply leaders in general (Exod. 18:25; Num. 25:4; Judg. 11:11).[24] These "heads" in the Old Testament were parts of a hierarchical leadership system (Exod. 18:21) in which each "head" played a specific role under or above other heads.[25]

In the New Testament, *kephalē* is also used in the basic sense.[26] But in the epistles of Paul, *head* and *body* are usually used as metaphors of Christ and the church, and occasionally *kephalē* is applied to the husband's role in the home (Eph. 5:25–27). It is again significant that the church, however, chose not to apply this word to apostles, overseers, elders, or deacons;[27] it was applied solely to Jesus Christ. The church is more than an institution; in fact, it is a living organism and living organisms have only one head.[28] Leadership functions in the church, therefore, are substantively different from those in other kinds of organizations. *Kephalē* does not point to a hierarchy as much as it does to a *relationship*. As "head" of the church, Christ is the One who sustains the body and provides for its growth.

κύριος *(kyrios)*

Originally an adjective with the meaning of "having power," *kyrios* is used only as a noun in the New Testament.[29] It was widely used in the ancient world to refer to leaders, perhaps because it combined the sense of "might" (power, ability to compel obedience) and "right" (legitimacy, legal authorization).[30] The word can refer to one who is in charge by virtue of possession, "owner," or a position of authority, "lord" or "master." The word was also used as a title rather than a name for the gods and earthly kings and emperors. In its verb form (*kyrieuō*), the word has strong connotations of control and dominance.[31] In the Greek Old Testament *kyrios* is primarily used to translate or stand in place of the Hebrew name of God, Yahweh.[32]

In the New Testament *kyrios* is used in general terms with regard to the ownership of land (Matt. 20:8; Mark 12:9; Luke 20:13, 15); of slaves (Matt. 24:45–51; Luke 12:36–37; John 15:15; Rom. 14:4); and of animals (Matt. 15:27; Luke 19:33). It is also used for positions of authority in society: the husband (1 Pet. 3:6), the father (Matt. 21:30), high officials (Matt. 27:63), respected individuals (Acts 16:30; Rev. 7:14), and even the emperor himself (Acts 25:25–26). While *kyrios* can mean either "owner" or "master," the line between the two is often blurred.

Kyrios is frequently used to translate Old Testament references to Yahweh, usually with reference to God the Father (Matt. 4:10; 5:33; Acts 4:26), but sometimes with reference to Jesus (Matt. 4:7; Phil. 2:9–11). It is also applied directly in the New Testament to God (Luke 1:6, 9; 2 Thess. 3:1–4; Heb. 8:2; Rev. 11:15); Jesus (Rom. 10:9; 1 Thess. 4:15; 1 Tim. 6:3, 14); an angel (Acts 10:4);

and pagan gods (1 Cor. 8:5). Interestingly, in contrast to other Greek leadership terms, it is not used with reference to demons.

In an interesting twist, Jesus applies *kyrios* to Himself and affirms its basic meaning, yet implies that its usual meaning is inappropriate for His disciples (John 13:13–17). He redefines the term in the context of humble service. It is in this text that Jesus illustrates servant leadership by washing the feet of His disciples. It is for this reason, perhaps, that the term *kyrios* is never used in relation to church leadership in the New Testament. It is used, however, to describe the way slaves and masters should relate to each other in the church (Col. 3:22).

προΐστημι *(proistēmi)*

Of all the general leadership words in the Greek language, the only one adapted to the concept of leadership in the New Testament church is the verb *proistēmi*.[33] Its fundamental meaning is "to put before," "to go first," "to exercise a position of leadership, rule, direct."[34] It is widely used in these ways in the non-biblical Greek literature. What may have made it particularly attractive to early Christians, however, is that it had a related meaning of "to have an interest in, show concern for, give aid."[35] So the verb combines a sense of leadership and direction with a strong sense of caring concern. This is, no doubt, why this leadership word was so attractive to the early Christians. That understanding becomes especially clear when contrasted with other words that could have been chosen.

Proistēmi is certainly used in this combined sense in Romans 12:8: "If it is encouraging, let him encourage; if it is contributing to the needs of others, let him give generously; *if it is leadership, let him govern diligently*; if it is showing mercy, let him do it cheerfully" (NIV, emphasis added). It is used both for leadership in the church (1 Thess. 5:12; 1 Tim. 5:17) and in the household (1 Tim. 3:4–5, 12), which qualifies a person for leadership in the church. Those described by this verb particularly function in the realm of pastoral care (1 Thess. 5:12–15).[36]

Summary of Common Leadership Terms

Most of the common leadership words in the Greek language occur in the New Testament, but not in relation to leadership or leaders in the church, in spite of the widespread usage of such terms in the Greek Old Testament, which was the Bible of the Early Church. Evidently, Christian leadership was unique enough that the use of traditional language might lead to misunderstanding and was therefore avoided. In the Christian context such language was applied mainly to Christ, the true Ruler, Lord and Head of the Christian church, but also to demonic powers as well as secular authorities. Within the church an alternative set of terms was adopted, expressing a distinction between Christian leadership principles and those commonly utilized in the wider world.[37]

EARLY LEADERSHIP ROLES IN THE NEW TESTAMENT CHURCH

In the earliest church, shortly after the death and resurrection of Christ, leadership was charismatic rather than appointed. People served as leaders because they had been particularly close to Jesus while He was on Earth and/or the church sensed a special working of God in their lives (e.g., Acts 1:15–26). Over time certain of these charismatic leaders became known by the titles *apostle* and *prophet*.

According to Luke 11:47–50, the ancestors of the scribes and Pharisees killed the (Old Testament) prophets (vv. 47–48), just as the scribes and Pharisees would kill the "prophets and apostles" that God sent to them (vv. 49–50). So both apostles and prophets in the New Testament are the successors of the Old Testament prophets (Eph. 2:19–22). The apostles and prophets together were agents of God's revelation to the fledgling church. As such, they naturally became visible leaders of the first generation of believers in Christ.

ἀπόστολος *(apostolos)*
The root meaning of *apostle* describes one who is "dispatched for a specific purpose," a messenger or ambassador of some kind. While used in Scripture as a noun, it is really an adjective, "the *sent* one." This word is related to the verbal form *apostellō*, which is usually translated as "send." The verb implies a commission or delegated authority aimed toward a goal.[38] The status of such an *apostle* depends on the status of the one who sends him or her (John 13:16).

The *apostle* can be simply a messenger between ordinary individuals. But when the *apostle* is sent by a king or by God, his or her status becomes extraordinary. It is as if the sender accompanies the one sent.[39] While the verb form is widely used in this way in both the Greco-Roman world and the Greek Old Testament,[40] the title *apostle* is rare in Greek outside the uniquely Christian context,[41] although it did have a Hebrew equivalent in rabbinic Judaism.[42]

In the New Testament, therefore, the apostle is highly honored by other believers as a special envoy from God.[43] In the fullest sense, Jesus is the ultimate apostle (Heb. 3:1–2), the One in whom the definitive revelation of God has taken place (Heb. 1:1–3).[44] All other apostles derive their authority from Him. These became prominent leaders of the church after the ascension of Christ. Although the term originally applied to the twelve disciples alone (Matt. 10:2; Mark 3:14; Luke 22:14; cf. Acts 1:26),[45] the body of apostles eventually extended beyond the twelve to include Paul (Rom. 1:1; Gal. 1:1; and so on); Barnabas (Acts 14:14; 15:2); James, brother of Jesus (Gal. 1:19); and others (Rom. 16:7).

The office was associated with some sort of direct calling from the New Testament Jesus—in Paul's case a call to reach out to the Gentiles (Acts. 9:15; Eph. 3:1, 8).[46] Powerful leaders of the second generation, such as Apollos and Timothy, who did not have a direct call from Jesus, were not called apostles (1 Cor. 3:3–9; 2 Cor. 1:1; Phil. 1:1; 1 Thess. 3:2). So the office seems to have been limited to the first generation of Jesus's followers (1 Cor. 15:8). The duties of the office centered on traveling from place to place proclaiming what the apostle had experienced with Jesus (1 Cor. 9:1, 5; Eph. 3:5). In the process, the apostles founded and administered new churches (1 Cor. 15:10–11; Eph. 2:20).[47] They appointed elders to head up those churches but retained an authoritative role among them.

προφήτης *(prophētēs)*

The Greek root of the word *prophet* is a compound word, combining a Greek word for "speaking" with the prefix *pro* which is ambiguous in meaning. It can mean "speaking openly" or publically, much like preaching. But it can also mean "speaking ahead of time" or "in advance."[48] In ancient Greece, the word came to be used to refer to appointed people through whom the gods revealed their will.[49] So by New Testament times the prophet was known as "a proclaimer or expounder of divine matters or concerns that could not ordinarily be known except by special revelation."[50]

We see New Testament prophets at work in the book of Acts (11:27–30; 15:30–32; 21:10–14). Their messages were accepted as authoritative by the church, and an obedient response was expected, so prophets had a significant leadership role in the earliest church. At the same time the church struggled on occasion with just how to apply the prophetic message to a specific situation (Acts 21:12–14).

It is interesting that although Paul speaks prophetically to the churches (1 Cor. 14:6),[51] he never calls himself a "prophet." This suggests that at the time *apostle* could include the gifts and activities of the prophet (2 Cor. 12:1–7; Eph. 3:3–7). In 1 Corinthians 12:28–31 the gifts of the Spirit are listed with ordinal numbers that may suggest a hierarchy of authority. So in terms of roles at the time, "apostle" is listed first and "prophet" is second. Apostles and prophets are equal when it comes to being the objects of direct revelation. The apostle's authority seems to have been greater because of the special commission of leadership and the unique association in time and proximity to the first-century Christ-event. The apostles were more directive in their counsel, while the prophets led by influence.

LATER LEADERSHIP ROLES IN THE NEW TESTAMENT CHURCH

Timothy and Titus are the clearest examples of how the church moved from leadership by charismatic apostles to appointees serving from their own calling and giftedness.[52] As a successor of the apostles, Timothy was ordained both by a council of elders (1 Tim. 4:13–15) and by Paul himself (2 Tim. 1:6) to leadership over multiple churches (1 Tim. 5:17–22). Titus not only exercised authority over multiple churches, he also appointed gifted elders and overseers to guide them (Titus 1:5–7), although Timothy likely did so as well. But although Timothy and Titus functioned like apostles, they were not themselves called "apostles." They were part of the transition to a second generation of leadership in the church, though they themselves did not carry any of the leadership titles.[53] This transition from apostles to appointed leadership is implied in the New Testament and directly stated in the writings of Clement of Rome (roughly 95 AD).[54] The second generation of leadership functioned under three titles in particular.

ἐπίσκοπος *(episkopos)*

The term *episkopos* was a common title in the Greco-Roman world and had Hebrew equivalents at Qumran.[55] The root meaning is "one who watches over," therefore, "overseer."[56] It means something like "supervisor," a position of responsibility within a wide range of contexts and applications,[57] "one who has the responsibility of seeing that something is done the right way."[58] In the non-biblical context *episkopos* was not an honorary title; rather, it was associated with very specific responsibilities.[59] In today's terms, the title came with a job description. In the Greek Old Testament it is used as a parallel to *archōn*. Broad usage of the term can carry an element of service and caring relationship.[60]

The word occurs only three times in the New Testament (Phil. 1:1; 1 Tim. 3:2; Titus 1:7), and the related noun *episkopē* occurs twice (Acts 1:20 and 1 Tim. 3:1).[61] From Philippians 1:1 we can determine that there was an identifiable group called "overseers," but the verse provides no details about their role in the church. On the other hand, 1 Timothy 3:2–7 and Titus 1:5–7 offer a lengthy list of qualifications and disqualifications for those holding the office, things like gentleness and ability to teach while avoiding arrogance and greed. That there is very little overlap in the two lists suggests that they had not yet been formalized, but contained a broad set of qualifications that were widely associated with the position.[62] Overseers had the same qualifications as deacons (compare 1 Tim. 3:2–7 with 3:8–12), with the one exception that they must be "able to teach." Blessed with spiritual gifts, such were expected serve the church in these roles.

πρεσβύτερος *(presbyteros)*

The root meaning of *presbyteros* is comparative, referring to someone of relatively advanced age in comparison with others.[63] But it also is used to refer to individual senior leaders in institutional operations.[64] Elders, as a leadership group, existed as far back as patriarchal times in the Old Testament.[65] They had great consultative influence but little direct authority.[66] In the New Testament, *presbyteros* is used to convey advanced age (Luke 15:25; John 8:9), but it normally has a strong leadership component as well. It is used with reference to a local leadership council in Luke 7:3. It is used more frequently for one of several groups of Jewish leaders.[67]

Based on usage within Judaism[68] and also in the Greco-Roman world,[69] *presbyteros* became a major title for church leaders in Jerusalem (the apostles and the elders, Acts 15:2, 4, 6, 22–23; 16:4) and much more widely throughout the Empire later on (1 Tim. 5:17; Titus 1:5; Heb. 11:2; James 5:14; 1 Pet. 5:1; 2 John 1; 3 John 1).[70] It is a position of great dignity and usually occurs in the plural, suggesting that elders did not normally function alone, but as part of a ruling council.[71] A heavenly example of such a council is found frequently in the book of Revelation.[72] According to 1 Timothy 5:17–18, elders were normally paid for their efforts, which implies that they were to have a full-time focus on their ministry. While not all elders engaged in teaching, many did. They may have been somewhat equivalent to congregational pastors today.[73]

To some degree the titles of *overseer* and *elder* seem to be used interchangeably, as a comparison of 1 Timothy 3:2–7 and 5:17–18 indicate. Titus 1:5–7 also seems to treat the two terms as equivalent. The hierarchical ranking between the two seen at the time of Ignatius does not seem present in Paul's day. According to Acts 20:17–35, the overseers and elders together are the guardians of the traditions of the apostles. Having said this, however, *episkopos* in the pastoral epistles is always in the singular and *presbyteros* is always in the plural, which would suggest that even here the overseer has a top leadership function. So it is likely that overseers were drawn from the council of elders as their giftedness was recognized.

διάκονος *(diakonos)*

The word *diakonos* is the noun form of the Greek verb *diakoneō*. The term *diakonos* originally designated a person who served at tables or took care of other people.[74] There are many terms for service in the Greek, but *diakonos* particularly emphasizes the personal touch, a one-on-one kind of service.[75] It is used with this original meaning in mind in Matthew 22:13 and John 2:5. Over time the verb form attained a primary meaning of "to function as an intermediary."[76] The noun form *diakonos,* therefore, was widely used in the Greco-Roman world to refer to an intermediary or a courier.[77] Like *apostolos* there is a sense of delegation; the *diakonos* does things at the behest of a superior. The term can also be used for secular rulers (Rom. 13:4).

Serving others was not highly regarded in the ancient world; ruling, not serving, was what brought dignity to a person. Service had a higher value only when rendered to the state. Within Judaism, on the other hand, service came to be seen in the context of love for neighbor (Lev. 19:18) and as an act of merit before God.

Diakonos is used in the New Testament, first of all, for Jesus Christ (Rom. 15:8), the ultimate *diakonos.* Jesus's view of service was built on the Old Testament command for love of neighbor. All human ideas of greatness were reversed, however, when the Son of God Himself not only served at table (John 13:13–17; 21:11–13) but also laid down His life for His friends (John 15:13). The Christian *diakonos* learns the position by serving Jesus and following Him (Luke 22:24–27; John 12:26).[78]

Over time the word naturally came into wide Christian usage for individuals singled out for special ministerial service in Christian communities (Rom. 16:1; Phil. 1:1; 1 Tim. 3:8, 12),[79] but these texts do not tell us much about the nature of the office. Evidently, both men and women were permitted to serve as deacons (Rom. 16:1). *Diakonos* seems to have been Paul's favorite leadership title after *apostle.* Deacons are closely associated with overseers in both Philippians 1 and 1 Timothy 3. So the original task of the deacon may have been to assist overseers in their work of caring for the church. It is possible that early Christians built on the synagogue model which had a "head of the congregation" (*archisynagōgos*) and an assistant, who was called a *hypēretēs* rather than a *diakonos.* The activities of these two leaders of the synagogue, however, were restricted to worship (the synagogue was led by elders).[80] Overseers and deacons in the church had a broader responsibility from the beginning.

The ministry of the deacon is often thought to have been established in the early Jerusalem Church under the direction of Peter in

Acts 6. But the title *diakonos* does not appear in the chapter. Instead the verb form (Acts 6:2, 4) and a related noun form (*diakonia*, see Acts 6:1) are used.[81] The seven "deacons" selected in Acts 6 all have Greek names and function more like Hellenistic counterparts of the apostles. But since they were appointed so that the apostles would not neglect "prayer" and "the ministry [*diakonia*] of the word," it may be inferred that the office of deacon came to focus more on the social and practical side of ministry than the teaching-oriented roles of overseer and elder.[82]

LEADERSHIP LANGUAGE IN THE FIRST-CENTURY CHRISTIAN CHURCH

Shortly after the close of the New Testament canon, the Early Church Father Ignatius (110 AD) describes a three-part system of leadership that had developed by his time:

> You must all follow the bishop [*episkopos*], as Jesus Christ fol-
> lowed the Father, and follow the presbytery [council of elders,
> *presbyteros*] as you would the apostles; respect the deacons [*diako-
> nos*] as the commandment of God. Let no one do anything that
> has to do with the church without the bishop. Only that Eucharist
> which is under the authority of the bishop or whomever he him-
> self designates is to be considered valid. Wherever the bishop
> appears, there let the congregation be; just as wherever Jesus
> Christ is, there is the catholic [universal] church. It is not permis-
> sible either to baptize or to hold a love feast without the bishop.
> But whatever he approves is also pleasing to God, in order that
> everything you do may be trustworthy and valid.[83]

In many ways an outline like this is more structured and defined than the realities exhibited in the New Testament. For the New Testament offices were the formalization of gift-centered min- istries and a means to an end, not the ends themselves.[84] For Ignatius, on the other hand, each office has a fixed place in a hierarchy: an overseer (bishop) at the head, a council of elders subordinate to him, and a group of deacons serving both.[85] The question to be addressed here is when such a structure developed and what stages led from the broadly distributed charismatic leadership of the earliest church to the situation described by Ignatius around 110 AD. The primary body of evidence for the leadership structure of the first-century church is in the New Testament itself.

The earliest church began with charismatic leadership roles including apostles and prophets, who emerged naturally through giftedness or a direct appointment from Jesus or the Twelve. As the church grew and the apostles spread out or died, a leadership of appointment was soon required. Appointment happened with guidance from the Holy Spirit and is described as based on spiritual giftedness. To be an overseer or a deacon was also based on a "gift" (Rom. 12: 7–8; 1 Cor. 12:28), but these gifts could only be exercised after a person was elected and called by the community to a position of leadership.[86] Gifts were exercised with the confirmation of the body. Overseers and elders were also the guardians of the apostolic tradition (Acts 20:17–35).

While the first-century cultural context was preoccupied with titles of office, Paul often refers to the leadership of churches without any reference to titles, and he does not mention the term *elder* until fairly late.[87] There seems to have been a concerted effort to discourage pride among those in leadership and hierarchy and to emphasize the broadly distributed and Christ-centered nature of Christian leadership. Nevertheless, offices and titles came to be needed for the sake of order within a generation of the church's first leaders.

One thing to keep in mind when assessing church organization in the first century is that most Christian gatherings occurred in private homes and were fairly small, even in urban settings.[88] A city like Rome or Ephesus might have hundreds of Christians, but they would be scattered in groups of ten to fifty all over the city (compare Rom. 1:7 with 16:5). The fact that an important qualification for the position of *overseer* is to be able to handle one's own family is a natural consequence of the house-church reality (1 Tim. 3:4–5). House churches were not much bigger than an extended family.

In developing offices and titles, the earliest churches had three major models of leadership to choose from in defining their own patterns of leadership: 1) what they had experienced in Judaism and the synagogue, 2) those displayed in the Greco-Roman family system, and 3) patterns of governance observed in the Greco-Roman state and society. We have observed evidence that the New Testament writers deliberately avoided the leadership language and titles associated with the Greco-Roman political and social environment.[89] Such titles and language were considered inappropriate to the servant model they had observed in Jesus Christ.

The Ignatian pattern, therefore, seems to have resulted from a somewhat awkward merging of the other two models of leadership: those found in the synagogue and the home.[90] The well-to-do Greco-Roman household had a head, an overseer, usually the patriarch of the family, and it also had a number of servants, who cared for the physical needs of the household. In a spiritual context, this could have given rise to the positions of overseer and deacon in a typical house church. From Judaism and the synagogue, the church inherited the concept of elder and a council of elders,[91] although, as we have seen, there were analogies to the positions of overseer and deacon as well.

Andrew Clarke, building on the work of R. Alastair Campbell, surmises that each house church might have come to be served by an overseer/elder. Over time, cities with multiple house churches would have developed a council of elders made up of the overseers of all the house churches. Eventually, in the absence of apostles, the council would select one of its members to be the overseer of the whole group of churches in a given city or region.[92] This hypothesis is supported by 1 Timothy 5:17, which indicates that all elders had a ruling role, but not all elders were teachers.

Since Paul does not use the title *elder* in his earlier letters, but only in the later letters to Timothy and Titus, the household model seems to have held sway at first in the Pauline churches, linking up with the synagogue model only toward the end of Paul's lifetime. It should not surprise us that church offices may have been loosely organized and defined in the earliest decades, when charismatic apostolic leaders were active and gift-centered leadership was widely accepted. But by the time of the pastoral letters (Timothy and Titus), the era of leadership by the apostles and prophets was drawing to a close and the formalization of structure was beginning to take shape.

CONCLUSION

This chapter began with a brief summary of the New Testament perspective on leadership. Christian leadership is grounded, first of all, in God the Creator. But the clearest revelation of God is in the Person of Jesus Christ, as He is revealed in the New Testament. And within the New Testament, the leadership principles of Jesus are most extensively exhibited in the letters of Paul.

There followed a survey of the leadership language found in the New Testament. While much of that language was drawn from the Greco-Roman state and society, and could be applied to God, Jesus, Satan, and state authorities, it was never used to refer to leadership roles in the church. Instead, the Early Church preferred language with a service-overtone—terms like *overseer*, *deacon*, and *elder*.

The above survey led to the conclusion that when the early Christians were choosing language to describe formal leadership roles in the New Testament church, they preferred language drawn from the synagogue and the everyday household over the language common in the institutions of the Greco-Roman society. The one exception to that rule (*proistēmi*) had a strong related meaning of caring concern and the giving of aid.

Early Christian leadership language had strong overtones of parental concern, service, divine guidance, and delegation of authority. In the earliest church, leadership was charismatic, recognized apostles were active, and all Christ-followers served in leadership in ways appropriate to their gifts. Toward the end of the first Christian century, appointed leadership became the norm and more hierarchical forms were adopted.

The bottom line of New Testament leadership is attention to God's way of leadership through observing the examples of Christ and the apostles. New Testament leadership exercises itself in loving concern for those being led and maintains the attitude of a servant. Followers of Jesus exercise leadership in ways appropriate to their gifts. For those seeking to learn from the language of the New Testament today, Christ-like, servant leadership must always be the goal.

FOR REFLECTION

Personal:

1. What is your favorite New Testament leadership text? If you applied that text consistently to your own leadership style, what would you need to do differently?
2. How can a church leader consistently place service ahead of self-interest in leadership decisions?

Organizational:

1. What specific things can the church do to ensure that organizational appointments are really made on the basis of demonstrated spiritual gifts rather than on cultural criteria?
2. What implications does the contrast between New Testament church leadership and Greco-Roman society have for the exercise of leadership in the church today?

ENDNOTES

1. Thomas Schirrmacher, *Studies in Church Leadership*, Edition Iwg—Mission Scripts, vol. 20 (Bonn: Verlag fur Kultur und Wissenschaft, 2003), 7.

2. Jon Paulien, *John: Jesus Gives Life to a New Generation*, Abundant Life Bible Amplifier Commentary Series (Boise, ID: Pacific Press, 1995), 209–243.

3. Steve Walton, *Leadership and Lifestyle: The Portrait of Paul in the Miletus Speech and 1 Thessalonians*, SNTS Monograph Series 108 (Cambridge: Cambridge University Press, 2000), 134–135.

4. Walton, *Leadership and Lifestyle*, 135, 184.

5. Darin H. Land, *The Diffusion of Ecclesiastical Authority: Sociological Dimensions of Leadership in the Book of Acts*, Princeton Theological Monograph Series 90 (Eugene, OR: Pickwick Publications, 2008), 196.

6. Walter Bauer et al., *A Greek-English Lexicon of the New Testament and other Early Christian Literature*, 3rd ed. (Chicago: University of Chicago Press, 2000), 16; Henry George Liddell and Robert Scott, *A Greek-English Lexicon*, 9th ed., with supplement (Oxford: Clarendon Press of Oxford University Press, 1940, 1996), 18.

7. Liddell and Scott, *Greek-English Lexicon*, 17.

8. Institute for New Testament Textual Research and the Computer Center of Munster University, editorial team, *Concordance to the Novum Testamentum Graece*

of Nestle-Aland, 26th Edition, and to the Greek New Testament, 3rd edition, with the collaboration of H. Bachmann and W. A. Slaby, 3rd ed. (Berlin: Walter de Gruyter, 1987), 779–780.

9. Bauer et al., *Greek-English Lexicon of the New Testament and Other Early Christian Literature*, 16.

10. Andrew D. Clarke, *A Pauline Theology of Church Leadership* (London: T & T Clark, 2008), 1–2.

11. Liddell and Scott, *Greek-English Lexicon*, 252.

12. Gerhard Delling, "ἄρχω," etc., in *Theological Dictionary of the New Testament*, ed. Gerhard Kittel, trans. and ed. Geoffrey W. Bromiley (Grand Rapids, MI: Eerdmans, 1964), 1:478.

13. Delling, "ἄρχω," etc., in *Theological Dictionary of the New Testament*, 1:479.

14. Bauer et al., *A Greek-English Lexicon of the New Testament and Other Early Christian Literature*, 138.

15. Scholars differ as to whether Revelation 3:14 should be translated "the beginning of God's creation" or "the ruler of God's creation." In either case, however, *archē* is clearly used with reference to Christ. See Delling (1:484) for a strong case that *archē* in Revelation 3:14 should be translated "ruler."

16. Liddell and Scott, *Greek-English Lexicon*, 254.

17. Delling, "ἄρχω," etc., in *Theological Dictionary of the New Testament*, 1:488.

18. Delling, "ἄρχω," etc., in *Theological Dictionary of the New Testament*, 1:489.

19. Bauer et al., *Greek-English Lexicon of the New Testament and Other Early Christian Literature*, 138.

20. Delling, "ἄρχω," etc., in *Theological Dictionary of the New Testament*, 1:487; Liddell and Scott, *Greek-English Lexicon*, 252.

21. Delling, "ἄρχω," etc., in *Theological Dictionary of the New Testament*, 1:487–488.

22. Bauer et al., *A Greek-English Lexicon of the New Testament and Other Early Christian Literature*, 541.

23. Bauer et al., *Greek-English Lexicon of the New Testament and Other Early Christian Literature*, 542.

24. Lawrence O. Richards and Clyde Hoeldtke, *A Theology of Church Leadership* (Grand Rapids, MI: Zondervan, 1980), 16.

25. Richards and Hoeldtke, *Theology of Church Leadership*, 16.

26. Richards and Hoeldtke, *Theology of Church Leadership*, 16–17.

27. Richards and Hoeldtke, *Theology of Church Leadership*, 20.

28. Richards and Hoeldtke, *Theology of Church Leadership*, 17.

29. Werner Foerster, "κύριος" etc., in *Theological Dictionary of the New Testament*, 3:1041; *International Standard Bible Encyclopedia*, Geoffrey W. Bromiley, gen. ed. (Grand Rapids, MI: Eerdmans, 1982), 3:157.

30. Foerster, *Theological Dictionary of the New Testament*, 3:1041–1047; Liddell and Scott, *Greek-English Lexicon*, 1013.

31. Bauer et al., *Greek-English Lexicon of the New Testament and Other Early Christian Literature*, 576.

32. B. W. Anderson, "Lord," in *The Interpreter's Dictionary of the Bible: An Illustrated Encyclopedia*, ed. George Arthur Buttrick (New York: Abingdon Press, 1962), 3:150–151; Bauer et al., *Greek-English Lexicon of the New Testament and Other Early Christian Literature*, 577; Foerster, *Theological Dictionary of the New Testament*, 3:1058–1062.

33. Clarke, *Pauline Theology of Church Leadership*, 2n6.

34. Bauer et al., *Greek-English Lexicon of the New Testament and Other Early Christian Literature*, 870; Liddell and Scott, *Greek-English Lexicon*, 1482; Bo Reicke, "*proistēmi*," in *Theological Dictionary of the New Testament*, 6:700.

35. Bauer et al., *Greek-English Lexicon of the New Testament and Other Early Christian Literature*, 870.

36. Reicke, *Theological Dictionary of the New Testament*, 6:702.

37. Clarke, *Pauline Theology of Church Leadership*, 2–3.

38. Liddell and Scott, *Greek-English Lexicon*, 219; Karl Heinrich Rengstorf, ἀποστέλλω, *apostellō* etc., in *Theological Dictionary of the New Testament*, 1:398.

39. Rengstorf, "ἀποστέλλω, *apostellō*" etc., in *Theological Dictionary of the New Testament*, 1:399.

40. Rengstorf, "ἀποστέλλω, *apostellō*" etc., in *Theological Dictionary of the New Testament*, 1:398–402.

41. Rengstorf, "ἀποστέλλω, *apostellō*" etc., in *Theological Dictionary of the New Testament*, 1:407–413.

42. Rengstorf, "ἀποστέλλω, *apostellō*" etc., in *Theological Dictionary of the New Testament*, 1:413–420.

43. Bauer et al., *Greek-English Lexicon of the New Testament and Other Early Christian Literature*, 120–122.

44. Peter K. Nelson, *Leadership and Discipleship: A Study of Luke 22:24–30*, SBL Dissertation Series 138 (Atlanta, GA: Scholars Press, 1994), 44–45; Rengstorf, "ἀποστέλλω, *apostellō*" etc., in *Theological Dictionary of the New Testament*, 1:423.

45. Jesus must have used the Aramaic form of a Hebrew word with similar meaning to the word *apostle* as later used by New Testament writers. So Jesus would be the origin of the Christian use of the word. See Rengstorf, "ἀποστέλλω, *apostellō*" etc., in *Theological Dictionary of the New Testament*, 1:413–420, 428, 430–437.

46. Eugene S. Wehrli, *Gifted by Their Spirit: Leadership Roles in the New Testament* (Cleveland, OH: The Pilgrim Press, 1992), 11–24.

47. Hans Dieter Betz, "Apostle," in *The Anchor Bible Dictionary*, ed. David Noel Freedman (Garden City, NY: Doubleday, 1992), 1:310.

48. Helmut Krämer, "προφήτης," etc., in *Theological Dictionary of the New Testament*, 6:783.

49. Krämer, "προφήτης," etc., in *Theological Dictionary of the New Testament*, 6:791; John J. Schmitt, "Prophecy (Preexilic Hebrew)" in *Anchor Bible Dictionary*, 5:482.

50. Bauer et al., *Greek-English Lexicon of the New Testament and Other Early Christian Literature*, 890; Liddell and Scott, *Greek-English Lexicon*, 1539.

51. Gerhard Friedrich, "προφήτης" etc., in *Theological Dictionary of the New Testament*, 6:850. There are many parallels between Paul's own biographical statements in his letters and the prophets of the Old Testament. Paul clearly understands his apostolic mission to be similar to their prophetic one. See M. Eugene Boring, "Prophecy (Early Christian)," in *Anchor Bible Dictionary*, 5:498.

52. Schirrmacher, *Studies in Church Leadership*, 31; Perry L. Stepp, *Leadership Succession in the World of the Pauline Circle*, New Testament Monographs, vol. 5 (Sheffield: Sheffield Phoenix Press, 2005), 183–191.

53. Schirrmacher, *Studies in Church Leadership*, 33.

54. In *1 Clement* 42:1ff., Clement notes a sequence of leadership in the church, moving from God to Christ to the apostles and finally to the bishops (*episkopos*) appointed by the apostles. The writings of Clement are a major non-biblical witness to the first-century setting.

55. Clarke, *Pauline Theology of Church Leadership*, 48.

56. Liddell and Scott, *Greek-English Lexicon*, 657.

57. Clarke, *Pauline Theology of Church Leadership*, 49.

58. Bauer et al., *Greek-English Lexicon of the New Testament and Other Early Christian Literature*, 379.

59. Clarke, *Pauline Theology of Church Leadership*, 50.

60. Kenneth Lyle Faught, "An Investigation of Selected Models of Group Leadership in the New Testament with Implications for Pastoral Leadership and Counseling" (EdD diss., New Orleans Baptist Theological Seminary, 1982), 49.

61. Clarke, *Pauline Theology of Church Leadership*, 47. Acts 1:20 uses the term with reference to Judas, so it is probably not useful for our purpose.

62. Clarke, *Pauline Theology of Church Leadership*, 50.

63. Bauer et al., *Greek-English Lexicon of the New Testament and Other Early Christian Literature*, 860.

64. Günther Bornkamm, "πρέσβυς, πρεσβύτερος," etc., in *Theological Dictionary of the New Testament*, 6:653. In Sparta, the term *presbyteros* even had a political connotation: "president." See Liddell and Scott, *Greek-English Lexicon*, 1462.

65. Note the extensive discussion of the Old Testament evidence in Bornkamm, "πρέσβυς, πρεσβύτερος," etc., in *Theological Dictionary of the New Testament*, 6:655–658. See also Land, *Diffusion of Ecclesiastical Authority*, 196.

66. Robert North, "Palestine, Administration of (Judean Officials)," in *Anchor Bible Dictionary*, 5:87.

67. There are at least four groups of Jewish leaders in the New Testament: rulers, scribes, chief priests, and elders; see the following examples: Matthew 16:21; Mark 8:31; Acts 4:5.

68. M. H. Shepherd, Jr., "Elder in the NT," in *The Interpreter's Dictionary of the Bible*, ed. George Arthur Buttrick (Nashville, TN: Abingdon Press, 1962), 2:73.

69. Bauer et al., *Greek-English Lexicon of the New Testament and Other Early Christian Literature*, 860; Bornkamm, "πρέσβυς, πρεσβύτερος," etc., in *Theological Dictionary of the New Testament*, 6:658–661.

70. Bornkamm, "πρέσβυς, πρεσβύτερος," etc., in *Theological Dictionary of the New Testament*, 6:662–672.

71. Clarke, *Pauline Theology of Church Leadership*, 52–53, 56–58.

72. The twenty-four elders: Revelation 4:4, 10; 5:5–14; 7:11 and 11:16, for example.

73. Schirrmacher, *Studies in Church Leadership*, 12.

74. Bauer et al., *Greek-English Lexicon of the New Testament and Other Early Christian Literature*, 230; Schirrmacher, *Studies in Church Leadership*, 15.

75. Beyer, "διακονέω…διάκονος," etc., in *Theological Dictionary of the New Testament*, ed. Gerhard Kittel, trans. and ed. Geoffrey Bromiley (Grand Rapids, MI: Eerdmans, 1964), 2:81.

76. Bauer et al., *Greek-English Lexicon of the New Testament and Other Early Christian Literature*, 229.

77. Bauer et al., *Greek-English Lexicon of the New Testament and Other Early Christian Literature*, 230. According to John N. Collins, *Diakonia: Re-Interpreting the Ancient Sources* (New York: Oxford University Press, 2009), quoted in Clarke, *Pauline Theology of Church Leadership*, 63. In fact, a full third of the Greco-Roman usage of the term has to do with conveying a message or making a delivery.

78. Nelson, *Leadership and Discipleship*, 131–136; Kenan B. Osborne, *Orders and Ministry: Leadership in the World Church* (Maryknoll, NY: Orbis Books, 2006), 97–98; Schirrmacher, *Studies in Church Leadership*, 15.

79. Bauer et al., *Greek-English Lexicon of the New Testament and Other Early Christian Literature*, 231. See Schirrmacher, *Studies in Church Leadership*, 16, for how Philippians 1:1 affirms the reality of the "office" of deacon in the churches of Paul.

80. Beyer, "διακονέω…διάκονος," etc., in *Theological Dictionary of the New Testament*, 2:91.

81. Shepherd, Jr., "Deacon," in *The Interpreter's Dictionary of the Bible*, 1:785.

82. Beyer, "διακονέω…διάκονος," etc., in *Theological Dictionary of the New Testament*, 2:90; Schirrmacher, *Studies in Church Leadership*, 15, 18–19.

83. Ignatius, *Letter to the Church at Smyrna*, 8:1–2, in *The Apostolic Fathers: Greek Texts and English Translations*, 2nd ed., ed. and trans. J. B. Lightfoot and J. R. Harmer, ed. and rev. Michael W. Holmes (Grand Rapids, MI: Baker Books, 1992), 188–191. See also Clarke, *Pauline Theology of Church Leadership*, 54.

84. Stepp, *Leadership Succession*, 201.

85. Bornkamm, "πρέσβυς, πρεσβύτερος," etc., in *Theological Dictionary of the New Testament*, 6:674–675 has a detailed analysis of the various parts of Ignatius's letters which help fill out the picture. The energy with which Ignatius defends this hierarchy suggests it is not yet fully in place.

86. Beyer, "διακονέω…διάκονος," etc., in *Theological Dictionary of the New Testament*, 2:92.

87. Clarke, *Pauline Theology of Church Leadership*, 47. In Acts 20:17 Luke refers to the church leaders of Ephesus as "elders," but Paul (in Acts 20:28) addresses the same group as "overseers." See Land, *Diffusion of Ecclesiastical Authority*, 196.

88. Clarke, *Pauline Theology of Church Leadership*, 45.

89. Beyer, "διακονέω...διάκονος," etc., in *Theological Dictionary of the New Testament*, 2:91.

90. Clarke, *Pauline Theology of Church Leadership*, 54.

91. Shepherd, Jr., "Elder in the NT," in *The Interpreter's Dictionary of the Bible*, 2:73.

92. Clarke, *Pauline Theology of Church Leadership*, 52–58. Cf. R. Alastair Campbell, *The Elders: Seniority within Earliest Christianity*, SNTW Series (Edinburgh: T & T Clark, 1995).

8 | The Gospels

Robert M. Johnston

Four books in the New Testament tell at length the story of Jesus of Nazareth, whom they declare to be the Messiah (the Christ),[1] the Son of God, and the Savior. Three of the books, Matthew, Mark, and Luke, are roughly parallel with each other and so are called the Synoptic Gospels. The fourth, John, stands apart from the others as quite distinct. They are four different portraits of Jesus,[2] but the portraits are like oil paintings, not photographs, because each Gospel presents Jesus in the light of the distinct message about Him to which the author is moved to bear witness.[3] In the light of this individuality of the Gospels, it is striking that they all speak with one voice about the nature of leadership as taught and exemplified by Jesus, a conception of leadership that was dramatically at odds with the understanding of the cultures of the time.

The Gospels all preface the story of Jesus's ministry with the story of another man whom they recognized as the forerunner of Jesus: John the Baptist.

JOHN THE BAPTIST AS LEADER

John the Baptist was a desert-dwelling ascetic in the mold of the Old Testament prophet Elijah,[4] a fiery preacher. He sternly denounced sin and corruption, preaching a baptism of repentance for the forgiveness of sins (Mark 1:4). Many regarded him as a prophet, and large numbers responded to his preaching; but he alarmed the religious authorities and political leaders, and he eventually met a martyr's death (Mark 6:16–29). Though John had a popular following, he was not a political leader; rather, he was a moral one who spoke truth to power.

John was fearless and forthright,[5] not hesitating even to denounce a king and queen whose marriage was unlawful. But he was humble and self-effacing, willing to defer to Jesus, whom he acknowledged to be the ultimate leader. He told the crowds, "After me comes the one more powerful than I, the straps of whose sandals I am not worthy to stoop down and untie" (Mark 1:7).[6] When it appeared that the movement led by John was being superseded by that of Jesus, John was willing to say, "He must become greater; I must become less" (John 3:22–30). He was a selfless leader: Even as his martyrdom in some measure foreshadowed that of Jesus, so did his self-abasement.

Jesus himself noted the difference between John's leadership and His own: "For John came neither eating nor drinking, and they say 'He has a demon.' The Son of man came eating and drinking, and they say, 'Here is a glutton and a drunkard, a friend of tax collectors and sinners!' Yet wisdom is proved right by her deeds" (Matt. 11:18–19).[7] It was not John's way to be gentle with wrongdoers, but that kind of leadership had its place, preparing the way for the very different style of leadership usually exhibited by Jesus.

JESUS AND HIS DISCIPLES

Matthew succinctly summarized the message of Jesus: "Repent, for the kingdom of heaven has come near" (4:17). The same had been the message of John (3:2). From this brief summary much can be unpacked. *Repentance* means "a radical reorientation of mind and life"; the *kingdom of heaven* means "the reign of God,"[8] which was being inaugurated by Jesus's ministry (12:28). But how was this message to be broadcast effectively?

It is often said that Jesus himself wrote no book and that is technically correct. But one should bear in mind that printing had not yet been invented, so books were expensive and rare. Furthermore many people were illiterate. In such a culture teachings were best published orally, and their propagation could be multiplied by attracting disciples who could memorize the teaching and transmit the message to others.[9] This is what Jesus did.

Our first written Gospel was produced about thirty years after Christ's crucifixion. During that time the memory of His words and works was preserved in the Christian community and propagated by the surviving apostles and by certain special persons of prodigious memory (who exist in all oral societies) whom Luke called "ministers of the word" (*hyperetai tou logou*, Luke 1:2). The latter are said to be eyewitnesses from the beginning and may have included the apostles (Luke 1:2).

Jesus followed the practice of the Pharisaic teachers of His time. In their oral tradition one of the basic maxims was "Raise up many disciples."[10] A group of students who joined together to partake of the Passover supper and to learn from a noted teacher was called a *ḥābûrāh*. Each of these students in turn might also become a teacher and thus a link in the chain of tradition, adding also his own opinions to the ever-widening stream of Torah. It was important for these disciples to be able to cite the opinions of those who went before them, and it was important for them to have a retentive memory. Thus Rabban Johanan ben Zakkai had five disciples, one of whom was Eliezer ben Hyrcanus, of whom Johanan said, "Eliezer ben Hyrcanus is a plastered cistern which loses not a drop."[11]

But in a significant way Jesus broke from this pattern. In Matthew 5, He broke with the tradition that had come down to Him, repeatedly introducing His own teachings with the formula, "You have heard that it was said to the people long ago.… But I tell you…" (Matt. 5:21–22; also vv. 27, 31, 33, 38, 43). Moreover, when He sent His disciples out to be teachers themselves, He told them not to be links in a chain, but rather conduits of His teaching:

"teaching them to obey everything I have commanded you" (Matt. 28:20). They were to raise up disciples of Jesus, not of themselves.

A leader must think not only of multiplying his or her effort, but also of preparing successors. Jesus surprises us in His choice of those who were to carry on His work. He appointed twelve men to be His understudies, "that he might send them out to preach and to have authority to drive out demons" (Mark 3:13–19). They were men of His own choosing (3:13), including Judas Iscariot, who was going to betray him. Judas, as a Judean,[12] would have felt himself superior to the others, who were probably all Galileans. Several were fishermen. Most remarkably, one was a tax collector and one was a terrorist. Tax collectors such as Matthew were regarded as traitors for collaborating with the Roman occupiers. Simon the Zealot[13] was, or had been, a member of the movement that rose up to oppose the Roman occupation and punish anyone who collaborated with it. That Jesus deliberately chose such a diverse and difficult group was, to say the least, counterintuitive. They were not the kind of disciples that the Pharisaic teachers would have chosen.

Jesus encountered these men in their daily occupations, be it fisherman (Mark 1:16–20) or tax collector (Matt. 9:9), and simply summoned them with the call, "Follow me!" The remarkable thing is that they left what they were doing and followed Him without hesitation.[14] He challenged would-be disciples to consider first the unconditional and costly commitment He expected of followers, but He brooked no half-heartedness (Luke 9:57–62; 14:25–33).

CLOSENESS AND DISTANCE

The Twelve whom Jesus especially called were first of all "to be with him" (Mark 3:14). A disciple is a learner. Jesus would teach them, and they would observe Him as He preached, taught the multitude, healed, and exorcised. They formed His *ḥābûrāh,* so their association was quite intimate. They traveled together, ate together, lodged together. Yet in spite of this closeness, Jesus also retained a certain mysterious distance from them. Jesus sometimes arose while they still slept and went off to be alone and pray (Mark

1:35; Luke 5:16), while other times He took a few of them with Him to pray in a deserted place. On one occasion He put them all on a boat to cross the Sea of Galilee while He stayed behind to pray on a mountain (Mark 6:45–51), from which He could see that they had run into difficulty in the rough sea. Near dawn He came to them, walking on the sea. But remarkably, Mark reports, "He meant to pass by them" (6:48, RSV), until they cried out, and only then did He speak to them and get into the boat.

The disciples found His teaching often cryptic or hard to understand (e.g., Mark 9:32), and His actions were often surprising. He would explain things to them in private (e.g., Mark 4:10–13; 10:10), sometimes enjoining them to secrecy (e.g., Mark 8:30). Yet when they did not understand, He could rebuke them as "men of little faith" (e.g., Matt. 8:26) or ask, "Do you still not see or understand?" (Mark 8:17). The same thing is seen in the Fourth Gospel, where the word "parable" never appears. Instead we find a series of puzzling sayings called *paroimiai*, which is translated "proverbs" or "figures" but can mean "riddles." In John 16:25 Jesus told them, "Though I have been speaking figuratively [*en paroimiais*], a time is coming when I will no longer use this kind of language but will tell you plainly about my Father." Until that time His sayings often puzzled them (e.g., John 6:60; 16:17–18). But the time came for Him to speak to them plainly and openly because they were His friends, not slaves (15:15). A slave does only what he or she is told, but a friend gets to share plans and obeys for a different reason.

We get a picture of a leader who concealed even when He revealed, who hid even as He disclosed. He did not spoon-feed His disciples but rather teased them into mental effort in order that they might understand. He aroused questions and then made them develop an appetite to learn the answers and work for them, constantly prodding them on. There was always something more—something beyond their understanding that they had not yet attained. One can also say that He planted a seed in their minds and hearts that did not germinate until He had risen from the dead (e.g., John 2:22). As a leader Jesus preserved a certain mystique even while He dwelled among people as one of them.

THE QUESTION OF AUTHORITY

After being with Jesus, the Twelve were "to be sent out to preach and have authority to cast out demons" (Mark 3:14). The Greek word for "send out" is *apostellō,* from which is derived *apostolos*, whence comes our word *apostle.* The Greek is equivalent to the Hebrew *šālîaḥ,* a word used for representatives sent out from the Jewish authorities in Jerusalem to the far-flung communities of the Jewish Diaspora. Such was Saul of Tarsus when he was carrying a letter to the synagogues of Damascus, authorizing him to arrest followers of Jesus (Acts 9:1–2).

Apostles represent the one who sends them and come with the authority of the sender to the extent that they faithfully fulfill the mission that is committed to them. Mishnah *Berakoth* 5:5 says, "A man's *šālîaḥ* is as himself." The twelve men were sent out by Jesus as His representatives with the assurance, "Anyone who welcomes you welcomes me, and anyone who welcomes me welcomes the one who sent me" (Matt. 10:40; cf. John 13:20). The authority of the person who is sent is derived from, and dependent on, that of the sender. In John 13:16 Jesus says: "Very truly I tell you, no servant is greater than his master, nor is a messenger greater than the one who sent him."

Jesus held no office or rank. He did not avail himself of any such shortcut to power (Matt. 4:8–11; Luke 4:5–8). Any authority that He had among people was generated solely by the power of what He said and did. But He was not reticent about claiming authority, even though the official authorities questioned it (Mark 11:28). We have seen how He broke with tradition on no other authority but His own (Matt. 5:21, 27, 31, 33, 38, 43), so it was said, "The crowds were amazed at his teaching, because he taught as one who had authority, and not as their teachers of the law" (Matt. 7:28–29; Mark 1:22). Before finally sending out the apostles, Jesus declared: "All authority in heaven and on earth has been given to me" (Matt. 28:18).

In all the Gospels, but especially the Fourth, Jesus consistently said that His authority was given to Him by the one who sent Him, who was God the Father. Thus John 5:26–27 declares: "For as the Father has life in himself, so he has granted the Son also to have life in himself, and he has given him authority to judge because he is the Son of Man," and even more clearly Jesus said, "By myself I can do nothing" (John 5:30). The apostleship of the Twelve was simply an extension of the apostleship of Jesus: "As the Father has sent me, I am sending you" (John 20:21). This seemingly hierarchical chain of command (Father to Son to apostles) might have suggested that it could be extended further, except for the teachings we note next.

THE EQUALITY OF JESUS'S FOLLOWERS

The position of Jesus was unique, not to be shared by any of His followers. They were to teach only what He commanded (Matt. 28:20) and acknowledge that His preeminence is His alone. In Matthew 23:1–12, Jesus excoriated the status seeking of the Pharisees and thus provides us with explicit teaching about the matter of rank and status:

> But you are not to be called "Rabbi," for you have one Teacher, and you are all brothers. And do not call anyone on earth "father," for you have one Father, and he is in heaven. Nor are you to be called instructors, for you have one Instructor, the Messiah. The greatest among you will be your servant. For those who exalt themselves will be humbled, and those who humble themselves will be exalted.

The word translated here as "instructor" is *kathēgētēs,* which is formed from a verb meaning "to lead the way,"[15] so though it commonly meant "teacher," it could also be translated "leader."[16] Here, then, is Jesus's definitive teaching about leadership, using the actual word *leader*: Do not be called leaders, because only Christ is the Leader. A different word translated "leader" (*hēgoumenos*) amplifies the point.

Two of Jesus's disciples asked Him to grant them top places in the government they expected Him to establish: "Let one of us sit at your right and the other at your left in your glory" (Mark 10:37). His answer was at first cryptic: "You don't know what you are asking. Can you drink the cup I drink or be baptized with the baptism

I am baptized with?" (v. 38). They did not understand that He was talking about death. Answering their request more directly, He told them: "To sit at my right hand or at my left is not for me to grant. These places belong to those for whom they have been prepared" (v. 40). When the other disciples heard what was going on, Jesus gave them His clearest instruction about leadership:

> You know that those who are regarded as rulers of the Gentiles lord it over them, and their high officials exercise authority over them. Not so with you. Instead whoever wants to become great among you must be your servant, and whoever wants to be first must be slave of all. For even the Son of Man did not come to be served but to serve, and to give his life as a ransom for many. (Mark 10:42–45; cf. Matt. 20:20–28)

Luke's version of this clarifies and reinforces the point:

> The kings of the Gentiles lord it over them; and those who exercise authority over them call themselves Benefactors. But you are not to be like that. Instead, the greatest among you should be like the youngest, and the one who rules [*hēgoumenos*, literally "leader"] like one who serves. For who is greater, the one who is at the table or the one who serves? Is it not the one who is at the table? But I am among you as one who serves. (Luke 22:25–27)

He then declares that all of them will have an honored place in His kingdom (vv. 28–30).

The idea that Jesus, the legitimate leader, came to serve rather than to be served is portrayed dramatically in the Fourth Gospel. John 13:1–20 describes how Jesus performed the role of a slave by washing the feet of His disciples. Then He explained the reason:

> Do you know what I have done for you? You call me "Teacher" and "Lord"; and rightly so, for that is what I am. Now that I, your Lord and Teacher, have washed your feet, you also should wash one another's feet. I have set you an example that you should do as I have done for you. I tell you the truth, no servant is greater than his master, nor is a messenger greater than the one who sent him. Now that you know these things, you will be blessed if you do them. (vv. 12–17)

With these words Jesus did not merely command the rite of foot washing,[17] He also acted out the principle, "I am among you as one who serves," and they as leaders were to follow His example.

In this teaching Jesus binds together two seemingly opposite roles. He can legitimately say that He is their leader, their lord, their teacher, even their king. His authority and His status are over them, and He is not renouncing that lordship.[18] But at the same time His Highness makes Himself His Lowness. He has dramatically abased Himself and humbled Himself before them, and He will do so even more when He dies the most humiliating death—death by crucifixion. He suffers to serve them. They will come to see that the way of self-abnegation is the way of exaltation by God. So here is the paradox of Christian leadership: "For all those who exalt themselves will be humbled, and those who humble themselves will be exalted" (Luke 18:14).

Jesus was the Good Shepherd who laid down His life for the sheep (John 10:14), and He called upon His disciples to follow His example and care for His followers as shepherds care for their sheep (John 21:15–23). The Good Shepherd stands in contrast to the bad shepherds described in Ezekiel 34:1–10, who exploit the sheep but do not feed them or care for them. Therefore, said the Lord, He Himself would be their Shepherd (vv. 11–16). The scriptures often use the metaphor of the shepherd to warn leaders against abuse of their position as well as to urge faithfulness in its exercise, as in 1 Peter 5:2–3: "Be shepherds of God's flock that is under your care, serving as overseers—not because you must, but because you are willing, as God wants you to be; not greedy for money, but eager to serve; not lording it over those entrusted to you, but being examples to the flock." Christ is the Chief Shepherd who will reward them (v. 4).

THE TEMPTATION OF HARD POWER

About forty years before Jesus was born, a man of Pharisee orientation wrote eighteen psalms that imitated the Psalms of David. He called them the Psalms of Solomon, and they are an expression of the longings of many Jewish people after the Roman general Pompey took Jerusalem and destroyed the independence of the

Jewish people. The seventeenth Psalm of Solomon expresses their hope for a righteous messianic king of the lineage of David, who would give the Jews victory over the Gentiles and expel sinners from the land:

> Behold, O LORD, and raise up for them their king, the son of David,
> For the time which thou didst foresee, O God, that he may reign over
>   Israel thy servant,
> And gird him with strength, that he may shatter unrighteous rulers;
> And purify Jerusalem of the nations which trample her down in
>   destruction.
> In wisdom, in righteousness, may he expel sinners from the inheritance:
> May he smash the sinner's arrogance like a potter's vessel. (vv. 21–22)[19]

Thus Israel would be restored, and the eternal reign of God on earth would be established.

And why not? Did not God give Israel victory in the past by force of arms? Was not the Lord with Joshua and David? Did He not bless the temporal rule of Moses the lawgiver, Josiah the reformer, and Nehemiah the zealous governor? In old times righteousness was established by the sword and the courts. Never mind that the righteous order did not endure. Political means did not for long solve a spiritual problem. Coercion can change behavior but not the heart.

This victorious king was the kind of messiah that the Jewish people hoped for, and that included the disciples of Jesus. But Jesus envisioned a different path to establishing God's rule. The kingdom of God was now a government in exile. One day the Son of Man would indeed return in glory to judge and eradicate sin from the earth. But first the reign of God must come to the hearts of human beings who choose to receive it, and that was Jesus's mission. The instrument for God's conquest of hearts was neither sword nor court of law, but love. But that is not an efficient way to bring people into harmony with God's will. Force is much quicker. So the temptation to obtain and use hard power was always there, but Jesus resisted it.

At the beginning of His ministry, Jesus went into the desert and was tempted by the devil, who showed Him all the kingdoms of the word and said, "All this I will give you, if you will bow down and worship me" (Matt. 4:9). Jesus refused. After Jesus miraculously fed five thousand men they wanted to make Him king, but He fled from them to a mountain (John 6:15). When He was about to be arrested, His disciple Peter tried to defend Him with a sword (Matt. 26:51–53; Mark 14:47; Luke 22:49–51; John 18:10), but Jesus rebuked him and healed the man Peter had injured.

Likewise He avoided civil litigation and refused to get involved in disputes of law. He warned against such conflict in the Sermon on the Mount (Matt. 5:23–26) and refused to take sides in a dispute about inheritance (Luke 12:13–14). Rather He praised mercy and peacemaking and going the second mile (Matt. 5:7, 9, 38–42). It is true that He outlined a protocol to be followed in the event of a dispute between His followers, but He insisted that forgiveness trumps everything else (Matt. 18).

He did not, however, avoid controversy, and He was as capable as John the Baptist of sharply denouncing hypocrisy and corruption (e.g., Matt. 23), but He saved His fire for people in power. He was, on occasion, so gentle with penitent sinners that He was criticized for befriending them (Luke 15:1–2). To appreciate how countercultural that was, we need only to hear a Pharisaic maxim: "Let a man never associate with a wicked person, not even for the purpose of bringing him near to the Torah."[20]

As mentioned above, Jesus's own disciples shared the popular expectation of a royal messiah who would vanquish Israel's enemies and cleanse the nation from sinners. This appears dramatically in Mark 8, which is the conceptual and structural center point of that Gospel. Jesus asked His disciples who they thought Jesus was, and Peter answered that He was the Messiah (v. 29). Jesus charged them to tell no one about Him (v. 30) because neither they nor the multitude understood what kind of a messiah He was. This is evident in what followed, for when He began to tell them that He was going to be rejected by the authorities and killed, Peter objected strenuously (vv. 31–33). That ending was not in the conventional script. It was not until Jesus was crucified that they began to realize what kind of messiah He was, but the ultimate recognition of who He is was given by a Roman centurion, who exclaimed: "Surely this man was the Son of God!" (Mark 15:39).

Jesus defeated pride by service, evil by good, hatred by love, and death by dying. Such leadership was bold and counterintuitive, but it ultimately defeated the men of hard power.

HOW JESUS SERVED

If Jesus came to serve, we can begin to understand what service meant to Him by observing what He did.[21]

First of all, He proclaimed the kingdom of God, which at that stage of history meant the reign of God was manifest in the ministry of Jesus. When John the Baptist sent messengers to Jesus asking for reassurance that He was the awaited Messiah, Jesus did not point to some political or military power. Rather He said, "Go back and report to John what you hear and see: The blind receive sight, the lame walk, those who have leprosy are cleansed, the deaf hear, the dead are raised, and the good news is proclaimed to the poor" (Matt. 11:4–5). More directly, Jesus told the Pharisees, "If it is by the Spirit of God that I drive out demons, then the kingdom of God has come upon you" (Matt. 12:28). The presence of God's power was manifest in the work of Jesus. No greater service to God or humanity can be done than to introduce them to the true God without distortion, and this is what Jesus did.

Second, Jesus healed and cast out demons. One of the words for "to serve" in Greek is *therapeuō,* which also means "to heal." Likewise, the word *sōzō* has two overlapping meanings: to save and to heal. The contemporaries of Jesus would have considered healing a very important part of His ministry. Jesus healed diseases, infirmities, and deformities, and He cast out demons. His ability to cast out demons was a sign that the kingdom of God had come and evidence of the powerful presence of God (Luke 11:20). Jesus even raised the dead. His ability to heal authenticated His messiahship, and His healing of the body was often a sign of healing of the soul (Mark 2:9–11).

Third, He forgave sins and fellowshipped with sinners. His healings were also proof of His authority to forgive sins (Mark 2:10). As a prophet, He knew the sins in the hearts and lives of human beings, but He forgave penitents (Luke 7:36–50). This is what He meant in His Nazareth sermon by "freedom for the prison-ers" (Luke 4:16–21). In the sabbatical year and the jubilee year, debts were forgiven and slaves were liberated. We should note that that in the Aramaic language, which was the vernacular in Galilee and which Jesus normally spoke, the word *hōba'* means both "sin" and "debt" (cf. Matt. 6:12). The sinful woman in Luke 7:36–50 was released from her debt of sins and freed from her burden of slavery to sin. Her response was love and gratitude.

There are sins against God, and there are sins against people. These sins separate people from God and from each other. Jesus had a ministry of reconciliation, and He invited His followers to share it when He said, "Blessed are the peacemakers" (Matt. 5:9).

As we have seen, the Pharisees frowned on association with sin-ners, and that included tax collectors. But Jesus made a point of associating with them, including table fellowship, which in that cul-ture was the ultimate sign of acceptance (Matt. 11:19; Mark 2:15–17; Luke 15:1–2). Jesus did not deny that the people He ministered to were sinners. He did not disagree with the Pharisees about that. The question was: What should be done about sinners? That is where Jesus disagreed with the Pharisees. The Pharisees said: Shun them. Jesus said: Save them.

Fourth, He taught radical new ideas about worship. In Judaism worship was linked to purity. Only pure, unblemished gifts could be offered as sacrifices in the Temple, and persons with physical defects were disqualified from the priesthood (Lev. 21:16–23, esp. v. 18). A person who was defiled was excluded from worship in the Temple, and defilement was considered a contagious thing. Physical contact with such unclean things as pigs, lepers, corpses, or persons with bodily discharges also conveyed uncleanness.

Against this background it is striking that Jesus often healed such people by touching them (e.g., Mark 5:21–42). He redefined defilement as something internal and spiritual (Mark 7:14–23); vis-ible sin was but the outworking of what was in a person. But a humble and contrite heart was acceptable worship (Luke 18:9–14). In the Fourth Gospel Jesus says clearly that the sort of worship God the Father desires is "worship in spirit and truth" (John 4:23–24). He also taught that worship had a direct relationship to forgiving one's neighbor and living at peace with him or her (Matt. 5:23–24), so that worship involves both the vertical relation to God and the horizontal relationship to other human beings.

CONCLUSION

By precept and example Jesus taught servant leadership—even sacrificial leadership. He reversed the secular understanding of success: "Anyone who wants to be first must be the very last, and the servant of all" (Mark 9:35). Jesus not only called His followers to humble service. He called upon them to sacrifice, and even to die for the sake of His cause, if need be. In all four Gospels we can find this saying: "Whoever wants to be my disciple must deny themselves and take up their cross and follow me. For whoever wants to save their life will lose it, but whoever loses their life for me and for the gospel will save it" (Mark 8:34–35). In John 10:11–12, He says, "I am the good shepherd. The good shepherd lays down his life for the sheep. The hired hand is not the shepherd and does not own the sheep. So when he sees the wolf coming, he abandons the sheep and runs away. Then the wolf attacks the flock and scatters it."

Jesus chose love and sacrifice over the ordinary sources of power such as office, religious authority, political influence, or military force. He established a relationship of fellow servant and friend (John 15:15) with those He mentored for service.

In the light of such teaching and such an example, the words of Jesus to Peter in John 21:17 must ring in the ears of every Christian leader as an especially high demand: "Feed my sheep." Such shepherds, as Jesus Himself was, are willing to give their lives for the sheep, the followers of Jesus that He commits to His servants' care.

FOR REFLECTION

Personal:

1. What mentoring or successor-building relationships do you foster? How would you describe those relationships?

2. Do you encourage questions? Are you comfortable with questions about the values you consider important?

Organizational:

1. What are the power resources in your organization? In what ways are you relying on them?
2. How is *success* defined in your organization? In what ways is that congruent with Jesus's model of leadership? In what ways is it incongruent?

ENDNOTES

1. The word *Messiah* is from the Hebrew language and means "Anointed One"; *Christ* is from its Greek translation, so the two words are synonyms.

2. This is recognized in the titles of many popular books, such as Richard A. Burridge, *Four Gospels, One Jesus?* (Grand Rapids, MI: Eerdmans, 1994); Michael R. Cosby, *Portraits of Jesus: An Inductive Approach to the Gospels* (Louisville, KY: Westminster John Knox, 1999); and Robert K. McIver, *The Four Faces of Jesus* (Nampa, ID: Pacific Press, 2000).

3. Thus in the Gospel of Mark we see what has been called the Messianic Secret. At the beginning only the demons know who Jesus really is, and Jesus tells them to be silent (Mark 1:23–25 *et passim*). Beginning in chapter 8 the real identity of Jesus as Messiah and Son of God gradually is revealed until at last He is crucified and a Roman soldier exclaims that He is the Son of God. In the Gospel of John, however, there is absolutely no secret about who Jesus is, for it is acknowledged in the very first chapter by John the Baptist (John 1:34) and the first disciples (1:41, 49).

4. In fact, when John burst upon the scene, he was wearing an Elijah costume. Compare Mark 1:6 with 2 Kings 1:8.

5. Jesus Himself testified concerning John: "What did you go out into the wilderness to behold? A reed shaken by the wind? Why then did you go out? To see a man clothed in soft raiment? Behold, those who wear soft raiment are in kings' houses. Why then did you go out? To see a prophet? Yes, I tell you, and more than a prophet" (Matt. 11:7–9).

6. Unless otherwise noted, Scripture quotations in this chapter are taken from the New International Version.

7. "Son of Man" was Jesus's usual self-designation. The term harkens back to Daniel 7:13.

8. This term goes back to Daniel 7:14, 18, 22. In the Judaism of Jesus's time, people feared to use God's name, lest they break the third commandment of the Decalogue, so they substituted euphemisms such as *Heaven*.

9. For a good discussion of the early Christian oral tradition, see James D. G. Dunn, *Jesus Remembered,* vol. 1 of *Christianity in the Making* (Grand Rapids, MI: Eerdmans, 2003), 173–254. I also owe much of the insight in this paragraph to Kenneth E. Bailey, from whom I heard it via an undated amateur video of a presentation he gave to a church group in Pittsburgh, PA.

10. Mishnah *Aboth* 1:1. The Mishnah is a written compilation made about AD 200 of the oral law. It consists of sixty-three tractates dealing with various topics. One of these is *Aboth,* a unique collection of pithy sayings of early rabbis. Mishnaic quotations are taken from the translation of Herbert Danby, *The Mishnah* (London: Oxford University Press, 1933).

11. Mishnah *Aboth* 2:8.

12. Iscariot is a transliteration of Ish-Kerioth, a man from Kerioth. There were two places called Kerioth, one in Moab and one in Judea. We know of no Kerioth in Galilee.

13. Mark calls him "Simon the Cananaean." The surname is a transliteration of the Aramaic word that the other Gospels translate as "Zealot." The Zealots were a liberation movement that arose when the Roman emperor ordered a census to be taken so that the people might be taxed. See David M. Rhoads, *Israel in Revolution: 6–74 C.E.* (Philadelphia: Fortress, 1976).

14. It may be that these encounters were not their first with him. The Fourth Gospel tells us that Jesus had an earlier Judean ministry in which He attracted some of the disciples of John the Baptist and their friends (John 1:35–51). But whatever it was that so immediately attracted followers to Jesus, as if they had been waiting for His invitation, it was not some kind of rank or office, for He held none; it was some quality that they recognized in Him.

15. Henry George Liddell and Robert Scott, *A Greek-English Lexicon*, rev. ed. (Oxford: Clarendon, 1996), 852.

16. This is the only place in the Bible where this word is used, but in the Apocryphal book of 2 Maccabees 10:28, we find the related word *kathemon* used metaphorically and also translated "leader." In Luke 22:26 the word *hegoumenos* also clearly means "leader."

17. This meaning is not excluded. John 13:10 indicates that the rite is a renewal of baptism.

18. Jesus accepts the appropriateness of *Lord* as a title for Himself in texts such as Matthew 7:21 and Luke 6:46.

19. Translation by S. P. Brock in H. F. D. Sparks, ed., *The Apocryphal Old Testament* (Oxford: Clarendon, 1984), 678.

20. *Mekilta Amalek* 3 (on Exodus 18:1–12), trans. in Jacob Z. Lauterbach, *Mekilta de-Rabbi Ishmael,* vol. 2 (Philadelphia: Jewish Publication Society of America, 1976), 166.

21. I am much indebted to an article by Craig A. Evans, "The Ministry of Jesus in the Gospels," in *Community Formation in the Early Church and in the Church Today*, ed. Richard N. Longenecker (Peabody, MA: Hendrickson, 2002), 59–72.

9 | The Acts of the Apostles

C. Adelina Alexe

The book of Acts provides a chronicle of the church in the time period immediately following Jesus's ascension to heaven. It recounts the beginnings of Christianity in upsurge, with all the challenges inherent within a new movement. Situated between the Gospels and the Epistles, Acts functions as a bridge between four narratives unfolding the life and mission of the Messiah and twenty-two letters addressing the followers of the Messiah—now members of established communities of faith. Three major shifts characterize this period of Early Church development: (1) the Holy Spirit takes the divine leading role in guiding the church after Jesus's ascension, (2) the wall of separation between Jews and Gentiles is broken as Gentiles are welcomed into the church as fellow-believers, and (3) new ministries and leadership roles develop. It is in the context of these changes that leadership roles are carried out in Acts. Thus, I have structured the chapter in three sections, each relating to a different transition and the aspects of leadership observed in the context of that transition. Naturally, newness accompanies change, and throughout the book we witness each of these facets expand from embryonic form to fuller and more integrated aspects of carrying out the Great Commission.

JESUS ASCENDS, THE HOLY SPIRIT DESCENDS

Acts 1:1–8[1] encapsulates and foreshadows the shift in divine presence that the disciples experienced throughout the time period covered in the book and beyond: Jesus ascended to heaven, and the Holy Spirit descended to guide the church. In this introduction, Luke recapitulates the last two commands Jesus gave the disciples before His ascension: to wait in Jerusalem until they received the Spirit (1:4–5), and then to go witness to the ends of the earth (1:8). The two commands stand together. The disciples would be able to accomplish their mission only in the power of the Holy Spirit (1:8) and, conversely, the power of the Spirit would prove so enabling that nothing could thwart the work. Thus, everything in Acts revolves around the fulfillment of the Great Commission, and the Holy Spirit is the leading divine Person assisting the church in this task. The number of references to the Holy Spirit in Acts (fifty-six: an average of twice in every chapter) further reflects the centrality of the Spirit. The purpose of this first section is to underscore the irreplaceable leading role the Spirit played in the establishment and expansion of early Christianity. His leadership is manifested primarily through two key functions—unifying agent and empowering agent. Each one is expounded separately, followed by an overview of the work enabled by the Spirit and a portrait of His leadership model.

The Holy Spirit Unifies

The concept of community and its concurrent unity is an important leadership principle, largely exemplified by the work of the Holy Spirit in the book of Acts. It is important to note first that the purposes and activity of the Holy Spirit are embedded in a relational Trinity whose members support each other in perfect unity. As the Spirit takes a leading role in Acts, He works harmoniously with Jesus and the Father on behalf of the human race. In 1:2, we read that Jesus gave the apostles commands through the Holy Spirit. Acts 1:4 describes the sending of the Spirit as the Father's promise, which Jesus revealed to the disciples. Peter reiterates this trinitarian idea in his sermon at Pentecost (2:33). Stephen, through the Holy Spirit, sees heaven open and Jesus standing by God (7:55–56).[2] In 5:30–32 the apostles witness about Jesus, whom God exalted to His right hand, and of whom the Holy Spirit testifies. With Jesus's enthronement (alluded to in 2:33), a new kingdom is inaugurated[3] and, throughout Acts, the Holy Spirit is actively involved in bringing together the members of the kingdom of God in community with each other, in common allegiance to the Lord. Thus, through the leadership of the Spirit, the unity of God will come to be reflected in divine-human and interhuman relationships crucial to the realization of the Great Commission.

Four intertwining aspects of church unity can be observed in Acts: soteriological, relational, social, and geographical. Unity among the followers of Jesus is expressed through "(1) holding to one body of teaching, (2) common meals, (3) prayer, and (4) having all things in common."[4] Unity of heart in harmony with divine principles is vital to the well-being of the community and is steadfastly protected by the Holy Spirit, as demonstrated in His dealing with Ananias and Sapphira, who unite with each other in deception to the Spirit (5:1–11).[5] In Acts 6, the provision for widows indicates obedience to the Torah in the context of a united community in which members take care of the needs of each other.

Through direct leading of the Holy Spirit, the boundaries of the Christian community are moved outside of Jerusalem and Judea in a unifying effort of ingathering the Jewish Diaspora and Gentile believers. A first step in this direction takes place after Pentecost (2:1–39), as Jews from all parts of the world, who had gathered in Jerusalem for the feast, take back home the news of salvation. The expansion of the Christian community continues with the encounter between Philip and the Ethiopian eunuch, who confesses his belief and is baptized, thus being soteriologically united with the Christian community (8:26–40).[6] In Acts 10:1–48, this soteriological unity between Jews and Gentiles takes place in conjunction with "relational unity expressed in table fellowship."[7] The wall of partition between Jews and Gentiles is broken under direct guidance from the Holy Spirit, and the ingathering of believers continues throughout the book as human leaders keep submitting to the leading of the Holy Spirit who "guides the movement across geographic and social lines."[8]

The Holy Spirit Empowers

The second chief role of the Holy Spirit in Acts is empowerment—another key leadership component. In the context of the Great Commission, the idea of empowerment is enveloped in the concept of baptism with the Holy Spirit and, therefore, dependent on the descent of the Spirit. This baptism took place first at Pentecost. As the disciples were gathered together (2:1), "suddenly there came from heaven a noise like a violent rushing wind, and it filled the whole house where they were sitting. And there appeared to them tongues as of fire distributing themselves, and they rested on each one of them. And they were all filled with the Holy Spirit and began to speak with other tongues, as the Spirit was giving them utterance" (1:2–4). The etymology of the word *baptizo* suggests that, at Pentecost, "the apostles have been 'immersed' or 'plunged' into the Holy Spirit."[9] The disciples' baptism echoes the baptism of Jesus. At Pentecost the Spirit came down as tongues of fire; at Jesus's baptism the Spirit descended upon Jesus in the form of a dove (Matt. 3:16; Mark 1:10; Luke 3:22). Just like Jesus would go forth in ministry anointed with the Holy Spirit, so the disciples would be equipped with the Holy Spirit at Pentecost.

The imagery of the Spirit's descent creates "a picture of a mighty, overpowering phenomenon"[10] that includes audible ("wind"), visible ("tongues as of fire"), and tactile ("sat upon the disciples") elements. The word *ekathisen*, translated with the expression "sat upon them" means more precisely "it established itself," thus denoting a "taking over" of the disciples.[11] The appearance of tongues as of fire suggests "the miraculous speech about to occur (2:4, 8, 11) that will twice again accompany a new outpouring of the Spirit (10:46; 19:6)."[12]

The descent of the Holy Spirit at Pentecost is both opportune and symbolic. It is opportune because, as a result of the Spirit's empowerment, the disciples witness to a great number of people gathered at the feast from many parts of the world (2:5–12) who repent and are baptized (2:37–41). It is symbolic because it occurred "on the feast day at which Judaism commemorated the promulgation of the Law and the creation of the Covenant between God and his people gathered in 'assembly' [at Sinai]. The Christian Pentecost, which celebrates the Spirit's coming, commemorates a New Covenant, which created a new people of God and constituted them a church."[13] While the promise of power is initially given to the disciples (1:8), who "inaugurate the mission of testimony,"[14] at Pentecost it is promised to the entire community of believers (2:38–39),[15] who will carry this mission to fulfillment.

Although the Pentecost event is unique in Acts, throughout the book we witness numerous occasions when the Holy Spirit infuses people. Two words are often used to describe the indwelling, empowering presence of the Holy Spirit: "fall" and "fill." Leadership figures in the book of Acts are filled with the Holy Spirit: Peter is filled with the Spirit when he addresses the Sanhedrin (4:8). Stephen was full of the Holy Spirit in his ministry (6:5) and on the threshold of death (7:55). When Ananias lays hands on Saul, the newly converted leader is filled with the Holy Spirit (9:17). Saul is filled with the Spirit when he exposes Elyma's allegiance to the devil (13:9). Barnabas was "a good man, and full of the Holy Spirit and of faith" (11:24). One time, after the apostles prayed, "The place where they had gathered together was shaken, and they were all filled with the Holy Spirit" (4:31). In Acts 13:52 we read that "the disciples were continually filled with joy and with the Holy Spirit." In Ephesus twelve disciples received the Holy Spirit when Paul laid hands on them (19:1–7). The Holy Spirit falls on the Samaritans when Peter and John lay hands on them (8:14–17), and, to the initial surprise of the apostles, the Holy Spirit falls on the Gentile Cornelius and his household gathered to hear the Word of God (10:44–45).

The Holy Spirit Directs, Guides, and Appoints

The reader of Acts often has the impression of a veil being pulled away, exposing supernatural involvement to such extent that its denial would dismantle the entire book. Taken at face value, however, Acts reveals a divinity that speaks to people, directs their steps, appoints them for specific roles, and guides them in decisions as they engage in leadership together. The Spirit asks four prophets and teachers to set Barnabas and Paul apart for a special work (13:1–2); having had hands laid upon them, the two are released, being "sent out by the Spirit" (13:4). The Spirit forbade Paul and Silas to preach in Asia (16:6) and Bithynia (16:7). He orchestrated an encounter between Philip and an Ethiopian wrestling with the writings of the prophet Isaiah (8:26–39) and instructed Peter to accompany the messengers of Cornelius (10:19–20). When leaders struggled with the issue of circumcision (15:1–29), the Holy Spirit guided their decision (15:28). The Spirit also directed prophets, as demonstrated in the ministry of Agabus, who prophesizes a great famine over the entire world (11:28) and foretells Paul's chains and death (21:11).

The Leadership of the Holy Spirit in Acts: Portrait and Outcomes

The Holy Spirit is the ultimate leader in Acts. Through many references to His Person and work, Luke reveals Him as a Spirit that pervades the mission of church leaders in His foremost role as empowerer and unifier. The Spirit is a relational being deeply involved in the formation of the church both at the individual and at the community level, yet One who respects the freedom of humans (can be received: 8:15, 17; 10:47; 19:2, or resisted: 7:51). His extensive participation in the fulfillment of the Great Commission portrays Him as a Spirit who comforts (9:31); falls upon and fills (2:4; 4:8, 31; 6:3, 5; 6:8–10; 7:55; 8:14–17; 9:17; 11:24; 13:9, 52; 19:1–7); sends out (13:4); snatches (8:39); forbids (16:6–7); speaks to people (8:29; 10:19; 11:12; 13:2; 21:11); makes overseers (20:28); binds (20:22); and testifies (20:23).

As the connecting agent between divinity and humanity, the Holy Spirit elicits a beautiful and tight collaboration with the followers of Jesus. It is in the power of the Spirit that the church grew at an astounding rate during the infancy phase of Christianity, as abundant verses indicate (2:41, 47; 4:4; 6:1, 7; 8:6, 12; 9:31; 11:19–21, 24; 12:24; 13:12, 48–49; 14:1, 21; 16:5, 13–14, 25–33; 17:10–12, 34; 18:4, 8; 19:1–5, 10, 18–20; 28:23–24a). In favorable and unfavorable circumstances alike, the gospel made inroads into more hearts and more territories. Aside from growing numerically, the church also grew spiritually and relationally in unity with each other and with God, as it continued to reflect the leadership of the Holy Spirit and submit to His guidance.

Leaders who desire to emulate the leadership model exhibited by the Holy Spirit in the various narratives of Acts can keep in mind that godly leaders:

1. Empower those they lead.
2. Enable those they lead.
3. Comfort those they lead.
4. Guide people in service.
5. Facilitate the utilizing of gifts.
6. Foster unity among those they serve.
7. Respect the freedom of others.
8. Cultivate a relationship with those to whom they minister.

BARRIERS ARE BROKEN

A second transition observed in this chapter is the inclusion of the Gentiles into the community of believers—a fundamental step in the development of early Christianity. The wall of separation between Jews and Gentiles had yet to be broken, and the first public breach occurs in Acts 10:1–11:18, an episode of church history profoundly instructive for leadership in regard to vision, growth, and submission to God. Luke gives considerable space to describing this event that marks publicly the transition from the exclusion of Gentiles to their inclusion into the church. The passage is a story in two parts. In the first part (10:1–48), two characters take turns occupying center stage until they are brought together in a meeting orchestrated by God. The two are the Gentile Cornelius, a generous, God-fearing Roman centurion, and the apostle Peter, one of the primary leaders of the Early Church. Not surprisingly, the Holy Spirit plays the role of unifier. The second part of the story (11:1–18) depicts the apostle's defense of his actions before the brethren in Jerusalem. Part two is a direct result of part one, and the implications of both are monumental for the development of Christianity and the fulfillment of the Great Commission. In this second section I give a brief narrative analysis of Acts 10:1–11:18 that helps illustrate several principles of leadership emerging from the story.

The passage begins with Cornelius, a devout man who feared God and prayed to him continually (10:2, *dia pantos*, literally "through everything")[16] having a vision in prayer (10:30) at the ninth hour. This would be three o'clock in the afternoon, the time of offering at the temple in Jerusalem[17] and of the Jewish daily prayer.[18] An angel of God addresses him by name and tells him that his "prayers and alms have ascended as a memorial before God" (10:4).[19] Then he instructs Cornelius to send for "a man named Simon, who is also called Peter" (10:5), and he gives specific instructions on where to find him. As soon as the angel leaves, Cornelius sends two servants and a devout soldier to Joppa.

As the emissaries near the city the following day, Peter, who "became hungry"[20] (10:10; likely after a fast), also receives a vision during prayer. He "saw the sky opened up, and an object like a great sheet coming down, lowered by four corners to the ground, and there were in it all kinds of four-footed animals and crawling creatures of the earth and birds of the air. A voice came to him, 'Get up, Peter, kill and eat!' But Peter said, 'By no means, Lord, for I have never eaten anything unholy and unclean.' Again a voice came to him a second time, 'What God has cleansed no longer consider unholy.' This happened three times, and immediately the object was taken up into the sky" (10:11–16).

As Peter seeks to decipher the vision (10:17), the three messengers arrive, and the Spirit instructs Peter to "get up, go downstairs and accompany them without misgivings, for [the Spirit has] sent them [Himself]" (10:19–20). The apostle's noncompliance to the voice in vision (10:11–16) softens into obedience to the voice of the Spirit, and from this point on the written record gives no indication of further resistance on his part. He hosts the emissaries overnight and leaves with them the next day, accompanied by six local brethren (10:23; 11:12).

The next segment of the narrative unveils a threefold divine purpose with the Gentiles: to mingle with the Jews, to receive salvation, and to share the news of salvation. These purposes transpire in the story through Peter's progressive understanding, artfully delineated by Luke through several narrative features: Peter's declarative statements (in italics below), the subject change in the main clauses of these statements reflecting language of understanding, Peter's personal involvement signaled by the tone of his speech, and the gradual fulfillment of God's purpose.

Upon arrival at Caesarea, Peter finds the house filled with relatives and friends of the host, thirsty to hear the gospel. Cornelius bows before him, but Peter declines the honors that are due to God alone, and then he addresses the assembly with an honest declaration that indicates his understanding: "You yourselves know how unlawful it is for a man who is a Jew to associate with a foreigner or to visit him; and yet *God has shown me that I should not call any man unholy or unclean*" (10:28, emphasis added). Here God is the subject of the main clause. He alone possesses understanding, which He imparts to Peter. The apostle is now willing to associate himself with the Gentiles, but his tone remains neutral.

After Cornelius shares his experience of seeing the angel and, on behalf of all present, expresses the desire to "hear all that [he has] been commanded by the Lord" (10:33b), Peter opens his mouth (10:34)—a solemn expression indicating that something of importance follows[21]—and says: "*I most certainly understand now that God is not one to show partiality, but in every nation the man who fears Him and does what is right is welcome to Him*" (10:34b–35, emphasis added). Peter now understands that God gives salvation without partiality. The apostle articulates this discovery in enlivened language and proceeds to preach the good news of salvation through Jesus.

As Peter declares that forgiveness of sins is available to everyone who believes (10:43), the Holy Spirit interrupts his speech with a powerful manifestation of His presence (10:44). To the amazement of the accompanying Jews, the Spirit falls upon the Gentiles who begin to speak in tongues and exalt God (10:45–46), which causes Peter to declare: "*Surely no one can refuse the water for these to be baptized who have received the Holy Spirit just as we did, can he?*" and orders them "to be baptized in the name of Jesus Christ" (10:47–48a, emphasis added). Thus the progression culminates with a rhetorical question Peter asks in a vibrant and passionate tone. The subject of the sentence, "no one," along with the implied answer to the rhetorical question, indicates that the apostle expects universal acceptance of God's plan for the Gentiles as fellow-believers and "participants in salvation history."[22]

With this meeting, God's purposes are met: The Jews and Gentiles associate with one another publicly,[23] and the Gentiles receive salvation and the Holy Spirit. The vision of Peter in 10:9–16 encapsulates both aspects of this shift, and it is partly elucidated by Peter's use of the term *athemitos* in 10:28, where he refers to the prohibition of Jews to mingle with Gentiles. The word means "forbidden" but implies social taboo, not unlawfulness.[24] Eventually, the apostle also understands that he "should not call any man unholy or unclean" (10:28b) because Jesus, through His blood, had cleansed both Jews and Gentiles. Thus the vision is meant to invalidate both the cultural norm that prohibited the Jews from gathering together with the Gentiles as well as the Jews' view of Gentiles as unfit for salvation. The two lessons God meant to teach Peter through this vision are interdependent. If the apostles were to follow Jesus's model of discipleship and evangelization, table fellowship and close association with people were inevitable. Thus both a cultural roadblock and a theological misconception had to be overcome in order for the Great Commission to be carried out.

Peter is the leader God chose for accomplishing the first breach of the wall between Jews and Gentiles, as the apostle himself recognizes during the council of Jerusalem (15:7b). Two narrative features indicate God's intentionality in selecting Peter for this task: the threefold repetition of the dialogue between God and Peter (10:11–18) and the expression "Simon, also named Peter."

The number three has personal history for Peter. In the Gospels we read that immediately preceding Jesus's sacrifice, Peter's professed devotion to Him (Luke 22:33) was invalidated by a threefold prophesized denial (Luke 22:34, 54–61) that brought him a bitter, tearful realization of his inadequacy (Luke 22:62). The third time Jesus showed Himself to the disciples after His resurrection (John 21:14), on the shore of the Sea of Tiberias, He asked Peter three times if he loved Him (John 21:15–17), and, in a sequence of three commissions, entrusted to him the feeding and shepherding of His lambs and sheep (John 21:15–17). The repetition recalling his disloyalty grieved Peter (John 21:17), yet the threefold denial needed to be addressed and acknowledged before being replaced with the stronger and sweeter memory of forgiveness and restoration.

In the accounts in the Gospels, Peter's yet unclear understanding of the Messiah's mission played a part in his denial. In Acts 10, the apostle is faced with a twofold misunderstanding needing correction: the wall of partition between Jews and Gentiles must be broken, and the Gentiles are to be partakers of the gift of salvation. The threefold repetition of the conversation between God and Peter (10:11–18) may indicate that God intended to make a point Peter should have already learned from previous dialogues with Jesus: God's all-knowledge is reliable and His purpose trustworthy, even when not yet clearly grasped by humans. God called the apostle to step away from exclusivist traditions and theological errors and align himself with His purposes. Despite initial reluctance, Peter obeys and the divine objective is fulfilled.

Peter's history is also recalled through the expression "Simon, who is also called Peter," which is repeated verbatim four times: when the angel appears to Cornelius (10:5), when the messengers ask for Peter (10:18), when Cornelius recounts the divine encounter before Peter (10:32), and when Peter relates the story to the brethren in Jerusalem (11:13). It is notable that, outside of this story, nowhere else in Acts is Peter mentioned with a reference to his birth name. Its employment in this context is likely intended to evoke the apostle's journey of transformation from fisherman to disciple of Jesus to influential leader. The recollection of the name change from Simon to Peter (*Chepas*, literally "rock"; John 1:42) gains particular significance with this story. It took a "rock" to break the wall, and Peter's act of obedience to the Holy Spirit was the first step in a phenomenal shift in the development of Christianity and the carrying out of the Great Commission. The spiritually mature leader, who has now grasped the true mission of the Messiah and has learned to trust God, is willing to follow the divine directions despite incomplete understanding. In fact, the story suggests that not only is it not necessary that a full understanding of God's purposes precede our obedience to God, but that sometimes a fuller understanding of divine purposes cannot take place unless we are willing to follow while we still "wonder" (10:17).

Peter's actions, although aligned with God's purposes, stir opposition from the "circumcised brethren in Jerusalem" who "took issue with him" (11:2b). Peter tells them the story in order and in detail and concludes his speech with a pronouncement of the same realization he grasped while in the house of the Gentiles, which the brethren eventually articulate after internalizing the news in silence: "God has granted to the Gentiles also the repentance that leads to life" (11:15–18). Thus, without any further discussion, the story ends here, even as the end becomes an open door that was never to be shut again. The response of the brethren in Jerusalem, although only given a few words' space in the narrative, has vast implications. Their acceptance of Peter's actions and, more importantly, of the divine revelation would allow the embryonic church to maintain unity while developing and moving forward in the Spirit's will and power.

It is remarkable that both the narrator as well as the characters (in the retelling of their story) see the beginning of the visionary experiences in prayer (10:2–3, 9–10, 30; 11:5). The divinely orchestrated meeting between two praying people suggests that the close relationship between each of them and the Holy Spirit opened the door for them eventually to connect to one another in an experience whose significance goes beyond the local and individual benefits of the actual, historical event.

Ultimately, as the story indicates, it was the Holy Spirit who staged and directed this episode. Yet even as we recognize the full merits of God in accomplishing this breach, the story clearly shows that God uses human agents to fulfill His plans. From this story we learn that a leader like Peter—a courageous door opener, refined in the school of human failures met with divine grace—is a leader who chooses to obey God first rather than human beings and will preserve and defend a conviction with grace and composure.

Several principles of leadership arise from this story. Godly leaders:

1. Are formed and informed through prayer.
2. Obey God despite internal or external opposition.
3. Follow God while their understanding is still partial.
4. Communicate their spiritual discoveries with conviction and courtesy.
5. Listen to one another.
6. Cultivate accountability.
7. Recognize divine involvement by the fruit of the Spirit.
8. Change views and adapt based on progressive divine revelation.
9. Value divine approval above cultural conveniences.

NEW MINISTRIES AND LEADERSHIP ROLES

While chapter 7 of this book provides a thorough description of leadership language in the New Testament and a review of the development of leadership roles after Jesus's ascension, I will now examine how each of the roles present in Acts is being played out and highlight the leadership aspects they reveal. I conclude the section with an overview of a leadership model in which all these roles intertwine as the Holy Spirit, through different gifts, guides service to and through the church.

Apostles

The apostles played a primary role in Acts, as is reflected in the number of references to the term *apóstólos* (twenty-nine, on average once in every chapter). They are messengers of Jesus sent out to bring the good news of salvation to the ends of the earth. It is on the basis of Jesus's authority that they are entrusted with the Great Commission (Matt. 28:16–20). In Acts, the concept of "apostle" is attached to the Twelve (including Matthias who took Judas's place; 1:15–26), Barnabas (14:14), and Paul (14:14).

The leadership role of the apostles is demonstrated in the activities they carry out. They perform many wonders and signs (2:23;

5:12); choose a replacement for Judas (1:15–26); send Peter and John to Samaria (8:14); preach Jesus (4:33); lay on hands (6:5–6; 8:14–17); discuss conflicts together with elders and the church (15:6); send letters to churches (15:22–29; 16:4); teach and fellowship; pray and fast (1:13–14; 10:9; 13:2; 20:36). They also initially assist with the distribution of money that people brought to their feet (4:32–41). However, this role acted out at the initiative of people is temporary as eventually the apostles decide that they should not "neglect the word of God in order to serve tables" (6:2), but center on devoting themselves to "prayer and ministry of the word" (6:4).

The apostles work closely with God in submission to His will and submit to one another. They listen for the guidance of angels, the Lord, and the Holy Spirit (9:3–6; 10:9–16, 19–20; 18:9–10; 22:17–21; 27:22–24). They also exhibit great familiarity with Scripture (2:14–36; 3:12–26; 13:16–42; 15:13–21; 17:1–14, 22–31; 20:19–36; 28:23) and testify of Jesus in the temple and in houses, in freedom or under the threat of persecution (5:42; 8:1–4; 9:20; 20:20, 24–27). The apostles refuse undue worship and give God the glory (3:12; 10:25–26; 14:8–18). Oftentimes they suffer for God (5:17–18, 41; 16:20–24; 20:19, 24; 21:30–33; 22:24–25; 23:2), even to death (foreshadowed in John 21:18; Acts 21:11). The apostles serve the Lord "with all humility and with tears and with trials" (20:19) with a single goal that reflects God's will for them: to "testify solemnly of the gospel of the grace of God" (20:24).

Acts also gives indication that the apostles fostered personal relationships with those they served and formed. In this sense, Paul's farewell to the Ephesian elders and overseers in 20:17–38 is as informative for leadership as it is moving and inspiring. Paul spent time with them (20:18), "night and day for a period of three years" (20:31) in humble service to the Lord (20:19), teaching them (20:20) and admonishing them with tears (20:31). The graphic reaction of the Ephesian elders and overseers, who "began to weep aloud and embraced Paul, and repeatedly kissed him" (20:37) as his departure time approaches suggests that a profoundly close relationship had been established between the apostle and the elders and overseers. Thus, the passage indicates that the apostle Paul follows Jesus's model of servant leadership, which consists in forming disciples through close association, teaching and admonishing them in humility and with a heart that is burdened for them to the point of tears.

Prophets

The prophetic activity in Acts is described in four passages:

1. *Acts 11:27–30.* The Spirit inspires prophet Agabus to foretell "a great famine all over the world" (Acts 11:28), which moves the disciples to come to the aid of the brethren in Judea.

2. *Acts 13:1–4.* The Spirit addresses five "prophets and teachers" from Antioch with a clear command: "Set apart for Me Barnabas and Saul for the work to which I have called them" (13:2). In obedience to the Spirit, they fast, pray, lay hands upon the chosen two, and send them into the mission field.

3. *Acts 15:30–33.* Prophets Judas and Silas, "leading men among the brethren" (15:22), are the two chosen to deliver the decision of the Jerusalem council concerning circumcision. They go to the Gentile brethren in Antioch and Syria and Cilicia, deliver the letters that cause great joy, and "[encourage] and [strengthen] the brethren with a lengthy message" (15:30–33).

4. *Acts 21:8–11.* During Paul's last journey to Jerusalem, prophet Agabus visits the apostle at Caesarea, in the home of Philip the evangelist ("one of the seven" and father of four virgin daughters who were prophetesses; 21:8–9). In a symbolic gesture, Agabus takes Paul's belt and binds his own feet and hands as he delivers a message from the Holy Spirit foretelling Paul's arrest and turning over to the Gentiles.

These four passages in Acts indicate that prophets seem to be concerned with both the here-and-now needs of the community of believers as well as with the anointing and mission of prominent church leaders.

Overseers

In the book of Acts, the term *episkop* is used only once, in the context of Paul's farewell to the Ephesian elders and overseers: "Be on guard for yourselves and for all the flock, among which the Holy Spirit has made you overseers, to shepherd the church of God which He purchased with His own blood" (20:28). The verse covers a few leadership principles worth noting.

First, the leaders are called to accountability for their own Christian walk before being asked to guard their flock. Second, the overseers were shepherds "among" the flock, not above the flock. This implies service to people in a humble attitude that regards those served as equals. Third, the overseers are appointed by the Holy Spirit (20:28), probably through leaders filled with the Spirit (14:23). Thus, they are accountable directly to God for their leadership. Fourth, the church belongs to God—the ultimate Leader; it is not the property of men. Lastly, the flock is to be the object of faithful service rendered by leaders who understand the value of men and women in light of the cross (20:28).

Elders

Aside from the passage discussed above and the indications that Paul and Barnabas appointed elders (14:23) and brought them aid from the disciples during famine (11:30), the term is applied to Christian leaders only in one more passage,[25] namely, Acts 15, where church leaders dealt with the conflict over circumcision. Several relational dynamics are noteworthy in this narrative.

1. The apostles Paul and Barnabas submit themselves to the brethren, who determined that they should "go up to Jerusalem to the apostles and elders concerning this issue" which had caused "great dissension and debate" (15:2).

2. Throughout the narrative, Paul and Barnabas's primary concern is to share ministry stories with the brethren (15:3–4).

3. The conjunction "but" in 15:5 underscores the difference in approach between, on the one hand, the elders and apostles who receive Paul and Barnabas and hear their ministry testimony (15:4) and, on the other hand, the Pharisees, who in a rather abrupt manner and hostile tone, stand up and raise the issue of circumcision (15:5).

4. The apostles and the elders came together to look into this issue (15:6). Several leaders take turns speaking: Peter (15:7–11), Barnabas and Paul (15:12), and finally James (15:13–21). In this passage, it is significant to note language reflecting listening. In 15:12, after Peter's speech, we read that "all the people kept silent, and they were listening to Barnabas and Paul as they were relating

what signs and wonders God had done through them among the Gentiles." This time they were heard without interruption (15:13), and only when they are done speaking does James take the floor, introducing his speech with "brethren, listen to me" (15:13). The listening-language present in this narrative indicates that the council of apostles and elders placed great emphasis on listening to one another.

5. The unanimous decision of the apostles, elders, and the whole church (10:22) not to impose circumcision upon the converted Gentiles is a joint result of Peter's recalling his experience with Cornelius, Paul and Barnabas's recounting the work God had done through them, James's showing from prophecy that the Gentiles are partakers of the gift of salvation, and the Spirit's guiding (15:28).

The episode of the council in Jerusalem indicates that the elders and apostles fostered a collaboration based on mutual submission and mutual respect and that they were committed to listening to one another and submitting to the guidance of the Holy Spirit (15:28) before settling the issue of circumcision.

Deacons

The description of the Christian community in Acts 4:34–35 suggests that no wanting person was found among Christians, as people joined material and financial efforts in order to meet everyone's needs. This passage, read in conjunction with 6:1–4, implies that the apostles were initially in charge of the distribution of donations. Perhaps with the growing number of disciples (6:1),[26] some church members came to be overlooked in the sharing of aid. As a result, the complaint of the Hellenistic Jews in Acts 6:1 that their widows were neglected brings the twelve apostles together with the congregation of disciples to work toward finding a solution. This issue seems to effect reflection on the part of the apostles regarding the nature and responsibility of their calling. Thus the controversy serves not only to solve a momentary issue, but also to provide a long-term solution both for the apostles' wish to fulfill their calling as well as for securing provision of food for all. The outcome of this episode is a new ministry concerned primarily with charitable work and table service to those in need. The ministry requires new leadership roles, for which leaders are selected by the brethren from among themselves. They are to be people "of good reputation, full of the Spirit and of wisdom" (6:3). With the approval of the congregation (6:5), the brethren choose seven individuals who are anointed for ministry by the apostles through prayer and laying of hands (6:6).

The book of Acts portrays a beautiful collaboration among the followers of Jesus united in heart and purpose with God and with each other. Under the guidance of the Holy Spirit, leadership roles interlace for both eternal benefits and the benefits of the here and now, and provide a leadership model worth imitating. This model endorses leaders who

1. Submit to God and one another.
2. Grow in personal relationship with God.
3. Pray and fast.
4. Maintain a humble attitude.
5. Exhibit familiarity with Scripture.
6. Preach Jesus.
7. Give God all glory.
8. Practice teamwork.
9. Encourage one another.
10. Listen to one another.
11. Respect one another.
12. Make decisions together.
13. Care for the needy.
14. Obey God despite persecution and even death.

It is essential to bear in mind too that leaders can be transformed by God and brought to alignment with His character and purposes. Both Peter and Paul, the major leadership figures in Acts, undergo profound change under God's influence. Peter's transformation (observed more closely in the Gospels) is gradual; Paul's conversion is a 180-degree turnaround from murderer of Christians to Christian martyr. Both transformations are radical yet different illustrations of God's relentless pursuit of human beings whose hearts wander hopelessly until they are filled with God.

CONCLUSION

Acts presents a portrait of godly leadership that requires complete dedication to God in submission to His will and obedience to His voice. This high profile may seem unattainable as we turn our eyes upon our sinful and limited nature. Yet the Christian leadership model in Acts shows that what is impossible without God is not only possible, but certain with God. He provides not only the model of servant leadership, but also, through the Holy Spirit, the enabling that we need. Godly leaders are not perfect people; they are people who grow in their relationship with God and in using their talents for God's glory, in service for God and their neighbors.

FOR REFLECTION

Personal:

1. What is a specific thing God asked you to do that you refused to do or delayed accomplishing due to feelings of inadequacy? How does the portrait of the Holy Spirit as Enabler inspire you to take action?
2. What steps can you take now to become more aware of ways in which the cultural norms surrounding you may conflict with the biblical model of servant leadership? How can you move toward greater conformity to Jesus's model?

Organizational:

1. How well do your church members listen to one another, especially in times of conflict? How can you help your community appreciate and develop listening skills?
2. How does your church practice accountability among leaders? What are some of the roadblocks to maintaining this practice, and how can those be overcome?

ENDNOTES

1. Scripture quotations in this chapter are taken from the New American Standard Bible.

2. George K. A. Bonnah, *The Holy Spirit: A Narrative Factor in the Acts of the Apostles* (Stuttgart, Germany: Verlag Katolisches Biblewerk, 2007), 97.

3. Allan J. Thompson, *One Lord, One People: The Unity of the Church in Acts in Its Literary Settings* (New York: T&T Clark, 2008), 64.

4. Thompson, *One Lord, One People*, 66–67.

5. Thompson, *One Lord, One People*, 73.

6. William H. Shepherd Jr., *The Narrative Function of the Holy Spirit as a Character in Luke–Acts* (Atlanta, GA: Scholars Press, 1994), 218.

7. Thompson, *One Lord, One People*, 100.

8. Shepherd, *Narrative Function*, 156.

9. Jacques Dupont, *The Salvation of the Gentiles: Studies in the Acts of the Apostles* (New York: Paulist Press, 1979), 44.

10. Shepherd, *Narrative Function*, 161.

11. Dupont, *Salvation of the Gentiles*, 42–43.

12. Shepherd, *Narrative Function*, 161.

13. Dupont, *Salvation of the Gentiles*, 58–59.

14. Joseph A. Fitzmyer, S.J., *The Acts of the Apostles: A New Translation with Introduction and Commentary* (New York: Doubleday, 1997), 236.

15. Craig S. Keener, *Acts: An Exegetical Commentary*, vol. 1 (Grand Rapids, MI: Baker Academic, 2012), 689.

16. David B. Woods, "Interpreting Peter's Vision in Acts 10:9–16," *South African Theological Seminary Conspectus* 13 (March 2012): 185.

17. Darrell L. Bock, *Acts* (Grand Rapids, MI: Baker Academic, 2007), 387.

18. Woods, "Peter's Vision," 185.

19. The term for "memorial" is used only here in the New Testament and carries the idea of sacrifice offering, suggesting that God regarded the Gentile's prayers as an offering.

20. The word for "hungry" (*prospeinos*) is also a unique occurrence in the New Testament. It is interesting that Peter's midday prayer did not take place at a "normal prayer time, which would be around either 9 a.m. or 3 p.m.," and considering that Jewish meals occurred in midmorning and later afternoon, neither was his hunger typical by daily norms. The fact that Luke uses a rare word in conjunction with the unusual time for prayer and meal suggest that Peter might have been fasting. This is of even greater interest since Cornelius had also fasted before he received the vision in prayer (Acts 10:30). See Bock, *Acts*, 388.

21. Biblical precedents of this expression include Job 3:1, Acts 8:35, Acts 18:14, and Matthew 5:2, where it "introduces Jesus's benediction." See Woods, "Peter's Vision," 188.

22. James B. Shelton, *Mighty in Word and Deed: The Role of the Holy Spirit in Luke-Acts* (Peabody, MA: Hendrickson, 1991), 133.

23. Association between a Jew and Gentile also occurs in Acts 8:26–39, which describes the encounter between Philip and the Ethiopian eunuch. Unlike in Acts 10, however, this episode indicates a private meeting.

24. The term *athemitos* occurs twice in the New Testament. It means "forbidden" and is distinct from *anomos*, meaning "unlawful." This prohibition was not warranted by the Old Testament or by the Jewish oral laws. Instead, it was a "strongly held social custom enforced as *halakha*." Some commentators suggest that a more appropriate translation of *athemitos* is "taboo, out of the question, not considered right, against standard practice, contrary to cultural norms." See Woods, "Peter's Vision," 182–183.

25. The term *presbuteros* ("elder") is employed in several other contexts in Acts, in reference to Jewish leadership.

26. It is debatable whether the beginning of the deacons' ministry has its roots in Acts 6:1–6, since the word *diakonos* ("deacon") is not used here (although the related verb form *diakovenin* and noun *diakonia* are employed). Whether this can ultimately be answered in the affirmative or in the negative, it is clear from this passage that a new ministry is set forth in the context of the food distribution.

10 | The Pauline Epistles

P. Richard Choi

The English word *leader* made it into the French language past the watchful eye of the Académie française, a national council of forty eminent French men and women who decide which foreign words will be admitted into French. The fact that this august body that forbade words such as *e-mail* and *software* admitted *leader* into French is evidence that the English word *leader* is difficult to translate, even into French. The reason for this difficulty is that in many cultures the term *leader* implies position and authority whereas it tends to have a more relational and egalitarian tone in English, emphasizing leadership quality. For example, the French word *derigeant* denotes a position as opposed to leadership quality. And in Germany, the word *Führer* is generally avoided because of its strong overtones of hierarchy and dictatorship. By contrast, the word *leadership* often denotes shared leadership attributes, such as teamwork and influence, without the negative overtones of hierarchy and position.

This egalitarian notion of leadership is a relatively recent phenomenon, even in English. This is evident from the way the term *leader* has been used in various English translations of the Bible. For example, the word *leader* never occurs in the King James Version at all. But in the Revised Standard Version, which was published between 1946 and 1952, the term *leader* occurs only twice, in Luke 22:26 and Acts 5:31. Interestingly, the King James Version translates these same passages with *chief* (ἡγούμενος) and *prince* (ἀρχηγός), which is what these words originally meant in the first century AD. Being a relatively modern American translation, the Revised Standard Version simply steered away from these status-conscious words—*chief* and *prince*—and instead chose *leader* in order to express a greater sense of collegiality and equality. But in the New Revised Standard Version, appearing in 1989 and guided by a philosophy of inclusiveness, the word *leader* appears a remarkable one hundred and twenty times.

Today the term *leadership* denotes various types of *influence* that one exerts on one's community. For example, Walter Wright defines leadership as "*a relationship in which one person seeks to influence the thought, behaviors, beliefs or values of another person.*"[1] Defining *leadership* as "influence" is somewhat simplistic, but the idea affirms that leadership does not denote hierarchy or control. This notion of leadership is especially true in sports and businesses that value teamwork. In the context of Christian leadership, the phrase *servant leadership* has been introduced to further stress the egalitarian character of leadership. For example, Kenneth O. Gangel describes "servant leadership" as follows: "1. leadership is servanthood.... 2. leadership is stewardship.... 3. leadership is shared power" and warns against "excessive individualism, extreme isolation, and self-centered empire building"—in other words, avoiding anti-egalitarian values.[2]

In his letters, Paul seems to have viewed his apostolic role differently, claiming divine authority as warrant for his leadership. For example, he insisted that his message could not be contradicted by anyone. He wrote, "If anyone proclaims to you a gospel contrary to what you received, let that one be accursed!" (Gal. 1:9, NRSV).[3] Also, according to 1 Corinthians 5:5, Paul handed over an immoral member of the church to Satan for the destruction of his flesh. Pastors and youth leaders today would not use this type of authoritarian language to deal with the problem of immorality in their congregations. Furthermore, Paul never relinquished his influence over his churches. He writes, "You have countless guides in Christ, you do not have many fathers" (1 Cor. 4:15). Kenneth Faught, a Christian leadership expert, correctly notes that Paul was "an *authoritarian* leader."[4] Paul was an ancient Mediterranean personality who was also an inspired apostle. In other words, the background of Paul's authoritarian leadership was both religious and cultural. Consequently, it would be anachronistic to use *leadership* or *leader*, in the contemporary sense, to describe Paul's apostolic work, which produced a rather hierarchical relationship with his congregations.

Therefore, this essay will distinguish certain *attributes* of Paul's leadership from his *authoritative style*. It would be highly inappropriate for ministers to imitate his style and, for example, write authoritative letters to their former congregations. Verging on absolute authority, Paul's leadership sometimes tended to alienate even his ancient readers. His leadership was shaped by three factors: the culture of his time, his own intense personality, and his inspiration. Therefore, the words *apostle* and *apostleship* will be replaced with *leader* and *leadership* in this essay to distinguish Paul's leadership style from his leadership attributes.

Although this distinction introduces a degree of anachronism, noted above, into the discussion, it is necessary for the purpose of this assignment that seeks to make Paul's apostolic work relevant to modern students of leadership whose aim is to find "a *framework* for understanding the [biblical] practice of leading."[5] The discussion in the following pages will be divided into nine sections based on nine attributes that comprised Paul's leadership: message, conversion, advantages, life, power, vision, the Holy Spirit, spiritual gifts, and character.

PAUL'S LEADERSHIP

Message

Paul had a clear message: Christ, the Son of God, died for our sins and rose on the third day (cf. 1 Cor. 15:3ff.) to demonstrate God's love for sinners (Rom. 5:8). But this message had many implications, as can be seen in the wide-ranging works on Paul's theology being produced today,[6] which range from doctrines like justification by faith[7] to individual commentaries on his letters to specific topics such as the sociology of Paul. This essay will focus on the Cross because his leadership was the Cross in action. First, the Cross played a central role in his proclamation (1 Cor. 2:2; Gal. 6:14) as both the fulfillment of the Old Testament prophecies (cf. 2 Cor. 1:20) and the focus of faith (cf. Rom. 3:25).[8]

Second, the Cross was a new paradigm of power that allowed one to see the conditions of human weakness as opportunities for manifesting divine power. Thus Paul often made conscious decisions that brought him hardship and suffering, such as imprisonment and rejection, so that God's power could be "made perfect" in his weakness (cf. 2 Cor. 12:9). Such a counterintuitive concept of leadership can be explained only in the light of his gospel that understood the Crucifixion as God's ultimate manifestation of power (cf. Rom. 1:16; 1 Cor. 1:17–18). Paul's leadership was an attempt to articulate this new concept of power in words and deeds.

Conversion

Paul's conversion stands as the single most important event in his life and the beginning point of his Christian leadership.[9] As a sharp distinction between Christianity and Judaism did not yet exist at the time of his conversion, Paul converted to the person of Christ rather than to a particular religion. In fact, he remained a Pharisee to the end of his life (cf. Acts 23:6). Yet the Damascus experience left him profoundly changed from being a fierce persecutor of the church to one of the staunchest defenders of the faith, causing him to relinquish much of his prior identity and learning, so that everything was impacted by this experience—his understanding of God, of humankind, and of the world. Paul described this experience of conversion in various ways: as a revelation of the Son of God, crucifixion, resurrection, and new creation (cf. Gal. 1:12, 16; 2:20; 6:14; 2 Cor. 5:17).

Paul's conversion also altered his concept of leadership. He writes: "I advanced in Judaism beyond many among my people of the same age" (Gal. 1:14, NRSV). From this statement, modern students of leadership might assume that Paul transferred his previous training and leadership skills to his leadership role in the church. But this assumption is a mistake—he actually gave up nearly all that pertained to his previous life, especially his people skills and notions of leadership, to live his life in imitation of Christ.

Advantages

Paul, transformed by the Spirit, rejected advantages that position offered. He wrote: "But what things were gain to me, those I counted loss for Christ." The word *gain* here means "advantage," and *loss*, "disadvantage." In other words, Paul rejected every advantage as a disadvantage. He even rejected advantages that would have given him the minimum comforts of life (cf. 1 Cor. 9:13–15). And he invited others to follow in his footsteps: "Be imitators of me, as I am of Christ" (1 Cor. 11:1). Judged from the perspective of business and politics, this was extraordinary because the tendency of a positional leader is to do what is advantageous for themselves and for their organization. But here is precisely where Paul demonstrated how Christian leadership differed from worldly leadership: Christian leaders model their leadership after Christ, who gave up the advantages of being equal with God and chose the ignominious death of the cross that was reserved for slaves and foreigners (cf. Phil. 2:6–7). So Paul wrote to his fellow believers in Philippi: "Let this mind be in you, which was also in Christ Jesus" (Phil. 2:5, KJV). Christian leadership is a call to take up the disadvantages of life represented by the Cross—even shame, defeat, rejection, and death—for the sake of the world, just as Christ did.

Life

Paul intentionally lived his life toward a definite goal. He wrote: "I do not run aimlessly, nor do I box as though beating the air," (1 Cor. 9:26, NRSV) and "I do it all for the sake of the gospel" (1 Cor. 9:23, NRSV). Paul's goal was to be a messenger through whom God offered eternal life to the dying world. Yet such aims were not unique to Paul, for almost all ancient religions had immortality as their goal. The uniqueness of his religion lay in the fact that he sought immortality through the Cross, "a stumbling block to Jews and foolishness to Gentiles" (cf. 1 Cor. 1:23, NRSV). In other words, Paul differed from other ancient religions not in his goal but in his methodology. He chose the methodology that Christ used to bring eternal life to humanity—humiliation, suffering, and death. So he wrote: "That I may know him, and the power of his resurrection, and the fellowship of his sufferings, being made *conformable unto his death*" (Phil. 3:10, RSV, emphasis added).

But why should the process of being a conduit of eternal life be such a painful experience requiring humiliation and offense? The reason is the sinful nature of this world. For Paul, the word *world* did not denote a locality, like some godless nation or habitation outside the church. Rather, it denoted the sinful principles active in untransformed people that caused them to turn away from God and to turn against each other. Therefore, to escape the world, one must undergo a transformation of character by the power of the Holy Spirit rather than simply change locations. To make this type of spiritual transition, one must first experience death, which refers to the experience of being offended by the gospel—humiliated before God and humans—until there is no hope left, except Christ. The calling of the Christian leader, then, is to help people make this painful transition from death to life, from sinful rebellion to a life of obedience, so that they can experience the resurrection in the present. This was why Paul wrote of the Galatians, "My little children, for whom I am again in *the pain of childbirth* until Christ is formed in you."[10] For, just as in the biological realm, there can be no birth without birth pangs, so it is in the Christian life.

Power

To become an agent of life, Paul's concept of power had to go through a fundamental change. In Greco-Roman society, as today, power was associated with such things as money, education, personal achievements, status, and friends in high places. The Greco-Roman society was a world of scarce resources that were unevenly distributed. Not surprisingly, then, Paul also claimed power (cf. 2 Tim. 1:7) and often mentioned it in his letters.[11] But he never used the word *power* in connection with education, money, status, or other such popular sources of power. Rather, he associated it with spiritual realities, especially God and His power to resurrect the dead. For example, he wrote: "I am not ashamed of the gospel of Christ: for it is the *power* of God unto salvation" (Rom. 1:16, KJV, emphasis added; cf. 1 Cor. 1:18). Yet Christ did not have any worldly power. Born impoverished and powerless, and belonging to the lower social rungs of Greco-Roman society,[12] He lived in abject poverty, and He died tragically. But for Paul, Christ was powerful, especially in His tragic death. For by His death He saved the world from sin. Christ's paradigm of power is this: One is powerful to the degree to which one is able to divest oneself of attachment to worldly power. So Paul wrote: "For though he was crucified through weakness, yet he liveth by the power of God. For we also are weak in him, but we shall live with him by the power of God toward you" (2 Cor. 13:4, KJV).

Vision

Paul's vision was to create a reconciled community that would exist in contradistinction to a world that was divided and hostile. Humans are by nature political animals.[13] For Paul, this meant that we are shot through with hostility in varying degrees of intensity. Indeed, history is replete with stories of humans resorting to whatever is at their disposal, be it religion or economy, to fortify barriers erected by hate and violence. Paul called these hostile human instincts *the flesh* (cf. 1 Cor. 3:1–3), responsible for division, jealousy, and anger (cf. Gal. 5:19–21). Paul's vision was to remove these hostile works of the flesh from the community by the power of the Spirit and create a reconciled community whose operating principle was "love, joy, [and] peace" (Gal. 5:22)—principles the exact opposite of those of the world.

For there to be such a reconciled community, people had to first catch the vision of God's great love manifested in Christ. Thus in Romans 5, Paul first presented a vision of God's love for sinners before asking the Jewish and Gentile Christians to put aside their hostility and come together in reconciliation. He wrote: "But God demonstrates his own *love* for us in this: While we were still sinners, Christ died for us" (Rom. 5:8, NIV, emphasis added). Then, in verse 10, Paul went on to further define this love as an act of reconciliation. He wrote: "while we were God's enemies, we were *reconciled* to him through the death of his Son" (NIV, emphasis added). This eloquent portrayal of God's reconciling love was an indirect call to both Jews and Gentiles to set aside their hostility toward each other in imitation of God the Great Reconciler.

In 2 Corinthians 5:19–21, Paul provides yet another powerful vision of God's reconciling love found in the Cross. Paul wrote in verse 20: "Be reconciled to God." In this passage, as in Romans, Paul presented God's gestures of reconciliation toward the sinful world as a paradigm for reconciliation. The difference was that, in 2 Corinthians 5, the parties in need of reconciliation were Paul and the Corinthian congregation, a congregation that had become estranged from him through mistrust and misunderstanding. So Paul yearningly wrote: "Our heart is wide open to you" (2 Cor. 6:11, NRSV). As in Romans, he once again based his appeal on the vision of God's reconciling action on the Cross. So Paul wrote: "In Christ God was reconciling the world to himself, not counting their trespasses against them" (5:19). In other words, before there can be a reconciliation, we must first catch the vision of a compassionate God who sacrificed all to win our hearts.

Notwithstanding, modern students of leadership tend to either overlook Paul's vision of reconciliation in 2 Corinthians or misunderstand it as a form of narcissism. For example, Doohan mistakenly criticizes Paul's tender gestures of reconciliation in 1 and 2 Corinthians as follows: "Paul's ability to empathize and to accept others is not demonstrated throughout these letters [1 and 2 Corinthians]. Rather, there is anxiety and distress in his all *too personal response.*"[14] However, Paul's point is that one cannot fully see the love of God until it has been exemplified by someone else's life of sacrifice. We comprehend God's love when we see a living example of Christians bringing life and hope to downtrodden people at an immense cost to themselves. This is what Christ did for humanity, and what Paul was doing for the Corinthians.

Peter Koestenbaum, founder and chairman of PiB and the Koestenbaum Institute, writes: "In the final analysis, leadership can be taught in only one way: through personal experience and through mentoring.... The role of the mentor is simple: *exemplify at all times exactly what you teach.*"[15] Paul employed three approaches in order to promote his vision: preaching, modeling, and establishing communities. He used preaching that rejected all messages that called for coercion, use of force, and even the rule of law because such methods of achieving unity were incompatible with his vision of love and reconciliation. Paul also exemplified the concepts of reconciliation in his own life by rejecting worldly advantages. As already noted, he believed that the best way to eliminate hostility in this world of limited resources was to relinquish the advantages that everyone was competing for: wealth, education, and status. But Paul not only preached reconciliation and exemplified it in his life. He also tried to establish model communities in which it would be safe to practice the principles of reconciliation. These model communities were churches in which reciprocating gestures of love would be realized.

The Holy Spirit

In Paul's theology, the Holy Spirit performs the duties associated with Christian leadership—and many more. The list is extensive:

- The Spirit gives life (Rom. 8:2, 6, 10; 2 Cor. 3:6; Gal. 6:8).
- The Spirit resurrects (Rom. 1:4; 8:11; 1 Tim. 3:16).
- The Spirit "searches the depths" of God and knows His thoughts (cf. 1 Cor. 2:11–12).
- The Spirit searches our hearts to know our thoughts (Rom. 8:27), so that He can supply the knowledge, discernment, and inspiration we need (cf. 1 Cor. 2:13–14; 7:40; 12:3, 8; Eph. 1:17; 3:5; Col. 1:19; 2 Tim. 1:14).
- The Spirit supplies spiritual discourses, such as sermons and exhortations (1 Cor. 12:10; 14:2, 14; 2 Cor. 4:13; Eph. 6:17).
- The Spirit imbues our words with authority and power (1 Thess. 1:5; 4:8; 2 Tim. 1:17) and guarantees their truth (cf. Rom. 9:1).
- The Spirit is the Agent that brings us justification. Paul writes: "Through the Spirit [we] wait for the hope of righteousness by faith" (Gal. 5:5, KJV).
- The Spirit provides us with sanctification (Rom. 15:16; 1 Cor. 6:11; 2 Cor. 3:18; 2 Thess. 2:13), producing in us holy desires (Gal. 5:17), obedience (Rom. 8:4–5, 11; Gal. 5:16, 18, 25), zeal,[16] and renewal (Titus 3:5).
- The Spirit is the Agent of the New Covenant (2 Cor. 3:3, 6, 8; cf. Gal. 5:2).

- The Spirit dwells in us individually and collectively (Rom. 5:5; 8:9; 15:30; 1 Cor. 3:16; 5:3; 6:19; Eph. 5:18; Col. 1:8; 2 Tim. 1:14), giving us freedom (2 Cor. 3:17), joy (Rom. 14:17; 15:13; 1 Thess. 1:6), peace, and hope (Rom. 15:13).
- The Spirit also builds communities (Eph. 2:22; 4:3–4; Phil. 2:1; Col. 2:5) and creates unity (1 Cor. 12:13; 2 Cor. 13:13) by supplying and organizing various types of spiritual gifts among members (1 Cor. 12:4, 7, 11; cf. 14:12).

Paul trusted the Holy Spirit to develop leadership in the churches rather than offering significant leadership training to his converts. Paul often had to quickly leave the cities where he planted churches, either because of his own itinerary or because of the persecution that arose from his preaching. For example, although Paul worked for relatively long periods of time in Ephesus (three years—cf. Acts 20:31) and Corinth (one and a half years—cf. Acts 18:11), in other places, such as Philippi, he was forced to leave the city almost immediately after he planted the church (cf. Acts 16:39). His letters provide no evidence of practical training. Although he sent weighty letters and capable envoys such as Timothy, Titus, Luke, and Epaphroditus to communicate with his churches,[17] he did not involve himself in the leadership of his churches. Gangel claims that "many of the church leaders were *personally trained* by the apostle Paul."[18] But Gangel does not reveal where he found this information. Nor does he discuss the methods and resources Paul might have used to train leaders. In fact, it is unlikely that Paul was directly involved in the training of leaders for his churches, given the "daily pressure" (2 Cor. 11:28, NRSV) he experienced on his trips, which included imprisonments and shipwrecks (vv. 23–29).

Although Acts tells us that "[the disciples] devoted themselves to the apostles' teaching" (Acts 2:42), no training manual found in the style of Cicero's *De Inventione* is found in any of Paul's letters—not even the pastoral letters are training manuals. This silence is an oddity because many ancient religions, such as the Hellenistic mystery religions, emphasized the importance of training and mastery of techniques, such as the techniques of trance and meditation. In stark contrast, Paul did not offer even one verse on methods of meditation or the times of the day when prayers would be most effective.

Nor did he offer much significant information on rhetoric, mathematics, music, history, or philosophy—the standard curriculum of Greek *paideia*.[19] In brief, Paul did not rely on professional training as a method of preparing leaders for churches.

He trusted the Holy Spirit to provide the necessary spiritual leadership and instruction for the new churches and the newly appointed leaders in his absence—from organization to training, from motivation to transformation. Without much significant administrative oversight or training, new churches grew rapidly because of the powerful activity of the Holy Spirit, who was able to supply what was lacking in human leadership. Paul was hardly alone in this experience, as history is replete with examples of how fledgling churches, such as those in early Adventism, grew rapidly in remarkably coherent and creative ways when they had no option but to trust the Holy Spirit for daily guidance and leadership.

Spiritual Gifts

Also integral to Paul's concept of leadership were spiritual gifts (cf. Rom. 12:3ff; 1 Cor. 12:4–10; Eph. 4:11–13). Spiritual gifts provided a natural way to organize and govern the budding community (Rom. 12:3–8; 1 Cor. 12:8–10, 28–30; Eph. 4:11–13). But more importantly, the spiritual gifts became Paul's way of describing how grace collectively operates in the context of a community. Still, Paul was unique among the New Testament writers in using the word *charisma* to describe the collective effects of God's grace on the life of service and cooperation in the community.[20] The reason was that grace was central to Paul's soteriology, and he wanted to ensure that grace did not remain a mere doctrine but also functioned at the community level, as a concrete reality for everyone. In our narcissistic age, it is easy to equate grace with one's assurance of salvation and think of it merely as an inner experience of God's acceptance and peace. But this is not how Paul thought of grace. For him, grace was synonymous with God's gracious gifts freely given, to be utilized by the entire community as a public good, rather than as a private good that fosters only self-preoccupation and competition—the two factors most often responsible for eroding the community's unity.

Ephesians 4:11–13 offers us an example of how Paul saw the correlation of spiritual gifts. He writes:

> The gifts he gave were that some would be apostles, some prophets, some evangelists, some pastors and teachers, to equip the saints for the work of ministry, for building up the body of Christ, until all of us come to the unity of the faith and of the knowledge of the Son of God, to maturity, to the measure of the full stature of Christ. (NRSV)

The opening words "he gave" (4:11) explain that Paul thought of the gifts as something graciously *given* and not as a result of training or self-discovery. One can see the gracious nature of the gifts more clearly in Greek: *kai autos edōken*—"and he gave." The pronoun *autos* (he) is placed at the beginning of the sentence to indicate emphasis and refers primarily to Christ.[21] However, the sense here is that it is the Triune God, and no one else, who supplies these gifts. Anthony Thiselton writes: "Paul's emphasis upon unity-in-diversity is grounded in the nature of one God, who is holy Trinity."[22] In other words, these were truly gifts, unmerited and not of human origin.

Yet the gifts listed in Ephesians 4:11–13 all concern leadership roles involving mostly speech: apostles, prophets, evangelists, preachers, and teachers.[23] This focus on speech in Ephesians underscores the fact that even the gifts that are not mentioned here—those that involve "service"—have to do with the transmission of the message of the gospel. In other words, whether one is an evangelist, a helper, or an administrator, the gifts refer to the type of role that one plays in explaining the redemptive significance of the Cross, either by words or by deeds. And explaining the meaning of the Cross in the most powerful way possible was the mission of the Early Church. For example, as an apostle, Paul was given a revelation that was foundational for the church. So Paul wrote concerning his own message: "According to the grace of God given to me, like a skilled master builder I laid *a foundation....* For no one can lay any foundation other than the one already laid, which is *Jesus Christ*" (1 Cor. 3:10–11, NRSV, emphasis added). Gifts are given in different forms to clarify and illustrate the love of God revealed in Jesus Christ.

The use of "equipping" in Ephesians 4:12, however, implies that some type of training went on in Paul's churches. Similarly, Paul writes in 1 Corinthians 3:6: "I planted, Apollos watered" (NRSV). "Watered" in this passage implies a sustained effort by human agents to cultivate the gifts that God has entrusted His church. So the development of competency through practical training in line with giftedness *is* supported in the epistles. The term "equipping" in Ephesians refers to the leader's ability to impart as well as to recognize and cultivate spiritual gifts in others. It appears that the Early Church had individuals who were recognized for this ability. For example, "ruler" in 1 Corinthians 12:28 and Romans 12:8 seems to refer to such individuals.[24] Furthermore, Paul wrote to the believers in Rome: "I long to see you so that I may *impart* to you some spiritual gift to make you strong" (Rom. 1:11, NIV, emphasis added). Apparently, such impartations of spiritual gifts were widely practiced in the early church by praying for others to receive the Holy Spirit and through teaching. For Ananias said to Paul in Acts: "Brother Saul, the Lord Jesus, who appeared to you on your way here, has sent me [to pray for you] so that you may regain your sight and *be filled with the Holy Spirit*." (Acts 9:17; NRSV; italics added).

In 1 Corinthians 12:7–11, Paul presents the Holy Spirit as the unifying and controlling force behind spiritual gifts by mentioning the Spirit throughout the passage, immediately after many of the gifts, as you can see in the italicized portions of the text:

> To each is given the manifestation of the Spirit for the common good. To one is given *through the Spirit* the utterance of wisdom, and to another the utterance of knowledge *according to the same Spirit,* to another faith *by the same Spirit,* to another gifts of healing *by the one Spirit,* to another the working of miracles, to another prophecy, to another the discernment of spirits, to another various kinds of tongues, to another the interpretation of tongues. All these are activated *by one and the same Spirit,* who allots to each one individually just as the Spirit chooses. (1 Cor. 12:7–11, NRSV, emphasis added)

But, in stark contrast, Paul does not once mention the Holy Spirit in Romans 12:6–8. Instead, each mention of the gift is followed by a corresponding Christian grace or virtue, as evident in the italicized portions of the text:

> We have gifts that differ according to the grace given to us: prophecy *according to faith;* ministry, *by ministry;* the teacher, *by teaching;* the exhorter, *by exhortation;* the giver, *by generosity;* the leader, *by diligence;* the compassionate, *by cheerfulness.* (Rom. 12:6–8; author's translation; emphasis added)

Paul's point here is that we exercise our spiritual gifts "according to the grace given to us." In other words, each spiritual gift is an outward activity that is performed based on the grace or virtue appropriate for that activity. Kenneth Berding sees the relationship between these pairs in Romans as one of "ministry functions" and "persons in their ministry functions." But this reading fails to adequately take into account the context of Romans 12:1–2, the focus of which is not on "function" but the transformation of the person providing the ministry.[25] For example, teaching is an outward activity performed based on one's inward capacity for teaching. Likewise, philanthropy is an outward activity performed based on one's inward capacity for compassion. Now, the catchall inward capacity that lends support to all of the spiritual gifts is a mind and body that has been transformed by the Spirit (cf. Rom. 12:1–2). But Romans 12 clearly emphasizes that God transforms each of us differently to meet different needs of the community. It is clear, then, that no one should possess just one or two gifts. Possessing and cultivating multiple genuine gifts accompanies sanctification in the Spirit.

But leaders must *use* their spiritual gifts for the gifts to become effective. Actually taking the plunge and mustering the courage to use one's spiritual gifts is often very difficult. The reason is not necessarily that people are lazy, unresponsive, or ignorant[26] but that their spiritual gifts often do not mesh well with their job descriptions because the gifts, being deeply spiritual and somewhat subjective, tend to collide with "the stated needs and goals of the group."[27] For example, when pastors arrive in a new church, they are confronted with job descriptions they will be expected to fulfill. It is hard to use one's spiritual gifts if one does not receive "support from top management."[28] This is where many fail, because, in order to be an effective leader, one must not only know one's spiritual gifts, but also find creative ways to *use* them in one's work. Paul, for example, knew that his spiritual gifts were all geared to the preaching of the gospel to the Gentiles, but it was no easy task for him to use these gifts within the administrative framework of the Early Church, which did not have much room for his Gentile ministry. So in Galatians 2:7–9, he describes how he found a way to use his unique gifts in his ministry. Please note how he uses the phrase "grace given to me" to denote his spiritual gifts. He writes:

> When they saw that I had been entrusted with the gospel for the uncircumcised…and when James and Cephas and John, who were acknowledged pillars, recognized *the grace that had been given to me*, they gave to Barnabas and me the right hand of fellowship. (Gal. 2:7–9, NRSV, emphasis added)

Paul, who had received his gifts directly from the risen Christ, sought acknowledgment of this fact from the other apostles so that he could use them in his apostolic ministry without hindrance. In other words, he did everything in his power to find a way to *use* his unique spiritual gifts as effectively and widely as possible within the framework of the expectations—that is, the "job descriptions" of the Early Church.

But one must not confuse spiritual gifts with one's natural talents or innate abilities, such as speaking abilities or organizational skills. Spiritual gifts are specific to a calling, given to enable an effective execution of the call received. For example, Paul was called to be an apostle to the Gentiles. To help him carry out this important calling, he was given the extraordinary grace, or gift, of articulating and applying the gospel for the Gentiles. And so Paul wrote: "*According to the grace of God given to me*, like a skilled master builder I laid a foundation…[and] that foundation is Jesus Christ" (1 Cor. 3:10, NRSV, emphasis added). In other words, the spiritual gifts are special graces given by God to explain and apply the gospel in a fresh and relevant way.[29] Natural abilities can become an asset as one exercises spiritual gifts, but it is clear that both the call and the gifts are *extra nos,* that is, they were not present in us before we received our calls. God gave Moses and David, as well as Paul, the power to do the work He called them to do, and none of them had the gifts needed for the job when they were called. For spiritual gifts are call and content-specific. In other words, they relate directly to the unique ways in which the gospel functions in one's life and community. For example, Paul may have been trained in leadership skills and had some superficial knowledge of Christianity prior to his conversion, but he had no understanding of his pro-Gentile gospel or what it meant to be an apostle before he was called.

Character

Ancient Greeks and Romans described the ideal character traits of a leader (virtuous man),[30] relying on stereotypes, known as *topoi.* For example, Aristotle, who believed that a leader must possess by nature virtues superior to those ruled,[31] described the virtues of continence and temperance in Book VII of his *Nichomachean Ethics,* as follows: "*continence* involves having strong and bad appetites…a *temperate* man will have neither excessive nor bad appetites."[32] Nearly three hundred years later,[33] the Roman writer Cicero used the same *topoi* to discuss the virtues of a leader: "*Temperance* is a firm and well-considered control exercised by the reason over lust and other improper impulses of the mind…. *Continence* is the control of desire by the guidance of wisdom."[34] The most desired character stereotypes of the Greco-Roman world were temperance, continence, confidence, courage, self-control, judgment, knowledge, and reason. Likewise, modern business theories often mistakenly rely on stereotypes to measure and evaluate desirable leadership traits, albeit in a more scientific way. For example, in a chart comparing the traits of a leader in 1948 and 1970, Ralph M. Stogdill lists judgment, knowledge, fluency of speech, alertness, originality, personal integrity, and self-confidence as desired leadership traits.[35] Although Stogdill argues that "the patterns of behavior acceptable in leaders differ from time to time and from one culture to another,"[36] it should be noted that he still discusses his situationalist approach to leadership using a set of character *topoi* called "traits." Of these, interestingly, self-confidence rates very high on the list.[37]

Paul marked a departure from this type of thinking when he assessed the character of a person because his concept of character was not defined in human terms, such as personal traits or relationship skills, but entirely in relation to God and resurrection. For example, for Paul, self-control—a valued virtue in the Greco-Roman world—was not some superior nature with which one was born, nor was it a disposition carefully cultivated; it was a *gift* from God given through the Holy Spirit. So he wrote: "The fruit of the Spirit is love, joy, peace…self-control [*egkrateia*]" (Gal. 5:22–23). In other words, these are not leadership traits one is born with or that one acquires by receiving training according to established stereotypes but a direct result of God's new creation. Therefore, for example, if Paul was confident, it was not self-confidence that he had, but God-confidence, not self-control, but rather, the control of God. While we need to cultivate the gifts that God has given us, it is a mistake to think that one "works on" one's traits, such as love, joy, and peace, to become a leader. Paul taught that humans lacked power to produce the attributes described in Galatians 5:22–23. They were given by the Spirit.

This view of human character had a rather dramatic effect on Paul's self-understanding of himself as a leader and caused him to depreciate himself in ways that were unprecedented in Greco-Roman literature. For example, he wrote: "Christ Jesus came into the world to save sinners—of whom I am the worst" (1 Tim. 1:15, NIV). Or "I am the least of the apostles, unfit to be called an apostle" (1 Cor. 15:9, RSV). Paul might be judged as displaying traits that are antonyms to those Bass assigns to leaders."[38] But the reason for Paul's behavior was not that he had a problem with confidence or false modesty. Rather, Paul spoke the way he did about his leadership because he measured his character against the yardstick of the image of Christ, and he found himself falling short.

Christ was the source of strength for Paul. Paul considered the strength of Christ and his own strength to be mutually exclusive. And so he wrote: "I will boast all the more gladly about my weaknesses, so that Christ's power may rest on me" (1 Cor. 12:9, NIV). As he became successful and as his apostolic work advanced, he wanted his sense of sinfulness and inadequacy to intensify so that

Christ would be magnified. Thus Paul wrote, "When I am weak, then am I strong" (2 Cor. 12:10, KJV). Now this preoccupation of Paul with weakness and lack of self-confidence finds no parallel in Greco-Roman literature. For example, Cicero wrote: "Confidence is the quality by which in important and honorable undertakings the spirit has *placed great trust in itself* with a resolute hope of success."[39] This preoccupation with confidence is true even in our contemporary context. Helen Doohan speaks for many Christian leadership experts when she writes: "leaders tend to be persons who emanate *confidence* and *self-assurance*."[40] In stark contrast, Paul placed his trust entirely in Christ and wrote: "I can do all things through him who strengthens me" (Phil. 4:13), meaning that he could not do anything on his own, something neither a Greco-Roman nor a modern leader would say, except perhaps to feign false modesty. The Jewish philosopher Martin Buber aptly notes: "It is 'against nature' that in one way or another the [biblical] leaders are mostly the weak and humble. The way in which they carry out their leadership is 'against history'…when [the Bible] announces a successful deed, it is duty bound to announce with utmost detail the failure involved in the success."[41] Yet the self-deprecating words of Paul were more than a gesture of humility. They were verbal imitations of Christ who "emptied himself" on the cross, humiliating Himself in the form of a servant (cf. Phil. 2:7). Paul sought weakness, and not confidence or self-assurance, because he ardently desired to conform to the weakness of Christ displayed on the Cross.[42] Paul's self-conceptions were, in the words of John M. G. Barclay, "moulded by the story of the crucified Christ."[43]

Weakness and brokenness, then, are typical of a Christian leader. And, as such, they also represent the softer, more vulnerable side of our human nature that enables us to connect with each other and erases the differences and barriers that stand between us. Even modern research seems to confirm the importance of such vulnerability in leadership, as Doohan eloquently notes: "Persons who understand and accept themselves, their needs and weaknesses tend to be more effective leaders and decision makers."[44] Still, the frequency with which Paul wrote of his woes and personal trials is unprecedented and surprising. In fact, it is something that no other New Testament writer attempted. For example, neither Peter nor James wrote much in their letters about their personal trials and weaknesses. In contrast, Paul repeatedly resorted to brutally honest and graphic portrayals of his character in order to crucify himself and drive home the point that, apart from Christ, he possessed no outstanding attributes. I agree with Brian Dodd that "Paul's letters display a diverse rather than uniform usage of self-portrayal."[45] Notwithstanding, Paul's use of constant and extreme self-depreciation as a leadership strategy is unique not only in the New Testament, but also in Greco-Roman literature.

CONCLUSION

Wilhelm Wrede called Paul "the second founder of Christianity."[46] Although we cannot accept such an overstatement about Paul's work, since Christ—Paul would protest—is the foundation of Christianity, it still testifies to the extraordinarily creative nature of Paul's leadership.

But, as an example of leadership, Paul is not one that modern students of leadership easily understand or follow because his style of leadership is seemingly counterintuitive and impractical. As we saw, Paul rejected advantages. He also relied on the Holy Spirit to perform leadership functions for him while he was planting churches elsewhere far away, often never to return again to the churches he planted. Paul was a leader in *absentia,* for the most part. He often allowed his spiritual gifts, his apostolic calling, to trump his job descriptions, the community's immediate needs and expectations, while parading his weaknesses in defense of his leadership. In most modern contexts such a leadership style would be considered inappropriate, if not outright offensive. Thus, for example, judging Paul from modern theories of leadership, Doohan unjustly censures Paul as follows: "He is sometimes too attached to his success and loses perspective in his response."[47]

For the purposes of this essay, we replaced the words *apostle* and *apostleship* with *leader* and *leadership* in order to discuss his leadership *attributes* apart from his authoritarian *style* of leadership. But, even if "the Bible makes no demands regarding *styles* of leadership,"[48] it would not be appropriate to further divest Paul of his unique style of leadership. For it was intentionally chosen to imitate the Cross, the symbol of rejection, shame, and loss—or, as Paul calls it, "a scandal" and "an offense." It was this unique, if offensive, style of leadership that made him what he was—a unique and powerful leader, indeed the Apostle of the Gentiles. Without his cruciform "style" of leadership, Paul would have been no more than an emaciated version of a Greco-Roman "virtuous man" who had courage, confidence, self-control, temperance, liberality, and so on. The truth is that even though Paul's cruciform leadership style may appear impractical to the sensibilities of modern leaders, it is the only way to bring life to this world. His aim was to bring love, joy, peace, and freedom to people who were without hope, so that they could live again and be restored to the image of Christ. For this goal, Paul could not have chosen a better style of leadership, one that leaders—such as Mohandas Gandhi and Martin Luther King, Jr.—have resorted to time and again to effect dramatic changes in human history.

But for such a lofty aim, Paul had to let God do the work. Again, this does not mean that Paul was lazy or encouraged irresponsibility. To the contrary, he worked very hard: travelling, teaching, working individually with small groups, and writing. But these activities alone could not explain Paul's leadership. Rather, the secret of his leadership lay in his unswerving trust in God who gave "the growth" (1 Cor. 3:6), a conviction that drove him to "boast in his weaknesses" (2 Cor. 11:30; 12:9) until he was reduced to nothing and forced to cry out in panic, "O wretched man that I am" (Rom. 7:24, KJV). For he knew that, only in such a state of weakness would the glory of God fill his life and the gospel would have the power to penetrate the world.

Paul understood his leadership in the same way he understood his doctrine of justification by faith, according to which one is justified by faith apart from any human effort. Paul applied this same principle to his leadership, fully convinced that God's power would be made manifest in his life to the degree that he was able to reduce himself to nothing. So Paul refused to give credit to any human effort for his success, just as he refused to give credit to any works of the law for justification. It was this refusal that led him to pen the following words: "So neither the one who plants nor the one who waters is *anything,* but *only God* who gives the growth" (1 Cor. 3:7, emphasis added). Paul wanted God to eclipse his ministry, fully and visibly, so that all could see that it was absolutely God, and no one else, who was doing the work.

It was Paul's vision of what the church could be that drove him to make these difficult and counterintuitive decisions. The church existed for one purpose: to impart life to the world. Everything else was peripheral. Assets such as universities, hospitals, and comfortable places of worship support mission. But Paul's leadership was not primarily concerned about these things because he was convinced that this world needed Christ, who alone could give life, joy, and peace to its dying denizens.

Unfortunately, these ideals of Paul often collide with our modern concept of training that bears more than a passing resemblance to Greek *paideia,* which devoted its time and energy to equipping students with skills and knowledge through training. I am not opposed to providing curriculum-based, rigorous training in biblical studies, theological interpretation, and practical ministry. But the values that marked Paul's leadership, such as rejecting advantages and relying solely on the Holy Spirit for leadership, must be front and center in our theological training. Our training methods tend to become focused on the human side of education—skills and methods. So even when it comes to the question of how to stimulate spiritual growth in our students, we tend to fall back on the standard method of providing core skills and concepts. In the words of Doug Bookman, "[This] world is addicted to methods,"[49] so that, even when we study "biblical leadership," we become preoccupied with the methods of leadership used by biblical characters. But, if we listen to Paul, no amount of skills, methods, or training can qualify one to become an effective Christian leader because the most important job of a Christian leader is to impart eternal life and to restore the image of Christ in fallen human beings—which only the life-giving power of God can accomplish.

FOR REFLECTION

Personal:

1. Do I relate to others as a fellow disciple? An authoritarian leader? An apostle? Why am I relating that way?
2. Am I placing myself in submission to the Holy Spirit as I go about my life? How?

Organizational:

1. Are disciples of Christ living in the world as ambassadors for Jesus, or have we come to depend on institutional programs to spread the gospel? How can we foster the right tension between the two?
2. Are denominational organizations expressing patient and confident trust in God? In what ways? How is trust in God evidenced in a Christian organization?

ENDNOTES

1. Walter C. Wright, *Relational Leadership: A Biblical Model for Leadership Service* (Exeter, UK: Paternoster, 2002), 2. It should be noted that Wright's concepts are heavily borrowed from contemporary business theories, and they are read into the Bible.

2. Kenneth O. Gangel, *Team Leadership in Christian Ministry* (Chicago: Moody Press, 1997), 58–59; see also Robert Greenleaf, *Servant Leadership* (New York: Paulist Press, 1977); for a history and critique of the concept of *servant leadership,* see Michael Cooper, "The Transformational Leadership of the Apostle Paul: A Contextual and Biblical Leadership for Contemporary Ministry," *Christian Education Journal,* 3rd series, vol. 2, no. 1 (2005): 49–50.

3. Different versions of English translations of the Bible will be cited throughout the essay to reflect the wording that, in the opinion of the author, best represents the intent of the original language.

4. Kenneth L. Faught, "An Investigation of Selected Models of Group Leadership in the New Testament with Implications for Pastoral Leadership and Counseling" (Ed.D. diss., New Orleans Baptist Theological Seminary, 1977), 139; emphasis added.

5. Faught, "Selected Models of Group Leadership," 59; emphasis added.

6. For a comprehensive overview of Paul's theology, see James D. G. Dunn, *The Theology of Paul the Apostle* (Grand Rapids, MI: Eerdmans, 1998); and Herman Ridderbos, *Paul: An Outline of His Theology,* trans. John R. De Witt (Grand Rapids, MI: Eerdmans, 1975).

7. For example, D. A. Carson, Peter T. O'Brien, and Mark A. Seifrid, *Justification and Variegated Nomism,* vol. 1, *The Complexities of Second Temple Judaism* (Tübingen, Germany: Mohr Siebeck, 2001); idem, *Justification and Variegated Nomism,* vol. 2, *The Paradoxes of Paul* (Tübingen, Germany: Mohr Siebeck, 2004).

8. For example, Philip F. Esler, *Conflict and Identity in Romans: The Social Setting of Paul's Letter* (Minneapolis: Fortress, 2003).

9. See Seyoon Kim, *The Origin of Paul's Gospel* (Grand Rapids, MI: Eerdmans, 1982); Kim rightly notes: "Paul's gospel and apostleship [i.e., leadership] are grounded solely in the Christophany on the Damascus road. The Damascus event is the basis of both his theology and his existence as an apostle [i.e., a leader]," 332.

10. Galatians 4:19, NRSV, emphasis added.

11. Paul refers to the following as the source of power: resurrection (Rom. 1:4; 1 Cor. 6:14; 15:13; 2 Cor. 13:4; Phil. 3:10, 21; 2 Thess. 1:11); the message of the gospel (Rom. 1:16); God's power to create (Rom. 1:20); God's actions (Rom. 9:17, 22); God (1 Cor. 2:5; 2 Cor. 4:7; 6:7; 10:4; 12:9; 13:4; Eph. 1:19; 3:7, 30); the Holy Spirit (Rom. 15:13, 19; 1 Cor. 2:4; 1 Thess. 1:5); the Cross (1 Cor. 1:17); the preaching of the cross (1:17); Christ (1 Cor. 1:24). Paul claims the following powers: to condemn and excommunicate sinners (1 Cor. 5:4), to interpret tongues (1 Cor. 14:13), to comprehend the love of God (Eph. 3:18), and to share in the suffering of Christ (2 Tim. 1:8).

12. Compare with John Dominic Crossan, *The Historical Jesus: The Life of a Mediterranean Jewish Peasant* (New York: HarperSan Francisco, 1991), 45–46. Although it is disputable whether Jesus would have been classed as a peasant by the Romans, one gets the picture of how the Roman society was structured.

13. Aristotle, *Politica* 1253[a] 1.

14. Helen Doohan, *Leadership in Paul* (Wilmington, DE: Glazier, 1984), 117; emphasis in original.

15. Peter Koestenbaum, *The Heart of Business: Ethics, Power and Philosophy* (San Francisco: Saybrook Publishing Company, 1987), especially 241–260; emphasis added.

16. Romans 12:11 ("aglow with zeal in the Spirit"—my translation [τῷ πνεύματι ζέοντες]); 1 Thessalonians 5:19 ("quench not the Spirit"—KJV).

17. Colossians 1:7; 4:12; Philemon 1:23. Walter Rebell, *Gehorsam und Unabhängigkeit: Eine sozialpsychologische Studie zu Paulus* (Munich: Chr. Kaiser Verlag, 1986), 75, lists Barnabas, Silas, Timothy, Titus, Aquila and Prisca, and Apollos as Paul's coworkers (*Mitarbeiter*). But Rebell recognizes that some of these are Paul's colleagues rather than his envoys and that "we unfortunately know precious little about these coworkers," 76 (my translation of *"leider ist unser Wissen über die Mitarbeiter nur sehr gering"*).

18. Kenneth O. Gangel, *Competent to Lead* (Chicago: Moody Press, 1974), 17, emphasis added.

19. For a more complete list of topics addressed by the Greek *paideia,* see Richard McKeon, ed., *The Basic Works of Aristotle,* intro. C. D. C. Reeve (New York: The Modern Library, 2001); cf. Abraham J. Malherbe, "Soziale Ebene und literarische Bildung," in *Zur Soziologie des Urchristentums: Ausgew. Beiträge zum frühchristlichen Gemeinschaftsleben in seiner gesellschaftlichen Umwelt,* ed. Wayne A. Meeks (Munich: Chr. Kaiser Verlag, 1979), 207.

20. For an excellent but succinct discussion on the various spiritual gifts from an exegetical standpoint, see Anthony C. Thiselton, *First Corinthians: A Shorter Exegetical and Pastoral Commentary* (Grand Rapids, MI: Eerdmans, 2006), 196–216; for a more practical approach, see Peter C. Wagner, *Your Spiritual Gifts Can Help Your Church Grow* (Glendale, CA: Regal Books Division, G/L Publications, 1979); Ronald E. Baxter, *Gifts of the Spirit* (Grand Rapids, MI: Kregel, 1983); Kenneth Berding, *What Are the Spiritual Gifts: Rethinking the Conventional View* (Grand Rapids, MI: Kregel, 2006); Leslie B. Flynn, *19 Gifts of the Spirit* (Wheaton, IL: Victor Books, 1986); and Robert J. Hillman, *27 Spiritual Gifts* (Melbourne, Australia: Joint Board of Christian Education, 1986).

21. See Ernest Best, *A Critical and Exegetical Commentary on Ephesians,* International Critical Commentary, ed. J. A. Emerton, L. E. B. Cranfield, and G. N. Stanton (Edinburgh: T & T Clark, 1998), 388.

22. Thiselton, *First Corinthians,* 197.

23. For an exegetical discussion of these gifts, see Best, *Commentary on Ephesians,* 389–395.

24. Compare with Baxter, *Gifts of the Spirit,* 207–228; but see also Best, *Commentary on Ephesians,* 391–392, who seems to equate these leaders with those mentioned in Ephesians 4:12.

25. Berding, *Spiritual Gifts,* 100.

26. For example, Flynn, *19 Gifts,* 17–19.

27. Faught, "Selected Models of Group Leadership," 30.

28. Koestenbaum, *Heart of Business,* 250.

29. Flynn, *19 Gifts,* 32–35, divides up the gifts basically into two categories: speaking and serving. I prefer to speak of *application* rather than *serving* because speaking is also done to serve the community's needs. The so-called service types of gifts represent the activities of saints that apply and exemplify (see above under "reconciliation") the message of the gospel.

30. See Aristotle, *Politica* 1277^a 14–32, trans. Benjamin Jowett, Modern Library Classics (MLC) (New York: Random House, 1941), especially 1277^a 20: "the virtue of a good ruler is the same as that of a good man."

31. Aristotle, *Politica* 1277^a 15–20; 3.1288^a 8–9: "a people who are by nature capable of producing a race superior in the virtue needed for political rule are fitted for kingly government."

32. Aristotle, *Nichomachean Ethics* 7.1146^a 9–12, trans. W. D. Ross (MLC) (London: Oxford University Press, 1966); emphasis added.

33. Aristotle (384–322 BC); Cicero (106–43 BC).

34. Cicero, *De Inventione*, Loeb Classical Library (LCL), 2.164.

35. See table 4 in Ralph M. Stogdill, *Handbook of Leadership: A Survey of Theory and Research* (New York: The Free Press, 1974), 75; for a detailed discussion and further evaluation of these *topoi* in the light of recent research on leadership, see Bernard M. Bass and Ralph M. Stogdill, *Bass & Stogdill's Handbook of Leadership* (New York: The Free Press, 1990), 78–221. Bass significantly modifies the format of Stogdill's original discussion and defines leadership in terms of transformational versus transactional styles and skills, on the one hand, and charismatic versus inspirational styles and skills, on the other. But Bass actually steers the discussion back to the "traits" approach, away from Stogdill's "situationalist" approach; furthermore, according to Bass, many major corporations rely on standardized tests to evaluate a person's aptitude for leadership and these tests utilize standard leadership skills and traits—in other words, modern *topoi* of virtues, 86–87.

36. Stogdill, *Handbook of Leadership*, 82.

37. See Bass and Stogdill, *Handbook of Leadership*, 220; cf. table 5.1, p. 80. To compare modern *topoi* with their Greco-Roman counterpart, see Aristotle, *Nicomachean Ethics* 3.1109[a 30]–7.1154[b] 33.

38. Bass, 78–221.

39. *Inventione* (LCL), 2.163, emphasis added.

40. Doohan, *Leadership in Paul*, 16, emphasis added.

41. Martin Buber, *Mamre: Essays in Religion,* trans. Greta Hort (Westport, CT: Greenwood, 1970), 50–51. In this light it should be noted that Paul's autobiographical description of his weaknesses and failures stands in the tradition of Psalms, especially of David, and the prophets, especially Jeremiah.

42. Eve-Marie Becker and Peter Pilhofer, *Biographie und Persönlichkeit des Paulus* (WUNT; Tübingen, Germany: Mohr Siebeck, 2005), 94–103, rightly note that Paul restricts his use of his personal stories to apologetic passages in which he defends his apostleship. Still, it is unlikely that Paul tried to defend his apostleship by soliciting pity from his readers, as such legal strategies were frowned upon by Greco-Roman rhetoricians. Cicero, *De Inventione* 1.109 [LCL], speaks for many when he quotes Apollonius's ridicule: *lacrima nihil citius arescit* ("nothing dries faster than tears," author's translation). Rather, Paul's intent in divulging his weaknesses was to crucify himself before the readers in imitation of Christ.

43. John M. G. Barclay, "Paul's Story: Theology as Testimony," in *Narrative Dynamics in Paul: A Critical Assessment,* ed. Bruce W. Longenecker (Louisville, KY: Westminster John Knox Press, 2002), 146; also 153, 155. But Barclay overstates his case when he writes that "Paul's own story is of ultimate significance," 155 because, by telling his own story, Paul tried to demonstrate life what the humbling effect of the cross looks like for Christian leadership.

44. Doohan, *Leadership in Paul*, 16; unfortunately, she does not develop this important idea in her book. And, although she mentions weakness as an important aspect of Paul's ministry numerous times (cf. 77, 104, and 110, 169) throughout

the book, she fails to apply the concept of weakness to Paul's leadership in a sustained manner—in passing, she merely links Paul's weakness to his "sincerity," 113. Her conclusion never once mentions the words *cross* or *weakness*.

45. See Brian Dodd, *Paul's Paradigmatic "I"; Personal Example as Literary Strategy,* JSNT Supplement 177 (Sheffield, UK: Sheffield Academic Press, 1999), 237, *et passim* for his insightful arguments on Paul's use of "self" in his letters.

46. W. Wrede, *Paul,* trans. Edward Lummis, pref. J. Estlin Campenter (Lexington, KY: American Theological Library Association Committee on Printing, 1962), 179.

47. Doohan, *Leadership in Paul,* 164.

48. Doug Bookman, "Biblical Leadership: Yieldedness—Not Style," *Fundamentalist Journal* 7.1 (January 1988): 19; emphasis in original.

49. Bookman, "Biblical Leadership," 20.

11 | The General Epistles

Thomas R. Shepherd

The theology of leadership found in the General Epistles is articulated in several ways. The first is through direct theological statements made by the authors about leadership, discipleship, power, and authority and the implications for Christian action that these entail. Second, since a theology of leadership always has linkages to other theological themes, the way in which the authors describe these other themes provides a context for their theology of leadership. Finally, the way in which an author describes his own experience and the way in which he leads the church by means of his writing display his theology of leadership. This series of three approaches for describing the theology of leadership in the General Epistles moves from the explicit to the implicit. When considered together, the descriptions provide a clearer understanding of the theology. To set the stage, brief introductory information for the seven books (four church settings) that form the General Epistles corpus will be presented.

INTRODUCTION

Except for 3 John addressed to Gaius, the seven General Epistles—James, 1–2 Peter, 1–3 John, and Jude—are unique letters in the New Testament due to their lack of linkage with individuals or individual congregations. Each of these letters does contain reference to the recipients, but the list is generally broad in nature and, in some cases, rather vague. James is addressed to "the Twelve Tribes in the Diaspora," 1 Peter to "the elect strangers in Pontus, Galatia, Cappadocia, Asia, and Bithynia," 2 Peter to "those who have obtained a faith of equal value to ours." First John's recipients are addressed simply as "you." Second John is written to "the elect lady and her children," and Jude is addressed to "those who are called." It is not surprising then that they are called General Epistles.

Each of the four authors writes to people facing particular problems. James addresses issues of disunity or inequality and matters of church function. Peter helps the people he addresses face persecution from without and false doctrines from within. John seems to speak to a church or churches that have just split and writes to bring healing to the members who stayed. Jude, like 2 Peter, addresses false teachings and brings warning while articulating protection to people under attack. These seven books contain a total of only twenty-one chapters, but they deal with varied problems in a variety of circumstances, addressed by authors with different gifts to diverse audiences. As such, they provide a unique window into Christian life and leadership in the first century with multiple lessons for us today. We begin then by looking at passages in these seven Epistles that are generally recognized as dealing with issues of leadership.

LEADERSHIP PASSAGES IN THE GENERAL EPISTLES

Though other passages could be included, five passages in the General Epistles can easily be described as dealing with issues of positional leadership in the culture of the time—James 2:1–7; 1 Peter 1:10–12; 3:7; 5:1–4, and 3 John 9–10. In each of these passages someone or a group of people uses a position to either help or hinder others around them. As we note each passage we will observe practices that the apostles affirm. These practices provide perspectives on important leadership principles.

James 2:1–7: Partiality to the Rich

> My brothers, show no partiality as you hold the faith in our Lord Jesus Christ, the Lord of glory. For if a man wearing a gold ring and fine clothing comes into your assembly, and a poor man in shabby clothing also comes in, and if you pay attention to the one who wears the fine clothing and say, "You sit here in a good place," while you say to the poor man, "You stand over there," or, "Sit down at my feet," have you not then made distinctions among yourselves and become judges with evil thoughts? Listen, my beloved brothers, has not God chosen those who are poor in the world to be rich in faith and heirs of the kingdom, which he has promised to those who love him? But you have dishonored the poor man. Are not the rich the ones who oppress you, and the ones who drag you into court? Are they not the ones who blaspheme the honorable name by which you were called?[1]

In this passage James presents his message about believers and, presumably, leaders showing partiality toward rich people who enter the congregation. Beginning the passage with his thesis that partiality is incompatible with the faith centered in Jesus Christ, the Lord of glory, James proceeds to argue his case via a vivid depiction of the bias taking visible form ("sit here in a good place," "stand there," "sit at my feet"). He indicts this bias as judging others and having an evil heart, contrasts it with the love of God for the poor, and concludes with two piercing rhetorical questions about rich people who oppress Christians and slander Jesus's name. This argumentation revolves around the concepts of honor and shame—core values in Greco-Roman society of the first century. The Christian community is showing honor to people who "show well" in public instead of respecting the person of real glory, Jesus Christ.[2] By contrast, James contends that God honors the shamed of earth, while the great ones on earth dishonor the Christians. This sets up a sharp moral tension in the discourse that can be resolved only by the leaders acceding to James's instruction. Thus partiality is unacceptable in the Christian community because of the countercultural, even topsy-turvy, values that arise from understanding who Jesus is and what God is doing in the world.

1 Peter 1:10–12: The Old Testament Prophets

> Concerning this salvation, the prophets who prophesied about the grace that was to be yours searched and inquired carefully, inquiring what person or time the Spirit of Christ in them was indicating when he predicted the sufferings of Christ and the subsequent glories. It was revealed to them that they were serving not themselves but you, in the things that have now been announced to you through those who preached the good news to you by the Holy Spirit sent from heaven, things into which angels long to look.

Before this point in 1 Peter 1, the apostle has set forth the great privilege of his readers in being brought into covenant relationship with God. Peter carries them through an amazing recital of how God has settled their *past* by His forgiveness and their rebirth experience, has secured their *future* redemption that will come to fruition at the return of our Lord, and thereby has made their *present* sufferings bearable. The apostle then continues by describing in verses 10–12 how the Old Testament prophecies pointed to the same outcome.

He describes the content of the prophecies, but he actually spends more time talking about the prophets who received them. He uses three terms to refer to their efforts at understanding the prophecies they received—"searched for," "inquired carefully," and "searched." Like good newspaper reporters, the prophets wanted to know the "who/what" and "when" of these prophecies. The "who" is Jesus, but the "when" is probably different from what the prophets expected, for the time of fulfillment was not to be in their time but in the time of the people receiving 1 Peter.[3]

Then the prophets received another revelation. This time it was not about the future but about the purpose of their work. It was revealed to them that they were not serving themselves but rather the recipients of 1 Peter. This is the key point about leadership in the passage. Christian ministry is not about self-aggrandizement or self-satisfaction for receiving or understanding a personal revelation. While revelation is attractive in itself and draws out intense inquiry, Peter teaches that its focus has to be outward, serving the needs of those who have not heard the good news and who need the affirmation that what the evangelists bring is indeed the message of salvation.

1 Peter 3:7: Husbands as Companions

"Likewise, husbands, live with your wives in an understanding way, showing honor to the woman as the weaker vessel, since they are heirs with you of the grace of life, so that your prayers may not be hindered." This verse is the conclusion of a section dealing with household relationships and even relationships to the wider community (2:13–3:7). It is not uncommon in modern discussions of the passage to dismiss its focus on hierarchy and submission as hopelessly outdated chauvinism from an ancient system of patriarchy.[4] That the ancient world held deep-seated patriarchal concepts of human relationships is without doubt. It is beyond the scope of the present work to critique that cultural characteristic in any detail. However, what we notice here in 1 Peter 3:7 is the way in which the apostle modifies this sense of male hegemony.

Peter begins his brief instruction to Christian husbands with a command.[5] They are to live with their wives in an understanding manner. The English does not quite catch the flavor of the Greek, which utilizes two compound words in verse 7 with the same preposition as the prefix: *syn* = "together with," *synoikeō* = "to dwell together with," and *sygklēronomos* = "inheriting together with."[6] The point Peter makes with his initial command is that the husbands are to dwell *together with* their wives. The command implies a sense of mutuality.

The dwelling together with the wife is to be done "in accordance with knowledge." That is to say, the mutuality of dwelling in harmony depends on the husband knowing something. What he is to understand is found in the phrase "as with the weaker feminine vessel." This phrase likely strikes the modern reader as demeaning to women in two ways. First is the concept of the feminine as weaker. In the ancient world, women were considered inferior to men physically, mentally and morally.[7] Peter, however, seems to have in view only the biological characteristic of women being physically less strong than men since he will go on to vouch that women are joint heirs with men of the grace of life.

The second way the phrase offends is by using the term "vessel," suggesting to many that women were considered chattel. But this is to misunderstand the term. While it can refer to furniture or property (cf. Matt. 12:29; Mark 3:27; Luke 8:16), in reference to people it denotes the body and is used of both men and women without pejorative connotation (cf. Acts 9:15, Paul as chosen vessel).[8] Peter's point is that harmonious home life depends upon a recognition of a difference in muscular strength between men and women and, consequently, suggests a protective role for the husband. He is not to use his strength for inappropriate purposes but rather for protection.

The next part of the verse calls for recognition not of weakness but of strength. The husbands are commanded to pay honor to their wives as joint heirs of the grace of life. As the first part of the verse involves dwelling *together with* their wives according to knowledge, so the second part of the verse involves a recognition that the husbands inherit eternal life *together with* their wives. The first is about dwelling in harmony in this world, the second is about our inheritance in the world to come.

Peter concludes his admonition to husbands with a warning. If husbands fail to dwell together in harmony or fail to honor their wives as joint heirs of life, the result is that their prayers are hindered or thwarted. This may seem like a small matter to some, but not to Peter. Prayer is the connection of the Christian to God and His will. A hindered or thwarted prayer indicates being out of step with the divine will. Thus Peter places the husband's mutual relationship to his wife on the moral level of the will of God. The implications for Christian leadership from this one verse are profound: First, proper use of power is a matter of being in tune with the will of God. All power derives from God and those who have it and use it are responsible to Him. Second, the will of God involves using power to protect and to honor others.

1 Peter 5:1–4: Shepherding the Flock

> So I exhort the elders among you, as a fellow elder and a witness
> of the sufferings of Christ, as well as a partaker in the glory that
> is going to be revealed: shepherd the flock of God that is among
> you, exercising oversight, not under compulsion, but willingly, as
> God would have you; not for shameful gain, but eagerly; not
> domineering over those in your charge, but being examples to the
> flock. And when the chief Shepherd appears, you will receive the
> unfading crown of glory.

Of the three passages from 1 Peter on leadership included in
this study, this is the clearest example. We can only briefly note the
apostle's instruction. Peter addresses the elders by identifying himself as a "fellow elder." It is the only use of the term *sympresbuteros,*
fellow elder, in the New Testament. Peter chooses not to use the
term *apostle* for himself but rather links himself *together with* the
elders he addresses. Like the words to husbands, he uses a word with
the *syn*: "together with" prefix.[9]

Peter next refers to two opposite roles he has, namely, witness
of the sufferings of Christ and partner[10] in the glory to be revealed.
This is not the first time in the letter that these themes of suffering
and glory have been united (1:6–7; 3:17–22; 4:12–13).[11] In each
case the suffering is a present earthly reality and the glory is an
eschatological one. It is a paradox of the Christian life: suffering
now but glory in the future. Peter will describe Christian leadership
in this context. In fact, in two steps he will illustrate what the elder
will do and suffer for now (5:2–3) and what the result in glory will
be later (5:4).

In a set of three antitheses Peter outlines honorable and dishonorable leadership. He places these antitheses within the context of a pastoral metaphor—"tend the flock of God which is
among you, giving oversight" (1 Pet. 5:2). Peter's use of this metaphor harks back to his own experience of denying Christ three
times and being confronted by Jesus's cutting threefold question,
"Do you love me?" (John 21:15–19). In restoring Peter to apostleship, Jesus used the very same metaphor—tending the flock,
feeding the lambs.

The set of three antitheses are most easily observed in table form.

Antitheses of Ministry

Dishonorable Leadership	Honorable Leadership
Under Compulsion	Willingly with Reference to God
In Fondness of Dishonest Gain	Eagerly, Freely
Domineering	Examples for the Flock

The antitheses are written mainly in an adverbial form modifying both the verb "shepherd" at the beginning of verse 2 and the participle "taking care of, overseeing" that comes just before the adverbial forms. The participle comes from the verb *episkopeō:* "to care for, look at, oversee." It has related forms (adjective and noun) that suggest the idea of visitation and a person who watches out for others—in this sense an overseer or superintendent. The noun form becomes the word that refers to the pastor or bishop of a church.

The adverbs on the dishonorable side of the table carry with them the sense of personal gain and domination. The first is interesting in that it suggests a situation in which a person was reluctant to take on the role of overseer. In the setting of persecution that Peter describes in 1 Peter, it is fair to assume that this reluctance would be based on fear of personal persecution or loss.[12] The second adverb in this list deals with personal desire for dishonest gain. It is as though the individual who did not want to enter leadership was pressured to do so and, to compensate for the personal pressure and risk involved, proceeded to chase dishonest gain. This desire for personal gain then finds its final form in power used to "lord it over" the flock (*katakyrieuō:* "to lord it over, rule, domineer"). Of course, any one of the three dishonorable traits could be present in any leader and would disqualify that person from leadership.

The adverbs on the honorable side of the table display a completely different quality. They are all other-centered—focused on ministry and forgetful of personal advantage. What seems to be the genius of this approach to leadership are two words in the first adverbial antithesis—*kata theon.* This literally means "according to God" or "with reference to God." It plays into a wider theme in 1 Peter dealing with the word "conscience" (*syneidēsis:* "conscience, consciousness";

1 Pet. 2:19; 3:16, 21). We normally think of conscience as an internal moral compass that tells right from wrong. But in the ancient world the moral compass was not so much seen as internal but as a consciousness of the values of your primary reference group.[13] The people to whom Peter is writing have shifted allegiance from the pagan world and its set of values to God and His value system.

Thus Christian life is a reorientation toward the will of God. Christian leadership is the same. The reference point of ministry is God and what He has done in graciously blessing us with salvation and hope (cf. 1:3–9). Christian leaders must willingly and freely serve without thought of personal gain or reference to regrets over sacrifices made. Leaders must be examples of self-sacrifice before the people they serve rather than masters who seek to dominate people within their sphere of influence. Put in mnemonic format for a homily, Christian leadership arises not from the push of people but the pull of God, not for the money but the mission, not to be a master but a mentor.

Peter concludes this passage with a return to the concept of glory. In verse 4 he reminds the leaders of their subordinate role to Jesus Christ, the *Chief Shepherd*. What is promised the leader who sacrifices for God now is the unfading crown of glory in the future. Some may find this emphasis on reward disturbing. But it has a striking parallel to Peter's question and Jesus's response in Matthew 19:27–30. When Peter says, "Behold, we have left all and followed you. What then will there be for us?" Jesus responds with a concrete recital of rewards for the faithful servant—thrones, one hundred–fold returns on lost relatives, homes and fields. This is not something earned in either Matthew or 1 Peter. Rather, it is God taking care of His faithful servants. They have lost all for Him here, so He provides all for them there. It is the assurance and action of grace from beginning to end.

3 JOHN 9–10: LEADERSHIP GONE WRONG

> I have written something to the church, but Diotrephes, who likes to put himself first, does not acknowledge our authority. So if I come, I will bring up what he is doing, talking wicked nonsense against us. And not content with that, he refuses to welcome

the brothers, and also stops those who want to and puts them out of the church.

The book 3 John is the shortest in the New Testament, a mere fifteen verses. Thus it is interesting that its focus is to contrast true and false ministry. Verses 9–10 are the expression of the false. The rest of the book concentrates on the true. The form of leadership expressed in Diotrephes's actions recalls the list of dishonorable leadership traits in 1 Peter 5, principally the domineering of one person over the flock. Diotrephes illustrates this problem in four ways. First, he likes to put himself first. Second, he does not acknowledge the authority of John and speaks against him. Third, he refuses to welcome a group called "the brothers" (probably itinerant Christian missionaries), and, fourth, he stops people who do so and expels them from the church.

John contrasts this sad set of actions with the principles of love and walking in the truth—two concepts that run throughout the three Epistles of the apostle. We will note below how these deep principles pervade John's theology, but we can close this section by summarizing what we have seen in the five passages. Based on who Jesus is and what God is doing in the world, James teaches an uncompromising equality and rejects partiality. Peter teaches that God's gifts are given for service to others. Proper use of power is about being conscious of, and sensitive to, the will of God. His will is plain: Power is to be used to honor and protect others. Ministry is not for self-aggrandizement but service, not for personal gain but willing self-sacrifice, not to be in charge but to be an example to others. John adds to these profound principles an emphasis on truth and love that mold ministry into gracious care and warm welcome for those seeking to spread the gospel in the world.

LEADERSHIP THEMES IN THE GENERAL EPISTLES

So far we have looked at passages in only three of the seven General Epistles. To broaden the perspective on the concepts of leadership in these writings, we will briefly summarize some major themes of the Epistles that relate to the question of leadership.

Themes in James

We have already noted a concept of equality in our discussion of James 2:1–7. This concept of fair and equal treatment runs throughout the letter. James particularly speaks up for the poor, not out of a sense that the rich are somehow evil because they are rich but rather out of a strong conviction that God treats all people impartially and wants us to do the same. God is the Judge and Lawgiver over all humanity. In light of this, people are to demonstrate humility before God and to show acts of charity and kindness toward others. Mere words are hollow. A person is a unity, and faith must show itself in acts of true compassion. The world and sin stand in sharp contrast with the principles of true religion. One cannot serve God and the world.

At the heart of James's theology of leadership is his clear concept of God and His will. God stands far above humanity as the Judge, Lawgiver, and gracious Father of Lights. Leadership must take place within this theological landscape. All people are equal, so partiality must be rejected and equality and compassion must characterize all the Christian's actions—toward the poor, the sick, the sinner, and anyone entering the church.

Themes in 1–2 Peter and Jude

For Peter all leadership begins with God. God the Father, Son, and Holy Spirit are active in a web of interaction, using their power to save, give rebirth, bless, protect, reward, judge, and punish. As in James, God is the moral arbiter of the world. All people must answer to Him for their lives. Christians in this realm are distinct in their orientation toward God and toward the world. God has chosen them ("election") for covenant relationship with Him and given them new birth. That new birth changes their relationship to the surrounding world ("strangers"). They no longer fit in and that creates tensions that Peter takes great pains to resolve.

In striking ways, Peter illustrates that both slaves and wives could exemplify leadership for the community in their practice of submission. Leadership is not usually thought of in terms of submission, but Peter presents Jesus as leading the way in His submission to suffering and death, resulting in salvation for humanity.

The Christian slaves in that ancient setting who walked in the path of Jesus presented an example for others to follow. The Christian wives who submitted to their husbands became silent evangelists winning their spouses to the faith. These underlying demonstrations of leadership—following Jesus's example, and silently evangelizing—undercut the common supposition that individuals in ordinate roles are the only ones called to illustrate leadership within the Christian community. Those who submit also lead.

In 2 Peter and Jude the central issue is attacks on Christian communities by false teachers.[14] This calls forth the protective nature of both writers. Jude is the shorter book, and its rhetoric is focused on two themes: the evil nature of the false teachers, on the one hand, and the connection of the community of faith with God, on the other. The book 2 Peter is longer and expands this rhetoric to include answers to the objections raised by the false teachers regarding the Second Coming of Christ.

The language used to describe and counter the false teachers in these two books is quite strong. This passion may raise for some the specter of a domineering form of leadership. But the authors speak so strongly because they recognize the threat to the church. The danger of the false teachings has raised their protective character as leaders. We do not whisper and speak calmly when a loved one is walking near the edge of a precipice.

Themes in 1–3 John

The books of 1–3 John read quite differently from the other General Epistles. In contrast to the straightforward step-by-step style of James and 2 Peter, the tight rhetoric of Jude, or the carefully interwoven theology of 1 Peter, 1–3 John consist of simple language having words with a depth of meaning repeated over and over—words such as *truth, lie, love, hate, witness, fellowship, commandments, light,* and *darkness.* First John is notoriously difficult to outline. The themes are introduced and then seem to digress in a seamless movement toward other concepts but then reappear once again.

Even so, the theological emphases of the books come through quite clearly. In 1 John, five strong themes come up again and again—sharp contrasts of opposites, eternal life through connection with Christ, testing doctrinal statements, showing love toward God and others, and sin and righteousness. Within the development of these themes, leadership concepts revolve around the test of truth, the call to fellowship, and witness to the light. For John, leadership has a clear sense of *Imitatio Dei*—"We love because He first loved us" (1 John 4:19). Over and over "we," "us," "you," "our" appear, expressing the close sense of fellowship and community John has with the people to whom he is writing.

But this sense of community is not simply built on an idea of abstract love. Rather, the basis seems to reside in truth (the term *alētheia*, "truth," appears twenty times in 1–3 John), and certain truths in particular—the doctrine of Christ being central. One of the great evidences for this emphasis on doctrinal truth in 1–3 John is the clear sense of being inside or outside of John's community. The same apostle who says, "love one another" (1 John 4:7) also states, "They went out from us but were not from us" (1 John 2:19). He even avers shunning one who holds a different teaching of Christ (2 John 9–10).

Thus, the books of 1–3 John seem to have a theology of leadership deeply tied to concepts of love and truth. *Love* creates the community sense of we/us and enhances relational aspects of leadership. *Truth* creates the boundaries and center of the community and highlights limits beyond which leadership cannot go.

LEADERSHIP DISPLAYED IN THE GENERAL EPISTLES

People may say one thing about leadership but demonstrate another in the way they use power or position. We can only briefly discuss the way in which James, Peter, John, and Jude display their own style of leadership in what they write. All the writers hold in common a very clear sense of religious authority. Without it they would not have written their letters. This authoritative voice is always rooted in a crystal-clear sense of connection with God. None of the writers sees himself *as God,* but rather presents the message *of God* to people.

We noted above how James presents a well-defined ethic of equality. It is interesting to ponder if one with such a clear sense of authority can also display a sense of equality in leadership. But this is exactly what James does. While his commands are clear, James nonetheless consistently *argues* his case for his readers. He treats them as thoughtful moral agents who deserve an explanation of the truth.

In 1 Peter the apostle demonstrates leadership through interlocking theological ideas that draw the reader into a higher realm of living in the presence of God. It is the beauty of the theological ideas and the power of the Spirit—an inspirational leadership—that draws the reader away from living as pagans do. But in 2 Peter the leadership on display is much more protective and pastoral as he seeks to guard the flock against ravenous wolves, the false teachers. But even then, Peter displays a leadership that persuades and answers questions in chapter 3. It is not enough to just tell the church that the false teachers are wrong; they need to see why they are wrong.

John has a leadership style of fellowship, witness, and truth. The fellowship aspect is warm and inviting and has led some interpreters to emphasize this to the exclusion of other ideas. However, the apostle is quite clear that love and truth combine to create the sense of community and define its borders. Love without truth is saccharine. Truth without love has no sense of "we." As John touched, saw, and experienced the Word of Life, his own life was infused with the fellowship, truth, and love that created the community he protects.

Jude, like 2 Peter, presents a pastoral/protective style of leadership, building up the church members in the true doctrine and exposing the false teachers who prey on the flock. Jude presents colorful examples of failure (Sodom and Gomorrah, Cain, Balaam, Korah) as well as powerful examples of holiness (Enoch and Michael).

CONCLUSION

In these seven epistles, written by authors of varied backgrounds, confronting widely different situations, we meet crucial leadership principles that continue to speak to the church today. Equality, service, leadership in submission by following in the footsteps of Jesus, personal self-sacrifice for the good of others, a balance of protection and warning, unmasking error yet answering honest questions, remembering we are not God but rather are entrusted with His message to build a community, expressing love in practical ways while maintaining the purity of truth—these are the principles of leadership that continue to find expression in Christian lives molded and guided by the deep truths of the General Epistles.[15]

FOR REFLECTION

Personal:

1. How do you understand the roles of follower and leader to be fluid? How has your experience shaped that understanding? How would it be changed by biblical understandings?
2. In what ways has the culture shaped your judgments regarding equality?

Organizational:

1. Is the mission of your organization built around others or its own interests? In what ways? Do you see that changing?
2. In what ways is your organization a learning organization? Is it changing?

ENDNOTES

1. Scripture quotations in the block quotations are taken from the English Standard Version. In other Scripture quotations, word and phrase translations are my own.

2. The colorful Greek term is προσωπολημψία (*prosōpolēmpsia*), which means literally "receiving the face." It has its roots in a Hebrew idiom of the Old Testament regarding showing favoritism (cf. Lev. 19:15; Deut. 1:17; Ps. 82:2). See Peter Davids, *Commentary on James*, NIGTC (Grand Rapids, MI: Eerdmans, 1982), 105–106.

3. See John H. Elliott, *1 Peter*, AB vol. 37B (New York: Doubleday, 2000), 345–346.

4. See Elliott, *1 Peter*, 585–599 for a long discourse on the meaning of the passage 1 Peter 3:1–7 in relation to modern values. Elliott maintains the passage

does reflect female inferiority, which he rejects, but he moderates more sweeping denunciations of the passage by others.

5. "Dwell together" is actually a participle in Greek, as is "show honor." Both are likely used as commands in this passage, with the phrase following each being explanatory. See Elliott, *1 Peter*, 575–579.

6. In the word συγκληρονόμος (*sugklēronomos*), the συν- (*syn*) prefix has shifted to συγ- (*syg-*) because of the following κ (*k*). It is easier for the tongue to pronounce the *g* sound in front of the *k* than the *n* sound, thus the shift.

7. See Elliott, *1 Peter*, 576–578, for the horrific type of statements about women that ancient authors made. Plato, *Leg.* 6.781B: "The female nature, in humankind, is inferior in virtue to that of males." *Letter of Aristeas*, 250–251: "the female sex is bold, positively active for something it desires, easily liable to change its mind because of poor reasoning powers, and of naturally weak constitution."

8. See Elliott, *1 Peter*, 578.

9. In συμπρεσβύτερος (*sympresbuteros* = "fellow elder"), the συν- (*syn* = "together with") prefix changes to συμ- (*sum*) in front of the π (p) for the same reason noted in endnote 6: ease of pronunciation.

10. The Greek term I translate as "partner" here is κοινωνός, *koinōnos*. The English Standard Version translates it as "partaker." The root meaning of the term is to participate in or have fellowship together in some experience. Peter observed Jesus's sufferings but, by the grace of God, he will be able to *participate* in the glory to be revealed when Christ returns.

11. See Elliott, *1 Peter*, 821.

12. See Elliott, *1 Peter*, 828.

13. See Elliott, *1 Peter*, 519.

14. Many scholars see 2 Peter as dependent on Jude. Space does not permit a discussion of this important matter here. For the purposes of this chapter, the issue of dependence does not impinge on the questions of leadership theology.

15. It is interesting to compare this list with typical concepts in the leadership literature. See Jerry C. Wofford, *Transforming Christian Leadership: 10 Exemplary Church Leaders* (Grand Rapids: Baker, 1999); Jim van Yperen, *The Shepherd Leader* (St. Charles, IL: Church Smart Resources, 2003); Loughlan Sofield and Donald H. Kuhn, *The Collaborative Leader: Listening to the Wisdom of God's People* (Notre Dame, IN: Ave Maria Press, 1995); James E. Means, *Leadership in Christian Ministry* (Grand Rapids: Baker, 1989); David Hocking, *The Seven Laws of Christian Leadership* (Ventura, CA: Regal Books, 1991).

12 | Revelation

Sigve K. Tonstad

Academic approaches to Revelation treat the opening word *revelation* (*apokalypsis*; Rev. 1:1) as an opportunity to discuss the literary genre of this remarkable piece of ancient literature. Quite a few interpreters are content to leave it at that. To my knowledge no one has attempted to explore this word as a declaration of ideology, and much less as a statement that this book is committed to a particular form of leadership. The following, therefore, is a consideration of the leadership implications of the word that gives the last book of the Bible its title. The working hypothesis is that the book of Revelation is committed to *transparent* leadership. This ideology is announced in the opening word. With such a reading, Revelation strikes a blow to religious, political, and other institutions that thrive on secrecy and concealment.

BEYOND THE QUESTION OF GENRE

Preoccupation with the genre of Revelation is legitimate, bolstered in part by force of habit and by the fact that the word *apokalypsis* has lent its name to the genre of apocalyptic literature. Awareness of genre, in turn, facilitates interpretation because it gives the reader a head start in terms of what to expect from the type of work he or she is reading.[1] Needless to say, such "knowledge" is less helpful if the reader gets the question of genre wrong.

The risk of error on this point is considerable. While many features of Revelation support the notion that this is an apocalyptic book,[2] it is not *only that.* Assigning it to the apocalyptic genre overlooks characteristics that align the book closely with the genre of prophetic literature.[3] John Wick Bowman is correct when he says that the use of the word *apokalypsis* in the opening verse of Revelation has had consequences that the author "neither intended nor foresaw."[4] As Morton Smith notes, we can be sure that this word was not a signifier of literary genre at the time of the writing of Revelation.[5] Elisabeth Schüssler Fiorenza sees the opening verses of Revelation in a similar light, arguing that the author meant to write "*a revelatory prophetic letter.*"[6] Interpretations that build on generic similarities alone should therefore be treated with caution. In comparing Revelation to the non-canonical apocalypses, R. H. Charles insists that the superiority of John's book "is not merely relative but absolute."[7] All of the above indicates that the genre of Revelation is elusive and that the word *apokalypsis* is not meant to cue the reader in to the genre of literature he or she is reading.

Moving beyond the question of genre, it is likely that the author used the word *apokalypsis* because it fit his message. We are thus well advised to begin by considering the root meaning of this term.

Looking at the word itself, it is best approached through its verbal counterpart, *apo-kalyptō*. This compound word consists of the verb *kalyptō* and the preposition *apo.* Starting with *kalyptō,* the action envisioned is straightforward. This verb means to "remove something from view," to *conceal, hide,* or *cover* the item in question. We might picture the action by imagining an item that is placed in a chest whereupon the lid is closed. The item has now been hidden from view. Transliterating the Greek word and giving it an English ending, the item has been *kalypted.*

If we wish to reverse the action, we can do it by placing the preposition *apo-* in front of the verb. *Apo-kalyptō* describes an *uncovering,* a removal of the lid in order to bring the hidden item into full view. The word itself pictures the opposite of concealment and is actually the reversal of concealment. In the context of Revelation, the notion of revealing what another party might wish to hide goes to the heart of the matter. When the concealed item is exposed in broad daylight, it has, in our makeshift Greek-English transliteration, been *apo-kalypted*.

It is not contrived to begin here, delineating the meaning of the word through this contrast and counterpart. The message of Revelation is not given in a vacuum. Anton Vögtle writes that God "is not the only one who is at work in this world—as the Apocalypse makes so abundantly clear."[8] Looking at the message of the book as a whole, we are justified in viewing the notion of *revelation* against the background of its opposite. We are, in fact, quite amiss if we do not keep this perspective in view. *Apokalypsis* confronts *kalypsis,* just as uncovering stands against cover-up. In Revelation, the attempted concealment is exposed and reversed.

This scenario does not weaken or diminish the value of the ideology of *uncovering,* providing transparency, which is central to the word we are exploring. What we find, as announced in the very first word of the book, is the ideology of transparency and transparent leadership. *Transparency* lies within the semantic field of the notion of revelation (*apokalypsis*). Transmuting this into an ideology and principle of leadership offers transparency as a core value in leadership relationships in the book of Revelation.

EXPLORING TRANSPARENCY IN REVELATION

Revelation leaves no doubt as to who is the prime mover in the expanding circle of initiates that come into view in the opening verses. "The revelation [*apokalypsis*] of Jesus Christ, which God gave him to show his servants what must soon take place; he made it known by sending his angel to his servant John, who testified to the word of God and to the testimony of Jesus Christ, even to all that he saw" (Rev. 1:1–2).[9] The initiative begins with God. God gives His revelation to Jesus in a way that makes Jesus both the mediator and the content of what is revealed. Jesus, in turn, sends His angel to John, the primary human recipient of the revelation. John, for his part, is not meant to keep the disclosure to himself. He put the message into letter form, addressing it "to the seven churches that are in Asia" (1:4). However, a wider audience was immediately assumed because the introductory greeting pronounces a blessing on "the one who reads aloud the words of the prophecy, and…those who hear and who keep what is written in it" (1:3). Broadly speaking, the message is addressed "to whom it may concern."

The verbal parameters in ever-widening circle are striking. At the center there is the *apokalypsis* itself, "the revelation of Jesus Christ." This revelation is transported from the center to the world's utmost periphery by a series of dynamic action verbs. It is given "to show"; it is "made known"; there is a person who testifies (John); there is writing; and there is a person who "reads aloud" (1:1–3). Whether as noun or as verbal action, the opening passage of Revelation resounds with openness, transparency, and publicity.

Transparency in leadership cannot happen unless there is access. In Revelation, the notion of access leads to God. In this book, John is given access not to an earthly hall of power but to the innermost chamber of the heavenly council. If we read this story as a text that brings to light a certain type of leadership, the scene is stunning, almost beyond comprehension. "After this I looked, and there in heaven a door stood open!" (4:1). The New Revised Standard Version (NRSV) appropriately adds an exclamation mark to its translation, emphasizing not only the sense of surprise at the open door, but also its location. Open doors have been in short supply in the halls of power throughout human history. If ever an exclamation mark was warranted, this must be the place. And what is the open door but a signifier of access? What is the open door but proof of transparency? What is the open door but a signal that the heavenly authority grants what earthly authorities often deny, even authorities that profess commitment to openness? John is certainly justified in conveying a sense of amazement at the discovery that "in heaven a door stood open!"

More is to follow. The open door is not a publicity stunt that has no bearing on policy. As if aware that John is unsure how to relate to the open door, the vision goes on to tell him how to proceed. "And the first voice, which I had heard speaking to me like a trumpet, said, 'Come up here, and I will show you what must take place after this'" (4:1). This, particularly, is a place to take seriously Richard Bauckham's contention that in Revelation "scarcely a word can have been chosen without deliberate reflection on its relationship to the work as an integrated, interconnected whole."[10] John recognizes that the voice in question is the voice he heard earlier, "speaking to me like a trumpet" (4:1; cf. 1:10). We are not amiss if we assume that the voice is still speaking "like a trumpet." The voice is at once prodding and commanding; it proclaims access without the slightest reluctance; it speaks in the tenor of the trumpet blast as if to make sure that the reluctance that must be overcome is on the human side and not on the side of the heavenly authority.

Spurred on by the open door and the voice speaking "like a trumpet," John, now in the Spirit, enters through the door (4:2). The open door leads into the very presence of God. Once more the New Revised Standard Version resorts to the exclamation mark: "there in heaven stood a throne, with one seated on the throne!" (4:2).

John's audience in the heavenly council has a substantive purpose. We cannot conclude otherwise if we allow ourselves to ponder the next item in the narrative. "Then I saw in the right hand of the one seated on the throne a scroll written on the inside and sealed with seven seals" (5:1).

Discretion and disclosure go hand in hand in this verse. The discretion, maintained consistently throughout Revelation, relates to John's depiction of "the one seated on the throne" (4:2, 9; 5:1, 7, 13). Disclosure is highlighted by the sealed scroll "in the right hand of the one seated on the throne" (5:1). Revelation could have tried to overwhelm John with an appeal to the senses, a dose of shock and awe. It could prioritize a display of pomp and circumstance, an aesthetic experience never to be forgotten, as the means by which to keep human beings obedient and submissive.[11]

But the core of Revelation's disclosure relates to policy. As Adela Yarbro Collins writes perceptively, "the heavenly council is faced with a serious problem."[12] The problem relates to God's way of dealing with a reality that seems long on disaster and short on hope. To this end, the sealed scroll must be unsealed. John has been invited into the heavenly council in order to witness the breaking of the seals. There, in his presence, one by one, the seals are broken by the Lamb that appears "in the middle of the throne" (5:6; 6:1–8:1). Breathtaking disclosures come to light. At last, when the seventh seal is broken, we read that "there was silence in heaven for about half an hour" (8:1).

Policy concerns are at the center of these disclosures. In leadership terms, God chooses the road of painstaking and principled openness. Secrecy is out, and transparency is in. What has been concealed, obfuscated, and misrepresented by the opponent in the cosmic conflict is revealed, explained, and made right in God's revelation of his ways through Jesus. A more complete account of the theological implications of this policy may be pursued,[13] but the leadership implications do not need the full account to be appreciated. "When the slaughtered Lamb is seen 'in the midst of' the divine throne in heaven (5:6; cf. 7:17), the meaning is that Christ's sacrificial death *belongs to the way God rules the world,*" says Richard Bauckham.[14] Jesus, the only One who can break the seals "in heaven, or on earth, or under the earth" (5:2–5), has confirmed that the heavenly leadership rests on the foundation of transparency.

The modus operandi of God's ways thus sets forth openness as a prized value. The first of Revelation's revelatory cycles, the cycle of the seven seals, is replete with transparency. There is an open door to God, a trumpet call to step into God's immediate presence, and a sealed scroll that will be opened before our eyes. We are brought face to face with leadership that is committed to openness. Trust in this leader rests on divine transparency and not on unquestioning submission. Revelation envisions faithful discipleship as much as any other book in the Bible (13:10; 14:4), but its notion of discipleship is predicated on understanding (13:18; 17:9).

The subsequent cycles of seven in Revelation do not retreat from this theme. In the trumpet sequence, it is precisely the policy of transparency that runs its course. As this cycle draws to a close, John's accompanying angel explains that "when the seventh angel is to blow his trumpet, the mystery of God will be fulfilled, as he announced to his servants the prophets" (10:7). If we allow the Old

Testament to illuminate this statement,[15] the transparency that under-lies the disclosure will shine even more brightly. God did speak to "his servants the prophets," as this allusion to the prophet Amos indicates. God did speak again and again in human history until the full account was out (Heb. 1:1) because transparency is not an acci-dental feature of what comes to light in Revelation. When we read Amos in his own context, we realize that transparency must be a core element in the divine ideology. God says, "Surely the Lord GOD does nothing, without revealing his secret to his servants the prophets" (Amos 3:7).

When the last of the cycles of seven, the bowl sequence, rolls across the screen, transparency, as principle and policy, completes its course. In this scene (Rev. 15:2–4), transparency is written on the structure of the scene. The final edifice of the redeemed is repre-sented as a sea of glass, as if to say that where God leads and reigns, obfuscation and concealment are banished.

> And I saw what appeared to be a sea of glass mixed with fire, and those who had conquered the beast and its image and the number of its name, standing beside the sea of glass with harps of God in their hands. And they sing the song of Moses, the servant of God, and the song of the Lamb: "Great and amazing are your deeds, Lord God the Almighty! Just and true are your ways, King of the nations! Lord, who will not fear and glorify your Name? For you alone are holy. All nations will come and worship before you, for your judgments have been revealed." (Rev. 15:2–4)

Here, too, the emphasis is on bringing things into the light, driving back the forces of misrepresentation and concealment. The proclamation that God's "judgments have been revealed" means that God's way of governing is incontrovertibly manifest. Those who sing this song, a song that recapitulates God's redemptive intent throughout human history, sing it with understanding.[16] God's way meets with admiration. Indeed, we should be prepared for the possibility that those who praise God in this song praise Him not only because "God's judgments" have met their compara-tively modest standards, but also even more because those judg-ments have far exceeded their standard and transformed their view of how to make right what has gone wrong.

Where there is transparency, there is also accountability. These are reciprocal and mutually dependent values. Accountability is impossible in the absence of transparency because the latter is the precondition for the former. On the other hand, transparency is the stance of one who has nothing to hide and who, for that reason, invites and solicits accountability. Two texts in Revelation are especially noteworthy as to how and why God will not lead in any other way. John says of the redeemed that they are people who "follow the Lamb wherever he goes" (14:4). The followers cannot follow unless they know where to go, and they know because the leader has led the way by personal example.

In the context of Revelation, it is implicit that followers prove the quality of their training by their ability to perform in the absence of their mentor. The principle that was modeled in the life of Jesus has been understood and internalized in His followers to the point that they will continue the course mapped out by the leader even when they are physically left to themselves. This, to be sure, is no easy task because, in the final analysis, Revelation describes the prospect of martyrdom. "If anyone is to go into captivity, into captivity he will go. If anyone is to be killed with the sword, with the sword he will be killed" (13:10, NIV). This text appears at one of the points in the story where there is direct eye contact between the reader and the audience so as to make sure that the take-home point is not missed.[17] "This calls for patient endurance and faithfulness on the part of the saints," the narrator interjects (13:10, NIV).

John also says of "those who share in the first resurrection" that "they will be priests of God and of Christ, and they will reign with him a thousand years" (20:6). From the point of view of the leader, the mentoring that has taken place is not meant to be passive. If transparency inevitably means accountability, it also brings empowerment. To be "priests of God and of Christ" suggests the ability to speak authoritatively on behalf of God and Christ; to "reign with him" suggests a genuine power-sharing arrangement. At this point those who were led have themselves become leaders. This was God's purpose from the very beginning. The redeemed have received the capacity to explain God's ways in a way that represents God correctly, and they have a mandate to execute policy.

On this point Revelation seems to be fully in tune with the leadership ideal that is envisioned by Jesus in the Gospel of John; "I do not call you servants any longer, because the servant does not know what the master is doing; but I have called you friends, because I have made known to you everything that I have heard from my Father" (John 15:15). This ideal is not scaled back or rescinded in Revelation, where disciples will be "priests of God and of Christ" and "reign with him a thousand years" (Rev. 20:6). In Revelation, too, the servant has been told everything that Jesus has heard from the Father (1:1–3; cf. John 15:15); the disciple knows what the Master is doing, and the relationship rests on the transparent rock of divine revelation.

REVELATION'S VIEW AS CORRECTIVE

In the Roman imperial system, the *imperator* lived according to the definition of his title: he was "the ruler answerable to none."[18] He ruled by decree, not by persuasion or consent. Accountability in the imperial system of government took the form of assassination. Transparency is decidedly not the first word that comes to mind in this type of governance and leadership. It goes almost without saying that Revelation's God is not an imperial figure even though notions of imperial sovereignty are widely diffused in Christian theology.

Plato (427–347 BC), the foremost political philosopher of the ancient world and probably of all time, did not advocate an outright imperial system of government, but transparency was low on the scale of values in his Utopian state. His ideal was stability. To achieve stability, expediency must trump transparency. "I mean," Socrates says in Plato's *Republic,* "that our rulers will find a considerable dose of falsehood and deceit necessary for the good of their subjects."[19] Lying is justified because it has a corrective medicinal purpose, in this case to facilitate Plato's vision of state-sponsored eugenics, to depersonalize motherhood, and to prevent parental bonding. The specifics are in the present context less important than the principle, and the principle is unequivocal: It is legitimate to practice falsehood if the governing body is doing it for the common good.

In *Laws,* another of Plato's books on statecraft and leadership, the ideal is for the subject to follow orders and have no mind of his or her own. To this end, it should not be in the mind of anyone "to do anything, either in jest or earnest, of his own motion, but in war and in peace he should look to and follow his leader, even in the least things being under his guidance."[20] Defenders of Plato have reacted with outrage at the suggestion that Plato deserves to be seen as the most beguiling ideologue of totalitarian systems of government along the lines suggested by Karl Popper,[21] but even Plato's most ardent defenders will be hard pressed to defend transparency, accountability, and the rule of law on the basis of Plato's writings. Indeed, as I. F. Stone suggests in his discussion of Plato's representation of the trial and death of Socrates, it is likely that Plato conveniently omits mentioning Socrates's opposition to Athenian democracy and his intimate relationship with some of the leaders who violently tried to overturn it. "In the elegant and seductive phrases of his *Apology,* Plato does not allow these political events to obtrude on the reader, though they were fresh in the memories of the judges. Nor does he mention them anywhere in his many dialogues," says Stone.[22] If this is correct, neither Plato nor those who try to honor his legacy are particularly fond of transparency.

Writing over a century before John on Patmos, Posidonius of Apameia (135–51 BC) is similarly unable to accommodate the values found in Revelation. In his view, too, genuine leadership values commands over explanations and authority over transparency.

> A law should be brief, so that the unskilled may grasp it more easily. Let it be like a voice from heaven; let it order, not argue. Nothing seems to be more pedantic, more pointless than a law with a preamble. Advise me, tell me what you want me to do; I am not learning, I am obeying.[23]

In this vision of leadership, the leader does not fret over process. Speaking to both sides of the issue, of the leader and of the person being led, Posidonius wants commands and not explanations from his leader. As Seneca later paraphrased this saying, "Tell me what I have to do...I do not want to learn. I want to obey."[24]

The leadership ideal in Revelation corrects this vision for leadership in two directions: the leader as well as the person being led.

Nicolò Machiavelli (1469–1527) ranks far below Plato in terms of influence, but he stands out in the annals of thinkers who have espoused enduring theories of leadership. In *The Prince,* Machiavelli writes approvingly of the cunning with which Pope Alexander VI (r. 1492–1503), the former Rodrigo Borgia and one of the great Renaissance pontiffs, managed to get his way in the power play of Europe. "Alexander VI was concerned only with deceiving men, and he always found them gullible," says Machiavelli. "No man ever affirmed anything more forcefully or with stronger oaths but kept his word less. Nevertheless, his deceptions were always effective, because he well understood the naivety of men."[25] The principle of transparency does not appear in Machiavelli's thought any more than in Plato's dialogues. For the Florentine political handyman, the good leader is results-oriented and not overly concerned with principles. To win the war counts more than to ascertain whether the war is just. The ruler who wins the battle will also win in the court of public opinion even if his cause is unjust. "For the common people are impressed by appearances and results," Machiavelli says knowingly.[26]

These thoughts on leadership have to do with affairs of government. A discussion of the leadership ideals in Revelation could obviously turn in other directions, to corporate leadership, church governance, or leadership in institutions. Revelation is in a sense a secular and world-oriented book, deeply concerned with issues of governance in the world. Beginning with the Roman Empire in the days of John, Revelation provides a sketch of powers vying for domination on the world scene until the return of Jesus. In Revelation 13, for instance, the topic of concern even extends to powers that appear to profess loyalty to God while actually subverting them.[27] For this reason it is appropriate, in closing, to allow Revelation's ideal of transparent leadership to speak to the ideals of both religious and political powers in the world today. In the religious arena, obviously one significant power in society is the Roman Catholic Church. In the realm of politics, the United States of America is obviously such a power. The message of Revelation reveals a principle of leadership—transparency—that applies throughout all creation, the political and social world as well as the spiritual.

How does Revelation's commitment to transparent leadership resonate in the leading democracy in human history and in the leading religious institution of all time?

The answer to this question has many facets, but the overall trend is unmistakable: Transparent leadership has fallen on hard times. The Roman Catholic Church may be the least transparent institution human civilization has ever seen, and, arguably, it reflects the nature of other religious institutions in that regard. It has successfully weathered modern demands for openness, substituting vigorous public relations for transparent policy. The sex scandals that have come to light in the church toward the end of the twentieth century and the beginning of the new millennium may be seen as aberrations in terms of priestly behavior, but they are not aberrations in terms of church governance.[28] Those who have tried to make headway against the terrible wrongs that have been committed against them have confronted a wall of silence.[29] It is not an anachronism to single out absence of transparent leadership as the most characteristic feature of this institution throughout much of its history. Its leadership, not unlike that of the Roman imperial system, is essentially and explicitly a leadership accountable to none. Where Revelation espouses a commitment to transparency, the church, in its ideology and arcane structure, embodies commitments that are imperiously contrary to the transparency that lies at the heart of Revelation's message. Again, this characteristic is reflective of other religious institutions as well, in Christianity and in other religious traditions.

The national and international affairs of nations have also been marked by an absence of transparency. For about a century or so, even the government of the United States has backed away from this commitment. In a book on government deception and secrecy in the United States in the twentieth century, David Wise writes that "the governed must know to what they are consenting" for democracy to work.[30] This requirement is in a precarious state. Wise shows that secrecy and state-sponsored deception are on the rise not in some underdeveloped foreign land but in the country that leads the "free" world. Concealment is in; openness and accountability are out. The

Orwellian vision is coming to fruition not only in totalitarian systems of government, but also in countries that profess a commitment to openness. Expediency, as in Plato's *Republic,* trumps transparency in the modern state. The late senator Daniel Patrick Moynihan, also chronicling the rise of secrecy in the US government, writes ruefully toward the end of his book, "The Cold War ended; secrecy continued as a mode of governance as if nothing had changed."[31] In the introduction to Moynihan's book, Richard Gid Powers quotes Lord Acton with the understanding that the latter gave a succinct account of what is at stake. "Everything secret degenerates, even the administration of justice; nothing is safe that does not show how it can bear discussion and publicity."[32]

Revelation concurs with this judgment. Trustworthy leadership must be transparent. This book offers no refuge to leaders who place results over principles or who bypass the pain of transparency for short-term gain. The transparency that comes to view in Revelation aims to expose deception at its source and to banish it from the society of created beings in heaven and on earth. Revelation looks to God as the source and defender of transparent leadership. It poses a formidable corrective to human expediency, speaking to the physician who relates to his or her patient with an attitude of paternalism; to the lender who conceals from the borrower the actual risk; to the board that votes in secret on some matter or person, knowing that they will not have to explain their decision; to the guardians of archives who try to limit access to information; to persons who censor books and opinions; and to religious institutions that behave as though they are absolved from accountability. Quite apart from the particular and specific attempts to subvert God's ways that are exposed in Revelation, this book holds its reader to a standard that those who claim to revere its message often miss.

CONCLUSION

This chapter has explored the leadership implications of the word that gives the last book of the Bible its title. The principle discovered in the nature of the book of Revelation is *transparent* leadership. This ideology is announced in the opening word. Revelation corrects religious, political, and other institutions that thrive on secrecy and concealment. "Blessed is the one who reads aloud the words of the prophecy, and blessed are those who hear and who keep what is written in it; for the time is near," says the narrator in Revelation (1:3). Blessed, too, is the leader who takes Revelation's quest for transparency to heart, and the fellow member of the community who demands transparency from all engaged in leadership.

FOR REFLECTION

Personal:

1. What would transparency in my personal relationships look like?
2. Do my colleagues see me as an approachable, open person? Why?

Organizational:

1. Is our organization comfortable with transparency? How could we be more transparent?
2. Are the needs of those we serve providing accountability for us? How?

ENDNOTES

1. E. D. Hirsch, *Validity in Interpretation* (New Haven, CT: Yale University Press, 1967), 86, defines *genre* as "that sense of the whole by means of which an interpreter can correctly understand any part in its determinacy."

2. John Collins and others give the following definition of the apocalyptic genre, a definition that is still widely accepted: "'Apocalypse' is a genre of revelatory literature with a narrative framework, in which a revelation is mediated by an otherworldly being to a human recipient, disclosing a transcendent reality which is both temporal, insofar as it envisages eschatological salvation, and spatial insofar as it involves another, supernatural world," John J. Collins, ed., *Apocalypse: The Morphology of a Genre*, Semeia 14 (Missoula, MT: Scholars Press, 1979), 9.

3. Frederick David Mazzaferri, *The Genre of the Book of Revelation from a Source-Critical Perspective*, BZNW 54 (Berlin: Walter de Gruyter, 1989). Greg

Beale, *The Book of Revelation,* NIGTC (Grand Rapids, MI: Eerdmans, 1999), 29, also sees Revelation as a prophetic work.

4. John Wick Bowman, "The Revelation to John: Its Dramatic Structure and Message," *Interpretation* 9 (1955): 437. See also Gregory L. Linton, "Reading the Apocalypse as Apocalypse: The Limits of Genre" in *The Reality of Apocalypse: Rhetoric and Politics in the Book of Revelation,* ed. David L. Barr (Atlanta: Society of Biblical Literature, 2006), 9–42.

5. Morton Smith, "On the History of *APOIKALUPTW* and *APOKALUYIS*" in *Apocalypticism in the Mediterranean World and the Near East,* ed. David Hellholm (Tübingen, Germany: J. C. B. Mohr, 1983), 9–20; cf. John J. Collins, *The Apocalyptic Imagination,* 2nd ed. (Grand Rapids, MI: Eerdmans, 1998), 3.

6. Elisabeth Schüssler Fiorenza, *Revelation: Vision of a Just World* (Minneapolis: Fortress Press, 1991), 23; emphasis added.

7. R. H. Charles, *The Revelation of St. John,* vol. 1 (Edinburgh: T. & T. Clark, 1920), lxxxvii.

8. Anton Vögtle, "Der Gott der Apocalypse" in *La Notion biblique de Dieu,* ed. J. Coppens (Gembloux, Belgium: Éditions J. Duculot, 1976), 383.

9. Unless otherwise noted, Scripture quotations in this chapter are taken from the New Revised Standard Version.

10. Richard Bauckham, *The Climax of Prophecy: Studies in the Book of Revelation* (Edinburgh: T. & T. Clark, 1993), x.

11. Fyodor Dostoevsky, *The Brothers Karamazov,* trans. Richard Pevear and Larissa Volokhonsky (New York: Farrar, Straus & Giroux, 2002), 255. Original Russian edition 1880.

12. Adela Yarbro Collins, *The Apocalypse,* NTM 22 (Dublin: Veritas Publications, 1979), 39.

13. Sigve K. Tonstad, *Saving God's Reputation: The Theological Function of* Pistis Iesou *in the Cosmic Narratives of Revelation* (London: Continuum, 2006).

14. Richard Bauckham, *The Theology of the Book of Revelation* (Cambridge, UK: Cambridge University Press, 1993), 64; emphasis added.

15. Bauckham, *The Climax of Prophecy,* xi, says that "Revelation's use of the Old Testament Scriptures is an essential key to its understanding.… Reference to and interpretation of these texts is an extremely important part of the meaning of the text of the Apocalypse. It is a book designed to be read in constant intertextual relationship with the Old Testament."

16. Tonstad, *Saving God's Reputation,* 149–154.

17. Ugo Vanni, "Liturgical Dialogue as a Literary Form in the Book of Revelation," *NTS* 37 (1991): 365–366. Similar exclamatory and hortatory phrases are found in Revelation 13:18, 14:12, and 17:9.

18. Nicholas Purcell, "The Arts of Government" in *The Roman World,* ed. John Boardman, Jasper Griffin, and Oswyn Murray (Oxford: Oxford University Press, 1986), 163.

19. Plato, *The Republic,* trans. Benjamin Jowett (New York: Bigelow, Brown, 1943), 190.

20. Plato, *Laws*, Book XII, trans. Benjamin Jowett. http://classics.mit.edu/Plato/Laws/html (accessed July 7, 2012).

21. Karl Popper, *The Open Society and Its Enemies,* 2 vols. (London: Routledge, 1945). The first volume deals with Plato, the second with Hegel and Marx.

22. I. F. Stone, *The Trial of Socrates* (New York: Anchor Books, 1989), 141.

23. *Posidonius,* vol. 2, ed. I. G. Kidd, Cambridge Classical Texts and Commentaries (Cambridge, UK: Cambridge University Press, 1988), 654.

24. Seneca, quoted in Patrick D. Miller, "The Ethics of the Commandments" in *The Ten Commandments: The Reciprocity of Faithfulness,* ed. William P. Brown (Louisville, KY: Westminster John Knox Press, 2004), 26.

25. Machiavelli, *The Prince,* ed. Quentin Skinner and Russell Price (Cambridge, UK: Cambridge University Press, 1988), 62.

26. Machiavelli, *The Prince,* 63.

27. Cf. Sigve K. Tonstad, "Appraising the Myth of *Nero Redivivus* in the Interpretation of Revelation," *AUSS* 46 (2008): 175–199.

28. Daniel J. Wakin and James C. McKinley, Jr., "Abuse Case Offers a View of the Vatican's Politics," *New York Times,* May 2, 2010.

29. Jason Berry and Gerald Renner, *Vows of Silence: The Abuse of Power in the Papacy of John Paul II* (New York: Free Press, 2004).

30. David Wise, *The Politics of Lying: Government Deception, Secrecy, and Power* (New York: Random House, 1973), 353–354.

31. Daniel Patrick Moynihan, *Secrecy: The American Experience* (New Haven, CT: Yale University Press, 1998), 202.

32. Powers, quoting Lord Acton in Moynihan, *Secrecy,* 1.

Section Three: Selected Biblical Narratives

13 | Nehemiah: The Servant Leader

Barry Gane

R obert Greenleaf offers the following thoughtful definition of *servant leadership*:

> The servant-leader *is* servant first…. It begins with the natural feeling that one wants to serve, to serve *first*. Then conscious choice brings one to aspire to lead…. The difference manifests itself in the care taken by the servant—first to make sure the other people's highest priority needs are being served. The best test…is: Do those served grow as persons? Do they, *while being served,* become healthier, wiser, freer, more autonomous, more likely themselves to become servants?[1]

His view is compatible with the understanding of servant leadership emerging from the remarkable experience of Nehemiah, a determined and unselfish postexilic Jew serving in the Persian court four centuries before Christ in the Persian Empire.

NEHEMIAH: THE SERVANT LEADER

Leaders make choices all the time. They can settle for what is—
or dream about what might be. When they devote themselves to such
dreams, they invite those around them to share the vision and travel
with them on a journey toward realization. One such visionary was
Nehemiah. Born into a displaced Jewish family in a foreign land, he
is introduced in the Hebrew scriptures one hundred and forty-one
years after the final sacking of Jerusalem. He had no personal knowledge of the city, but like other Jews in captivity, he looked to the
ancient capital as his ultimate home, the place his heart resided. It was
a place that gave meaning to his existence. We see just how much he
cared about his distant homeland when news of the broken and
crumbled walls and the burnt gates came to his attention.

Feeling helpless, he did the only thing that made sense to him:
he prayed. This prayer is the first of nine recorded in the book that
bears his name. We witness his anguish as he fasts, weeps, mourns,
and prays. Despite being a slave of the king, he refers to himself as
God's servant. The reality is that he was a slave, a dispensable person, a cupbearer. [2] His job was to taste the wine before it was passed
to the king. Since predecessors to the current king had lost their
lives through poisoning, his role was uncomfortably vital to the
ongoing existence of the king! He lived under the shadow of death.

Nehemiah's prayer was one of intercession. Three prerequisites
for this type of prayer can be identified: "jealousy for God's reputation, love for one's fellows, and indifference for one's own life and
destiny."[3] Although the recorded prayer of chapter 1 is brief, it was
part of four months of Nehemiah's persevering intercession before
God, which opened an opportunity for him to raise the issue with
Artaxerxes, the king. Nehemiah, noted as a cheerful person of hope
and courage, had never allowed emotions of sorrow or suffering to
show while in the king's presence. It may have been because of his
demeanour that he secured his position in the king's court. But the
sadness he experienced for Jerusalem and his people spilled over
into his working life and was noted by the king. Immediately
Nehemiah became dreadfully afraid—he could have at that moment
come under suspicion, and it could have cost him his life. But again

he prayed. And God granted him vision as well as the extraordinary courage to follow through with his petition.

Four months of praying had given him the courage to present to the king the reason for his sadness. When the king demanded, "What is it you want?" (Neh. 2:4),[4] Nehemiah was quick to pray and swift in his answer. Although he had no skills as an architect or builder, expertise that would seem requisite for the task that lay before him, he pled, "Send me to the city in Judah where my ancestors are buried so that I can rebuild it" (2:5).[5] A vision was clearly announced. The king, touched by the courageous heart of his servant, asked how long such a project would take. He demanded a time frame and assurance of Nehemiah's return. Although Nehemiah had never been to Jerusalem and had only mental pictures of chaos and destruction, he ventured to define the time needed to rebuild the walls and the city. He likely asked for and received permission to take a few years, not the twelve he eventually needed and was granted for the task. Those residing in Jerusalem had not accomplished the rebuilding after more than fifty years. Rational analysis would confirm it was an impossible task even in a lifetime. Yet a servant leader waits on God for vision and has courageous faith.

Nehemiah was so committed to the vision that he was not afraid to ask for help. Miraculously the king gave him letters of introduction to the surrounding leaders, an armed escort, and the means to get the job done. This servant leader is an example of this principle: If you are to receive, first you must ask.

THE CHALLENGE

It should not be overlooked that the rebuilding of the Temple took place under Ezra at which time a spiritual revival had begun in Jerusalem. Nehemiah was not just a leader who arose in a vacuum. God had been preparing the way for the next step in the journey, and He used leadership to further His purposes.

Visionary leadership evokes both the worst and the best in people. Whenever a leader begins a project, calls out vision from the community, or promotes a direction embraced by the community, there will be opposition. Nehemiah was dogged by local leaders opposed to what he was doing. They quickly moved from being opposers to outright enemies. Nehemiah encountered opposition before he even arrived in Jerusalem. Sanballat and Tobiah quickly moved from feeling disturbed by this new leader to engaging in caustic sarcasm. Their mockery was interspersed with laughter and derision. As Nehemiah remained committed to his vision, their sarcasm turned to threats, and the threats became outright guerrilla warfare. Ultimately they sought to use an insider, a trusted confidant, to lure the man of God into a death trap. Strong leadership evokes equally strong reaction. Few people remain neutral; sides are clearly taken.

External opposition is easier to handle than internal strife. Conflict and misunderstanding are common when one casts vision, even when the community embraces it, because some persons involved have their own agendas. Often the leader of leaders will become a mediator between members of a team. The challenge calls for an understanding of the underlying interests, attention to the process, excellent communication techniques, and especially negotiating skills. We see these skills used effectively in chapter 5 when Nehemiah learns that the wealthy are using the opportunity to profit from the poorer workers.

Nehemiah spent his first three days in the city watching and listening. Several thousand years later Greenleaf[6] identified twelve characteristics that are seen in the life of the servant leader. The first is "listening," followed by "empathy." These are characteristics demonstrated by Nehemiah. He listened to the reports, then merely observed what had been happening. In both processes he was deeply empathetic. He did not share the vision of the rebuilding until he had a good understanding of the situation and the challenge he faced. He said, "I had not told anyone what my God had put in my heart to do for Jerusalem" (2:12). He did a full survey of the needs so that he could comprehend the task in detail. He then spelled out the vision and issued his challenge: "See the trouble we are in.... Come, let us rebuild the wall of Jerusalem, and we will no longer be in disgrace" (2:17).

Greenleaf traces the attributes of a servant leader in progression from empathy to awareness and then persuasion. Kouzes and Posner also endorse this flow from empathy to awareness and persuasion: "To truly hear what constituents want—what they desperately hope to make you understand, appreciate, and include within the vision—requires periodically suspending regular activities and spending time listening to others."[7] Nehemiah engaged with the community in their shared sense of God's will for them, which required listening and empathy. In the process, awareness was advanced, and he was able to persuade them to embrace a latent vision God was stirring in the hearts of His people.

This inspirational and persuasive servant leader was met with the response: "Let us start rebuilding" (2:18). After analyzing what the project entailed, Nehemiah laid out the objectives and then delegated responsibilities to various teams or family groups. Each knew clearly what was expected of him or her. Thus, Nehemiah provided a lesson on motivation for the Christian leader. Motivation is about moving people toward a goal. It is most easily achieved when it meets a need in those being led, or when they can see that they are achieving the mission to which they are committed. The leader clarifies the need, giving the team a reason to celebrate what they do. The leader's conviction can be very compelling, and this conviction is heightened in followers as the leader walks the talk. Motivating other leaders is essentially looking ahead and feeding back. We do not find out until the third chapter that there were a number of people who preferred to stand back and watch rather than bend their backs to the task. It is not surprising that these were the nobles, the *adirim* (exalted), the failed leaders of the past (3:5). It was expected that Sanballat and Tobiah would create difficulties, but it is another thing altogether to have opposition from within. Despite the opposition, Nehemiah was quick to give credit to those involved in building the wall and he acknowledged the group leaders individually. He recognized the need to affirm and acknowledge the team.

Nehemiah became remarkably effective in casting the increasingly shared vision to rebuild the walls of the city. A wide cross section of the community joined in. The high priest bought into the vision, and together with other priests, he took responsibility for the building of the Sheep Gate. Seven local rulers became involved in the reconstruction, as did a perfume maker, a city guard, goldsmiths and merchants, as well as Levites and other priests. All of these people were acknowledged by name for their involvement.

The Nehemiah model is one that is endorsed by the respected and admired founder of the Willow Creek Community Church, Bill Hybels. He believes that the church is the most leadership-intensive enterprise in our society. It is his contention that positional leadership does not work in organizations staffed by volunteers. Leaders in churches have only their influence to make things happen. They cannot force people to follow or buy into their dreams, but under the power of the Holy Spirit, they can nudge people toward their vision and the mission of the church.[8] Nehemiah's life testifies to the truth of this proposition.

LESSONS FROM NEHEMIAH

It is amazing what a leader can achieve when he or she is happy to share the credit. This adage is especially true when the leader does not mind who gets the credit. Nehemiah was a servant who became a leader of leaders who then merged with a company of leaders.

Focusing on a contagious, God-given, heart-stirring vision with other servant leaders is very different from the role of a company CEO to whom others are answerable. Unlike the role of a corporate CEO, church leaders face a great challenge: most frequently they lead volunteers. The process of seeking a God-given shared vision, then articulating it effectively in an environment of volunteer leaders, is one of prayerful submission, careful listening, challenging the community to openness and negotiation. All leaders discover that a variety of personal agendas generate alternate visions when a group of talented leaders come together. Nehemiah had to submit his impression of the vision to rebuild first to God that he might understand God's will for the community. His submission required the joining of the spiritual qualities of a servant, respect for the body of God's people, the relational skills of a diplomat, and intensive strategic corporate and one-on-one conversations as he sought to help others to adopt and own the vision.[9]

Often the *servant of servants*—a term that describes Nehemiah's calling and ours—will be viewed as the one responsible for merely oiling the machinery: maintaining the organization so that other people can get the job done. But a key role of the servant leader is

to make the whole greater than the sum of its parts. It means bringing together multiple talents and building on them, a process that happens more readily when those led know they are part of a community with shared mission, values, and ideas. This process is evident as the team is involved in decision making and planning. Knowing history will enhance direction. There is evidence of this cooperative decision-making process in chapter 3 of Nehemiah as the diverse groups pull together to realize the vision. Nehemiah knows the power of *team,* and his actions reflect the reality that "No one of us is as smart as all of us!"

Reflect for a moment on Nehemiah's timeless demonstration of the power of team and how he went about forming teams. The effective team is built on the premise that everyone has something valuable to contribute and will do so, if the environment is right. Hence an effective team needs to have a clear purpose that it knows can best be met by using the skills and abilities of all the members of the group. The team will develop a sense of ownership if it is empowered and given the flexibility to look at the task in a creative way, and if the team members are nurtured to increase the variety and depth of their skills.

It is a basic proposition of the Bible that people have a great deal of potential, and Paul makes it clear that each person has something worthwhile and important to offer to the growth and health of the church (1 Cor. 12). Each individual has much more to offer than many in leadership realize. The servant leader's task is to create an environment that is safe, nurturing, and, through empowerment, one that encourages contributions from all members. Empowerment is the key—the driving force behind successful teams. There is a powerful interplay among empowerment, team satisfaction, and task performance.

Wellbourn puts his finger on an important factor when he says, "In principle, team based organizations and formal bureaucracies are incompatible. Teams work on group processes, whereas bureaucracies work on the basis of individuals giving instruction to other individuals. Therefore, an attempt by senior management to gain the benefits of teamwork without changing the system that supports individualism is likely to fail."[10] Nehemiah does not try to pull rank; in fact, he does not use the power invested in him by the king to make things happen but rather repeatedly casts the shared vision and inspires the team. "The success attending Nehemiah's efforts shows what prayer, faith, and wise, energetic action will accomplish. Living faith will prompt to energetic action. The spirit manifested by the leader will be, to a great extent, reflected by the people."[11]

As the wall began to grow, so did the opposition, and lives were threatened (4:1). When the wall reached half its final height, the people had almost unstoppable momentum, but the opposition embraced open warfare, and Nehemiah's enemies attacked a number of places at once. Yet his rallying call instilled courage: "Don't be afraid of them. Remember the Lord, who is great and awesome, and fight for your families, your sons and your daughters, your wives and your homes" (4:14). He did not just use inspirational words; rather, he did the hard, sacrificial work of coordinating working parties into fighting groups. Shields and soldiers protected the stonemasons. Trumpets were used to indicate when the fighting became too intense in one place and reinforcements were needed. An expectation of the servant of servants is that that leader will have a loyalty and duty to care for those he or she is leading.[12]

John F. Kennedy said, "Leadership and learning are indispensable to each other."[13] In fact the word *educate* comes from the Latin *educere*—"to lead forth." It is a crucial task of the servant leader to educate. The education process involves understanding where growth needs to take place and how to build on the strengths that already exist. The process often means creating a learning context in which the leader can take the group on a journey of discovery. At other times, a one-on-one learning experience rather than group instruction may have advantages including dealing with power blocks by isolating the power group. The leadership challenge requires careful consideration of how learning can proceed in order to invite genuine participation and engagement. Nehemiah invited many of the troubled and the troublemakers to his table and here sought to engage and reeducate. He was not just passionate about wall building—the main task—but he was also concerned about social justice. He related his anger about the way some were treating the poor in the community (5:6), and he responded, not only with words, but also with decisive action. As a servant leader, Nehemiah sought transformation in his colleagues and his community.

Nehemiah shows us what singleness of purpose can achieve. He did not stop to deal with external opposition. He started with the end in mind. But as he witnessed the internal damage being done, he was prepared to deal with an issue that could destroy the project. Some of the wealthier people were profiting by selling food to the poorer families involved in the building project, and many poor folk had to sell their families into slavery simply to pay the resulting obligations. Nehemiah was not naïve. He confronted the business practices of those taking advantage of the poor, and he brought an end to the practice of charging interest. "Learning is the essential fuel of the leader, the source of continually sparking new understanding, new ideas and new challenges. Very simply, those who do not learn do not long survive as leaders."[14]

The most often quoted words of Nehemiah come in the final days of the wall building. He did not slacken the pace or ease off the task. When his enemies sought to entice him away from his mission, he thundered, "I am carrying on a great project and cannot go down. Why should the work stop while I leave it and go down to you?" (6:3). The pressure intensified as he was told of the conspiracy afoot to destroy him. A remarkable scenario unfolds in the biblical narrative. A planted and treacherous informer encouraged Nehemiah to run to the Temple for safety—when in fact an assassin waited there to take his life and end the work. His response was memorable: "Should such a man as I flee? And who *is there* such as I who would go into the temple to save his life? I will not go in!" (6:11, NKJV, emphasis added). Nehemiah's account reveals that Eliashib the priest (some believe the high priest) later actually provided a room in the temple courts to Tobiah, Nehemiah's nemesis. Nehemiah carried out his work in the midst of treachery that likely included the cooperation of the temple leaders.

Foresight demands that leaders understand the past, engage the future, and remove their blinders in order to develop creativity. Nehemiah achieved what was apparently impossible: The wall was completed in fifty-two days! Demonstrating a servant's heart, he took none of the glory but declared, "And it happened, when all our enemies heard of it, and all the nations around us saw these things, that they were very disheartened in their own eyes; for they perceived that this work was done by our God" (6:16, NKJV). He takes none of the glory for himself but ensures that it is given to God.

Ken Blanchard asserts, "Leaders who are servants first will assume leadership only if they see it as the best way to serve. They are called to lead, rather than driven, because they naturally want to be helpful. They aren't possessive about their position. They view it as an act of stewardship, rather than ownership."[15] We see that Nehemiah was committed to the growth of the people as well as convinced that he was doing more than just building a wall.

The last half of the book is the record of *people building*. The administrative tasks of building, managing the project, were carried out to accomplish the purposes of the people. As with leadership, managing is done for people, not for the sake of controlling them.

> With the traditional pyramid, the boss is always responsible and the staff are supposed to be responsive to the boss. When you turn the pyramid upside down, those roles get reversed. Your people become responsible and the job of management is to be responsive to their people. That creates a very different environment for implementation. If you work for your people, then what is the purpose of being a manager? To help them accomplish their goals. Your job is to help them win.[16]

Indeed Nehemiah began the work knowing only that at its completion he would return to Persia. He was committed to leave the city wall completed and in the control of those who built it.

The community around the servant leader is enriched by his or her leadership both in the organization where he or she serves and within the wider world around them. There is a real hunger for community, and when people find it, they will do all they can to remain within it. Real community is contagious. Being part of a community and doing a good job are seen as more important by workers in an organization than getting ahead or making a good living. "The values and interests of freedom, self-actualization, learning, community, excellence, uniqueness, service, and social responsibility truly attract people."[17] Nehemiah successfully negotiated the process to create and foster community. He was not tempted to settle for pseudo-community. Chaos visited the building group as different agendas arose, but the willingness of Nehemiah to empty himself of self-interest created a new paradigm that gave rise to true community.

CONCLUSION

When it comes to change, the leader has the choice to be either transactional (political and incremental in approach), or transformational, and this choice will inform him or her in the process of personal change as well as organizational change. Nehemiah is a transformational leader who "attends to the future, remains up-to-date with emerging trends, focuses on purpose and direction, and communicates a sense of where the company will be over the long term. In the motivator role…[he] attends to commitment, emphasizes…values, challenges people with new goals and aspirations, and creates a sense of excitement."[18] After Nehemiah completed the wall, he then set about to rebuild the nation through reformation and revival. This process of change is described in the final chapter of the book, as Nehemiah walks forward in obedience to God, with *faith and courage.* Both are essential qualities of effective leaders.

Agreeing with the wisdom of Nehemiah, Robert Quinn made the following insightful statement: "The land of excellence is safely guarded from unworthy intruders. At the gates stand two fearsome sentries—risk and learning. The keys to entrance are faith and courage."[19] Transformational leaders are willing to risk and then to learn from both their successes and failures. Nehemiah demonstrates that to move toward real change there has to be an unswerving faith in the direction (vision) and courage to stay the course despite opposition.

We can learn much from the life of Nehemiah, and this learning lends credence to George Weber's assertion: "The successful leader of the future must have one more attribute that weighs perhaps as much as all the others on the scale of effectiveness; he or she must be a tireless, inventive, observant, risk-taking, and ever-hopeful builder and enabler of management and leadership teams within and among the organization's constituent parts."[20]

Nehemiah epitomizes the truth of the following statement: "The future is not a result of choices among alternative paths offered by the present, but a place that is created, first in mind, next in will, then in activity. The future is not some place we are going to, but a place we are creating. The paths are not to be discovered, but made: and the activity of making the future changes both the maker and the destination."[21] Servant leaders dream, then believe enough to see the dream become reality.

FOR REFLECTION

Personal:

1. Nehemiah's discourse with the king was undergirded by four months of prayer and petition to God. What inferences can you make about Nehemiah and your own spiritual life?
2. Servant leaders assume positions of leadership when they perceive that position affords them the best capacity to serve. How have you personally discerned that your position is the best way for you to serve others?

Organizational:

1. Nehemiah honestly assessed the situation and its corresponding challenges. How does your organization approach the process of assessment and planning?
2. Nehemiah's effective leadership was evident in his singleness of purpose as he overcame external opposition that threatened to deter him. How does your organization react to challenges?

ENDNOTES

1. Robert Greenleaf, *Servant Leadership* (New York: Paulist Press, 1977), 13–14.

2. There are some commentators who believe that the position of cupbearer was one of privilege and not of slavery since Nehemiah's brother, Hanani, was the one who shared the news of Jerusalem after returning from a visit there. Yet the language that Nehemiah uses in the first seven chapters is rough and coarse. This

leads many commentators to the conclusion that he was not well educated, which lends credence to the idea that he was in fact a slave.

3. John White, *Excellence in Leadership: The Pattern of Nehemiah* (Leicester, England: InterVarsity Press, 1987), 23.

4. Unless otherwise noted, Scripture quotations in this chapter are taken from the New International Version.

5. Scripture references are taken from the book of Nehemiah unless noted otherwise.

6. Larry C. Spears and Michele Lawrence, eds., *Practicing Servant Leadership: Succeeding through Trust, Bravery, and Forgiveness* (San Francisco: Jossey-Bass, 2004), 9–24.

7. James M. Kouzes and Barry Z. Posner, *The Leadership Challenge* (San Francisco: Jossey-Bass, 2003), 150.

8. John C. Maxwell, *The 21 Irrefutable Laws of Leadership* (Nashville: Thomas Nelson, 1998), 18.

9. For an excellent guide on how to lead leaders, see Jeswald W. Salacuse, *Leading Leaders: How to Manage Smart, Talented, Rich and Powerful People* (New York: AMACOM, 2006).

10. Michael Wellbourn, *Understanding Teams* (Frenchs Forest, NSW: Prentice Hall, 2001), 138.

11. Ellen G. White, *Christian Service* (Nashville, TN: Southern Publishing Assoc., 2009), 177.

12. Salacuse, *Leading Leaders,* 131.

13. Salacuse, *Leading Leaders,* 131.

14. W. Bennis and B. Nanus, *Leaders: The Strategies for Taking Charge* (New York: Harper Collins, 1985), quoted in Spears and Lawrence, *Practicing Servant Leadership,* 148.

15. Ken Blanchard, *Leadership by the Book: Tools to Transform Your Workplace* (New York: Random House, 1999), 42.

16. Ken Blanchard, "Servant-Leadership Revisited" in *Insights on Leadership,* ed. Larry C. Spears (New York: John Wiley and Sons, 1998), 25.

17. Kouzes and Posner, *The Leadership Challenge,* 152.

18. Robert E. Quinn, *Deep Change: Discovering the Leader Within* (San Francisco: Jossey-Bass, 1996), 149.

19. Quinn, *Deep Change,* 165.

20. George B. Weber, "Growing Tomorrow's Leaders" in *The Leader of the Future,* ed. Frances Hesselbein, Marshall Goldsmith, and Richard Beckhard (San Francisco: Jossey-Bass, 1996), 309 quoted in Kenneth O. Gangel, *Team Leadership in Christian Ministry* (Chicago: Moody Press, 1997), 15–16.

21. Arthur Costa and Bena Kallick, *Assessment in the Learning Organization* (Alexandria, VA: Association for Supervision and Curriculum Development, 1995), quoted in Gwendolyn Hallsmith, *The Key to Sustainable Cities: Meeting Human Needs: Transforming Community Systems* (Gabriola Island, BC: New Society Publishers, 2003), 215.

14 | Women in the Old Testament: Leadership Principles

Jo Ann Davidson

Old Testament narratives frequently highlight leadership principles within the experience of women who contributed leadership at crucial moments. Textual details in those narratives, often overlooked, are especially illuminating in discovering principles of spiritual leadership.[1] Biblical history spans thousands of years and includes accounts of families, kings, queens, wars, political alliances, and business ventures. Yet these records are very compactly written, which means details become all the more significant.

No historical record is exhaustive. Historians comb evidence of past people and events to determine what they consider to have had the most impact. In one perspective, the biblical canon is also a history book. Its details have been carefully selected by the writers. In that light, it is significant to note that women in leadership emerge in the Old Testament, often demonstrating important leadership principles. The biblical writers have intentionally provided the details of their service.

One significant discovery should precede the examination of the following narratives. While it is not the purpose of this chapter to press this discovery as a comment on culture, it is the purpose to apply the discovery to the lessons regarding biblical leadership. It actually reveals an essential leadership principle. The discovery has to do with the equality of women in the creative initiative.

Cultures may embrace a variety of viewpoints, but from the foundation of Scripture, rightly understood, women are regarded as equals with their male counterparts in God's call to the service of leadership. Role distinctions of either gender in the human creation do not establish essential inferiority or superiority, at least in regard to the challenges of leadership. This obviously supports the idea that the Scriptures insist on the high dignity of women as being made in God's image, joint heirs with men of eternal life. Often historical texts in their cultural milieu do no better than to treat women as expendable, connected to evil influences, and/or less than men in terms of intrinsic worth. But this is counteracted in the first chapter of the Old Testament where the Deity speaks:

> Then God said, "Let Us make man in Our image, according to Our likeness; let *them* have dominion."…So God created man in His own image; in the image of God He created him; male and female He created them. (Gen. 1:26–27, emphasis added)[2]

Scripture expresses a positive portrait of human nature, both male and female, and God joins them in the leadership challenge. The implications of this are far-reaching and evident in Scripture.

The core of this chapter is developed around five female figures from the Old Testament. (This is obviously not intended to be an exhaustive treatment.) Other significant figures are mentioned in the chapter for the purpose of underscoring that the five narratives dealt with are not extraordinary. That is, women are often engaged in ministry and lessons of leadership emerge in their stories across centuries of time and diverse cultures. The chapter contributes understanding of leadership principles by identifying those principles in concluding remarks following each of the five narratives, and they are then summarized in the conclusion of the chapter. The reader can rest assured that these principles are not in any way intended to be unique. On the contrary, the principles in themselves both underscore the universality of biblical leadership principles and contribute to a single affirmation: God distributes leadership opportunity to all His human creation. He calls all to service. Men and women join in service to God. That is the larger idea regarding leadership that is the discovery of this chapter.

The conclusion affirms that this single idea contributes an important leadership principle grounded in our understanding of God. It is an understanding emerging from the theological reflection this chapter encourages. God equally regards all His creation. As we engage in leadership, we should be transformed to exercise the same principle of equality for all.

MIRIAM

The daughter of Jochebed exhibits intelligence, diplomacy, and courage. She probably never married for the biblical narratives make no mention of a husband or offspring, which they do for her two brothers.[3] Yet her important role in the founding of the covenant people is obvious. We typically only recall her one great sin and thus underestimate her role in the Exodus narratives, where she is depicted as formidable and charismatic: a prophetess, poet, musician, and leader.

Narrative studies now recognize her high profile in Scripture. In the book of Exodus she brackets the exodus event: appearing at the Nile as the book of Exodus opens and again at the Red Sea deliverance (Exod. 2:1–10; 15:20–21)—the latter in her mission as a prophetess, musician, and leader of the people of Israel along with Moses and Aaron, her two brothers.[4] She is called a prophet (Exod. 15:20), only the second person in the Pentateuch thus designated to that point. The Song of Moses and the Song of Miriam are both found in Exodus 15. The antiphonal Song of Miriam led by this inspired prophet is placed by the narrator as the grand climax of the exodus deliverance from Egypt.

> The subtle emphasis on the importance of the roles of women in the fate of Moses…and thereby the whole people of Israel, culminates in the duet of Moses and Miriam, where the reader is invited to remember and acknowledge the audacious roles of women, particularly Miriam.[5]

She was Jochebed and Amram's firstborn child. And once the exodus from Egypt commences, the focus of attention is generally on the lives of her two brothers. But God insists: "For I brought you up from the land of Egypt, I redeemed you from the house of bondage; and I sent before you Moses, Aaron, *and Miriam*" (Mic. 6:4, emphasis added). Another text includes a telling genealogical notation suggesting Miriam's stature among the covenant people. She is listed as a child (*ben,* literally "son") of Amram: "The children [literally, "sons"] of Amram were Aaron, Moses, and Miriam" (1 Chron. 6:3). The fact that Miriam is mentioned among Amram's "sons" in an entire chapter of fathers and male sons surely confirms her prominence.

Her death and burial are also recorded. It is noteworthy that, whereas other figures mentioned in the Exodus narratives (e.g., Hur, Eldad, and Medad, Moses's wife and father-in-law) disappear without their deaths being mentioned, the inclusion of Miriam's death in Numbers 20:1b highlights her significance. Miriam's stature and importance during the Exodus must not be underestimated. Indeed, most of the passages in the Pentateuch that mention Miriam by name represent her as a leader.[6]

Among the leadership principles notable in the experience of Miriam is communication. Consider first the natural intelligence and composure she was blessed with that accompanied her leadership. When she observed that the daughter of Pharaoh had discovered her infant brother floating in the basket among the reeds, she quickly discerned the compassion of the woman and offered a solution that could spare her brother's life, the encouragement Pharaoh's daughter needed at just the right moment. "Shall I go and call a nurse for you?" she asked (Exod. 2:7). Further, she had the confidence to present her mother as the nurse without showing any indication of her initiative to reunite the infant with his natural mother!

Miriam's song on the edge of the sea expressing the joy of deliverance suggests the inspiration of God joined with her own human intelligence and creativity. The song offered leadership through casting a vision of God's providence in the future of Israel. That vision had been formed and nurtured by God's calling of Moses, and by God's demonstration of His presence in signs and wonders accompanying the Exodus. The people embraced that vision of God's calling to some limited degree, though struggling with faith and human hesitancy. Miriam offered not only a refrain of creative praise, but she also confidently led the women of Israel in a celebrative moment, as they sang together to deepen their shared confidence in God. Miriam's abilities were blessed by God and become creative gifts to advance a vision of His will.

She cast this God-honoring vision with unusually artful and creative ability, demonstrating her leadership skills as a communicator. "Sing to the LORD, for He has triumphed gloriously! The horse and its rider He has thrown into the sea!" (Exod. 15:21). Today, believers in God still recite the lines of Miriam's song to strengthen their faith in God.

DEBORAH

It is generally recognized that the book of Judges serves as a continuation of the covenant history of the Pentateuch and Joshua. Chronologically, it comes between the conquest of Canaan under Joshua and the later emergence of the monarchy. After the death of Joshua, the Israelites do evil in the eyes of Yahweh and violate the covenant by turning to the gods of Canaan. Thus rejected, God withdraws His protection and surrounding peoples attack them. But when they finally cry to Him for deliverance, He sends deliverers, the judges, to relieve them of their oppressors. However, after the judges die, the people return to their old ways, sinking even deeper into apostasy, sometimes with a new judge leading the way. This progressive moral degeneration in Israel is one of the main themes in the book of Judges. But the faithfulness of the female judge Deborah is noted as an exception in this downward spiral.

In response to Israel's cry for help, Yahweh raises up courageous Deborah to bring His judgment on an oppressor of His people. The narrative presents Deborah reporting the commission from Yahweh— "Has not the LORD [Yahweh] the God of Israel commanded?" (Judg. 4:6). While the soldiers are fearful, Deborah's summons is emphatic, employing God's very words. Barak will accept the battle plan only if Deborah will go with him. He speaks for the first and only time in the narrative to insist that she come. He will not act upon Yahweh's command alone. Resolutely Deborah responds, "I will surely go with you" (Judg. 4:9), for she believes the divine promise.

Through Deborah, Yahweh brings reluctant Barak into action against a king with nine hundred iron chariots (Judg. 4:13)—a powerful military force for this time. Leadership is taken up by a prophet and judge—in this case a woman—who exhibits the dauntless courage missing from Israel's warriors: "Up! For this is the day in which the LORD has delivered Sisera into your hand. Has not the LORD gone out before you?" (4:14).

Once again Yahweh is gracious to His faithless people, for the "LORD routed Sisera" (Judg. 4:15). The expression is the same one found in Exodus 14:24, where it says that Yahweh "overthrew the army of the Egyptians" in the Red Sea, and also in Joshua 10:10: "So the LORD routed them…[with Joshua]." Thus we are instructed that this deliverance is another decisive miracle in spite of a great imbalance of military force. Twice in the narrative the reader is pointedly reminded that fearsome iron chariots offer no advantage when the God of heaven is in action! Superior military implements are no help then—just as the Egyptian army learned earlier at the Red Sea. Even mighty Sisera himself is brought down by a woman—Jael (Judg. 4:17–23).

This decisive victory is attributed to God as Deborah sings a victory ode (Judg. 5:1–31). The action is retold, but now through poetry. In contrast to Barak's initial hesitancy, Deborah proclaims: "Hear, O kings! Give ear, O princes! I, even I, will sing to the LORD; I will sing praise to the LORD God of Israel" (Judg. 5:3). Deborah unabashedly invites neighboring kings and princes to consider Israel's God and be reminded of their inferiority to the God of Israel. Deborah praises this divine victory as equal to that which Israel experienced earlier at the Red Sea when creation again fought on behalf of God's people. She insists that the God who has just liberated Israel is the God of Sinai.[7] She is obviously honoring His glory here early in Israel's history in the Promised Land. Her song of victory is considered a supreme example of a triumphant ode in Israelite literature—and it comes from the inspired and artistic soul of this great woman, joyfully perceiving God's work in history.

Deborah is the only judge called a prophet in the book of Judges. And this is mentioned even before naming her husband. She sat in judgment at the "Deborah-palm" (Judg. 4:5), settling disputes that lower courts likely referred to her because they were unable to adjudicate them. She was like the Supreme Court justice of Israel, the recognized political leader of the nation, "one of Israel's chief executive officers."[8] Deborah appears in the book of Judges without any apology, explanation, or suggestion that it was irregular for a woman to fill such a position.

The appointment of Sandra Day O'Connor as the first female Supreme Court justice in the history of the United States elicited much excitement. Yet Israel was far advanced in this respect. Deborah was, apparently, Chief Justice of the Supreme Court of ancient Israel, a judge to whom the entire Israelite culture turned for legal counsel and to settle court cases (Judg. 4:5). In addition, she is a political leader through whom God initiates a war, conscripting the nation for combat.[9] It is two women, Deborah and Jael, rather than Barak, who provide the leadership Israel needs in a time of crisis.

> The plot of Judges 4 signals the conceptuality of Deborah's predominant status and superior role in comparison with Barak.... Deborah is the initiator and Barak the reluctant follower. Deborah is the strategist and Barak the executor. Against this background the story develops with the subtle implication that the real heroic honor goes to the women, Deborah and Jael, as opposed to the men, Barak and Sisera.[10]

In Deborah's time, legal duties, military leadership, and prophecy were three recognized areas of authority. The book of Judges portrays her as serving in all three of these roles, for she decides disputes, summons people to war, and is a prophet. This great "mother in Israel" (Judg. 5:7) who chants a triumphant hymn of praise is also a wife and musician (Judg. 4:4; 5:1–30).[11]

Biblical history has recorded several female prophets urging God's will. Nothing in the biblical text ever suggests that it was a shocking thing for God to do nor is their service ever criticized as opposed to the divine will for women. It is never even hinted as extraordinary that women were chosen by God to communicate His will and to lead in its execution. These women were clearly accepted by the covenant community in their roles and blessed by God in their positions.

It should not be overlooked that she is the only judge described in the book of Judges with any detail without including serious character flaws: "Among the major judges, she escapes unscathed as a spiritual leader."[12] Indeed, "the only judge who combines all forms of leadership possible—religious, military, juridical, and poetical—is a woman!"[13] In her case, one sees teamwork and mutual cooperation between Deborah and Barak, with Barak following Deborah's leadership.

Several leadership principles emerge in the narrative of Deborah. She has confidence in God. Her confidence leads her to accompany soldiers to battle and to inspire them with her own unwavering faith. This is not the confidence of a prideful soul; rather, it is confidence emerging from deep, enduring faith. She also demonstrated, as did Miriam, creative casting of vision in the art of song. With that leadership she inspired hope. The principle of the courage to speak truth to power is expressed in her narrative as well.

It is character that distinguished her in her time. Deborah provided leadership during a time when the prevailing influence of her own culture was idolatrous and faithless. Enemies of the people whom God wished to form for His mission threatened to destroy the young nation. The temptation to adopt the culture of the surrounding nations, even to abandon their identity, was strong. In fact, the people of Israel were ready, with their leaders, to deny all that made them unique in God's providence. But Deborah withstood those influences. It is difficult to comprehend the power of such character, unswerving in devotion to God. God preserved a nation through the resolutely devout character of Deborah.

Today spiritual leadership calls for such strength of character. Only through submission, devotion, spiritual exercise, and the grace of God's presence can we serve with such character. Every Christian leader is reminded by Deborah's story of the importance of constant prayer and dependence on God. It is not intellect, talent, energy, or education that equips one for leadership. Transformation of character is at the heart of leadership, and such transformation is where leadership development begins.

QUEEN OF SHEBA

This female potentate sets out on a lengthy and perilous journey (at that time) to seek truth in an audience with king Solomon. This effort stands in contrast to the tasks that male kings were then generally noted for: "Now it came to pass in the spring of the year, at the time when kings go out to battle" (2 Sam. 11:1).

King Solomon is considered the wisest man in the Old Testament:

> He spoke three thousand proverbs, and his songs were one thousand and five. Also he spoke of trees, from the cedar tree of Lebanon even to the hyssop that springs out of the wall; he spoke also of animals, of birds, of creeping things, and of fish. And men of all nations, from all the kings of the earth who had heard of his wisdom, came to hear the wisdom of Solomon. (1 Kings 4:32–34)

Thus one of the rulers who comes "to hear the wisdom of Solomon" is a woman, the Queen of Sheba. She travels a great distance to learn from Israel's king. Fabulously wealthy, traveling "with a very great retinue" (1 Kings 10:2) to the court of Solomon, she gives him the modern equivalent of several million dollars (one hundred and twenty talents of gold), rare spices, and precious jewels.

Solomon and the Queen meet as equals, a "meeting of minds" it might be said—she comes to "test him with hard questions" (1 Kings 10:1). This implies she is no ignorant consort! Through the testimony of this queen, we learn that God's promise to give Solomon "a wise and understanding heart" (1 Kings 3:12) has been signally fulfilled:

> Now when the queen of Sheba heard of the fame of Solomon concerning the name of the LORD, she came to test him with hard questions. She came to Jerusalem…[and] spoke with him about all that was in her heart. So Solomon answered all her questions; there was nothing so difficult for the king that he could not explain it to her. And when the queen of Sheba had seen all the wisdom of Solomon…she said to the king: "It was a true report which I heard in my own land about your words and your wisdom. However, I did not believe the words until I came and saw with my own eyes; and indeed the half was not told me. Your wisdom and prosperity

exceed the fame of which I heard. Happy are your men and happy are these your servants, who stand continually before you and hear your wisdom! Blessed be the LORD your God, who delighted in you, setting you on the throne of Israel! Because the LORD has loved Israel forever, therefore He made you king, to do justice and righteousness." (1 Kings 10:1–9)

It is apparent that this queen is a very discerning woman for she determines to take this lengthy journey for the purpose of seeking wisdom—instead of political advantage. And she returns home praising God (v. 9). This is a unique occasion in all Scripture: two reigning monarchs discussing truth and wisdom instead of military strategy or alliance. The Queen of Sheba is a rare reigning sovereign of whom no war or battle is recorded. No wonder composers such as G. F. Handel were inspired to write a composition about her singular visit to Solomon's court.

The leadership principle of collegiality is demonstrated in the narrative of the Queen of Sheba. Positional power, such as was held by a monarch in biblical times and is now experienced by those serving in a role assigned some authority by a community in our time, is often accompanied by insular judgment. Position is a challenge to spiritual leadership. Humans allow the power assigned to positions to delude them into thinking they have knowledge and wisdom that others do not have.

Communities form structure to accomplish shared mission. That structure requires persons willing to serve in designated positions with authority to perform certain functions assigned with such positions. But human nature, suffering from millenniums of sinful experience, struggles with power. When given positions of power, human beings too often act alone, regard themselves above others, and abuse power. It was not so with this biblical character. She considered herself a learner at the same time that she served as a monarch.

Not enough is known of this leader's story to assume this principle was demonstrated in all her dealings with the nation she served, but in this one narrative we see extraordinary collegiality. She sought wisdom, she observed, and she learned.

HULDAH

This Old Testament prophetess is portrayed as the primary religious authority in her time and place. The King of Judah sends Hilkiah the priest, Shaphan the scribe, and several others equally prominent in the state and church at that time to this woman: "Go, *inquire of the* LORD [Yahweh] for me, for the people and for all Judah, concerning the words of this book that has been found" (2 Kings 22:13, emphasis added). Huldah's voice is considered authoritative. She responds, "Thus says the LORD [Yahweh] God of Israel: 'Tell the man who sent you to me, "Thus says the LORD: Behold, I will bring calamity on this place and on its inhabitants—all the words of the book which the king of Judah has read'" (2 Kings 22:15–16). A woman is called to certify that the scroll found in the Temple is authoritative scripture.

Huldah does not coddle those sent to her with pleasing, gentle words, nor does she take time to defend the book's authenticity. She amplifies the conviction already voiced by Josiah in verse 13: "Great is the wrath of the LORD [Yahweh] that is aroused against us." Whereas Josiah locates the guilt of the people of the past ("our fathers have not obeyed the words of this book"; 2 Kings 22:13), Huldah places the burden on the current inhabitants who, says Yahweh, "have forsaken Me and burned incense to other gods, that they might provoke Me to anger with all the works of their hands" (2 Kings 22:17).

Huldah is the authoritative interpreter of Scripture for her day. Note her "hermeneutical principle": She accepts the veracity of the book, including its announcement of doom, because of Judah's current condition. The Hebrew Scriptures are officially recognized as authoritative—validating our present canon. The king recognizes the words of Yahweh written in the book, and Huldah is called upon as the authorized interpreter. The king knows and accepts her authority to declare the present will of God. Huldah's role is significant. She places herself, her people, and the king under the divine text by declaring its judgment against them.

The scroll of Deuteronomy had been found as the Temple was being repaired and refurbished. This particular book deals chiefly with Israel's religious practices as Moses records his final address to the people. Thereby the authority that the king recognizes in Huldah is profound.

The Hebrew text specifically states that Huldah is a prophetess and a wife (2 Kings 22:14). She is consulted at the very time that Jeremiah, a prominent prophet in the Old Testament, is already well established in his prophetic office.

Leadership is everyone's opportunity. People do not necessarily become prophets in the sense of Huldah's calling while serving with a community in leadership. But understanding biblical leadership helps us realize that we are to speak truth within our communities. That truth involves discernment of God's will. Speaking truth suggests the study of Scripture combined with the quality of spirituality established in prayer. For all those engaged in the leadership challenge, it means clarity in speaking truth and the courage to speak to the issues of our time and place.

ESTHER

The book of Esther presents a complex interplay of narrative elements, yielding a fascinating plot whereby God's people are delivered from a deadly death decree. And a woman is the agent of deliverance. The timing of her courageous acts is crucial to the survival of the Hebrew people.

The men in the story, with the exception of Mordecai, are not the heroes. It is the women, Vashti and Esther, who display the most admirable characters. Vashti has the courage to refuse the drunken suggestion of the king to appear in a manner that does not suggest moral purity. Esther, when an extreme emergency arises for her people, displays incredible courage in dealing with the king's rash and deadly proclamation, even courageously revealing her ethnicity at this dangerous time. To prevent genocide, she bravely discloses herself and even her threatened nationality to the king who made the death decree. She demonstrates her ability to analyze, strategize, and execute a possibly fatal course of action—and persevere in its fulfillment. God uses Esther when a whole nation's existence is at stake. And her name is mentioned fifty-five times in the text, more than any other woman in the Bible.

The narrator wants the reader to notice what this brave woman was able to do in a Persian culture where women were considered possessions for men's entertainment and where queens were powerless—royal in name only. Esther, an exile and an orphan, becomes queen of the mightiest empire on earth and is able to avert genocide—all because of her courage.

The courage that leadership requires takes many forms. Sometimes it is the simple courage to challenge the status quo, asking hard questions about policies and procedures in the interest of improving service or advancing mission. Those questions are not always welcome. Even though offered in a kind or gentle spirit, they can trouble others.

Courage is frequently the willingness to process change. Though carefully processed, with inclusion of stakeholders across the breadth of any group's shared mission, leading change still involves risk and requires courage. The characteristic of creativity, often taken for granted, is a helpful quality, even an essential one in the leadership challenge, equipping people to process change and move beyond their current experience. To think and form strategy outside the identified bounds of a group's prior experience requires courage.

Esther demonstrated courage in all these ways. She refused to conceal her identity and thus allow events to take their natural course. She would not accept the status quo. She became determined to change the way things were, and she invented a creative way to approach the problem.

Her most evident demonstration of courage is seen in her determination to act. Knowing the truth of God's will, knowing providence had placed her in a position of opportunity, she had the character to act, knowing it could cost her life. An anonymous saying asserts: "Courage is fear that has said its prayers." That describes the source of Esther's courage. She finds courage by dedication to a purpose higher than her our own life. We would do well to emulate this essential leadership quality.

IN CONCLUSION: MANY OTHERS...

The leadership principles evidenced in the lives of these five Old Testament characters are consistent with the leadership principles found woven throughout the narratives, instruction, and prophecies of Scripture. They are not isolated revelations. Their stories remind the thoughtful reader of the power of vision and of the process of inspiring others by communicating that vision. The characters demonstrate confidence in the providence and calling of God. They show unusual discernment of right and of justice. They act with courage. Theirs is not a prideful courage grounded in their own physical or even intellectual strength. Instead, it is courage emerging from submission to a higher purpose. It is evidenced in persuasion and dedication. They express collegiality, a sense of belonging to a community beyond themselves.

One final leadership lesson should be noted. These five characters are all females whose stories help us understand leadership in a context across centuries of history when women were generally not empowered in their cultures. To grasp this last lesson, consider that many other women were noted as leaders in similar ways in Scripture. Hannah initiates an act of worship though her husband is a Levite.[14] The wise woman of Tekoa is sought to instruct David in a complex situation, assuming the highly regarded role of sage. New Testament women follow in this same tradition (2 Sam. 14). The Gospel of Luke, the only biblical book written by a Gentile, highlights many women. For example, he records the eighty-four-year-old widow Anna as the prophetess who announces the birth of Jesus in the capital city of Jerusalem: She "spoke of Him to all those who looked for redemption in Jerusalem" (Luke 2:38). The first "apostle" to the Samaritans was a Gentile woman: "Then they [the Samaritans] said to the woman, 'Now we believe, not because of what you said, for we have heard for ourselves and know that this is indeed the Christ, the Savior of the world'" (John 4:42). Paul acknowledges many women in ministry in the last chapter of Romans. One of those is Phoebe (16:1–2), whose "servant of the Lord" translation hides her role as "deacon"—and deacons were preaching and baptizing at this time[15] (not just taking up the offering). The book of Acts speaks of the church at Philippi being organized by women (Acts 16:11–15). This occurred at a time when Jewish men were still thanking God that they were not born women. The new church becomes a great political, gender, and ethnic equalizer (Gal. 3:27–29) and echoes the original plan of God in Eden: "let *them* have dominion" (Gen. 1:26)—fulfilling God's promises to Abraham of the covenant blessing extending to the whole world. And the psalmist is right: "The Lord gave the word; great was the company [literally, "of females," in Hebrew] of those who proclaimed it" (Ps. 68:11).

What unique leadership understanding does this plethora of women in the account of Scripture provide? The lesson, or the principle, is so apparent that the casual reader may miss its importance.

The essential core equality of all human life is grounded in the character of God. It is apparent that God does not discriminate between male and female in those moments when He calls and blesses leadership. Our usual arguments about how humans view male or female, or about how gender roles express themselves in culture, pale before this significant insight into the character of God. He values all His human creation, gifts them, calls them, and utilizes their lives in His service. Racial, personal, or gender differences do not create inequality in the view and purposes of God's calling. Equality in the spiritual realm, and in the presence of God, transcends intellectual capacity, physical strength or energy, talent, and physical distinctives such as ethnicity, race, or gender. We all serve one God, who pours His blessing out on all. Spiritual leaders, transformed by the Spirit of God, share this deep and essential view of equality, and they express it in their leadership.

FOR REFLECTION

Personal:

1. What influences in your life situation have shaped your view of the leadership women bring to the church and society?
2. In your experience, how have women contributed to helping or forming your life and service?

Organizational:

1. How is your organization benefiting from the service and gifts of women in leadership?

2. How does your organization develop women for service and endeavor to create appreciation for the service of women?

ENDNOTES

1. "A literary approach to narrative yields practical benefits in bibliography, comparative literature, exegesis, and exposition. While source criticism remains alive, its health is deteriorating. Current biblical scholarship is reassessing source criticism's 'assured results,' partly due to literary studies of the Bible. By concentrating on the form of biblical texts, a literary approach often identifies unifying patterns that challenge traditional source criticism," Don Parker, *Using Biblical Hebrew in Ministry: A Practical Guide for Pastors, Seminarians, and Bible Students* (Lanham, MD: University Press of America, 1995), 118–119.

2. Scripture quotations in this chapter, unless otherwise noted, are taken from the New King James Version.

3. Of Moses and Aaron, her two brothers: we know the names of Moses's wife and sons, and also the names of Aaron's sons (which implies he had a wife).

4. "The horses of Pharaoh went with his chariots and his horsemen into the sea.… Then Miriam the prophetess, the sister of Aaron, took the timbrel in her hand; and all the women went out after her with timbrels and with dances. And Miriam answered them: 'Sing to the LORD, for He has triumphed gloriously!'" (Exod. 15:19–21).

5. Hyun Chul Paul Kim, "Gender Complementarity in the Hebrew Bible" in *Reading the Hebrew Bible for a New Millennium: Form, Concept, and Theological Perspective,* vol. 1 of *Theological and Hermeneutical Studies,* ed. Wonil Kim, et al., Studies in Antiquity and Christianity (Harrisburg, PA: Trinity Press International, 2000), 274.

6. Exodus 15:20–21; Numbers 12:1, 4–5, 10, 15; 20:1; 26:59; Deuteronomy 24:9.

7. Exodus 19–20; Deuteronomy 33:2; Psalm 68:7–8; Habakkuk 3:3.

8. Jo Ann Hackett, "In the Days of Jael: Reclaiming the History of Women in Ancient Israel" in *Immaculate and Powerful: The Female in Sacred Image and Social Reality,* ed. Clarissa W. Atkinson, Constance H. Buchanan, and Margaret R. Miles (Boston: Beacon Press, 1985), 22.

9. In the earliest history of Israel, "Localized and sporadic defense problems existed during this period, but they were met…without the formalized structure of a standing army, [so] women could and did contribute to the defense effort. Female participation in the military realm is in fact a typical feature of pioneer societies," Carol Meyers, *Discovering Eve: Ancient Israelite Women in Context* (New York: Oxford University Press, 1988), 174.

10. Kim, "Gender Complementarity," 277. Kim also shows evidence for this conclusion in the narrative's contrast between the cowardice of Barak and the courage of Deborah. Robert Alter does the same in *The World of Biblical Literature*

(New York: Basic Books, 1992), 40–43; also Mark A. Vincent, "The Song of Deborah: A Structural and Literary Consideration," *JSOT* 91 (2000): 64–65.

11. There are other songs of victory, besides this one in Judges, found in the Old Testament: Exodus and First Samuel—each also directed by a woman. In fact, notice the godly Israelite women who lived in the time of Judges: Deborah, Mrs. Manoah, Jephthah's daughter, Ruth, Naomi. The time of the Judges was a bleak period in Israelite history. By contrast, the lives of these women in the time of Judges/Ruth exhibit even greater luster. Deborah's oracles concern the entire community and indicate that a prophetess was duly authorized, as any male prophet, to articulate matters of national and sacral concern to the whole body of the people.

12. Charme E. Robarts, "Deborah—Judge, Prophetess, Military Leader, and Mother in Israel" in *Essays on Women in Earliest Christianity*, vol. 2, ed. Carroll D. Osburn (Joplin, MO: College Press, 1995), 76.

13. Mieke Bal, *Death and Dissymmetry: The Politics of Coherence in the Book of Judges* (Chicago: University of Chicago Press, 1988), 209.

14. "Now when she had weaned him, she took him up *with her,* with three bulls, one ephah of flour, and a skin of wine, and brought him [Samuel] to the house of the LORD in Shiloh" (1 Sam. 1:24, emphasis added).

15. For example, Philip—see Acts 6:5; 8:5–13, 26–40; 21:8.

15 | Jesus and Leadership

R. Clifford Jones

B ooks on leadership continue to be published by the ton and are consumed by the general public whose appetite for more of the same seems insatiable. The shelves of Christian bookstores are heavy with books about leadership. Yet hunger for a true understanding of leadership among Christians should not surprise us, because Jesus devoted His ministry to developing the spiritual leadership of the people who would launch the first Christian communities.

For the Christian, leadership must be viewed and understood on Jesus's terms, not those of modern leadership texts or manuals. What did Jesus say to His disciples about leadership? More importantly, how did Jesus model leadership for them? In this chapter, the leadership of Jesus will be examined, beginning with an investigation of Jesus's understanding of His mission and an exploration of His use of two important terms: *diakonos* and *doulos*. The following is a reflection on the leadership of Jesus and the insight it provides for Christian leaders today.

JESUS AND MISSION

The point of departure for an exploration of the leadership of Jesus must be *mission.* Jesus understood His leadership to be grounded in His mission. He affirmed, "For I have come down from heaven not to do my will but to do the will of him who sent me" (John 6:38).[1] Jesus led from His mission, and that mission was primary, formative, and guiding. It shaped all that He did. It was His sense of mission that fueled His passionate pursuit of goals and objectives transcending the earthly domain. It was His clarity of mission that powered His success in transforming the people and culture He encountered while on earth. Implicit in the notion of Jesus being on a mission is the thought that He was sent to earth, suggesting, if not underscoring, that Jesus did not aspire to leadership in and of Himself. As He led, Jesus never lost sight of the fact that His leadership was not about Him; it was always about His Father and the mission that had been entrusted to Him. Jesus could lead because He was led; He was led by the mission of the Triune God, a mission He formulated with the Father and the Spirit from the foundation of the world. Jesus continually sought His Father's will, submitting His agenda, if it could be said that He had one, to what had been foreordained.

Christian leaders, therefore, are men and women who have been invited by God to join in the mission of the church. They are people who view leadership as mission, not career, and they know that without mission, leadership is destined to lose its focus and lapse into a worship of the cult of personality. These leaders know that leadership is, as Henry and Richard Blackaby assert in the title of their work, "moving people on to God's agenda."[2]

SERVANTS AND SLAVES

Even a cursory reading of the Gospels will reveal that Jesus practiced—even embodied—what is known today as servant leadership.[3] Christ never aspired to overwhelm those He led with His power and authority, declaring instead, "For even the Son of Man did not come to be served, but to serve, and to give his life as a ransom for many" (Mark 10:45). Over and over, Jesus sought to drive home the truth that leadership is about servanthood by using two terms—*diakonos* and *doulos*—and their derivatives. The first term captures and conveys the idea of serving, as in serving at tables, and connotes humility and attitudes associated with service. The second conveys service grounded in obedience rendered because one has given up certain rights, willingly or otherwise.

While the disciples of Jesus were traveling to Capernaum, an argument about who would be the greatest in the kingdom of God erupted among them, prompting Him to say, "Anyone who wants to be first must be the very last, and the servant of all" (Mark 9:35). The feud continued in the days that followed, ending with Jesus using the occasion to differentiate between the authoritarian rule of those outside God's kingdom and those He would commission as His disciples. "You know that the rulers of the Gentiles lord it over them, and their high officials exercise authority over them. Not so with you. Instead, whoever wants to become great among you must be your servant, and whoever wants to be first must be your slave—just as the Son of Man did not come to be served, but to serve, and to give his life as a ransom for many" (Matt. 20:25–28). Earlier, in a stinging repudiation of the hypocrisy of the Pharisees, who by precept and practice viewed leadership as synonymous with position, power, and prestige, Jesus had stated, "The greatest among you will be your servant. For those who exalt themselves will be humbled, and those who humble themselves will be exalted" (Matt. 23:11–12).

Laurie Beth Jones poignantly articulates how service defined and shaped the ministry and leadership of Jesus. She writes, "Jesus, the leader, served his people. Most religions teach that we are put here to serve God; yet, in Jesus, God is offering to serve us. Some people are shocked by the inference that God serves us. Yet this man who represented God—who was imbued with all the power of God—walked up to people and asked, 'How can I help you?'"[4]

The notion of service inherent in the word *diakonos* means that Christian leaders will follow Jesus wherever He leads them, even to the foot of the Cross. As Jesus prepared to offer His life in sacrifice, He desired to convey an important truth about service: He appealed to the imagery of a kernel of wheat dying in the ground to become more productive. Jesus informed His disciples that "anyone who loves their life will lose it, while anyone who hates their life in this world will keep it for eternal life," concluding by affirming that "Whoever serves me must follow me; and where I am, my servant also will be. My Father will honor the one who serves me" (John 12:25–26). The lesson could not be clearer: The one who serves Jesus Christ must be willing to follow Him into death.

Jesus said, "You are my friends if you do what I command. I no longer call you servants, because a servant does not know his master's business. Instead, I have called you friends, for everything that I have learned from my Father I have made known to you" (John 15:14–15). In saying that He no longer viewed His disciples as servants (*doulos*) but as friends (*philous*), Jesus was underscoring not only the significance and centrality of the servant-slave metaphor, but, more importantly, the core value of relational leadership. To the extent that Christian leaders continually encourage one another in love, going so far as to champion the causes of each other and celebrate the successes of each other, backbiting and ugly striving for position will be minimized, if not eradicated altogether. That is the call and challenge of Christian leadership: a leadership model that is radical and transforming to the core. Yet this model is viewed with suspicion by those who have not experienced the grace of Jesus Christ.

LEADING WITH HUMILITY

According to Jesus, the call to servant leadership is a call to humility. Jesus did not affirm the accomplishments of people who clamored for positions and places of primacy. In fact, God calls the humble, not the proud and self-important, into leadership. Luke records an incident in which Jesus, noticing how guests to a dinner positioned themselves in the coveted places of honor at the table, said:

> When someone invites you to a wedding feast, do not take the place of honor, for a person more distinguished than you may have been invited. If so, the host who invited both of you will come and say to you, "Give this person your seat." Then, humiliated, you will have to take the least important place. But when you are invited, take the lowest place, so that when your host comes,

he will say to you, "Friend, move up to a better place." Then you will be honored in the presence of all the other guests. For all those who exalt themselves will be humbled, and those who humble themselves will be exalted. (Luke 14:8–11)

The lessons and implications for Christian leadership embedded in this teaching of Jesus are fundamentally significant. Just as salvation is the free gift to humankind from a loving and gracious God, so is Christian leadership. Opportunity for Christian leadership is bestowed on all. More significantly, Christian leadership is manifested by the humble, the man or the woman who is free from selfish ambition and drive. Christians serve out of devotion to Jesus and His mission, and as servants, they exercise leadership in whatever context God places them. They operate under the assumption that it is God who not only has called them to lead, but also called them to *serve*. They exercise leadership to advance His mission and fulfill the responsibilities placed upon their shoulders. They know that they are servants of God, and they take joy in the success of others rather than becoming covetous or jealous.

The humility that Jesus expected His followers to imitate was demonstrated in the incarnation and crucifixion of Jesus. According to Paul, Christians "should have the same mindset as Christ Jesus: Who, being in very nature God, did not consider equality with God something to be used to his own advantage; rather, he made himself nothing by taking the very nature of a servant, being made in human likeness. And being found in appearance as a man, he humbled himself by becoming obedient to death—even death on a cross!" (Phil. 2:5–8). Humility was at once the core and content of Jesus's being and mission. The ambition of Jesus was never to be first or foremost, but to do His Father's will. When Jesus challenged the worldview of religious leaders, or cleared the Temple of those who defiled its ministry, He was acting in selfless service to the will of God, not to accomplish His own plans or realize vain ambitions. When Jesus was the focus of the admiration and appreciation of clamoring throngs, He deflected and redirected such to His Father. Ego was never a problem with Jesus Christ, who was subjected to the vilest and most heinous death known at that time: death on a cross. Jesus died as a common criminal, between two common criminals, while people around the Cross jeered and taunted. The death Jesus Christ experienced was hardly the kind expected of a prominent world leader. Thus from the very beginning of His life on earth, to His crucifixion on Calvary, and then to His burial in a borrowed tomb, Jesus modeled humility.

Between His life and death, Jesus led by serving, the most poignant example of His service taking place in the Upper Room when He washed the feet of His disciples. John records,

> Jesus knew that the Father had put all things under his power, and that he had come from God and was returning to God; so he got up from the meal, took off his outer clothing, and wrapped a towel around his waist. After that, he poured water into a basin and began to wash his disciples' feet, drying them with the towel that was wrapped around him (John 13:3–5).

Note that Jesus does this at the very moment of His fullest realization and actualization of divinity. In washing the feet of His disciples—an assignment usually performed by servants on such occasions—Jesus showed an amazing picture of God: that He was willing to surrender His exalted position at the table to serve those He was leading, even the one who would betray Him. As a servant leader, Christ rose above the temptation to retaliate, a temptation to which not a few leaders succumb. And in washing the feet of Peter, who would later deny Him, Jesus showed that meeting the needs of those whom they serve is paramount on the agenda of true servant leaders. To wash the feet of His disciples, Jesus had to bend His knees, an act that is infused with symbolism and meaning, including that of submission.

In his seminal work, *Jesus on Leadership,* C. Gene Wilkes asserts that what drove Jesus to serve His disciples in the Upper Room was the acute sense Jesus had that God was in complete control of His life. Wilkes states,

> When we trust that God is in control of our life, we can take big risks. We can relinquish impressive positions. We can act like true servants without being insecure or defensive. A servant can risk her place of leadership for the purpose of service. A servant leader trusts that in her relationship with Christ, God has placed

all power under her, that she has come from God, and that she is returning to God.[5]

In his call for Christian leaders to emulate the humility of Christ, Paul affirms that God raised up Jesus. "Therefore God exalted him to the highest place and gave him the name that is above every name, that at the name of Jesus every knee should bow, in heaven and on earth and under the earth, and every tongue acknowledge that Jesus Christ is Lord, to the glory of God the Father" (Phil. 2:9–11). Christian leadership is a paradox, as is Christianity itself. Just as Christians give away in order to keep and are richest when they seem poorest, Christian leaders rise up when they bow low. Jim Cress characterizes this as "the greatness of descent."[6] So too does Bill Hybels, who says, "The message of Philippians is this: If you want to be truly great, then the direction you must go is down. You must descend into greatness."[7] Henri Nouwen picks up the refrain when he reminds us that "the way of the Christian leader is not the way of upward mobility in which our world has invested so much, but the way of downward mobility ending on the cross.… It is not a leadership of power and control, but leadership of powerlessness and humility in which the suffering servant of God, Jesus Christ, is made manifest."[8]

DEVELOPING LEADERS

Jesus did not gather power and authority to Himself. Though He was God, He emptied Himself and clothed Himself in humanity, complete with humanity's limitations and inclinations. One of the most significant inclinations He rose above was humankind's penchant to hold on to and not share power and authority. Jesus demonstrated an amazing ability to empower others, to trust others with leadership, to allow others to stumble and fail without condemning them, and to share whatever and all He had with those He led. In a true sense, Jesus was all about developing and multiplying leaders, doing so at any and all costs. Jesus developed the leadership abilities latent in every disciple.

Toward the end of His time with His leadership team, Jesus said to them, "All authority in heaven and on earth has been given to me. Therefore go and make disciples of all nations, baptizing them in the name of the Father and of the Son and of the Holy Spirit, and teaching them to obey everything I have commanded you. And surely I am with you always, to the very end of the age" (Matt. 28:18–20). After His resurrection and just before His ascension, Jesus promised His disciples that the Holy Spirit would be bestowed upon them, thereby empowering them to be effective witnesses for Him throughout the world (Acts 1:8). Focusing on the importance of Jesus's promise, Wilkes writes:

> We often overlook the fact that Jesus stated his authority to send before he sent his followers on the mission. Leaders who send others out without the authority to make decisions send powerless followers to defeat. As leader, Jesus claimed his authority to send those he had recruited before sending them out. Jesus shared his authority along with his responsibility to make disciples of all people.... Servant leaders share their responsibility and authority to meet a greater need.[9]

Secure leaders are able to share power and authority, and leadership that is shared generally results in growth: in the individual person and their spiritual walk, and in the organization as a whole.

Mark records: "Then Jesus went around teaching from village to village. Calling the Twelve to him, he began to send them out two by two and gave them authority over impure spirits" (6:6–7). Jesus did not engage in ministry by Himself. Our Lord constantly had people with Him sharing ministry: He called and formed a band of men and women known as His disciples (John 1:35–50). Jesus delighted in inviting people to join Him in ministry, essentially sharing leadership with those whom He called. On the mount where He was transfigured, Jesus was accompanied by Peter, James, and John, the same three disciples He had asked to watch and pray with Him as He prepared to enter into His agony in the Garden of Gethsemane (Mark 14:32–33; Luke 9:28).

Did Jesus need to build a team to be effective in ministry? Obviously not. As the Son of God, Jesus possessed all power and had all authority. Why then did Jesus prioritize building a leadership team? It was His nature to do so. In doing so He modeled leadership lessons, one being that Christian leaders include others in what they do. Wilkes writes,

> Servant leaders team with others to serve. They know that effective leadership is not a solo venture. Leadership is a team sport. Servant leaders also know that teams move the ball down the field to reach a goal. They know that they are most effective when they can team with others who are equipped to meet a specific need. Jesus' earthly ministry revolved around building a team of close followers. He called, equipped them, and mobilized them for ministry. After Jesus had completed His mission on earth, these disciples would carry the message of God's salvation to the world. Jesus modeled team ministry for those He called to be servant leaders.[10]

The literature on the importance of team building and on the vital role teams play in the achievement of the goals and objectives of organizations is extensive. Today, leaders who function as the proverbial Lone Rangers are frowned upon and not generally successful or effective, while team building is considered a core responsibility of leadership.[11] Teams maximize the strengths of people while minimizing their weaknesses. As team members complement each other, striving together in pursuit of a shared vision and exercising a diversity of skills, effective service is assured. A team of people will accomplish more than an individual on his or her own.

Yet teams also call for humility on the part of the more gifted and a willingness on the part of the leader to share authority and responsibility. Leaders who hoard power stifle the creativity and abilities of team members. Such leaders reveal their own insecurities and fears while demonstrating a woeful inability to trust people. In the end, such leaders will wear themselves out trying to do everything on their own.

Jesus was willing to empower those whom He called to serve with Him. He saw that each individual can exercise leadership in the mission of God. He promised His disciples the power of the Holy Spirit, and nearing the end of His time on earth, Jesus told His disciples that He would share the authority of heaven with them as they set forth to disciple the world (Matt. 28:18–20; Acts 1:8). Jesus had spent an inordinate amount of time mentoring His disciples:

instructing, qualifying, and encouraging them for service (Matt. 13; Mark 4:35–41; 10:32–34; Luke 14:26; 17:7–10; John 14).

A fundamentally significant element of team building is leadership succession. It has been said, and rightly so, that there is no sustainable success without a successor. John C. Maxwell views legacy as one of the indispensable laws of leadership, saying that the success of leaders should be gauged by whether their organizations thrive after they leave.[12] Leaders who do not build up others or who fail to multiply the leadership potential in those who serve alongside them neglect to perform one of their key roles.

LEADING WITH INTEGRITY

In his seminal work *The Spiritual Formation of Leaders,* Chuck Miller bemoans the shift in focus from character to personality as the dominant virtue required for effective leadership, asserting that the shift is responsible for the prevalence of moral failure in leaders.[13] Character is the most important element of Christian leadership. Being is foundational, and being is infinitely more critical than doing. History is littered with the human wreckage of leaders whose lack of character both derailed their leadership and hurt others.

The leadership of Jesus Christ was grounded in His being. Jesus led with who He was, from what He thus believed and thought, more than from a skill set—as important as those competencies were. In leading with His being, Jesus demonstrated that Christians lead most transformationally when they lead out of their personal relationship with God rather than rely on the formulas and slogans derived from leadership manuals and books.

The relationship that Jesus nurtured and sustained with His Father led to a life of transparency, authenticity, and honesty. Responding to Thomas who questioned Him about the way he and the other disciples would travel with Jesus, He said, "I am the way and the truth and the life" (John 14:6). Jesus was at once the incarnation and embodiment of truth—His life was a model of integrity for Christian leaders. Ellen G. White says, "The greatest want of the world is the want of men—men who will not be bought or sold; men who in their inmost souls are true and honest; men who do not fear to call sin by its right name; men whose conscience is as true to duty as the needle to the pole; men who will stand for the right though the heavens fall."[14]

Prayer was the medium through which Jesus maintained His relational connection to His Father; this activity was anything but a pastime for Him. Jesus sometimes prayed through the night, in order to access the will and strength of God (Matt. 14:23; John 17:1–25). The prayer life of Jesus demonstrates that the source of power required for the successful promulgation of ministry lies outside of Christian leaders. The most effective Christian leadership is that which emanates from prayer because it gets to the heart of integrity in leadership. The power of leadership is not in technique but in prayer, which is what moves the arms of God and is a critical element in equipping people for service.

Yet Christian leaders need people who are constantly praying for them too. Far too often, Christian leaders are the only ones praying within an organization, spending themselves physically and emotionally as they intercede on behalf of others. Just as leaders will fail to adequately and appropriately equip people for service if they neglect to pray for them, so too will they fail to lead effectively if they do not have people praying for them. Of course, to have people praying for them, leaders will have to humble themselves. They will have to be vulnerable and transparent about areas in their lives in which they are in need. Yet it is in the very act of being vulnerable that they will become strong and experience the power of God in their ministry.

JESUS THE VISIONARY

The life of Jesus on earth was a journey of vision casting. As He launched His public ministry on earth, Jesus spoke of a time when life would be radically different. Jesus envisioned a time of possibility and betterment, a preferred future in which the principles of the kingdom of God would reign. In His Sermon on the Mount, Jesus spoke of a vision He hoped would be broadly shared. Over and over, Jesus intoned, "You have heard.... But I tell you..." to drive home the difference between what He envisioned and what was (Matt. 5:1–48). And when He was questioned by Pilate concerning whether He was the king of the Jews, Jesus responded, "My kingdom is not of this world.... But now my kingdom is from another place" (John 18:36).

John Maxwell considers *vision* to be one of his twenty-one indispensable qualities of a leader.[15] Vision is foundational, central, and integral to leadership, and a vision-less leader is a living, breathing contradiction. Scripture asserts that without vision, which George Barna defines as foresight with insight that is based on hindsight,[16] people are destined to desolation and dissolution (Prov. 29:18). Little else besides a God-given vision for the future motivates people to mission. It was no different with Jesus, who stated, "Do not let your hearts be troubled. You believe in God; believe also in me. My Father's house has many rooms; if that were not so, would I have told you that I am going there to prepare a place for you? And if I go and prepare a place for you, I will come back and take you to be with me that you also may be where I am" (John 14:1–3).

CONCLUSION

Jesus came to earth for a specific purpose, one that He alone could pursue and fulfill. That purpose was to redeem humanity through His atonement, and in doing so influence people to follow Him in living lives of obedience to God that bring glory to God's name. Even though He was born under humble conditions and raised in humble circumstances, Jesus lived a life of influence from the start. Yet Jesus did not emerge as a leader because of circumstances, or even the historical moment, though He was mindful of the context of time and history. Jesus was a dynamic leader because He was empowered by the Holy Spirit and led from His being. If ever one led with integrity, that person was Jesus Christ. Filled with the Spirit, Jesus was a compelling figure who attracted the admiration of multitudes, drawing followers to Himself (Matt. 2:1–12; Luke 2:53; John 6:2).

For Christian leaders, Jesus remains the prototype and model of leadership. Our Lord viewed mission as the basis for His leadership, and in His incarnation and crucifixion He demonstrated that Christian leaders achieve their purpose not by climbing the corporate ladder but by traveling the path of humility. Only to the extent that Christian leaders are self-effacing will they become great. Over and over, Christ emphasized that He came to earth to serve, identifying as friends those He assembled on His leadership team. Never one to hoard, Jesus Christ sought to develop leadership skills in others by sharing His authority and power. Our Lord focused on others, placing value on people, and inspiring them with a clear vision of the future to which they were called by the will of His Father. People felt welcomed and affirmed in the presence of Jesus, and not a few left Jesus's presence feeling liberated and empowered for mission and ministry.

To lead as Jesus led requires that one be emptied of self and all worldly ambition, and calls for courage and a mind-set that places a premium on valuing others. In short, servant leadership calls for conversion—and the heart of Jesus Christ.

FOR REFLECTION

Personal:

1. Implicit in Jesus's robust prayer life was the conviction that the success of the servant leader's endeavors would come from God. How does your personal prayer life reflect your level of dependence upon God?
2. Jesus deflected the accolades of society, refusing selfish ambition as the governing power in the accomplishing of His Father's mission. How difficult is it for you to resist succumbing to human praise and approval during your attempts at being mission minded?

Organizational:

1. How have the externals of personality and charisma obscured your organization's ability to assess the potential in every individual?
2. Jesus's acute sense of His Father's complete control of His mission was instrumental in His investment in others and in

His sharing of authority with His colleagues (disciples). How has your organization modeled and/or encouraged a climate conducive to empowering individuals?

ENDNOTES

1. Scripture quotations in this chapter, unless otherwise noted, are taken from the New International Version.

2. Henry T. and Richard Blackaby, *Spiritual Leadership* (Nashville: B&H Publishing Group, 2011).

3. The scholarship on leadership theory and practice is extensive. A useful summary of leadership theories and a tenable definition of leadership may be found in Richard L. Draft, *The Leadership Experience* (Mason, OH: Thomson; Southwestern, 2005).

4. Laurie Beth Jones, *Jesus, CEO: Using Ancient Wisdom for Visionary Leadership* (New York: Hyperion, 2011), 250–251.

5. C. Gene Wilkes, *Jesus on Leadership* (Wheaton, IL: Tyndale House Publishers, Inc., 1998), 131–132.

6. See James A. Cress, "How to Destroy Your Leadership," *Ministry* (January 1996): 30.

7. Bill Hybels with Rob Wilkins, *Descending into Greatness* (Grand Rapids: Zondervan, 1993), 16.

8. Henri Nouwen, *In the Name of Jesus: Reflections on Christian Leadership* (New York: Crossroad, 1989), 62–63.

9. Wilkes, *Jesus on Leadership,* 182–183.

10. Wilkes, *Jesus on Leadership,* 103.

11. See, for example, John Maxwell, *The 21 Indisputable Laws of Teamwork* (Nashville: Nelson Business, 2001). For an insightful look at the dysfunctional aspects of teams, see Patrick Lencioni, *The Five Dysfunctions of a Team* (San Francisco: Jossey-Boss, 2002).

12. John C. Maxwell, *The 21 Irrefutable Laws of Leadership* (Nashville: Thomas Nelson Publishers, 1998), 215–224.

13. See Chuck Miller, *The Spiritual Formation of Leaders* (Longwood, FL: Xulon Press, 2007).

14. Ellen G. White, *Education* (Mountain View, CA: Pacific Press Publishing Association, 1903), 57.

15. John C. Maxwell, *The 21 Indispensable Qualities of a Leader* (Nashville: Thomas Nelson Publishers, 1999), 148–154.

16. George Barna, *The Power of Vision* (Ventura, CA: Regal Books, 2003).

16 | Peter: A Narrative of Transformation

Douglas Tilstra

The story of Peter in scripture is a case study in transformation. The story describes Peter's shift from community disrupter to community facilitator. This transformation introduces profound implications for a biblical understanding of leadership. The process of leadership as described in Scripture demonstrates the healthy development of community, sometimes prompted by the destabilization of community. Jesus exercised discernment in that process, often bringing instability as a path to repentance, personally and corporately. Peter did not have that spiritual quality until he had been transformed by Christ. Thus Peter's life demonstrates transformation that leads to healthy community and Christ-like leadership.

Jesus mentors Peter and transforms him from a disrupter and destabilizer of community to a facilitator of community.[1] Peter starts as a would-be leader who often disrupts and distracts. He becomes a true leader who gathers people into collaborative community. This progression unfolds in the three phases of Peter's life presented in scripture: Gospels (Peter in training), Acts (Peter in apostolic function), and Epistles (Peter in pastoral function).

This brief evaluation of Peter's life and transformation will focus on five community disrupting characteristics evidenced in Peter's early life. Then, Jesus's mentoring intervention with each of those destabilizing characteristics will be explored. Finally, drawing from the historical accounts of the book of Acts and the evidence found in Peter's Epistles, the author will suggest the consequences of Jesus's mentorship—a life transformed from a stumbling block to a building block. No longer does Peter destroy community; rather, he is part of the leadership process that builds community. Jesus's transformational work for Peter has been effective.

The community disrupting elements of Peter's early experience center around the five issues of (1) vision, (2) limitations, (3) relationships, (4) power, and (5) climate. Peter tended to exhibit a flawed and self-serving *vision*. He seemed often to not recognize his own *limitations* and to overestimate his own abilities. His *relationships* appear to lean toward the dysfunctional. Peter's early understanding of *power* seems to indicate his penchant for centralizing power and decision making in himself rather than empowering others. Finally, Peter in the Gospel accounts appears to promote *climates* of instability rather than safety and collaboration. The Gospel accounts allow us to examine Peter's style in each of these five areas prior to his transformation.

SELF-SERVING VISION

Various researchers have studied the leadership phenomenon known as "charismatic leadership."[2] One of the primary negative characteristics of charismatic leadership is an inflated ego.[3] There is a sense in which Peter could be considered a charismatic leader.[4] Each of Peter's five community-disrupting traits described above are endemic to charismatic leaders and have as their driving force an untamed ego.[5] The effect of an inflated ego is probably most obvious in the first of the five issues to be examined, a flawed and self-serving vision.

Peter's flawed and self-serving vision is perhaps most evident in his question immediately following Jesus's conversation with the rich young ruler. After the young man walks away, Peter exclaims to

Jesus, "We have left everything to follow you! What then will there be for us?" (Matt. 19:27).[6] Peter seems to view discipleship as a utilitarian transaction at this point. He hopes for a reward that will justify the decisions the disciples have made to join with Jesus.

One might see additional indications of Peter's self-serving vision in other comments he makes to Jesus. "Everyone is looking for you" (Mark 1:37) Peter says to Jesus the morning after a night filled with miraculous healings. The critical point here is that everyone in Peter's hometown had lined up at Peter's door in search of Jesus and healing. It is not hard to imagine Peter's pride in his connection to this Miracle Worker and boasting that Jesus was housed in his own home. Jesus's response to Peter is decisive and reveals a vision contrary to Peter's, "Let us go somewhere else—to the nearby villages—so I can preach there also. That is why I have come" (v. 38).

Other revealing comments from Peter to Jesus include his horror and disdain at the thought of following a suffering Messiah. He says, "Never, Lord!... This [betrayal and cruel death] shall never happen to you!" (Matt. 16:22). Consider Peter's ill-timed quip on the Mount of Transfiguration in an effort to memorialize (and trivialize) the occasion, "Lord, it is good for us to be here. If you wish, I will put up three shelters—one for you, one for Moses and one for Elijah" (Matt. 17:4); or his outburst in the Upper Room at the disgusting prospect of a servant-leader Messiah, "No...you shall never wash my feet" (John 13:8); or his boast later the same evening just hours before a triple denial, "Even if all fall away on account of you, I never will" (Matt. 26:33). In each situation Peter expressed a vision vastly different from Jesus's vision. Peter envisioned an earthly kingdom and a reputation of honor.

Leadership thrives best in a community free from inflated egos. Jesus knew that and mentored Peter accordingly, as we shall see later.

OVERESTIMATED ABILITIES

Research indicates that charismatic leaders tend to downplay their own limitations, overestimate their own ability, and often succeed in leading others to look at them in similar light.[7] Overestimated abilities minimize cooperative efforts in the community since all are more focused on the strengths of the charismatic leader than on the individual abilities of each community member. The Gospel stories show Peter overestimating his own ability. The defining story on this point is Peter's denial of his denial of Jesus. All four Gospel accounts record Peter's stubborn affirmation of loyalty to Jesus even to the point of death (Matt. 26:31–35; Mark 14:26–31; Luke 22:31–34; John 13:36–38). The affirmation of loyalty is clearly an overestimation of his own abilities and an underestimation of his own limitations.

Peter's declaration is not an isolated example. Only a few hours later Peter again overestimates his own abilities when he single-handedly pulls a weapon to defend Jesus against a large mob armed with swords and clubs and accompanied by a detachment of Roman soldiers (Matt. 26:47–57; Mark 14:43–50; Luke 22:47–51; John 18:1–11). Peter had, in previous experiences, also overestimated his ability to walk on water (Matt. 14:22–32), his ability to correctly read and respond to a delicate social/political situation (Matt. 17:24–27), his ability to enhance a moment of divine revelation (Matt. 17:4), his own generosity and forgiving spirit (Matt. 18:21–35), his understanding of Jesus's mission (Matt. 16:21–23), his contributions to the kingdom of God (Matt. 19:27), his loyalty to Jesus in comparison to that of the other eleven disciples (Matt. 26:33), and his ability to even stay awake and pray with Jesus (Mark 14:37–38). No less than seven times,[8] Scripture records Peter saying "No" to a statement or request of Jesus. In these moments Peter overestimates his own understanding and abilities while underestimating Jesus's knowledge and abilities.

Leadership thrives best in a community in which people recognize their own limitations and compensate by cooperating with one another. Jesus knew that and mentored Peter accordingly.

DYSFUNCTIONAL RELATIONSHIPS

Many dysfunctions can plague relationships. Some noted in leadership research are manipulation, unreasonable demands, breaking promises, unchecked power, pathologic narcissism, unethical means of winning support, and taking personal credit for the contributions of others.[9] The Gospels do not give evidence of all such dysfunctions in Peter's early relationships; however, some are present. Perhaps most notable is Peter's apparent disregard for the effect of his words and actions upon others. When Jesus predicts Peter's denial, Peter not only denies Jesus's prediction, but he also competitively compares himself to the other disciples. He assesses himself positively and everyone else negatively. The other disciples appear defiant as they refute Peter's assessment of them (Matt. 26:31–35).

Another evidence of Peter's dysfunctional relationships surfaces in his emotional reaction to the matter of paying the Temple tax, a challenging situation, one in which Jesus apparently felt it necessary to do damage control "so that we might not offend them" (Matt. 17:24–27). Other examples include Peter's broken promises (Matt. 26:69–75; Mark 14:66–72; Luke 22:54–62; John 18:15–27); his inability to mind his own business (John 21:20–22); his inclination to speak "when he did not know what he was saying" (Luke 9:33); and his unforgiving spirit and apparent preoccupation with the limitations and mechanics of forgiveness rather than with the transformation of his hard heart (Matt. 18:21–35).

Leadership thrives best in a community characterized by healthy relationships, not dysfunctional relationships. Jesus knew that and mentored Peter accordingly.

RETAINED POWER

Communities, especially communities of faith, thrive on shared and decentralized power. In terms of leadership this distribution of power often includes mentoring, delegating authority, sharing decision making, preparing successors, and fostering interdependence among members rather than either independence of, or dependence upon, a dominant leader.[10] The scriptural evidence for Peter's use of power early in his life is fragmentary and more suggestive than conclusive. However, the clues seem to reveal Peter leaning toward power retention rather than power sharing.

Peter is often the spokesman for the Twelve. He corrects and even rebukes Jesus (Matt. 16:22; Luke 8:45; 22:31–33); is quick with unsolicited suggestions (Matt. 14:22–33; Mark 9:5–6; John

21:3); presumes to speak officially yet unadvisedly on behalf of Jesus (Matt. 17:24–27); evokes Jesus's stern rebuke after a spontaneous solo and disruptive action (John 18:10–11); reacts almost violently to Jesus's abandonment of positional power (John 13:2–8); and questions Jesus regarding the offering of forgiveness (Matt. 18:21–35).

The final clues about Peter's relationship to power are found in his behavior during the last twenty-four hours before Christ's death. He grasps frantically for power. He refuses to accept Jesus's predictions of his denial and forces a different meaning onto Jesus's words (Matt. 26:31–35; Mark 14:26–31; Luke 22:31–34; John 13:36–38); he tries to force a different outcome to Jesus's arrest (John 18:10–11); and, finally, he uses anger, intimidation, and swearing to force a different response from his accusers (Matt. 26:69–75; Mark 14:66–72; Luke 22:54–62; John 18:15–27). Peter uses his dwindling sense of power in a frantic effort to bolster his sense of control. It is the opposite of Jesus's use of power and the opposite of Jesus's plan for leadership and power in the new community of faith.

Jesus demonstrates a different relationship to power in the same context. Jesus demonstrates His words, "No one takes…[my life] from me, but I lay it down of my own accord" (John 10:18). With that attitude toward His own power, Jesus steps toward the murderous mob rather than attempting to flee from it (John 18:4–5); waits for the mob to regroup after they fall to the ground (John 18:6–9); refuses a violent counterattack (John 18:10–11); calmly challenges His accusers on their unjust charges and tactics (John 18:19–24); reframes the interrogation process with Pilate in order to make a spiritual appeal to a confused and lost man (John 18:33–37; John 19:7–11); makes extended elder-care plans for His mother from the cross (John 19:25–27); prays for His executioners (Luke 23:34); and offers Kingdom hospitality and eternal life to the dying man next to Him (Luke 23:39–43). In short, Jesus exercises His power in the final twenty-four hours of His life to give power away. Jesus consistently modeled a community leader capable of sharing rather than grasping at power. Jesus mentored Peter and the rest of the disciples accordingly.

UNSTABLE CLIMATES

One of the characteristics of a healthy church community is the characteristic of a safe and collaborative climate. Paul describes that mature community climate with the words, "we will no longer be infants, tossed back and forth by the waves, and blown here and there by every wind of teaching.... Instead, speaking the truth in love, we will in all things grow up into him who is the Head, that is, Christ" (Eph. 4:14–15). Speaking the truth in love is a concise description of the safe community that is able to confront as well as support; that is able to collaborate and yet encourage individual responsibility; that can provide both nurture and accountability. As Paul says, that type of community is comprised of mature people, not infantile people. Leaders with infantile, bloated egos tend to destabilize communities rather than encourage safe and collaborative climates.

Leadership research in various settings confirms this fact.[11] Specifically, healthy communities need leaders who will encourage group problem solving without allowing their egos to get in the way of the group's best interest. They also need a willingness to back one another up during difficulties, to build trust, and to focus on maintaining the climate of safety within the group. Leaders who are intolerant of dissent, sensitive to criticism, driven to gain personal power and glory, and unable to listen well, and who are unnaturally competitive and unsympathetic do not facilitate safe environments.[12] Such leaders destabilize rather than stabilize communities.

Peter's early life is tainted with destabilizing tendencies rather than stabilizing ones. Again, the information is suggestive rather than conclusive, but the clues are there. Peter seems to be disrupting, distracting, and destabilizing in many of the Gospel accounts. Often he seems to interrupt Jesus and draw the attention of others away from Jesus's main point at the moment. It happens in the incident of the bleeding woman Jesus meets en route to the home of Jairus (Luke 8:40–48). It happens soon after Peter's Great Confession (Matt. 16:21–23), on the Mount of Transfiguration (Luke 9:28–33), during the foot washing in the Upper Room (John 13:1–8), and during the arrest and trial of Jesus (John 18:10–27).

Jesus encouraged Peter to promote a gracious environment. The dialogue regarding forgiveness illustrates such teaching: "Then Peter came to Jesus and asked, 'Lord, how many times shall I forgive my brother when he sins against me? Up to seven times?'" (Matt. 18:21). The subtlety in this story is Peter's apparent desire to create a safe, forgiving climate. Jesus's parable in response reveals the desire to mentor Peter and the disciples (Matt. 18:22–35). Peter wants to appear forgiving, but not overly so. He looks for the reasonable position, not the highest possible reason to extend grace. Peter's attitude illustrates counterfeit safety in communities. Communities can offer the appearance of forgiveness and grace but harbor the spirit of exacting demand. If churches are to become safe and collaborative communities of grace they will mentor leaders and members who internalize the lesson Jesus offered Peter in this encounter about safety and stability.

Leadership thrives best in a community with a safe and gracious climate. Jesus knew that and mentored Peter accordingly.

JESUS'S MENTORING INTERVENTION: PETER IN TRAINING

In each of the stories mentioned above, Jesus intervenes with corrective mentoring. In a few cases Peter responds positively and appears to learn from Jesus's intervention. In other cases the opposite occurs. Though each situation elicits from Jesus a mentoring response, only one or two representative responses from Jesus for each of the five issues will be considered.

Vision

Jesus repeatedly works to inspire Peter and his companions with the vision that motivates His own life.[13] He calls them away from flawed and self-serving visions to a clear vision of reconciliation through self-sacrifice. That vision united them and eventually served to unite the Early Church. Perhaps one of the most pointed and poignant mentoring moments between Peter and Jesus occurs just hours before the Cross, when Jesus says, "Simon, Simon, Satan has asked to sift you as wheat. But I have prayed for you, Simon, that your faith may not fail. And when you have turned back, strengthen your brothers" (Luke 22:31–32). Jesus not only exposes the source of Peter's flawed and selfish vision, but also holds before him the vision of his life transformed by a ministry of reconciliation through selfless service. It is characteristic of virtually every interaction between Jesus and Peter over the issue of his flawed vision.

Limitations

Jesus appears to work with Peter on at least two levels regarding his overestimated abilities. One is Peter's limitations and need for Jesus. The other is Peter's limitations and need for other people. Peter is blind to both. A dramatic event addresses Peter's need for Jesus. "Peter got down out of the boat, walked on the water and came toward Jesus. But when he saw the wind, he was afraid and, beginning to sink, cried out, 'Lord, save me!' Immediately Jesus reached out his hand and caught him. 'You of little faith,' he said, 'why did you doubt?'" (Matt. 14:29–31). A quieter yet equally dramatic event addresses the second level, Peter's need for other people. In Gethsemane Jesus "returned to his disciples and found them sleeping. 'Could you men not keep watch with me for one hour?' he asked Peter" (Matt. 26:40). Jesus's desperate cry for prayer support and companionship in His suffering is a contrast to the independent spirit of Peter, who seems to rarely ask for help from anyone.

Relationships

Jesus fosters healthy relationships among the Twelve merely by living in close proximity to them, speaking the truth in love, and holding them accountable while offering grace. One of the closing incidents in the Gospels exemplifies the healthy nature of Jesus's relationship with Peter. "When they had finished eating, Jesus said to Simon Peter, 'Simon son of John, do you love me more than these?' 'Yes, Lord,' he said, 'you know that I love you.' Jesus said, 'Feed my lambs.' Again Jesus said, 'Simon son of John, do you love me?' He answered, 'Yes, Lord, you know that I love you. Jesus said, 'Take care of my sheep.' The third time he said to him, 'Simon son of John, do you love me?' Peter was hurt because Jesus asked him the third time, 'Do you love me?' He said, 'Lord, you know all things; you know that I love you.' Jesus said, 'Feed my sheep'" (John 21:15–17). In this final face-to-face encounter recorded in the Gospels, Jesus not only restores Peter to his role among the other disciples, but does so with both grace and accountability. Jesus speaks the truth in love, speaks with hope of Peter's future, and calls Peter to step from dysfunction into health.

Power

Jesus constantly empowered His followers. "He called his twelve disciples to him and gave them authority to drive out evil spirits and to heal every disease and sickness…. 'Freely you have received, freely give'" (Matt. 10:1, 8). Far from centralizing and monopolizing power in Himself, Jesus gives it freely to His disciples and invites them to participate in leadership and ministry with Him. It is noteworthy that the passage cited above continues with a listing of the Twelve, "These are the names of the twelve apostles: first Simon (who is called Peter; Matt. 10:2). Peter heads every list of the twelve apostles. His positional power seems to have been asserted among the Twelve.

It takes the repeated mentoring of Jesus to transform Peter into a leader among other leaders, one who can freely give because he freely receives. It is that transformation that finally enables Peter to lead the new community of faith.

Climate

Peter seems to step into relatively stable environments and destabilize them without spiritual discernment (Matt. 16:21–23; 17:24–27; 18:21; Luke 8:40–48; 9:28–33; John 13:1–8; 18:10–27). Jesus stepped into certain environments and destabilized them, and, at other times, He stepped into chaotic environments and introduced safety and stability (Matt. 14:22–32; 26:6–13; Luke 22:47–51; John 8:1–11). Perhaps Jesus's most notable mentoring moment with Peter occurred immediately after Peter's denial of Jesus. "Peter replied, 'Man, I don't know what you're talking about!' Just as he spoke, the rooster crowed. The Lord turned and looked straight at Peter. Then Peter remembered the word the Lord had spoken to him: 'Before the rooster crows today, you will disown me three times.' And he went outside and wept bitterly" (Luke 22:60–62). During the chaos and torture of His own trial, Jesus offered

Peter a message. His message is spoken only with His eyes, and it reminded Peter of Jesus's warning words earlier that night. Jesus's warning had been preceded by the assurance, "Simon...I have prayed for you" (Luke 22:31–32). The memory of Jesus's words led Peter to repentance and safety within the community of faith. Though this example is notable for its poignancy, it is nonetheless representative of the many other times and ways Jesus mentored Peter in the establishment of climates of safety. Such climates allow community and Jesus-inspired leadership to flourish.

Leadership thrives best in a community with shared selfless vision, cooperation born of realization of personal limitations, healthy relationships, shared power, and safe climates. Jesus knew that and mentored Peter accordingly.

A LIFE TRANSFORMED: PETER IN APOSTOLIC FUNCTION

"When they saw the courage of Peter and John and realized that they were unschooled, ordinary men, they were astonished and they took note that these men had been with Jesus" (Acts 4:13). The continuation of the Christ story in the book of Acts is also the continuation of Peter's story. Now, however, Peter is a man transformed by the mentoring process of Jesus and the outpouring of the Holy Spirit. He is able to lead rather than disrupt community. Jesus has transformed Peter from stumbling block to building block. A few representative examples from the book of Acts illustrate the point.

The opening story of the preparation for Pentecost (Acts 1) reveals Peter with a reconciling vision. He seems to recognize his own limitations, takes the matter of Judas's replacement to the entire group of one hundred and twenty believers, then leads the group in a process of scriptural reflection, prayer, and decision making. Peter's influence appears to share power rather than centralize it and encourage collaboration rather than the destabilization of the group.

The story of Pentecost features Peter speaking on behalf of the group of apostles, yet he does it in partnership with them (Acts 2:14), and the crowd responds to "Peter and the other apostles, 'Brothers, what shall we do?'" (Acts 2:37). Peter is leading a team, not acting independently. In addition, his sermon reveals how thoroughly the mission and vision of Jesus had become his own, and the results of his preaching that day establish a fellowship of more than three thousand believers who begin living in generous and gracious community with one another (Acts 2:42–47).

The next story of Peter in Acts centers around the healing of a man crippled from birth (Acts 3–4). Peter acknowledges his limitations. He says, "Silver or gold I do not have" (Acts 3:6), and later, "Why do you stare at us as if by our own power or godliness we had made this man walk?" (Acts 3:12). Contrary to his preoccupation two years earlier with Jesus as a physical healer (Mark 1:35–39), Peter now urges the amazed onlookers to see beyond this physical healing to the grander spiritual healing God offers them (Acts 3:11–26). Again, Peter works not alone but with John and later the entire congregation (Acts 3:1; 4:19–31). And again, as after the Pentecost story, the net effect is described in terms of the benefit to the entire community. "All the believers were one in heart and mind. No one claimed that any of their possessions was their own, but they shared everything they had" (Acts 4:32).

Even in the troubling story of Ananias and Sapphira, where one might interpret Peter's bold remarks as a return to centralization of power or overestimation of his own abilities, there are clues to the contrary. The large donations are laid "at the apostles' feet" (Acts 4:37), not merely Peter's feet. Peter makes it clear to both Ananias and Sapphira that their sin is not against him, but against the Holy Spirit (Acts 5:3, 9). In the aftermath of the dramatic events, "Peter and the other apostles replied" (Acts 5:29), once again indicating collaboration rather than the hoarding of power. Finally, the results of the story are reported in Luke's repeated formula for recounting the story of the formation of the new community of faith: "The apostles performed many signs and wonders among the people. And all the believers used to meet together in Solomon's Colonnade. No one else dared join them, even though they were highly regarded by the people. Nevertheless, more and more men and women believed in the Lord and were added to their number" (Acts 5:12–14).

Peter and John's missionary trip to Samaria (Acts 8:14–25) contains several evidences of Peter's transformation, but none is more notable than his new attitude toward power and personal gain. Peter had once asked Jesus, "What then will there be for us?" (Matt. 19:27). Now he confronts another man, ironically also named Simon, for exhibiting that same spirit. When Simon the Sorcerer attempts to buy the power of the Holy Spirit, Peter's response is reminiscent of some of Jesus's strongest rebukes to him, "May your money perish with you, because you thought you could buy the gift of God with money! You have no part or share in this ministry, because your heart is not right before God. Repent of this wickedness and pray to the Lord in the hope that he may forgive you for having such a thought in your heart. For I see that you are full of bitterness and captive to sin" (Acts 8:20–23).

Peter's experience with Cornelius and later his explanation of his actions to the church leaders in Jerusalem reveal a transformed man who is still in the process of maturing (Acts 10–11). Peter did initially say no to Jesus and refused to cooperate (Acts 10:9–16). Eventually he did obey and is later criticized for entering a Gentile home and baptizing Gentile believers. Peter's past track record would indicate a reactive or defensive posture to such criticism (Matt. 17:24–27, esp., but also Matt. 16:22; 26:33–35; Luke 8:45; John 13:8). Instead, Peter answers their questions, explains his position, and the story ends with a variation on Luke's formula about the effect on the community: "When they heard this, they had no further objections and praised God, saying, 'So then, even to Gentiles God has granted repentance that leads to life'" (Acts 11:18).

The final two stories of Peter in the book of Acts (the raising of Dorcas to life and his release from prison) also give evidence of various aspects of Peter's transformation. Most notable among them in this context is the high level at which Peter is interacting as an integral part of a community (Acts 9:32–43; 12:1–24). Both stories end with Luke's formula comment regarding the impact on the larger community of believers, "This became known all over Joppa, and many people believed in the Lord" (Acts 9:42), and "the word of God continued to spread and flourish" (Acts 12:24).

Leadership thrived in the Early Church community. Jesus had mentored Peter to contribute to that thriving rather than disrupt it.

A COACH FOR FUTURE LEADERS: PETER IN PASTORAL FUNCTION

In his Epistles, Peter functions as a wise pastor, advising future church leaders, drawing upon his own experience, and reflecting the very principles he learned under Jesus's mentorship. It is clear in Peter's Epistles that his self-serving vision has given way to a larger and nobler vision that compels him and those he addresses (1 Pet. 1:3–7; 2:11–12; 2 Pet. 1:3–11). Peter no longer overestimates his own abilities (1 Pet. 1:24–25; 2:24–25; 5:5–6; 2 Pet. 2:12–15). He is now mindful of healthy relationships and appears to know what comprises them (1 Pet. 1:22; 2:1; 3:7–9; 4:7–11; 2 Pet. 1:5–9). He reflects on the use and abuse of power, and he centers his reflection on the closing hours of Jesus's life—where Jesus's masterful use of power contrasted so sharply with Peter's own abysmal attempts to use power.[14] Apparently Peter has learned from Jesus and has passed on what he learned to the next generation of leaders. Finally, Peter crafts both letters with an overarching message of encouragement to create safe, collaborative communities characterized by patient endurance rather than destabilizing reactivity (1 Pet. 2:23; 3:9–17; 2 Pet. 2:1–22; 3:14).Virtually everything that Peter learned from Jesus about leadership in community is summarized in his closing words to the church elders:

> To the elders among you, I appeal as a fellow elder and a witness of Christ's sufferings who also will share in the glory to be revealed: Be shepherds of God's flock that is under your care, watching over them—not because you must, but because you are willing, as God wants you to be; not pursuing dishonest gain, but eager to serve; not lording it over those entrusted to you, but being examples to the flock. And when the Chief Shepherd appears, you will receive the crown of glory that will never fade away. (1 Pet. 5:1–4)

CONCLUSION

The story of Peter is a story of transformation. Jesus transformed a man, Peter, and thus laid the groundwork for transforming leadership in the infant church. Leadership thrives in communities where vision is shared and selfless, where cooperative effort replaces ego-driven arrogance, where healthy relationships prevail, where power is shared rather than hoarded, and where safety and stability are rightly nourished. Jesus knew the power of community and of shared leadership. As He shared that truth with him, He transformed Peter's leadership from a stumbling block into a building block.

FOR REFLECTION

Personal:

1. How do you, like Peter, struggle to identify and lead reasonably within the borders of your abilities and limitations? What are some ways to distinguish between personal limits and unrealized potential?

2. Peter refuted Jesus's prediction of his denial in order to preserve his inordinate self-esteem. In the process, Peter diminishes the integrity of the other disciples' commitment to Christ. Do you find yourself eager to maintain a certain image or reputation at the expense of others?

Organizational:

1. Implicit in Peter's question on forgiveness was an apparent method to embrace a false system of grace where forgiveness had a calculated limit. Does your organizational climate exude an atmosphere of grace, or is "grace" used to cover up a spirit of exaction? How can grace be balanced with expectations?

2. How can your organization accept the immature Peters while still nurturing their process of transformation?

ENDNOTES

1. Much has been written about the rock motif in Peter's life and his subsequent writings. For an excellent discussion of the use of the word *rock* in Peter's life, see Tremper Longman III and David E. Garland, *Expositors Bible Commentary,* vol. 9, *Matthew & Mark* (Grand Rapids, MI: Zondervan, 2010), 414–430. While

it is not the purpose of this article to repeat that discussion, it is useful to note Jesus's words to Peter in Matthew 16:18, where He refers positively to Peter's role as a rock on behalf of the church, and moments later in 16:23, where Jesus refers negatively to Peter's role as a stumbling block, or rock, on behalf of Jesus and His church. This incident seems to capture the essence of Jesus's mentoring work with Peter—transforming him from stumbling block to building block—a theme that appears to be echoed elsewhere in the New Testament (Eph. 2:19–22; 1 Pet. 2:1–8; Rev. 21:14).

2. See R. Birchfield, "Creating Charismatic Leaders," *Management* 47.5 (2000): 30–31; Jay A. Conger and Rabindra N. Kanungo, *Charismatic Leadership in Organizations* (Thousand Oaks, CA: SAGE, 1998); J. M. Howell and B. Shamir, "The Role of Followers in the Charismatic Leadership Process: Relationships and their Consequences," *Academy of Management Review* 30.1 (2005): 96–112; Michael Maccoby, "Narcissistic Leaders," *Harvard Business Review* 78.1 (2000): 69–77; and B. Shamir, "Charismatic Leadership in Organization (Book Review)," *Journal of Occupational and Organizational Psychology* 74.1 (2001): 112–114.

3. Conger and Kanungo, *Charismatic Leadership,* passim; Frank M. Lafasto and Carl E. Larson, *When Teams Work Best* (Thousand Oaks, CA: SAGE, 2001), passim.

4. A four-point summary definition of a charismatic leader emerges in the literature: (1) a leader who communicates high performance expectations to followers, (2) a leader who exhibits confidence in the ability of followers to reach goals, (3) a leader who takes calculated risks that oppose the status quo, and (4) a leader who articulates a value-based overarching vision of collective identity. These are the basic positive traits. On the negative side, charismatic leaders have been observed to be grandiose, exploitive, and self-promoting, J. A. Raelin, "The Myth of Charismatic Leaders," *Training and Development* 57.3 [2003]: 46–51. Charismatic leaders tend to destabilize organizations (R. Khurana, "The Curse of the Superstar," *Harvard Business Review* 80.9 (2002): 60–66. They tend to be poor listeners, overly sensitive to criticism, lack empathy, and be overly competitive, Maccoby, "Narcissistic Leaders," 69–77. For descriptions of charismatic leaders, see Bernard M. Bass, *Bass and Stogdill's Handbook of Leadership,* 3rd ed. (New York: Free Press, 1990); Jay A. Conger and Rabindra N. Kanungo, "Toward a Behavioral Theory of Charismatic Leadership in Organizational Settings," *The Academy of Management Review* 12.4 (1987): 637–647; M. G. Ehrhart and K. J. Klein, "Predicting Followers' Preferences for Charismatic Leadership: The Influence of Follower Values and Personality," *The Leadership Quarterly* 12.2 (2001):153–179; R. J. House, "A 1976 Theory of Charismatic Leadership" in *Leadership: The Cutting Edge,* ed. James Hunt and Lars Larson (Carbondale: Southern Illinois University, 1977): 189–207; B. Shamir, R. J. House, and M. B. Arthur, "The Motivational Effects of Charismatic Leadership: A Self-Concept Based Theory," *Organization Science* 4.577 (1993): 594; and Douglas A. Tilstra, "Charismatic Leaders as Team Leaders: An Evaluation Focused on Pastoral Leadership," *Journal of Religious Leadership* (Fall 2010).

5. Conger and Kanungo, *Charismatic Leadership,* passim; Lafasto and Larson, *Teams,* passim.

6. Scripture quotations in this chapter are taken from the New International Version.

7. See Conger and Kanungo, *Charismatic Leadership,* passim; Maccoby, "Narcissistic Leaders," 69–77; and R. Khurana, "Curse of the Superstar," 60–66.

8. (1) Peter's initial resistance to let down the fish net, Luke 5:1–11; (2) Peter's resistance to Jesus's question, "Who touched Me?" Luke 8:40–46; (2) Peter's contradiction to Jesus's statement about His death on the cross, Matthew 16:13–28; Mark 8:27–33; (3) Peter's initial refusal to allow Jesus to wash his feet, John 13:3–10; (5) Peter's denial of his denial of Jesus, Matthew 26:31–35; Mark 14:26–31; Luke 22:31–34; John 13:36–38; (6) Peter's denial of Jesus, Matthew 26:69–75; Mark 14:66–72; Luke 22:54–62; John 18:15–27; (7) Peter's refusal to eat the animals let down in the sheet, Acts 10:14. In fairness, Peter usually relents and says yes to Jesus after his initial no. Nonetheless, Peter's initial response shows his spontaneous overestimation of himself.

9. Conger and Kanungo, *Charismatic Leadership,* passim; and Conger and Kanungo, "Theory of Charismatic Leadership," 637–647.

10. Vanessa U. Druskat and Jane V. Wheeler, "Managing from the Boundary: The Effective Leadership of Self-Managing Work Teams," *Academy of Management Journal* 46.4 (2003): 435–457; Vanessa U. Druskat and Jane V. Wheeler, "How to Lead a Self-Managing Team," *MIT Sloan Management Review* 45.4 (2004): 65–71; Elspeth McFadzean, "Developing and Supporting Creative Problem-Solving Teams: Part 1—A Conceptual Model," *Management Decision* 40.5–6 (2002): 463–474; Raelin, "Myth of Charismatic Leaders," 46–51.

11. Conger and Kanungo, *Charismatic Leadership,* passim; Lafasto and Larson, *Teams,* passim.

12. See Bass, *Handbook of Leadership;* Conger and Kanungo, *Charismatic Leadership;* Ehrhart and Klein, "Charismatic Leadership," 153–179; Howell and Shamir, "The Role of Followers in the Charismatic Leadership Process," 96–112; Khurana, "Curse of the Superstar," 60–66; Lafasto and Larson, *Teams* (2001); Maccoby, "Narcissistic Leaders," 69–77; McFadzean, "Creative Problem-Solving," 463–474; and Raelin, "Myth of Charismatic Leaders," 46–51.

13. For example, Jesus's invitation to make His disciples "fishers of men" (Matt. 4:19; Mark 1:17; Luke 5:10); His demonstration of what that "fishing life" looks like (Mark 1:21–31); His clarity about his own mission that focused on service rather than popularity (Mark 1:38–39); His realistic expectations about persecution that accompanies mission (Matt. 10:16–26); or Jesus's reminder to Peter that washing dirty feet had deeper meaning than any of the Twelve realized (John 13:3–10).

14. 1 Peter 2:13–25; 3:13–17; 4:12–17; 5:3; 2 Peter 2:1–22 (where Peter warns of false leaders who exhibit characteristics similar to his own previous behaviors, i.e., greed, 2:3; false words, 2:3; bold and willful actions, 2:10; speaking loud to boast of folly, 2:18; and enslaved by corruption, 2:19).

17 | Paul: Principles for Leadership and Contextualization

Leslie N. Pollard

L eadership in our world is changing rapidly. The leadership environment of the twenty-first century is more globally connected than at any other time in history. Communications technology, international media activities, global immigration patterns, online educational institutions, and access to global travel are bridging continents and connecting diverse groups. This dynamic interaction unavoidably influences perceptions and expectations about leadership. Thus, versatility, adaptability, and fluency in leadership appear to be requisite skills in the current leadership environment. Christian leaders, now as before, must process their development of these new skills through the sieve of Scripture.

With these rapid changes in leadership culture in mind, the purpose of this chapter is to identify principles of leadership adaptation arising from an analysis of ministry of the apostle Paul. The assumption behind this chapter is that modern adaptations to cultural and social variation, while affirming modern consciousness, have not been limited to our times. Adaptation is assumed and effected in the ministry life of Jesus Christ, is inherent in the gospel commissions of Matthew 28:18ff and Revelation 14:6–12, and is consciously explicated in the ministry of the apostle Paul.

PAUL: THE SLAVE-LEADER OF GENTILE MISSION

The concept of servant leadership in Scripture is not to be confused with how *servile* leadership is construed in many cultures. *Servile* leadership suggests weak, groveling, and beggarly service. Servant leadership, on the other hand, carries a dignity grounded in the leadership of Christ and his apostles.

In fact, in the Christian community, the social contamination of the term *servant* is exactly the cultural attitude that scripture challenges. The word *servant* occurs in the New Testament more than one hundred and fifty times. The ancient Greek word *doulos* is one of the original words translated as "servant." The word *doulos* in New Testament times encompassed a range of meaning that often included the complete and degrading loss of personal autonomy, with possible horrific treatment, an idea conveyed well by our twenty-first-century understanding of the word *slave.* Just as some cultures despise the word *servant* today, the surrounding culture of the New Testament writers despised the word *slave* for many of the same reasons. Slaves lost autonomy, respect, dignity, and independence due to war, kidnapping, sale, and a variety of other reasons. But biblical writers, such as the apostle Paul, consciously labeled themselves as *douloi* (slaves) of Jesus Christ and His people (Romans 1:1 and 6:22; 1 Corinthians 9:19; 2 Corinthians 4:5; and Galatians 1:10). Make no mistake about it; biblical writers were bold in their decision to transform a term—a term often accompanied by social derision—into a term that captures the dignity of and calling to selfless service to God and for others.

No writer in the New Testament was more insistent in the redemption of the term than the apostle Paul. The word *doulos* is a crucial term in the world of Paul the apostle. Slavery played an essential role in the economy and culture of the Roman Empire. Slaves provided labor, education, and, in some rare instances, civic guidance within the Roman Empire. The one common theme to such service, regardless of severity or interpretation of context, is the loss of autonomy. In the pages of the New Testament, slavery is frequently referenced. As noted, this term appears to be a favorite term that Paul applies to himself. In passages such as Romans 1:1, Philippians 1:1, Titus 1:1, and Colossians 1:23, the term is used, and this "slave" self-designation, meaning at least a forfeiting of autonomy, is a counter-cultural declaration by Paul. Thus, when Paul describes himself as a slave of Jesus Christ, this language of his new life indicates that he had lost his previous autonomy in service to Jesus Christ.

Paul, the slave-leader apostle to the Gentiles, faced a dilemma. How should a Jewish apostle influence his Gentile contacts while retaining his commitment to mission? Would his Jewishness impede his reception by Gentiles? Would Jews find him guilty of betraying his unique heritage?

It is the argument of this chapter that careful examination of Paul's self-explication concerning his practice of contextualization instructs us by both word and example regarding the appropriate use of what is commonly called servant leadership. While Paul's thoughts are pervasive in the books that he has penned in the New Testament, this discussion will focus on a single passage that crystallizes Paul's perspective: 1 Corinthians 9:19–23. This is one of the few passages in which Paul took the time to engage in a methodological explanation of his influence (leadership) tactics both within and without the diverse Jewish and Gentile communities he encountered.

The text of 1 Corinthians 9:19–23 opens a window on the thinking of Paul on the issue of adaptation and contextualization of one's leadership influence. Paul says:

> For though I am free from all men, I have made myself a servant to all, that I might win the more; and to the Jews I became as a Jew, that I might win Jews; to those who are under the law, as under the law, that I might win those who are under the law; to those who are without law, as without law (not being without law toward God, but under law toward Christ), that I might win those who are without law; to the weak I became as weak, that I might win the weak. I have become all things to all men, that I might by all means save some. Now this I do for the gospel's sake, that I may be partaker of it with you.[1]

In 1 Corinthians 9, Paul's discussion of freedom and responsibility frames his understanding of leadership adaptation. He
defends his apostleship against attack, while having argued for the
regulation of the freedom of the strong in chapter 8. By the time
we get to verses 18 and 19 of 1 Corinthians 9, Paul launches into
a full-blown discussion of his leadership and mission effectiveness.
Here is one of the few places in his writings where Paul discusses
how he implements his servant leadership.

This chapter, focused on the principles and practices of Pauline
leadership, will address principle-based practices of Paul, the leader, as
observed in 1 Corinthians 9:19–23. The first line of the passage introduces the first principle from Paul on servant leadership. He writes,
"For though I am free from all *men,* I have made myself a servant to
all, that I might win the more" (1 Cor. 9:19, emphasis added).

LEADERSHIP PRINCIPLE 1

**The Voluntary Use of Leadership Influence Is Subordinated
to the Saving Purpose of God.** We know that leadership influence
is subordinate to God's purpose because Paul unites two contradic-
tory concepts: "freedom" (ἐλεύθερος) and "enslavement" (δουλόω).
To any Greco-Roman, freedom was a badge of social status and self-
value. When Paul asserts that he is "free from all men," this claim of
freedom would have sat at the apex of the values pyramid of his
Corinthian hearers. Freedom had a grip on the Greco-Roman imagination that is difficult for modern-day readers to appreciate.
Throughout the letter of 1 Corinthians, Paul frequently remonstrates
with the Corinthians over how to use their freedom. Corinthian
believers felt fully free to belong to the Peter party, or the Apollos
party, or the Christ party (1 Cor. 1:11–13). They felt free to take
their fellow believers to public courts (1 Cor. 6:1–6). The Corinthians
felt free to tolerate an incestuous relationship between a son and his
stepmother (1 Cor. 5:1–7). Some Corinthians felt free to eat meat
offered to idols (1 Cor. 8:4–13). But in 1 Corinthians 9:19–20,
Paul moves away from the prerogatives of his personal freedom by
deconstructing his personal leadership and by delineating how he lived
out freedom's missional purpose. Paul offers a theory of surrendered

freedom in the interest of effective mission. "Though free," Paul declares that "I enslave myself to all men." Paul introduces a paradox: the concept of redeemed freedom to submit to being slave versus unregulated freedom. Leaders make sacrifices that voluntarily arise from a personal freedom that has been redeemed by Jesus Christ.

LEADERSHIP PRINCIPLE 2

Christian Leaders Engage in a Reformulation of Personal Identity. Scholars know that 1 Corinthians 9:19–23 forms a chiasm. This means the parallel sections of the structure of the verses correspond to emphasize his message. A and A' tell us that Paul's leadership and service strategy are framed by his "slave" self-understanding. B and B' tell us that Paul saw himself through a new identity understanding. Read the text and note the commentary that follows it. Paul writes:

> A I made myself a slave to all in order that I might win the more (v. 19).
>> B I became to the Jews as a Jew, in order that I might win Jews (v. 20a).
>>> C To those who are under the law as [one] under the law…to win those who are under the law (v. 20b).
>>> C' To those who are without law, as without law…that I might win those who are without law (v. 21).
>> B' To the weak I became weak, that I might win the weak (v. 22a).
> A' I have become all things to all men, that I might by all means save some (v. 22b).[2]

Paul opens verse 19 by asserting that "to the Jews" he became "as a Jew." How can Paul take this stance? The answer is in the immediate context. Paul, the apostle to the Gentiles, had the difficult task of working among multiple cultures. But he takes up his task because he is bound to Christ. Paul is free to serve the Corinthians because he has not accepted any compensation from them (1 Cor. 9:15). Further, because he is free, he is able to "enslave" himself to people in need of the knowledge of Jesus Christ (1 Cor. 9:19). At minimum, Paul is free because of his encounter with

Jesus Christ (1 Cor. 9:1). Thus he is released from the old identity anchors that he once embraced. His freedom is grounded in a new experience. He affirms: "If anyone is in Christ he is a new creation" (2 Cor. 5:17).

Thus Paul says, "I became *as* a Jew" (emphasis added). The apostle is saying that he no longer considers himself a Jew in terms of primary values, commitments, and allegiance. The word translated "as" or "like" in 1 Corinthians 9:20 comes from the Greek comparative particle *hos*. In this verse it is the pivotal word. It introduces a simile into Paul's discussion. A simile is a figure of speech that compares one distinct idea, person, or object to another. By saying that he became "as" a Jew, Paul asserts that he is no longer defined "Jew." He enjoys the freedom of a new self-understanding. He is free from the limiting prejudices, preconceptions, and presuppositions of his early understandings of ethnic and religious Judaism.

When Paul says "to the Jew, I became as a Jew," Paul actually rattles the prison doors of identity idolatry. Suppose I said while speaking to a group of African Americans, "To the African American, I became as an African American." Would someone not reasonably respond, "But Les, you *are* an African American." Well, I would respond, "Paul spoke similarly and who was more Jewish than he?" Paul's autobiographical references in his letters clearly outline his biological, religious, and cultural classification as a Jew of the Jews. "I am an Israelite, of the seed of Abraham, of the tribe of Benjamin" he declares in Romans 11:1–2. In Philippians 3:5 he recalls that he was "circumcised the eighth day, of the stock of Israel, of the tribe of Benjamin, an Hebrew of the Hebrews…a Pharisee."

But when Paul says "To the Jews I became as a Jew," Paul is saying that he has experienced a reformulation of his base identity. He is a new creature with a new identity (2 Cor. 5:17). The convert Paul, the former persecutor who loved Judaism enough to kill to protect it, now refuses to be enslaved to the identity politics of either his times or his culture of origin. Paul is free in Christ! At Damascus, Paul received an identity transplant (Acts 9:1–6). The transforming encounter with the risen Christ deconstructed his inherited identity and replaced it with another primary identity. Paul became a new creature in Jesus Christ. New perceptions of the world, new perceptions of society, new priorities, new ambitions, and new criteria of perception—all these and more constituted a reformulation of Paul's former self-understanding and identity.

LEADERSHIP PRINCIPLE 3

Leaders Cross Ethnic, Racial, and Cultural Boundaries in Service to God and Jesus Christ. While Christian Paul was not Judeocentric, 1 Corinthians 9:18–22 reveals that he was deeply Judeo-sensitive. Similarly, as leaders we are not called to be ethno-centric, but Christ-centered and ethni-sensitive. Like Paul, we will require an intimate knowledge of our own history and culture. Self-awareness assists us as leaders in coming to terms with our own personal identity and history. Modern leadership experts often call this knowledge emotional intelligence. Emotional intelligence assists us in learning to speak the cultural language of our people of origin. By critically analyzing the strengths and weaknesses of the culture and worldview that has been passed on to us, we will better be able to relativize and utilize our personal history. This practice is absolutely essential in the modern leadership environment.

Effective leadership also requires that we undertake the specific study of the culture of the people that we lead. Effective missionaries do this all the time. It will require situationally appropriate methods. We should consult with persons from the cultures we are serving, read their history books, and find a cultural mentor.

LEADERSHIP PRINCIPLE 4

Leadership Is Inseparably Connected to Stewardship. In Paul's thinking, everything that he had inherited or acquired was a part of his leadership resource bank for the execution of mission. Modern leadership theorists now recognize that leadership is nothing if not the intentional deployment of one's influence for the advancement of the mission of the organizations we serve. Interestingly, in 1 Corinthians 9:19–23, Paul uses everything associated with bio-physical existence, including his talents, and the markers of his birth ("to the Jew, as a Jew"). Thus, life is a gift (Gen. 2:7), with all of its responsibilities (Gen. 1:27–28): race, ethnicity, education, class, and status. For Paul these are clearly resources to be stewarded; they are not possessions to be worshiped or protected. Paul retreats from the racial and ethnic idolatry that had served only to divide and alienate in the first century. Paul's intimate experience as a Jew is engaged so that he can be "as" a Jew. Paul works for his own ethnic group, but only as an ambassador from another kingdom (2 Cor. 5:20) to his racial and ethnic group. Paul adapts himself to the customs of the Jewish people when working among them. He takes a Nazarite vow (Acts 18:18). He has Timothy circumcised (Acts 16:13). He takes part in purification rituals and pays Nazarite expenses for the sacrificial offering (Acts 21:23ff). But he can also be as one "without the Law," that is, a Gentile. While he is with Gentiles, he does not enforce Jewish ceremonial ritual upon them (Gal. 2:11–14; Col. 2:11, 16). Here Paul lays out the possibility for cross-cultural ministry. Paul will work for his "own" but will not be limited to them. All people are within the scope of his stewardship.

Clearly, two tracks of ministry emerge in Paul's vision of leadership and service. One track is grounded in ethnic particularity. Paul "the Jew" works sensitively with his Jewish kindred (Rom. 10:1). He knows their history, culture, and social outlooks. But he also exemplifies another radical track of cross-cultural leadership and ministry. Paul "the apostle" works among Gentiles as one who deeply understands them (Acts 17:16–31; Rom. 11:13).

LEADERSHIP PRINCIPLE 5

Leadership Is Grounded in Love. What is most energizing about Paul is his deep understanding of the relationship between love (*agape*) and leadership. In 1 Corinthians 9:19–23, the service motivation guiding Paul is his passionate love for the redemption of souls. Love for Christ is the law under which Paul functions (v. 21; also Gal. 6:2). His mission is to lead as many as possible to Christian discipleship. He considers this opportunity his blessing (1 Cor. 9:23). *Agape* love has great meaning in the address of Paul to the Corinthians. Paul is assisting a congregation attempting to resolve problems that are threatening to destroy its witness and life. A thoughtful reading of 1 Corinthians makes clear that leadership is needed. By the time Paul comes to 1 Corinthians 13, he is attempting to establish harmony and collegiality within the rancorous church at Corinth. Perhaps that explains why the apostle Paul uses the word *agape* ten times in 1 Corinthians 13.

Corinth is clearly the most contentious church of all the churches mentioned in the New Testament. Personality cults and factions (1:11–13), notorious examples of sexual immorality (5:1–7), adversarial and litigious confrontations between believers in public courts (6:1–6), flawed and false teaching regarding marriage (7:1–5), debates over the eating of meats offered to idols (8:4–13), battles over Paul's call and apostleship (9:1–18), fights over the Lord's Supper and worship (11:20–34), and disputes over the greater versus lesser spiritual gifts (12:15–27) have left the congregation divided and fractured. But it is into this bubbling cauldron of church conflict that Paul interjects his most extended treatment of what he considers the greatest of all gifts to the church—the one which if exercised would bring the body of Christ into harmony and unity. "LOVE" says Paul, is the greatest gift and it is the one that every believer should covet (1 Cor. 12:29–31, emphasis added). The fact that Paul deposited this teaching into the swirl of Corinthian conflict tells us that this teaching on love is not theoretical, but immensely practical! *Agape* in the hearts of believers solves conflicts, heals relationships, initiates peace, seeks the good for others, regulates egotism, and opens up dialogue between former enemies. *Agape* love transforms failing marriages, reconciles alienated parents and children, creates high-trust supervisors, and produces loyal employees. In the 1950s and 1960s, Dr. Martin Luther King Jr. revolutionized American society with a Civil Rights movement based on the principle of redemptive and self-sacrificing love. And we could cite a hundred other examples to show that *agape* love is practical in its outcomes.

LEADERSHIP PRINCIPLE 6

Leadership Imitates the Slave-Leadership of Jesus Christ. What we see of Paul in 1 Corinthians 9:19–23 is, in fact, Paul's application of the self-dispensing leadership of Jesus Christ referenced in

Philippians 2:1–5. For Paul, Jesus Christ was the *exemplar* of servant-oriented love. Paul speaks in chapter 11 of the Passover meal Jesus experienced with His disciples. It is hard to imagine the narrative being shared with Paul apart from the act of Jesus's washing the feet of the disciples. Paul knew, it can be assumed, that a problem arose: There was no *doulos* to wash the feet—the dirty, crusty, muddy feet of the disciples that evening. Because this work was our modern equivalent of cleaning the toilets, there were no volunteers. Jesus waited for the disciples to move, and the disciples waited for a servant or a volunteer to appear. After many minutes of pained silence, John, the writer of the fourth Gospel, records that Jesus "rose from supper and laid aside His garments, took a towel and girded Himself. After that, He poured water into a basin and began to wash the disciples' feet, and to wipe them with the towel with which He was girded" (John 13:4–5).

Christ's revolutionary act on that Thursday evening turned the concept of dominance leadership on its head forever. Jesus had already taught the disciples that leadership in His community is not modeled after the very familiar Gentile domination of others. In Mark 10:42–45, Jesus told His disciples, in response to their request for the highest seat in His kingdom, that "You know that those who are considered rulers over the Gentiles lord it over them, and their great ones exercise authority over them. Yet it shall not be so among you; but whoever desires to become great among you shall be your servant. And whoever of you desires to be first shall be slave of all. For even the Son of Man did not come to be served, but to serve, and to give His life a ransom for many." Then, in John 13, at the end of His last class session with His disciples, Jesus did more than tell them what Christian leadership should look like. He proceeded to dramatize servant-leadership before their very eyes. He had already disclosed His mission by presenting Himself as one who came "not to be served, but to serve" in Mark 10:45. But on this Thursday evening in the Upper Room, Jesus reenacted the great condescension that would be later described by the apostle Paul in Philippians 2:1–5. Just as Christ divested Himself of His robe in the Upper Room, He had also divested Himself of His glorious divinity in a preexisting eternity. Just as He girded Himself with a towel (a universal instrument of service) in the Upper Room, He had also girded Himself with humanity in preparation for the universal service of redeeming the human family back to God (John 3:16). His leadership was prompted by a love commitment that knew no bounds or depths. He chose to become a slave, bound to humanity, for our salvation.

Christ's sacrificial service best reflects the love that is described as *agape* love in the New Testament. Paul seeks to follow Jesus Christ in His practice of slave-leadership, and so we should as well.

CONCLUSION

Paul reveals in his life and teaching the nature of a servant leader transformed by an encounter with Christ. In a culture in which the nature of servitude involved abandonment of autonomy at best, Paul considers it an honor to be a servant, to imitate Christ in doing so. He lives the life of a servant in obedience to Christ, aware of the model of servant leadership that Jesus commanded His disciples to follow after His own example (Mark 10:42–45). Paul's words in 1 Corinthians 9:19–23 summarize his perspective on what servant leadership is. From the passage, Christian leaders can extract the six principles that challenge us to serve as Jesus served:

1. Though free toward all men, spiritual leaders voluntarily become their servants.
2. Christian leaders redefine their identity within an encounter with Christ.
3. Christian leaders appreciate ethnic/cultural distinctives and are able to cross such barriers.
4. Christian leaders engage in service with awareness that they are stewards of leadership opportunities that can change lives.
5. Christian leaders serve because their lives are transformed by love.
6. Christian leaders are imitators of Christ as they serve.

Jesus redeems us because it is in His nature to do so—to love His creation so deeply that He identifies with them and substitutes

His life for theirs. Paul served Christ and others *from a heart* transformed by love. In like manner, Christians serve out of love. Service given in grudging obedience is not the service of which Paul speaks.

One may identify the horrific abuses of slavery at its worst, or understand that service at least suggests the giving up of autonomy. In either view, service abandons self and requires sacrifice. To abandon our own self-interests for others can be done only in love. There is no substitute. The sacrifice is so great that it demands extreme love. This love comes only from a life transformed by the Spirit.

In his poem "Outwitted," Edwin Markham penned these words that summarize the active practice of servant leadership:

> He drew a circle to shut me out,
> Heretic, rebel, a thing to flout.
> But Love and I had a mind to win,
> We drew a circle and took him in!

Servant leadership represents an ever-widening circle designed to take in persons we are called to serve and to love.

FOR REFLECTION

Personal:

1. Do you think of yourself as a person who serves? How do others see that reality manifested in your life?
2. Has God's calling determined your purpose in life? How has that shaped your identity?

Organizational:

1. In what practical ways are people of various cultures valued in your organization?
2. Describe the mission your organization is steward of. Evaluate its stewardship.

ENDNOTES

1. Scripture quotations in this chapter are taken from the New King James Version.

2. D. E. Garland, *1 Corinthians,* Baker Exegetical Commentary on the New Testament (Grand Rapids, MI: Baker Academic, 2003), 427.

18 | Barnabas: A Study in Empowering Leadership

The author of Acts is commonly understood to be Luke, who also authored the gospel that bears his name, and he selected for his narrative persons whose stories were recorded within the oral or written sources available for his research and complementary to his purpose (Luke 1:1–4). Those characters he discovered as having devoted themselves to Christian mission are seen as Christian leaders. Luke describes these leaders' participation in mission not only by using the verb to lead (*ago* and its family), but also by describing how they influenced individuals and groups to learn about the gospel, to decide to receive it, and to adopt a Christian way of life.

Luke shows his readers that the Christian message is rooted in the Jewish religion with its Scriptures, Temple, and culture, but that it had to become a universal faith in order to be able to reach Rome, the capital city of the Roman Empire. On its way, the gospel had to be appropriately received by the closest human groups to the orthodox Jews of his time—the Hellenist Jews, the Samaritans, the proselytes (of whom the Ethiopian eunuch is an example), and the God-fearing friends of the Jews (such as Cornelius)—to be able to reach the most distant human groups, those with no link at all to the God of the Bible.

This chapter will focus on the leadership principles demonstrated by one character in the expansion of mission described in Acts: Barnabas. These principles will emerge from eight biblical narratives in the book of Acts involving Barnabas, whose ministry itself reveals the general principles evident in Acts and in the context of his time. The chapter will first introduce Barnabas, and the eight narratives will then be examined.

BARNABAS IN THE BOOK OF ACTS

Paul mentions Barnabas twice in his letters: Galatians 2:11ff and 1 Corinthians 9:6. But the book of Acts provides the greatest detail concerning this early Christian leader. He is present in all three divisions of the book.[1] Peter and Paul are the only others to have this distinction.

The first reference to Barnabas appears in the first division of Acts (1:1–8:1), which represents different steps in the progress of the gospel, based on Christ's prophetic commission in 1:8. This first division can be called *Jerusalem,* because it is the city where the action takes place from the beginning of the book to 8:1; and Jerusalem is representative of the Jewish people living in the Promised Land and willing to remain faithful to the Temple and the Hebrew Scriptures.

The reader meets Barnabas again in the second division of Acts, which can be called *Judea and Samaria* (8:2—9:31). These geographical areas of reference in the narrative point not only to the regions that surround Jerusalem, but also to the populations close to the Jewish religion but more peripheral than central: the Samaritans because they are of mixed origin and could not collaborate with the rebuilding of the Temple after the Babylonian exile,[2] the proselytes represented by the Ethiopian eunuch who had come to Jerusalem to worship the true God but who could not be included in God's people because of the law,[3] and Saul of Tarsus, the public enemy of the Christians.

After the conversion of Cornelius and his household, Barnabas plays a very important role with Paul in the first section of the last division of the book of Acts, which can be called the *Ends of the Earth.* This geographical reference represents those who are religiously and culturally far away from the roots of Christianity. This last step in the progress of the gospel, as described in the third division of the book, is itself divided into three parts: (1) the transition from Peter to Paul (9:32–15:39); (2) the Pauline mission (15:40–21:16); (3) the explanation and details of Paul's inexorable journey to Rome (21:17 to the end of the book). And Barnabas is the key person in the first part. It is in this narrative, when Paul took over from Peter in mission activity, that the specific principles of Barnabas's leadership surface.

This chapter will now explore eight passages in Acts concerning Barnabas. These passages unfold more detail of his life and ministry, and they provide a grounding for leadership principles within the text.

ACTS 4:36–37

These two verses belong to the second summary describing the life of the Jerusalem Christian church. Its main emphasis is to show the community spirit of that church.

In these verses Barnabas is introduced by his name, Joseph, a Hebrew name famous because of the great leader of the last part of the book of Genesis. But he does not belong to one of the two tribes coming from Joseph. He belongs to the tribe of Levi, which was in charge of the Hebrew sanctuary and of the religious education of the people in ancient Israel. This gives a certain stature to this person. As the book is dedicated to Theophilus, an influential character, Barnabas is established as a religious notable who contributes to the credibility of the Christian message and mission.[4] But nothing in the text would lead the reader to think that this man is a leader because of this position he inherited by birth.

The apostles gave him a surname, Barnabas—an Aramaic name—that Luke translates for his readers as "son of encouragement." The etymology of the Aramaic name Barnabas is not clear. One possibility is "son of Nabu," one of the gods of ancient Babylon, but it does not fit the context at all. The best possibility is "son of nebouah, prophecy."[5] A prophetic ministry is attributed by God Himself; it cannot be authentic if it is a self-proclaimed mission. God speaks to the prophet by various means, and the prophet transmits God's message in written or oral form according to circumstances and his natural abilities. And as one of the roles of a prophet is to encourage, exhort, and comfort (Acts 13:15), this ministry well fits the abilities of Barnabas.

This explanation of the name is unique in the book of Acts. Saul of Tarsus also has a surname—Paul—but Luke does not explain where it came from. No one else bears a name given by the apostles. This insight shows that he had companionship with the apostles for enough time and of sufficient quality to be observed by them and to impress or influence them. And this name describes one of his gifts: to comfort or encourage others through the words he pronounces as a prophet.[6] This prophetic ministry is to be understood as a manifestation of God's Spirit in his life: It gives him an authority that comes from God and is recognized and affirmed by the official leaders of the Early Church appointed by Jesus Himself. It also shows the human and relational dimension of this ministry, which is not limited to communicating information from God but consists in bringing emotional support, such as comfort, to people who go through uncomfortable situations. And this positive ministry based on a God-given capacity for relationships of quality is not a boast coming from him but an affirmation recognized and attested to by the apostles.

He came from Cyprus. He was a Jew by birth, but from the Diaspora. He, or his parents, had been confronted with people of another culture, another religion, and another mentality. But he lived in Jerusalem and shared the life of the first Christian church there. His Hebrew name and Aramaic surname, as well as his Levite ascendance, seem to indicate that he was not viewed by the author of the book as a Hellenist Christian but as an orthodox Jew, a Hebrew Christian in his right place in Jerusalem. This is very important in Luke's viewpoint. Barnabas would be an authoritative bridge between the Jerusalem church and the mission outside of Israel.[7]

His first action mentioned is an act of generosity: He sold a field and brought the money to the apostles' feet. This act is mentioned in a summary about the quality of life inside the first Christian community. That makes Barnabas a model in the eyes of the readers, a positive example of Christian charity. We will never know if the field he sold was in Cyprus, his native land, or in Judea, where he lived. Even if the Levites had no portion in the Promised Land distributed among the twelve tribes in Joshua's time, they had villages and fields and were able to buy and sell land, as Jeremiah, who belonged to a sacerdotal family, did.[8]

The price of his field is brought to the feet of the apostles. By means of this detail, Luke shows that Barnabas is a Christian giver, not a *benefactor* according to the Roman model.[9] Unlike the typical recipient of gifts in Roman culture, the church is not put in a position of debt toward him. His generosity cannot be suspected of interest, pride, or manipulation. He belongs to the community and lives out practical communion.

After reading those two verses, the reader feels that the character thus described will have "an important stature"[10] in the remainder of the narrative. Barnabas is a leader in the eyes of Luke. His generosity was a positive model for the Christian community of Jerusalem and beyond, and he has been seen by the apostles themselves as a prophet able to comfort. His sense of *koinonia* is a principle of leadership in the community.

ACTS 9:27

The second mention (9:27) is very short but important for our study because Barnabas led (*êgagen*) Saul to the apostles. Lead, here, conveys the sense of meeting someone where he is, showing him the way, and walking with him until he reaches a new place where he feels better and where he belongs. It seems ironic that Saul, the one who sought to lead captured believers to Jerusalem (9:2), is now led to the apostles by someone who puts his hand, a friendly hand, on him.[11] The Christians in Jerusalem did not believe that their previous enemy had become their brother in faith, and they were afraid.

But Barnabas did not fear Saul. On the contrary, he took him with him, and led him to the apostles. This implies that he knew where the apostles were, and he had a positive relationship with them. But it also means that Barnabas possessed some courage along with the capacity for building a trusting relationship with Saul.

328 | Servants and Friends

The explanations given by Barnabas in 9:27 are a theological interpretation (*diegesato*) of what happened to Saul on the Damascus road. As a prophet, he receives from God understanding about what is going on. He is convinced that Saul had seen the Lord, a special privilege after the Ascension, which gives Saul a status comparable with that of the apostles.[12] Barnabas is sure that the Lord had spoken to Saul and that he had preached boldly in Damascus in the name of Jesus. How did Barnabas know these things? The only assumption available for the reader is either that he received a revelation from God or that he listened to Saul before introducing him to the apostles. Even if he had felt some fear in front of Saul, knowing his past as a persecutor, he believed what Saul had told him and trusted his testimony; he was not suspicious when he saw him trying to get closer to the disciples. If he shared the natural prejudice of the believers, he was able to overcome this prejudice, to control his fear.

Barnabas was an open-minded leader; he was able to face new situations with courage and a strong will to communicate, an ability to trust the word of a previous enemy, to share and to build community. Where did he develop that capacity? At this point in the narrative, Luke gives us no real clue. It is clear, however, that the Early Church and its mission benefit from that gift.

Barnabas also has a strong relationship with God that leads him to receive revelations as the prophets of the past or simply to recognize God's action in Saul's life. For Barnabas, God is sovereign, and his role, as a believer, is to submit to His sovereignty. He believes that God's power has been able to transform Saul. This kind of belief in the capacity and willingness of God to change the lives of people, even the lives of those who are considered the worst or the farthest from the church, is certainly an important characteristic for a leader. It could be the best explanation of the word *faith* used in Acts 11:24.

ACTS 11:22-26

The third time Barnabas appears in the book is in the planting of the Christian church in Antioch (11:22–26). This narrative comes immediately after the longest story of the book, presenting Cornelius as the first God-fearing, converted non-Jew and concluding with the

Jerusalem believers admitting that the Gentile nations can become Christians as well. It is here that Luke turns to tell more of the story of those Christian Jews scattered by the persecution following Stephen's martyrdom. That story began in 8:4 with Philip going to Samaria. Now it continues with other Christians who were from Cyprus (as Barnabas was) and from Cyrene and who went to Antioch in Syria and spoke to Greek people.

When the news of this came to Jerusalem, the church chose Barnabas and sent (*aposteilo*) him to Antioch. Recall that after the first conversion of non-Jews, in Samaria, the church sent Peter and John, two of the Twelve (Acts 8:14). By now they trusted Barnabas as if he were an apostle, and he will be called an apostle later on (Acts 14:14). As the number of believers increased, leadership had to be delegated and new leaders were to take up new tasks. Thus, after the seven Hellenists of Acts 6, Barnabas was entrusted with an official leadership role. Barnabas's mission was not his own initiative. He was a servant, ready to accept the challenges given him by the community to which he belonged. Barnabas was chosen for this mission because of the qualities he possessed. There is no detailed explanation about the purpose of his mission. Was it just one of information? Was it oversight? Did it reflect suspicion that the conversions were not genuine, as could have been behind the mission of Peter and John to Samaria and as was clearly the attitude of the circumcised in Jerusalem when Peter came back from Cornelius's home (Acts 11:1–2)? Was it a mission of integration of the new Antioch community into the spiritual fellowship of the Christian church and evangelism (v. 22)?

Whatever the mission, Barnabas was identified as a trustworthy leader: He seems to have had the confidence of the Jewish Christians in Jerusalem as well as that of the Hellenist Christians who dared to share the gospel with Greeks in Antioch.

Barnabas went to Antioch; he saw God's grace, rejoiced in the work done by others, and exhorted the new believers to stand firmly attached to the Lord (v. 23). Barnabas, as in the case of Saul, was able to see God in action in the population of Antioch. The initiative of the Christians who shared the gospel also with Greek people was led by God. The effects of this divine intervention were interpreted as manifestations of God's grace. For Barnabus it was a source of joy. He did not try to attach people to his person but to the Lord. A leader has followers, according to one of the simplest definitions of leadership. But as a Christian leader Barnabas made followers of the Lord.

Then Luke describes (v. 24) his character: a good man, full of the Holy Spirit and of faith. Here is the core of Barnabas's leadership. The verb *prostithemi* (meaning "to put to, to add") and the adjective *ikanos* (meaning "large, sizeable") are typical tools for Luke to bring to his readers' minds the golden age of the Early Church in Jerusalem, with participation from the new church in Antioch. It is remarkable that Luke calls Barnabas a good man. In his two books, Luke uses that description for only two men: Barnabas, and Joseph of Arimathea (Luke 23:50). Readers will remember that, according to Luke, Jesus gently reminded a man who called Him good that only God is good (Luke 18:18–19). Luke thus presents Barnabas as a transformed man—he is a man who has godly character. And we understand why Luke insists on the influence of the Holy Spirit in Barnabas's life as on many of the first Christian leaders.[13] For him a leader is first a follower of Christ resurrected and exalted and present through the Holy Spirit. And Luke adds that Barnabas is full of faith.

Then (v. 25) Barnabas moves on from his mission post in Antioch. He goes to Tarsus to join efforts with Saul, whom he had introduced to the apostles sometime before. What he understood about Saul and was able to explain to the Christians of Jerusalem (9:27) is enough to give him a vision of Saul's potential. Moved by that vision, he goes and finds the coworker he needs. He finds him: The verb *anazêteo* used here seems to indicate that the search was not easy and that it required some perseverance and will to find.[14] Then he leads (*ago*) him to Antioch. He must either have arrived when Saul was already convinced by God himself that he should go with him, or have been persuasive enough to convince Saul to come with him. But the result is the same: both of them go to Antioch and act as leaders, gathering (*sunago*) with the converted as a church and teaching them.

Their leadership and teaching made the Antioch community call the believers *Christians,* not disciples of Barnabas or Saul but of Christ.

ACTS 11:29

Barnabas and Saul are mentioned in this passage as a team sent (*aposteilo*) by the Antioch church to carry the money gathered to help the disciples living in Judea who would suffer from a famine predicted by Christian prophets (11:30). Both men were considered trustworthy. To carry funds was not an easy matter at that time of traveling on foot, animals, carriages drawn by animal, or by boat. We can suppose from what Paul says in his Epistles that the number of persons who accompanied him on his trip to Jerusalem (Acts 20:4) was to increase the safety of the money he carried.

The money was taken to the elders in Jerusalem. This is the first mention of the word *presbuteros* in the book of Acts. Nothing is said about those elders. There were elders among the Jewish authorities in the city of Jerusalem, as in any city of ancient Israel. One third of the Sanhedrin was made up of elders of the Jewish community. The money carried could have been given to those Jewish elders, but here Luke, by using the word *brothers,* seems to point to elders inside the Christian church in Jerusalem. They are there, receiving the money sent to help the victims of the famine. They have been appointed because they were perceived as trustworthy and able to handle that gift correctly.

Barnabas had taken the money from the sale of his field to the feet of the apostles. The seven were called to serve at the tables.[15] But we have no explanation for the origin of the ministry of these elders. It indicates once more that leadership in the Early Church is shared with more and more people as the mission grows.

ACTS 13:1–3

The next mention of Barnabas is in the short calling narrative of Acts 13:1–3. He belongs to a small group of leaders of the Antioch church, a group of prophets and teachers. This is the only time when these ministries are directly attributed to Barnabas. Both of these ministries require a gift for communication. The first one can be easily associated with the surname he was given by the apostles. The second one reminds the readers that Jesus is the subject of teaching in the Christian community and that the apostles are in charge of this teaching.[16]

He is the first on the list, probably as the official church planter. His leadership is recognized by the local church members. His spiritual gifts are seen and appreciated by them. Nobody seems to contest his leadership initiative in that church. As a prophet and teacher, he is included among those who lead the congregation in the worship (*leiturgo*) of the Lord. While they were fasting, the Holy Spirit spoke and told them that Barnabas, together with Saul, was called for a special work. The Antioch church affirmed their calling by fasting, prayer, and the laying on of hands. They already had confidence in this team as preachers and as stewards of the contributions that would sustain the Judean church.

ACTS 13:5—14:28

The account in Acts follows Barnabas during the long narrative of the first missionary trip (13:5—14:28). After the editor changes Saul's name to Paul (13:9), he ceases to call the two missionaries Barnabas and Saul (13:7), instead referring to the team as Paul and Barnabas (13:43, 46, 50). Paul seems to take the first place. He is the one who speaks. He speaks as somebody who is filled by the Holy Spirit (13:9) to stop the magician Elymas's efforts to prevent Sergius Paulus from receiving the gospel. Barnabas is apparently one of Paul's companions and his name is not mentioned when they leave Cyprus (13:13). When they are invited to speak in the synagogue in Antioch in Pisidia, Paul stands up and speaks. Even when both men are associated after the long missionary speech of Paul in Antioch, Barnabas seems to play the secondary role. There is an exception. During the episode at Lystra, after the healing of the crippled man, Barnabas is called Zeus and Paul Hermes by the crowd (14:12), and then (14:14) we find the original order with Barnabas first and Paul (not Saul) second but preceded by the title *the apostles*. We agree with those who see a logical order for the two apostles to be called Zeus and Hermes. Paul is the speaker. To give him the name, Hermes, the messenger of the gods in Greek mythology, is a fitting way to describe him. Barnabas is like Zeus because he needs a speaker to go with him when he visits the humans.[17]

The end of the episode is puzzling: Paul is stoned, but not Barnabas (14:19). Why? Because a positive view of the courage of Barnabas is retained in Acts, it seems he simply was not immediately present when that stoning took place. But he obviously was nearby because the text says that the following day, Paul, together with Barnabas, left for Derbe (14:20).

ACTS 15:2–26

Barnabas next appears in the narrative of what is usually called the Jerusalem Council. The conflict began because of questions some had raised about the work that Paul and Barnabas (15:2) had been doing. It was decided that Paul, Barnabas, and several others would go to the apostles and the elders in Jerusalem to settle the matter (15:2). This shows that Paul and Barnabas, and those opposing them, recognized the authority of the leaders in Jerusalem. During the meeting, Barnabas and Paul related the signs and wonders done by God through them among the nations (15:12).

Why is Barnabas named first here? Was it because Barnabas as a Levite had a better reputation among the Jerusalem church than Paul, the previous persecutor? Was it because Barnabas had been a member of the Jerusalem church, the one which had sent him with total confidence to Antioch?

When a decision was reached, two delegates were sent with Paul and Barnabas (15:22). Why now was Paul first? When the letter explaining the decision was written, the order is once more reversed: with Barnabas and Paul (15:25). Is the order of the two names important? Has it a meaning? It may be likely that the author views all who contribute leadership in mission as equal partners, not in a hierarchical or positional authority with one another, and thus, the order of the names is insignificant.

One thing is certain: for Luke, these two men are dear to the apostles and elders in Jerusalem because they are men who have dedicated their lives to the name of the Lord Jesus (15:26). This is probably the strongest evidence of their leadership among the early Christians, according to Luke.

ACTS 15:35–39

After the Jerusalem Council, Paul and Barnabas returned to Antioch where they, with many others, taught and preached the good news (15:35).

Then we reach the last mention of Barnabas in the book of Acts. After some period of time (without any chronological detail), Paul invited Barnabas to join him and visit the churches they planted during that first missionary trip. Barnabas was ready to go but wanted to take John, called Mark, with them (15:37). But Paul insisted that it would not be good to take with them someone who had renounced their mission (13:13) during the previous trip (15:38). And that became a *paroxysm* (meaning "provocation, angry dispute"), a point of conflict, and they separated. Barnabas took John Mark, and they boarded a ship to Cyprus (15:39), while Paul took Silas and left (15:40).

For Luke the conflict between the two coworkers was just a matter of a team agreeing to divide. And the disagreement ended up with two missionary teams instead of just one, a positive result for Luke. The message to the reader is clear: Barnabas was a positive mentor and exceptional leader. He was able to empower John Mark, just as he had earlier been used by God to empower Saul.

Even when Paul took the first place on their team, Barnabas remained happy with the second one. He demonstrated humility. But the departure of Barnabas leaves the reader with some questions. Luke seems to send him and John Mark away quickly, without even giving them the brotherly recommendation to God's grace that Paul and Silas received (15:40). We know that the thirteen remaining chapters of the book are focused on Paul.

There had been another conflict between Paul and Barnabas. Paul related it in his letter to the Galatians (2:1–14). When people from James's group came from Jerusalem to Antioch, Peter changed his practice of associating with Gentiles, and he drew Barnabas after him in what Paul called a *hypocrisy* (2:13).

CONCLUSION

Several principles of leadership emerge in the narratives of Barnabas. The first is the calling and gifting from God of all who follow Him. For Luke, Barnabas and Paul were chosen by God and appointed apostles. Even if Barnabas had natural or educational qualifications, received at birth or acquired by any kind of training, they did not constitute his leadership. God chose him, trained him, qualified him, empowered him, and equipped him for the leadership he gave to the Christian mission. And Barnabas was willing to cooperate with God for this mission.

Another principle is dependence on the empowering of the Holy Spirit. Barnabas was filled with the Holy Spirit, and he was recognized by the apostles and by the local church of Antioch as a prophet and teacher. Even if he was not a gifted orator like Peter and Paul, he was able to see and understand situations and to communicate efficiently and in a comforting way. He had many gifts and capacities given by God. He was the one whose vision was able to see God's hand on Saul, even if it was difficult for others to believe that this persecutor could become a missionary.

But Barnabas was not only a man of vision, he was also a man of action: He went, searched until he found Saul in Tarsus, and brought him into an active ministry in Antioch. He was ready to disagree with Paul because he had a different vision concerning John Mark. His humbleness allowed him to be a leader able to recruit and train the greatest missionary of the first century, Paul, and, if traditions are correct, the author of the first gospel, Mark. This might be of interest for Luke who took the initiative to write another gospel on the model of at least a previous one, and a second book concerning the Christian mission.

In his early relationship with Saul, Barnabas illustrates a leadership principle: risk-taking. As a result of his Spirit-led risk, Barnabas can be seen as the missiological bridge between the apostles of the original mission and the universal Christian mission.

Barnabas demonstrates in an extraordinary way the leadership principle of empowering others. It is impressive to review the great number of Christian ministries in nearly all denominations that use the name of Barnabas in their official name—ministries related to health care, education, youth ministry, mission, and nurture.[18] This would never have happened without the perception Luke had of this early Christian leader and without choosing, under Inspiration, to memorialize it in the book of Acts.

Barnabas was a true leader in the early Christian movement. The characteristics and leadership principles Barnabas clearly demonstrated include acceptance of God's vision and mission for him and others, generosity, integrity, faith, courage, commitment, the empowerment of others, and humility.

FOR REFLECTION

Personal:

1. How do I empower others in leadership?
2. Do I desire to see the work or ministry of others increase beyond my own effectiveness?

Organizational:

1. How do we respond to the failings of people in our organization? Are we willing to give them hope and further opportunity?
2. When God seems to be doing something extraordinary, are we able to trust and wait patiently for His working to be evident?

ENDNOTES

1. I have chosen to favor a three-part plan of the book of Acts, and I explained why and how in Louis Ségond, *La Nouvelle Bible Ségond: Edition d'étude* (Paris: Société biblique française, 2002), 1427–1429.
2. 2 Kings 17:2–41; Ezra 4; Nehemiah 4 and 6.
3. Deuteronomy 23:2.
4. See Ben Witherington III, *The Acts of the Apostles: A Socio-Rhetorical Commentary* (Grand Rapids, MI: W. B. Eerdmans; and Carlisle, PA: Paternoster Press, 1998), 212.

5. See, for instance, Ernst Haenchen, *The Acts of the Apostles: A Commentary* (Philadelphia: Westminster Press, 1971), 231–232; Daniel Marguerat, *Les Actes des Apôtres (1–12),* Commentaires du Nouveau Testament, Va, deuxième série (Geneva, Switzerland: Labor et Fides, 2007), 171.

6. See E. Earle Ellis, "The Role of the Christian Prophet in Acts" in *Prophecy and Hermeneutic in Early Christianity: New Testament Essays* (Tübingen, Germany: J.C.B. Mohr [Paul Siebeck], 1978), 131.

7. See Marguerat, *Les Actes,* 171.

8. Jeremiah 1:1; 32:6ff.

9. Marguerat, *Les Actes,* 172.

10. Marguerat, *Les Actes,* 164.

11. This is the meaning of the verb *epilambanomai* used in Acts 9:27.

12. It seems to be a kind of "apostolic legitimating" as Marguerat calls it in *Les Actes,* 343.

13. D. Marguerat, *La première histoire du Christianisme,* Lectio Divina 180 (Paris: Cerf; and Geneva, Switzerland: Labor et Fides, 1999), 152–154, shows how the mentions of the Holy Spirit decrease in number when we advance in the book and the Holy Spirit is given less to communities and more to individuals.

14. See E. Delebecque, *Les Actes des Apôtres,* Collection Budé (Paris: Les Belles Lettres, 1982), 57.

15. Acts 6:1–6.

16. Acts 2:42.

17. Many think that the crowd named the apostles with names of local gods (see Haenchen, *Acts of the Apostles*), and that Luke or his oral or written sources changed these names into Zeus and Hermes to make it easier for the readers to understand. But Lystra was a city founded around 6 BC in Lycaonia as a Roman colony peopled by Roman veterans. See M. J. Mellink, "Lystra," *The Interpreter's Bible Dictionary,* vol. 3, ed. George Buttrick (Nashville: Abingdon Press, 1962), 194–195. Therefore, it is not surprising that Luke uses the names of Greek gods well admired among the Roman gods.

18. For example, Barnabas Ministries in Zeeland, Michigan, focuses on reaching at-risk youth and families; http://barnabasmin.org/new/want-to-help (accessed on October 17, 2013). Barnabas International in Rockford, Illinois, "exists to edify, encourage, enrich and strengthen servants in ministry," http://www.barnabas.org/index.php (accessed on October 17, 2013).

Section Four:
A Biblical Theology
of Leadership

19 A Reflection on Leadership Principles in the Old Testament

Skip Bell

God's relationship with humankind from creation to the first advent of Christ demonstrates principles contributing to a biblical theology of leadership. Such principles give shape to an understanding of leadership and form the foundation for the ideas we commonly call servant, or incarnational, leadership. Those principles also contribute to the foundation for our work, *Servants and Friends*. The principles include relational leadership, shared leadership, vision, initiative, creativity, communication, and service.

The purpose of this chapter is to reflect on the biblical context of selected significant, reoccurring principles and then emphasize their application to the leadership challenge we face in the present. While the previous chapters provide the content for this reflection, new material is provided to help stitch these concepts together. Therefore, the treatment of these principles is not limited to the articulations of the contributors. The principles selected for this reflection are significant, but the list should not to be considered exhaustive. A thorough reading of the first part of this volume—and indeed continued biblical study—will reveal many other principles that help form a biblical theology of leadership. The principles selected are arguably the most comprehensive, and they also enfold related principles such as integrity, faith, and courage. First and perhaps most broadly expressed is relational leadership.

LEADERSHIP IS RELATIONAL

The most apparent principle regarding leadership emerging from the Old Testament is the idea of relational leadership. It is evidenced in the purpose for initiating creation, the manner of creation, the revelation of God Himself, the nature of relationality in community, and communication between God and humankind throughout the Old Testament record.

Humankind was created for relationship. The environmental condition in which humankind was to exist and flourish was designed for relational community. Humankind engaged relationally with the living forms of their created environment by nourishing and caring for plants and interacting with animals. Animals themselves, though lacking some aspects of relationality, were created in pairs and with distinguished kinds that multiplied and found association, together with other species and with humankind. Humankind also pursued daily life in a more intimate company with their own kind, having been created male and female. Adam and Eve were created with the other in mind and complemented the being of the other. Thus within creation God designed and affirmed that humankind was to live in a relational community; it was not good to live alone. Leadership is experienced within relational community.

Assumptions regarding the nature of creation in regard to relational community often go unnoticed. These assumptions, with appropriate reflection, provide principles of leadership. The creation narrative reveals relationships that imply shared respect. Humankind tended the world of plants with appreciation and regard for that life form on its own. There is a certain respect for the inanimate creation of air, soil, and water. Humankind did not see them as objects to be exploited for their own purposes; rather, the inanimate creation provided a rich contribution to relationality. Humankind existed alongside of animal life without a sense of threat. Interdependence, mutuality, respect, and care are implied within the relationship with animal life. The same attributes of relationship are inherent in the relationship of Adam and Eve. Both are created in God's image, and thus mutuality and respect are expressed.

The relational nature of God is seen first in the creative act, but also it is evident throughout the Old Testament. Creation helps us understand that He desires relational community. God is relational. When approaching creation, He counseled within that triune relationship—God the Father, God the Son, and God the Holy Spirit. God exists Himself as community, not in the singular. He said: "Let us make man in our own image."[1] He imagined creation with the relational aspects that reflect His own nature. He walked and talked with humankind in the original space of their existence before sin broke the relationship. He spoke with Abraham. He called Moses in a very personal way. He gave evidence of His presence in the wilderness experience of Israel. He has spoken through His prophets.

The relational nature of God's initiatives with humankind implies that leadership happens in relationships formed within relational communities, not as acts imposed on communities. As we engage with others in leadership, we must be guided by this principle: Leadership is a relational process. The principle should be demonstrated by interdependence, mutuality, respect, and care. Leadership is not primarily directing, or making decisions, though such activity is often required. Leadership is better understood in the formation of strength in others within the relational community we share with them.

LEADERSHIP IS SHARED

The Old Testament reveals the principle of shared leadership. The idea of family and the resulting notion of tribe and nation idealize shared leadership. God formed humanity to live in the context of family. Family structure suggests sharing space, resources, opportunity, and identity within loving relationships offering capacity for enlargement as the family expanded. Families could share leadership by forming identity as tribes. Children could grow to independence while retaining access to guidance and wisdom from family, tribe, and the judges or prophets providing wisdom for the nation. The idea of developing maturity in children in a family context was a reflection of God's nature as He delighted in our capacity to grow and mature. However, families, as seen in the Old Testament account, generally fell short of the ideal for which they were created. As with the institutions created by humankind, dominance and control were substituted for loving relationships.

Among the most remarkable evidences of shared leadership are the narratives of God's counsel with humankind. Abraham reasons with God over the destruction of Sodom and Gomorrah. Moses reasons with God over the stated intent to destroy rebellious Israel. God calls His servants, and, like Moses, David, Elijah, and Jonah, they question God regarding the call itself. God, the all-powerful Creator of Earth and the infinite universe, pauses to counsel with us, His creation.

Expressions of mutuality in the Old Testament record further emphasize shared leadership. The relationship of Adam and Eve in creation expressed mutuality; they helped each other. Mutuality transitioned to subordination after sin; the domination experienced by Eve was not in the original thought. Hierarchy entered following the Fall; and, though not evil of itself, hierarchy is universally accompanied in the social structure of humankind by a struggle for power and dominance—the antonym of mutuality.

Distributed authority further revealed the nature of shared leadership in the historical contexts of the Old Testament. The designation of the firstborn (Gen. 48) indicated the assignment of certain leadership functions in the family setting. Nothing in the biblical record suggested that families considered the firstborn to possess qualities inherently superior to those who differed in birth order. While arguments cannot be made from silence, the silence suggested the designation of the firstborn recognized that passing on of certain leadership functions was important to assure order in the family. Further, since each new family extension provided leadership in the community, leadership was multiplied.

Two significant concessions to human limitation within the history of the Old Testament are notable as the concept of distributed leadership is considered: (1) the appointment of the tribe of Levi to serve as priests in place of the firstborn within the reality of Israel's continued unfaithfulness (Num. 3), and (2) God's decision to grant the request of the elders to appoint a king over Israel (1 Sam. 8). It is beyond the scope of this chapter to treat the idea of the redeemed community and the integration of the priesthood of every disciple as pressed in the New Testament narratives, but it is evident from the record that the challenges of spirituality and worship were met by new structures seeking distribution of leadership. The desire of Israel for a king marked a departure from God's vision for shared leadership in human experience. The biblical record portrays the institution of kingship as a concession to a request for centralized authority in the nation, similar to what was experienced by other nations of people. God counseled Israel regarding the loss they would experience in copying the neighboring cultures, but the people insisted. God granted freedom for Israel to determine its destiny, though suffering would result. He permitted the people to be self-determinative. The affliction of central and authoritarian leadership exercised by kings was seen in the subsequent years of Israel's history.

Evidence of God's intention for transition of leadership functions emerges in God's instruction to Moses that Joshua should exercise authority (Num. 27:15–20). God recognizes that leadership and authority are to be distributed in order that the community might function well.

Shared leadership is a biblical principle that guides our leadership. Craig Pearce and Jay Conger define *shared leadership* as "a dynamic, interactive influence process among individuals in groups for which the objective is to lead one another to the achievement of group or organizational goals or both."[2] Our society often demonstrates centralized authority rather than shared leadership. We coexist with theistic cultures in which spiritual leaders exercise rule over people with a sense of divine direction and authority. Populations in some contexts embrace theistic governments as right. In business structures we experience people who believe the most effective leadership for their organization is centralized, or even dogmatic. More pervasively, we see our corrupt human natures gathering authority to serve selfish ends or appease a need for dominance. These experiences are substitutes for shared leadership.

Christian leaders grounding their experience in biblical leadership principles practice shared leadership patiently and persistently. The principle is not sacrificed to obtain a particular end. It may appear that to centralize authority or to dominate in the interest of expediency is the right thing to do, but, with rare exception, such leadership behaviors transgress a principle of biblical leadership and contradict the nature of God. Shared leadership is a biblical principle and inherent in a biblical theology of leadership.

LEADERSHIP IS VISIONARY

A further principle emerging from the Old Testament is the nature and function of vision. Arguably no Old Testament narrative is as powerful in defining vision as that of Moses. His compelling, God-given vision for the Hebrew nation led to years of sacrificial service through the wilderness experience and defined his humble submission to death on the doorstep of the Promised Land. It might be easy to overlook the value God places on vision as a principle of leadership. The capacity for vision is a God-given potential and principle of spiritual leadership. God envisioned a great nation from Abraham's seed. He envisioned hope for Israel on the edge of the Promised Land (Deut. 32). He envisioned the rebirth of a nation out of the captivity in Babylon (Jer. 29). God is a God of vision.

A God inspired, passion-stirring vision is essential for every Christian leader. George Barna states: "If you want to be a leader, vision is not an option; it is part of the standard equipment of a real leader."[3] Kouzes and Posner define *vision* as "an ideal and unique image of the future."[4] Scott Rodin emphasizes that we do not form a vision; instead, we are stewards of vision given by God.[5]

Vision is a clear mental image of a preferable future imparted by God to His chosen servants that transforms their lives and communities and is based upon an accurate understanding of God, self, and circumstances. Vision is formed as an image in our minds. It means the act or faculty of seeing. A vision is much more than a mere idea—it is a clear picture of the idea or concept. In the context of religious leadership the guiding work of God within the community is a prerequisite for a God-honoring vision. The terms with which we describe this image imply what we hope for. It is a cherished ideal representing the values we hold—something better than our current experience. Vision suggests future orientation; it is forward-focused and inspires us.

The formation of Israel out of Egypt portrays God-given vision and the risks inherent when vision is lost. When a community loses vision, communication breaks down. Appreciation fades to criticism. Mission is clouded, misunderstood, or forgotten. Problems occupy attention. Little thought is given to the future. Lost in the fog of uncertainty, a community, church, school, or other organization, like Israel, begins to drift.

Vision carries with it an implied and urgent need to create a desired future. "Vision plays a key role in producing useful change by helping to direct, align, and inspire actions on the part of large numbers of people. Without an appropriate vision, a transformation effort can easily dissolve into a list of confusing, incompatible, and time-consuming projects that go in the wrong direction or nowhere at all."[6] Vision transforms a community only when it is developed within the hearts of people, when it is a shared and common image that inspires them corporately.

Shared vision is built on careful consideration of the biblical foundations for calling and mission. A God-given vision is born in the context of a Spirit-led community. It has acknowledged God's providence. In a God-given, shared vision, the values underlying such vision are referenced by a community to form images of the future. Vision is not the popular wish of the community; rather, it is a God-given picture of His will. One such example from the biblical record is the entire book of Deuteronomy, in which Moses recounts God's dealing with Israel and portrays prospective vision for God's blessing of Israel in the Promised Land. Moses portrays a vision for a people obedient to God (Deut. 10:12–13) and for a land promised and blessed by God (Deut. 30:19–20).

What makes the difference between a shared vision and a vision owned and forced on a community by a leader? The answer is in how vision is formed. Leadership implies a relational community in its vision-driven journey, empowering and influencing colleagues rather than dominating. Again, God-honoring vision is fostered in spiritual inquiry within the community, not from human longings. So we must make every effort to lead others in a shared commitment to listening to God's will for our communities.

Perhaps the most remarkable biblical account of this is the final chapter of Moses's leadership experience. The book of Deuteronomy closes with an appraisal of his life (34:10–12): forty years in the palace of Pharaoh, forty years a refugee in Midian herding sheep, and forty years serving Israel in the desert. Here is a man possessing profound spiritual insight; unparalleled godly knowledge; noble, uncompromising character; astounding, remarkable ability; amazing, powerful love; abundant, overflowing enthusiasm; keen, wise judgment; exuberant, unflinching dedication; and dauntless, consistent courage. Told he will not enter the Promised Land (Deut. 3:23–27), Moses offers a blessing and exhortation to the people we read in the pages of Deuteronomy.

He cherished a vision in his mind, lived by a vision in his soul, and served from that vision with love. Moses devoted his final days not in complaining but in blessing the people. The mountain into which God led Moses was in the range named Abarim—it is perhaps Jebel Neba, rising 2,600 feet from the plain, or perhaps Pisgah, a nearby peak. At the age of one hundred and twenty, having sung his last song, offering praise to God before Israel, announcing his last blessing to God's people, Moses went to the mountain alone.

Imagine the heart of Moses. Leaving the people, knowing he would not see them again, he offered a song of praise! He made his way arduously up the mountain. From the mountaintop God provided for him a vision of the Promised Land, and Moses gloried in the vision! He was not absorbed in self-pity.

There are many implications to this final chapter of Moses life. Perhaps the most powerful is the primacy of a God-inspired vision. Moses submitted to that vision with joy, and he encouraged others to hear God's will as they submitted their lives to God as well. Moses did not set foot in the Promised Land, but the vision was enough to carry him through his life. God provides what is required for leadership along with that gift of vision. Leadership is visionary; vision draws us to serve, and communities find life in their God-given, shared vision. Visionary leadership is a principle of biblical leadership that empowers our mission.

LEADERSHIP EXPRESSES INITIATIVE

The Bible begins with God's initiative, "In the beginning, God" (Gen. 1:1). The Old Testament reveals a God of initiative. He creates, He comes to communicate, He lays out a plan for salvation, He forms a nation, He redeems His people from Egypt, He reveals His law, He redeems from Babylon, and He redeems His people from their enemies. A biblical theology of leadership embraces this notion of going before, of preceding, namely, the principle of initiative.

Leadership requires initiative. Initiative implies that, at times, a person is willing to move into empty space where nothing yet exists and create. The space may be a void in ministry, a need, a challenge, or an opportunity. Exercising initiative to fill those spaces requires imagination. A God-given vision may suggest a blessed imagination, ideas born out of prayerful reflection. Such spiritual reflection, when experienced in a life of faith, necessarily engages one with the community in which his or her faith is nourished.

A word of caution is needed. Initiative requires careful reflection on motive and timing. This evaluation must also determine whether the initiative to fill the empty space will actually advance mission. God blesses initiatives that are dedicated to His service, not to our own selfish interests. Sometimes an initiative causes undue damage. Responsible initiative is not foolish. It does not proceed without prayerful consideration. The elders of Israel took the initiative to carry the Ark of the Covenant into a battle they had initiated for the expansion of their interests when God had not ordained the battle. The result was a disastrous defeat of Israel's army and the capture of the Ark (1 Sam. 4:3–11).

Courage is required in our communities as initiative is considered. The best considered and most evident initiative requires it. Since initiative means we are willing to move into empty space where nothing yet exists and create, it suggests change, and change is always accompanied by risk. It follows, then, that communal leadership demonstrates risk-taking courage. An individualistic desire to be known as a person of courage—who takes arbitrary "courageous" stands or engages in a personal initiative supposedly on the behalf of the community—is self-serving. Courage emerges from a selfless, sacrificial, communal commitment to mission.

The principle of initiative implies that any person in the community is able to take initiative. Thus God's view of leadership expresses a harmony among individual initiative, relationality, and shared leadership. With this understanding of initiative, wise leadership empowers others for service. It does not remove initiative, thereby positioning people as followers who lack the power to think, create, process, and fill a void.

LEADERSHIP IS CREATIVE

The principle of creativity is evident in the Old Testament. Human beings are given creative potential; they are, for example, entrusted with the ability to procreate. We are urged: "Be fruitful and multiply; fill the earth and subdue it; have dominion over the fish of the sea, over the birds of the air and over every living thing that moves on the earth" (Gen. 1:28). By expanding the human race, humankind participates in the creation of Earth. "Subdue" and "have dominion" suggest both management and creative leadership in the context of our physical environment, thus connecting leadership and creativity. Creative activity is one expression of leadership.

Scripture reveals a God of creativity and the creative work of His people. God took the city by having the Hebrews march around it thirteen times—certainly a creative way to go about conquest! The Sanctuary demonstrates the creativity of the Designer in its intricate color and design, the Psalms are written beautifully, God uses creativity in showing signs and wonders, and the prophets convey their messages in creative ways. Beauty is seen in the Temple. God enjoys creativity and encourages His people in their creativity.

The connection between leadership and creative beauty is often marred because leadership is seen only in management terms. Such a view of leadership is incomplete. Asaph, the musician, psalmist, and contemporary of King David, illustrated creativity. Because creative beauty was important to God in establishing patterns of worship, He set aside families of the tribe of Levi to be full-time musicians. Asaph, a Levitical priest, was one of these. His responsibility was to work in the tabernacle, a Levite ordained by God to perform various functions within the Tabernacle. "So he [David] left Asaph and his brothers there before the ark of the covenant of the LORD to minister before the ark regularly, as every day's work required" (1 Chron. 16:37). Asaph's function within the Tabernacle was that of a musician (1 Chron. 9:33). He is referred to as a singer (1 Chron. 15:19). He wrote at least twelve of the Psalms: 50, 73, 74, 75, 76, 77, 78, 79, 80, 81, 82, and 83. He was not only a singer, but also a songwriter and composer. He was a spiritual leader, and his music was considered exhortation.

As a creative musician, Asaph was providing spiritual leadership for Israel. He was a holy, sanctified, spiritual leader who communicated God's truths and his love for the Lord in his musical worship. Leadership that is creative produces productivity and life. Creativity is motivated by service; it finds its highest expression when accompanied by the service of life. In the context of leadership, creativity is unselfish; it is meant to serve.

Keri Wehlander envisions the transforming power of art: "We can be certain that we will be transformed by what we create—and in turn, this finished creation may become a source of transformation for others."[7] Creative arts provide a signpost for the future and guide us through creative risk to immense personal change and to subsequent transformation in our churches and communities. God connects with us in His own creative nature, and thus we experience truth about God. Wehlander describes in her introduction that the choice to create is a choice to risk. The capacity to take risks provides transformative power and the element of change.[8]

Diana Butler Bass, in an insightful essay, asserts that God is "elegant," and that His universe is proven equally elegant by the discoveries of scientists and physicists. Christianity, she suggests, is transformed from being a truth discovered by rational formulation to being an exploration of the nature of God revealed in beauty.[9] Bass concludes her essay by asserting that we are called to imitate God's creative life—shaping the clay of our experience with voices and hands.

Leadership is creative. As noted above, the principle of initiative means we often seek to fill a void or meet an opportunity. That implies change rather than maintaining the status quo. The object of initiative is creative action, creating something that has not existed before. Creativity means that ideas, ministries, procedures, or actions themselves are new. Leadership imagines the potential of people and communities, empowering others to reach those potentials. Creativity in leadership adds beauty to God's creation.

LEADERSHIP FOSTERS COMMUNICATION

Communication is a biblical principle of leadership. "In the beginning...God said" (Gen. 1:1–3). As Jacques Doukhan points out in the first chapter, in creation God spoke directly to His creation: Then "God said to them, 'Be fruitful and multiply'... And God said, 'See, I have given you every herb" (Gen. 1:28–29). God communicates; He has done so in many ways, including through theophany (Exod. 33:21–23); in audible voice (Exod. 3:2; 19:19; 1 Kings 19:12); through angels (Gen. 32:22–32) (although this also seems to be a theophany); in dreams (Gen. 28:10–22, 37:5–10); and in prophetic action (Hos. 3).

The Scriptures reveal communication that is strongly communal. God actively seeks an ongoing, just, and loving relationship with what is created. God sometimes encourages this relationship to be interactive, involving qualities of initiative and response, question and answer, closeness and distance, complaint and reassurance, on both sides. Even in revealing Himself, God gives people the freedom to participate, to see or not to see.

God created humankind with the capacity and nature to communicate. Mutuality is further evidenced in the nature to communicate. This art of good communication sheds light on communication in leadership.

Communication, in its highest form, is a process marked by mutuality and respect. It is an interaction between persons that is multidirectional; there is no real communication if, in the process, the other is dominated. Communication takes time and implies caring for the other. Christian communication is a reflection of God's nature and God's way of doing things: establishing, maintaining, and developing full and robust relationships. This perspective should guide us in evaluating not just the content of communication, but also the method of communication. The central message of the Christian gospel is that the method by which God's redemptive love was shown was by being present with fallen creation personally in Jesus Christ. The method by which we communicate as Christians has meaning, not just the content of our communication.

Leadership, whether it occurs on a vertical level between God and humans or on a horizontal level between humans, requires relationship expressed in communication. A community marked by good leadership is one that communicates. Such a group has strong interpersonal communication; they exercise basic communication skills for improving interpersonal relationships. The interpersonal gap is bridged as members increase their understanding of each other through good communication. Shared understanding means that each has accurate information about the other's ideas, suggestions, feelings, intentions, emotional responses, and assumptions. Good communication is marked by a spirit of joint inquiry.

Improving communication requires listening with a desire to understand, reflecting on one another's opinions, keeping open-minded attitudes, and, ultimately, discovering common ground amidst diversity. The fact that God communicates in the exercise of His own leadership, and implanted that necessity of communication in the creation of humans, contributes to our understanding of leadership. We have been called to communicate well, whether it is in sharing the gospel or in relating to people in our own churches, families, or workplaces. It is incumbent upon us to listen to what God wants to say to us about communication, to develop communication skills, and to be doing the task of communicating.

LEADERSHIP IS SERVICE

Service is a biblical principle of leadership. God reveals Himself as one who creates for the joy of humankind. God provides for humankind: "I have given every herb that yields seed which is on the face of all the earth, and every tree whose fruit yields seed; to you it shall be for food" (Gen. 1:29). Jacques Doukhan points out that God provided abundantly; everything He created, including

Adam and Eve themselves, were "*very* good" (Gen. 1:31, emphasis added). God creates for the purpose of relationship and expresses relationship at least partially through serving humankind.

The words of Jesus regarding servanthood among those who follow Him are familiar: "Whoever desires to become great among you, let him be your servant. And whoever desires to be first among you, let him be your slave" (Matt. 20:26b–27). The notion of servanthood is not a new idea that Jesus is presenting to the disciples; the idea has existed from the beginning of God's plan, and it is rooted in the Old Testament.

The Old Testament contains numerous references to God's concern for the widow and the orphan (or fatherless) as well as multiple references to His concern for the alien (Zech. 7:10). Widows, orphans, and aliens were the most vulnerable members of society, and God expected His people to serve them (Deut. 24:19). God will pass judgment on those who fail to provide for the needs of the most vulnerable members of society (Mal. 3:5).

The Old Testament describes the Messiah as a Suffering Servant. God embodies the idea of servanthood. In demonstrating His nature, He calls us to likewise focus on others, to be servants as He is a servant. As godly servants, we must look past ourselves and see others. We exist for the sake of others. His church exists for the sake of others. Leadership is not selfish; it is service for others. It comes from an experience of humility. It demonstrates sacrifice, not as a means of atoning for one's own guilt but for the sake of others. Christian servanthood can manifest itself in our daily lives if we are willing to lead by serving.

CONCLUSION: A SUMMARY

The wisdom of the Old Testament has been shared from generation to generation and offers important guidance for Christian leaders today. In the creation stories, and in the formation of God's people in the historical books, the wisdom literature, and the prophets, a biblical theology of leadership can be formed. Through the principles demonstrated in the historical situations, the counsel of God, and the lives of God's people, vital leadership principles emerge that guide the church today.

A biblical theology of leadership is rooted within a highly relational community. Leadership is not a solo journey. Leadership is an activity engaged in as one within a community, not standing outside or over a community. We are one with the community in the process of leadership. Leadership is shared; it is not a hierarchal position that separates leaders from others. Thus leadership and followership are mutually identified and exchangeable. One leads and follows, and if one loses the ability to follow within a community, one loses the ability to lead as well.

The vision that properly moves a Christian faith community is a God-given one; it is not the imagination of one person. It is shared within community. Thus understood, vision is not what one gives another, though it can be inspired within others by one's devotion to vision. It is a gift of God to a community. Some within their community relationships foster and surface vision more than others; they promote God's vision for the community, and in that process they serve. Communication of God's will for us happens within our relationships and is an outflow of the highly relational communities we serve.

The Old Testament lends the idea of initiative to a biblical theology of leadership. God has created us with a nature that seeks to go forward into empty spaces and create in order to fulfill mission. Creativity is thus affirmed. Newness and invention are part of God's vision for life. Just as initiative and creativity are reflections of God, so is service. Going forward in creative initiative suggests the idea of service. An Old Testament theology of leadership directs our motives; we prioritize the needs of others over our own agenda and sacrifice for others. In leadership, we are servants to God's servants.

FOR REFLECTION

Personal:

1. When you take initiative, is it affirmed by those you are closest to? Why? How?
2. How has the way you lead been transformed over the last five years?

Organizational:

1. How does your organization foster relationality?
2. How does your organization build shared vision?

ENDNOTES

1. Scripture quotations in this chapter are taken from the New King James Version.

2. Craig L. Pearce and Jay A. Conger, *Shared Leadership* (Thousand Oaks, CA: SAGE, 2003), 1.

3. George Barna, *Leaders on Leadership* (Ventura, CA: Regal, 1997), 47.

4. James M. Kouzes and Barry Z. Posner, *The Leadership Challenge* (San Francisco: Jossey-Bass, 1995), 95.

5. R. Scott Rodin, *The Steward Leader* (Downers Grove, IL: IVP Academic, 2010), 121–122.

6. John P. Kotter, *Leading Change* (Boston: Harvard Business School Press, 1996), 7.

7. Keri K. Wehlander, ed. *Creating Change: The Arts as Catalyst for Spiritual Transformation* (Kelowna, BC: CopperHouse, 2008), 8.

8. Wehlander, *Creating Change,* introduction.

9. Diana Butler Bass, quoted in Wehlander, *Creating Change,* 18.

20 | A Reflection on Leadership Principles in the New Testament

Stanley E. Patterson

A reflection on New Testament leadership principles begins with the foundation laid in the Gospels. It is here that we hear the words and observe the behaviors that demonstrate Jesus's leadership in the context of His human development, His personal calling and vision, His building and equipping of a team, and His initiation of the Christian church. Jesus's teachings, and to a greater degree, His modeling of leadership behavior provide the basis upon which a New Testament theology of leadership is built. His words and model serve as the standard for Christian leadership and, as such, take precedence over all factors—cultural, organizational, and political—that inform the practice of leadership in the church.

Jesus's incarnation placed Him in the context of an ancient and rich culture that had well-established norms and traditions. He entered His earthly ministry as a Jew with all that the Torah, the prophets, the wisdom literature, and their national history brought to bear. The political domination of Israel contributed Roman traditions and norms to the context of His life, which melded with the residual influence and divisiveness of Greek culture. All of this was a part of the mix into which He came and from which we draw our understanding of His teachings and behavior that inform our twenty-first-century practice of Christian leadership.

The books and Epistles that follow the Gospels illustrate the manner in which the Early Church practiced what Jesus had taught and demonstrated regarding leadership. Each unit of the New Testament contributes something to our understanding of the practice of Christian leadership. The apostle from Tarsus provides unique insights into the spiritual design that makes Christian leadership distinct and undeniably spiritual. The letters of Paul unfold the plan of diverse spiritual gifts (Rom. 12; 1 Cor. 12; Eph. 4) devised by the Master to provide the competencies necessary for the church to accomplish its work. This provision enables each believer to contribute meaningfully to the mission of the church. Paul also makes us aware of the Holy Spirit's provision of character formation by means of spiritual fruit (Gal. 5:22–23) that guarantees a sustainable relational context in which these competencies are practiced in the course of proclamation, discipling, and baptizing as commanded in Matthew 28:18–20. The General Epistles further reveal the practical application of Christian principles of leadership.

This reflection provides a conceptual overview of the New Testament teaching and practice of leadership while endeavoring to draw together the insights of the scholars who have contributed to this volume.

THE NEW TESTAMENT MODEL OF INCARNATIONAL LEADERSHIP

The transformation of Jesus that earned Him the title of "Immanuel…God with us" (Matt. 1:23)[1] is built upon the act of the Son of God being made flesh and dwelling among us (John 1:14). Taking on human form was not only a means of revealing the love and character of the Father to fallen humankind, but also represented a commitment by the Messiah to identify with us for all eternity. It is this empathic willingness to identify with us that provides a powerful insight into Christ-like leadership.

Jesus spoke quite directly to His disciples regarding His preference for their relationship with Him. His choice to become one with us is consistent with His desire to lay aside His titles of position (Phil. 2:7) and take up the relationship of friend (John 15:15). This announcement reveals an aspect of His incarnation that goes beyond the physical and engages the socio-relational. The text itself reveals His choice of titles for the disciples rather than for Himself. *Servant* presumes the positional counterpart of *master* while His preferred descriptive is *friend* for which there is no positional counterpart.[2] This choice is made powerful by the fact that Jesus, part of the Triune community active in creation, was proclaimed "Creator of heaven and earth." His choice challenges every claim to title that any in the church might wish to leverage as a distinctive that would set one above another in an assertion of dominance or power. It further challenges the tendency to give greater deference to one who holds high position in the church's hierarchy of order.

Incarnational leadership as modeled by Jesus requires a willingness to descend in order to serve (Luke 22:25–27) all humanity even as He descended for the purpose of serving (Matt. 20:28). Seeking dominance over one another aligns us with the ascendant behavior attributed to Lucifer in Isaiah 14 and is a "Gentile" behavior (Matt. 20:25–26) judged by Jesus as emphatically inappropriate in the New Testament church. Jesus's incarnational model champions the value of all the members of the body apart from the preeminence of their position, the privilege of their birth, or any distinctive by which the world might tend to measure the value of people (Rom. 12:3). Such leadership is devoid of the search for dominance over others or the desire to ascend the ladder of position at the expense of others. "Whoever desires to become great among you, let him be your servant" (Matt. 20:26) lies at the root of Christian leadership and must be absorbed and integrated by the Christian leader in the context of "a community of friends."

THE PARADOX OF LEADING AS A SERVANT

The washing of the disciples' feet (John 13:5–17) stands as the preeminent example of service and egalitarian attitude modeled for the church. But how do we lead as a servant so as to relieve the tension of that paradox? In some cultures the chasm between servant and leader is so great that it is almost impossible to bridge. The mystique and honor granted to leaders simply cannot be formed into a concept of the leader as servant without violating cultural norms. For others it is less difficult to implement service as the defining element in leadership.

Once again, Jesus provides an answer. He had three and a half years to transform twelve ordinary men into world-class leaders—leaders who could competently and with godly character bear the burden of establishing the Christian church upon this earth. He entrusted the Twelve with meaningful responsibility during that period of time. His service to them was focused upon their development, and He never did for them what they needed to do for themselves. Ministry service is not intended to contribute to the leisure or luxury of those served but rather to their growth in meaningful service to others. Jesus trusted them with responsibilities, such as baptizing, that constituted service to others.

THE SERVICE OF TRANSFORMATION

Jesus's service was relational and process-oriented, directed toward the transformation of those who would plant the Christian church. He served them by serving their developmental needs—spiritual, social, and personal. Leadership service should not be seen in the context of the servant who does for members those things God intended for them to do themselves. Jesus took the raw human material that He found in Peter, James, John, and the others and transformed their characters and their competencies in a manner that qualified them for the responsibility of leadership. He directed all of His resources to that end—teaching, encouraging, modeling, rebuking, and whatever else was needed to create leaders who would honor the Father by emulating[3] Him in a world that was perched on the edge of monumental change.

If the model of Jesus was about developing leaders to engage in the revision and expansion of the kingdom of God, then it stands to reason that the primary function of Christian leaders is the stewardship of developing leaders.[4] Parents who model leadership in their children's lives bear the responsibility of developing them not only as faithful followers of Christ, but also as capable leaders who can serve others.[5] Some pastors are tempted to look upon their congregations as an assemblage of followers who must be managed and directed. The New Testament model would have them viewed as a gathering of potential leaders for whom experienced leaders bear the responsibility of training and equipping for leadership service according to their gifts.[6]

Task accomplishment grows out of the development of spiritual leaders. Discipleship is the New Testament model of leadership development, even though we commonly think of it as being follower development. Jesus took followers and transformed them into leaders! The tendency for leaders to function as managers who coordinate the human resources of members can overshadow the spiritual leader's call to "make disciples." The spiritual and leadership development of others as modeled by Jesus is a primary responsibility mandated in the Great Commission (Matt. 28:18–20). Secular leadership development specialists[7] have learned that the relational development model leads to greater and more consistent productivity. Jesus demonstrated that the development of competent and committed leaders would result in the accomplishment of mission more effectively than efforts to direct compliant followers to accomplish the same end.

THE BODY METAPHOR FOR THE CHURCH

The New Testament presented a model of church that could not be illustrated by a graph of power or control. The organizational structure of the church was presented in terms of parts and systems of a body where none could rightfully claim preeminence over another (1 Cor. 12:14–27), but, rather, each part honored every other part as being interdependently connected to the system as a means of functioning in a holistic healthy manner. Such "systems-thinking is a discipline for seeing wholes."[8] This diverse model, with harmonious parts, assumes the incompleteness of all of those individual parts until they achieve effectiveness in union with the others to produce the completeness of the whole.

The metaphor of a body with interdependent systems is a reversal of the secular understanding of service. The New Testament metaphor allows for a leadership model that must move away from the concept of the singular positional leader that directs the whole to a model that recognizes the interdependence of all who are called to service in God's kingdom. The church, like the body, depends upon each member to contribute his or her giftedness and faithfulness as a service to the leadership process of the collective whole.

DIVERSITY OF COMPETENCE

This diversity of systems and parts results in an interdependent model that disallows any single member, regardless of position or prominence, to claim completeness or glory apart from the counterparts in the body.[9] The church body is composed of specialized parts and systems made possible by a Spirit-controlled distribution of skills or competencies (Rom. 12:4–5; 1 Cor. 12:4–11) that the apostle Paul refers to as the "spiritual gifts" (1 Cor. 12:1). The Holy Spirit assumes responsibility for building this network of skills that makes the body complete, and members are individually accountable for the right use of these gifts of grace (Matt. 25:14–30). Giftedness and accountability create the expectation that the individual thus gifted assumes leadership responsibility in the context of that gifts. Every member of the body of Christ is thus expected to lead in the context of the gift he or she has been given. For some that giftedness and leadership responsibility will be high profile and involve major influence on the body, while for others it may be relatively obscure but nonetheless necessary to the healthy function of the body.

Where does the follower fit in? The answer is found in the dynamic relationship between leading and following. Leadership as influenced by the universal distribution of spiritual gifts disallows the fixed-position singular leader. Followership is a constant companion of leadership that involves flexing between leading and following, depending upon the ministry need and the gifts available in the body.

The ubiquitous nature of leadership responsibility is not restricted to the ecclesiastical context alone; it is also recognized in the secular context "that in the course of their lives, most people must take on leadership roles and participate in leadership processes."[10] This organizational leadership design assumes a dynamic exchange of leader and follower roles as the system recognizes and honors the functions of its diverse parts.

It is essential that spiritual leaders recognize this interdependence and view their own contributions as reflections of their giftedness. Remaining respectful and grateful for the contribution of all while at the same time holding a prominent leadership position is not always an easy task. Self must always be kept in perspective as it resides in the context of community.[11] The allure of power and the tug of ego are constant influences that can marginalize the spiritual aspects of Christian leadership and feed the natural tendency to dominate others in the community.

THE CHURCH AS BODY

When we speak of members as leaders, it can cause some confusion due to our general mental model of what constitutes leadership. We should be reminded that *leadership* is a relatively new word and remains embedded primarily in Western thought. Until the nineteenth century,[12] our choices of words to describe what we know as leadership were limited to *king, ruler, commander, head of state,* or *master*—all of which assume dominance and hierarchy. These terms clearly delineate leaders and followers, lords and subjects, sovereign and ruled, and controller and controlled. Such organizations and relationships could be charted on hierarchical graphs of power. Everyone knew his or her place in the order of things.

Paul's defining metaphor (1 Cor. 12:12–31) for our diversely gifted community—the church—is the metaphor of the body. It is the body of Christ and this chapter in Paul's writings that serve as the revelation of God's plan for organizing the church He has gifted. This metaphor needs little or no interpretation. The church is not defined by the charismatic gifts; rather, it is defined by its spiritual nature—a living organism made alive through the presence of the Holy Spirit. The diversified and interdependent model is His plan and His choice, "But as it is, God arranged the members in the body, each one of them, as he chose" (12:18, ESV).

ACCOUNTABILITY FOR SPIRITUAL GIFTS

The gifting and the calling of God are one. We are by covenant bound to God and are consequently responsible and accountable for the ministry gifts granted us by the Spirit. These gifted competencies must be developed through discipleship and use, but they do not find their origin in learning. They are chosen and matched to us by the wisdom and action of the Holy Spirit.

The parable of the talents recorded in Matthew 25:14–30 makes it clear that each of the servants bore personal responsibility for stewardship of the talent(s) entrusted. No one was assigned as a buffer between the master and the steward's responsibility for attending to the entrusted property. We must assume that stewardship of the competencies is the personal responsibility of the member who can expect at some point to give an account of how the gift was employed in the body of Christ.[13] The conclusion we can draw is that God expects the members of the body to proactively lead through the exercise of their spiritual gifts in ministry.

The body was designed with the expectation that all members would proactively apply their spiritual gifts as need for them arose, even as the human body proactively coordinates its systems and parts for healthy and productive function. Again, each member is a leader within the context of his or her specialty and functions in an interdependent manner with all other parts of the body. "But God composed the body, having given greater honor to that *part* which lacks it, that there should be no schism in the body, but *that* the members should have the same care for one another" (1 Cor. 12:24–25).

INTERDEPENDENT MODEL OF COMMUNITY

The community-based interdependent model was introduced to us at creation. The first negative expression in the creation story,

"It is not good" (Gen. 2:18), was a recognition of Adam's incompleteness rather than a lack of individual perfection. The solution for the first man's incompleteness was the creation of a "helper" (Gen. 2:18, 22) that allowed them together to represent the image of God (Gen. 1:26–27)—sharing that which was necessary to make them whole as a team or community. Adam was not created to live as an individual but was rather created to live as a person in community with others. Eve's qualities complemented Adam's and created wholeness. Neither was complete alone. This act of God established a relational model that revealed His organizational plan for His people. We complement one another through diversity in both our human and our organizational relationships and are thereby made complete in recognizing and honoring our dependence on one another.

We must consider this reality as we formulate our understanding of Christian leadership. By the gifting of the Holy Spirit, we are all set apart *within* the community of the church (as contrasted with being set apart *from*). Positional leaders are gifted first by the Spirit and then chosen by the community to exercise their giftedness as leaders within the community. The description of leadership among the gifts of the Spirit does not limit leadership to one receiving an exceptional gift.[14] Some will be gifted and called to a service that is as visible to the body of Christ as are the eyes on the face of a person we meet. Others will lead in relative obscurity even as there are parts of the body that will never be seen but are equally as important to the health of the body.

This truth has enormous impact upon how we lead. The worldly view of leadership follows a heroic model. Western culture in particular tends to emphasize the individualistic aspects of leaders and often grants them exaggerated importance. Leaders' salaries and benefits in the corporate world testify to this reality. But the church is an interdependent world of freely associated members. As Steven Covey notes, "you cannot think and live independently in an interdependent world."[15] We must be crystal clear on the fact that leadership in the church is an interdependent community process rather than the product of a solitary person or even a small group of leaders. The individual leader and the small group or committee of leaders contribute to the process of leadership but do not constitute leadership as a process apart from the whole body, any more than the heart can sustain life apart from the collective contribution of the entire body.

The Spirit selects and provides a *variety of gifts* (competencies) (1 Cor. 12:4). This diversity of giftedness allows for a *variety of ministries* which the apostle credits to the Lord (12:5). In addition, the text reveals a *variety of activities* which Paul specifically attributes to God (12:6). This diverse distribution of ministry competencies among members of the church is presented to us as the work of a diversified pattern of involvement of the Godhead. The organization of the New Testament church and the acts of creation (Gen. 1:1–2, 26; John 1:3; Col. 1:15–16; Heb. 1:2) have in common the diverse distribution of responsibilities. God functions in the context of community—Father, Son, and Holy Spirit—and demonstrates a diversification of responsibilities but exists as one. Likewise the diverse ministry competencies expected of the church are not designed to bring glory to any individual member or part of the body but rather honor the faith community as a whole.

THE RELATIONAL CONTEXT OF CHRISTIAN LEADERSHIP

Leadership is not a person or a select group of persons. Leadership is a relational process. In spite of the fact that we commonly refer to a leader or a small group of leaders as "leadership," leadership is a process in which God designed all of us to participate.[16] We should not speak of a positional leader or leaders as "leadership" without understanding that, in so doing, we are failing to recognize the members of the body who are mandated by God to contribute to the process of leadership as surely as are those visible and well-known leaders who coordinate and direct the work of the body. Leadership is a community process.

Covey and Merrill[17] divide the essence of trust and, by extension, leadership into two essential elements: "character and competence." Most leadership scholars[18] agree that these two elements constitute the essence of leadership. But what does the New Testament present in this regard? The spiritual gifts (Rom. 12:3–8; 1 Cor. 12:1–31; Eph. 4:1–16) are clearly presented as the source of our ministry competence. By these gifts we contribute to the advance of the mission of the church in response to our commissioning (Matt. 28:18–20). A careful look at all three of the spiritual gifts passages above reveals a relational context that cannot be ignored without cost.

In Romans 12:3 Paul prefaces his presentation with these words, among others: "For I say, through the grace given to me, to everyone who is among you, not to think *of himself* more highly than he ought to think, but to think soberly, as God has dealt to each one a measure of faith." If the gifting of the Holy Spirit mandates that we contribute to the leadership of the body by means of our spiritual competencies, then Paul is addressing leaders with the counsel to be careful not to inwardly assume an attitude of superiority over others within the body. He thus introduces spiritual gifts in the context of personal relationships within the body. After presenting spiritual gifts in verses 4–8, he follows in verses 9–21 with one of the New Testament's most powerful exhortations to foster healthy relationships within the community of faith.

The two primary elements of spiritual leadership, character and competence, are joined together in each of the primary texts relating to spiritual gifts. In 1 Corinthians 12 the discourse on spiritual gifts is followed by a passionate appeal for unity based upon the metaphor of the body wherein he says, "care for one another. And if one member suffers, all the members suffer with it; or if one member is honored, all the members rejoice with it" (vv. 25–26). This relational exhortation is followed by chapter 13, the "love chapter." This chapter reveals a consistency between the combination of spiritual gift competency discussed in Romans 12 and 1 Corinthians 12 in that they both cast the introduction of spiritual gifts in a nest of relational health.

Ephesians 4 follows suit in that the first six verses address the relational context of the church. It includes this counsel: "with all lowliness and gentleness, with longsuffering, bearing with one another in love, endeavoring to keep the unity of the Spirit in the bond of peace" (vv. 2–3).

DUAL SERVICE OF THE HOLY SPIRIT

The elements of the fruit of the Spirit placed alongside Paul's discussions of ministry competence (gifts) would seem to suggest that Covey's "character and competence" are mirrored in the New Testament. Paul consistently joins the relational health of the members through character formation with spiritual gifts that provide ministry competence. This establishes an essential principle of New Testament leadership: These primary functions of the Holy Spirit, spiritual gifting for ministry and engendering spiritual fruit for Christ-like character, are inseparable.

The fruit of the Spirit as detailed in Galatians 5 (and in 1 Pet. 1:5) reveals a standard of character possible to those being transformed by the indwelling Spirit. These items constitute the relational standard of spiritual leadership—love those we lead; contribute joy and peace to their lives; and extend patience, kindness, goodness, faithfulness, gentleness, and self-control. Though character may be treated as a desired trait but not necessarily required in some secular contexts, the expectation of consistent Christ-like character patterned after the relational standards of Galatians 5 is an essential component of spiritual leadership. Spiritual leadership is not built on competency alone. The attitude of spiritual oversight that Thomas Shepherd describes (see chapter 11) as emerging from the Christian leader in place of the more common ruler compulsion is not possible apart from the Holy Spirit. The spiritual aspect is forfeit without the elements of the fruit of the Spirit that provides the relational context for the practice of Christian leadership.

Spiritual gifts are distributed at the will of the Holy Spirit in quantities and combinations determined solely by the Spirit. As such, the diverse distributions of these gifts among the members of the body of Christ are almost infinite. The fruit of the Spirit, however, carries with it a uniform expectation of Christian character. Our temperaments may differ, our mind styles may reveal different ways of thinking and ordering life, our mental orientation of right and left brain will vary, but the standards of character are the same for all. Leaders do not, by conferral of position, inherit the privilege of demonstrating impatience or loss of self-control simply because they occupy positions of authority. Positional leaders (persons appointed or elected by a community to formal positions of authority) and ministry leaders who serve without distinct appointment to positions within the body are both subject to the standards established by the fruit of the Spirit.

The good news regarding this combination of competence and character is that both emanate from the Spirit of God. Leaders, both those who are highly visible and those who serve in more obscure roles, have the assurance that competence for ministry and leadership contribution is ours as a result of the willingness of the Spirit to dwell within us. A transformed character and a calling with the gifted competencies to support it are ours to claim according to the promise of God.

DISCIPLESHIP

Discipleship and the process of developing a disciple are often associated most closely with following. We hear the invitation of Jesus, "Come follow me." And we rarely take the time to consider that discipleship implies taking someone to a destination.[19] Consider for a moment what lay before the twelve disciples: three and a half years of intense, socially connected spiritual and intellectual conditioning with the Messiah. But was that the terminal point Jesus had in mind when He voiced the invitation? They were still on the journey with Him when He informed them that He would be leaving them—but not as orphans (John 13:33–35). At Pentecost their Spiritual companion took up residence within them (John 14:17), but their function changed dramatically in that transition. They went from being disciples to being apostles. The discipleship process developed them as leaders, and, under the influence of the indwelling Spirit, these sent men planted the Christian church and changed the world—forever.

Discipleship has as its goal the making of a leader who remains a follower of Jesus. It is a leadership development process. His intent for us on this earth is that we become effective ministers regardless of our specific calling, whether lay or clergy, whether gifted as pastors or gifted as healers, we are called to become leaders in the context of our giftedness. Our call to make disciples is to identify giftedness and develop spiritual leaders for the Kingdom.

Transformational Calling

Jesus demonstrated a method in the process of transforming common men from being fishermen, tax collectors, farmers, and so on, to becoming effective spiritual leaders. It started with a selection process and an invitation to enter into a journey of personal transformation. His words "I will make you fishers of men" (Matt. 4:19) revealed a purpose in the mind and heart of Jesus that communicated value to these men and superseded the value of their current occupations. Jesus's call was an invitation to personal transformation, and they followed Him. The discipling relationship was personal, intense, and accompanied by risk. But they followed, and their lives were forever changed.

The Invitation to Discipleship

The first step in discipleship today is the same as it was on the day that Jesus called Peter, James, and John from their boats and nets—selection and invitation. The invitation was personal and involved the promise of relationship. Discipling is personal, and it must be intentionally relational in nature. Our modern obsession with efficiency tends to relegate relational elements of leadership development to the dark corners of ministry while we apply economy-of-scale principles and make assessments on the basis of efficiency rather than effectiveness. We need to consciously seek out and identify giftedness in people and invest personal effort and time to aid the Spirit in transforming them into effective spiritual leaders who will contribute to the mission of God's church.

Discipleship Leads to Mentoring

The invitation leads to discipleship. It is in discipleship that the relationship is developed, allowing the sort of learning that Frank Smith[20] refers to as *classical learning*. This is learning that takes place in a natural, relational context of mentoring in which the learning is most often immediately connected to events and activities of life. This context of mentoring offers the experience of learning enjoyed by children. Observation prompts questions that are answered in the context of doing. It is a form of learning that is effortless and effective. Most of the questions associated with this learning find their origin in the learner rather than the teacher—a condition that increases the effectiveness of teaching and learning. Such mentoring requires close personal contact and honest relational commitment, which greatly enhances retention of the lessons learned.

Mentoring Leads to Empowering

The disciples enjoyed such an environment with Jesus. They learned as they lived together. They were transformed in the context of observing their Leader, even as a child's formative introduction to leadership behavior occurs in the relational environment of the home.[21] This prepared them even as good parenting behavior prepares a child for the empowerment that attends responsibility and authority for effective contribution to the needs of the family.

Empowering Leads to Sending

The leader must also assign responsibility and empower others to effect growth. Barnabas was an empowered leader who modeled the generous extension of authority in the empowerment of others. As such, empowerment is not only for task accomplishment; it also has a generative and maturing effect on the learner. Once done, sending is the next step.

The sending of the seventy (Luke 10:1–24) had a mission focus and reveals the connection between empowerment and sending. The assignment was clear and the parameters of empowerment were clear—proclaim the presence of the Messiah and heal the sick (10:9). Only in executing these two assignments did they discover that their empowerment also authorized authority over demons, which says something about the abundant nature of the Master's empowerment.

Sending Leads to Leader Multiplication

The plan of sending the seventy had an essential link to leadership development. Pairing them in teams of two created a relational learning context that prepared the learners to adjust to a new paradigm for learning when Jesus was not immediately present for a mentoring relationship. After His ascension, His Spirit worked with them, two by two, in the continuing mentoring context of co-learning. The disciples had the advantage of a social group plus an active contextual environment necessary for optimal learning.[22] In a sense the two-by-two model provided a weaning strategy in the leadership development process that resulted in less dependence upon the physical presence of Jesus and paved the way for the internalized influence of the Holy Spirit. Thus disciples were multiplied to form an army of spiritual leaders.

Multiplication Leads to the Priesthood of All Believers

The New Testament presents a leadership model enriched by a cultural history of internal tension relating to divine expectation and human failure but also impacted by external tensions of war, occupation, and captivity. The universal priesthood of God's people was predicated by God's service as ruler of His people under a covenant relationship that involved no human buffer between Him and them and provided a distributed leadership model down to the family level. God reluctantly submitted to Israel's request to place a king as ruler but characterized the request as a rejection of Him as their Leader (1 Sam. 8:7). The centralized monarchial leadership model and the consolidation of priestly responsibility in a tribe instead of the familial model of the firstborn ended the direct role and relationship of God as their Ruler (Judg. 8:23). This separation between God as personal Ruler and His people was radically reversed in the New Testament record when Immanuel was realized and the Spirit of God took up residence in the hearts of His people (John 14:17; Acts 2:4). The need for the intermediate ruler was no longer present, because God and the individual were once again bonded in the Spirit.

Christian churches emerged with no formal ecclesiastical structure to govern them beyond that of the Holy Spirit, the ministry of the apostles, and the Scriptures. Yet leaders emerged from the body in what seems to be an egalitarian process of selection and commissioning by the church, although the apostles and their disciples involved themselves intimately in the ministry of spiritual formation and leadership development.

CONCLUSION

The natural human tendency to dominate others was modified by efforts to instill in the body of believers a sense that all members, regardless of position, gender, or giftedness, had equal value and dignity. A leadership role was determined by spiritual giftedness and a spiritual character that demonstrated Christ-like relational behavior. These two Spirit-given and interwoven qualifications—character and competence—establish the spiritual foundation for leadership in the New Testament.

Today, each member serves as a steward of his or her spiritual gift and contributes specific service to the process of leadership that addresses the mission to which the church has been called by the Master who calls us friends.

FOR REFLECTION

Personal:

1. If our natural human nature is predisposed to ascendant behavior that moves us toward a position of dominance relative to others, what evidence do you have that the Spirit of God is directing you toward leadership behavior marked by service?
2. How might you explain your personal sense of wholeness as a leader within the understanding that you are a connected part of a much larger spiritual body?

Organizational:

1. How might you approach the tension between following and leading as it relates to the "make disciples" directive of Matthew 28? Is it possible that leadership development is an expected outcome of learning to follow Jesus?
2. Since the title of *priest* is traditionally linked to the expectation that some are set apart for spiritual leadership, how should

the church interpret the radically inclusive New Testament concept of the priesthood of all believers?

ENDNOTES

1. Scripture quotations in this chapter are taken from the New King James Version.

2. C. S. Keener and InterVarsity Press, *The IVP Bible Background Commentary: New Testament* (Downers Grove, IL: InterVarsity Press, 1993), John 15:15.

3. Frank Smith, *The Book of Learning and Forgetting* (New York: Teachers College Press, 1998), 9.

4. Larry C. Spears, ed. *Reflections on Leadership: How Robert K. Greenleaf's Theory of Servant-leadership Influenced Today's Top Management Thinkers* (New York: J. Wiley, 1995), 207.

5. James MacGregor Burns, *Leadership* (New York: Harper & Row, 1978), 77–78, 98–99.

6. James D. Berkley, ed. *Leadership Handbook of Management and Administration*, rev. and exp. ed. (Grand Rapids, MI: Baker Books, 2007), 355.

7. Cynthia D. McCauley, Russ Moxley, and Ellen van Velsor, eds. *The Center for Creative Leadership Handbook of Leadership Development*, 2nd ed. (San Francisco: Jossey-Bass, 2004), 85–115.

8. Peter Senge, *The Fifth Discipline: The Art and Practice of the Learning Organization* (New York: Currency, 1994), 68.

9. Russ S. Moxley, *Leadership and Spirit: Breathing New Vitality and Energy into Individuals and Organizations* (San Francisco: Jossey-Bass, 1999), 117.

10. McCauley et al., *Creative Leadership Handbook*, 2.

11. Edwin H. Friedman, Margaret M. Treadwell, and Edward W. Beal, *A Failure of Nerve: Leadership in the Age of the Quick Fix* (New York: Seabury Books, 2007), 138–140.

12. B. M. Bass, *Bass and Stogdill's Handbook of Leadership: Theory, Research, and Managerial Applications* (New York: Free Press, 1990), 11.

13. Warren S. Kissinger, *The Parables of Jesus: A History of Interpretation and Bibliography* (Metuchen, NJ: Scarecrow Press, 1979), 33, 40.

14. For a thorough treatment of this matter, see Henry Blackaby and Richard Blackaby, *Spiritual Leadership: Moving People on to God's Agenda* (Nashville, TN: B and H Publishing, 2011), 51 and following.

15. Stephen R. Covey, *The Eighth Habit: From Effectiveness to Greatness* (New York: Free Press, 2004), 57.

16. George Barna, ed., *Leaders on Leadership: Wisdom, Advice, and Encouragement on the Art of Leading God's People* (Ventura, CA: Regal Books, 1997), 65.

17. Stephen M. R. Covey and Rebecca R. Merrill, *The Speed of Trust: The One Thing That Changes Everything* (New York: Free Press, 2006), 31.

18. Henry Blackaby and Richard Blackaby, *Spiritual Leadership: Moving People On to God's Agenda* (Nashville: Broadman & Holman, 2001), 19. See also Barna, *Leaders on Leadership,* 134–135; Berkley, *Leadership Handbook,* 45; Covey, *Eighth Habit,* 149, 235.

19. Colin Brown, *The New International Dictionary of New Testament Theology,* vol. 1 (Grand Rapids, MI: Zondervan, 1975), 481.

20. Frank Smith, *The Book of Learning and Forgetting* (New York: Teachers College Press, 1998), 5.

21. Bass, *Handbook of Leadership,* 807–811.

22. John D. Bransford, Ann L. Brown, and Rodney R. Cocking, eds., *How People Learn: Brain, Mind, Experience, and School,* exp. ed. (Washington, DC: National Academy Press, 2000), 119, 279.

21 | A Biblical Theology of Leadership for the Church

Skip Bell

The introduction for this work asserted that Christian leadership principles and practices emerge from a theological foundation for persons whose worldview is spiritually oriented. As I noted, the contribution of theological reflection to understanding leadership includes three essential and helpful elements: (1) it provides a ground for defining leadership beyond cultural context, (2) it seeks the root of Christian leadership understanding in universal experience, and (3) it reveals a capacity within leadership to both transcend and transform people and culture.

Readers should remember that the dilemma for theological reflection is the truth that leadership understanding must not be limited to, or determined by, culturally defined phenomenon. One cannot do theology without thinking critically about culture. Culture consists of patterns of believing and behaving emerging out of our worldview in the place and time we share with others. People of faith remain in their culture but are distinctly transformed, or at least should be, as they think and form beliefs in submission to the teaching and leading of God.

Biblical theology provides a source for theological thinking that potentially transcends culture. The starting point in leadership development is theology, and the starting point of theology is the inspired text. It is not that biblical theology replaces a more expansive theology, or that we choose one or the other. It is simply that for people of faith who embrace a high view of revelation within the sacred text, a biblical theology provides perceptions of leadership within universal truths, which transcend culture.

As stated in the beginning, it is the purpose of this book to provide a biblical theology of leadership that transforms people and culture and informs the definition and practice of leadership. Such a Scripture-centered theology of leadership preserves Christ's headship of the church by acknowledging His revealed will as the source of understanding. It is also apparent that in seeking a biblical theology individuals must divest themselves, in so far as is prayerfully possible, of their own cultural bias. We have endeavored to do that, and the reader must in their own investigation judge our success. The limits of revelation within human language, and its inherent cultural interpretation, must also be reckoned with.

Applying a biblical theology to leadership understanding offers the opportunity for persons of faith to extricate themselves from the dominance of time and culture as they approach their vocation, because it draws them beyond the barriers of their own experience. This is especially true when a biblical theology is approached with confidence in the inspiration of the text. Confidence in Scripture that transcends our reflection on liturgy and experience, history and ethics, teaching and pastoral care, literature and story, is needed.

We operate from the assumption that Christian Scripture exists as revelation from God and provides the clearest, most objective starting point and the best hope to preserve a church's leadership from being formed by a particular personality, the peculiarities of a specific culture, or even the bent of a specific faith tradition, including our own.

Readers must also remember that this is a book about leadership, not about skills demanded by particular roles. It is important to distinguish among leadership, the focus of our theological inquiry, and leading, or leaders. Leadership is everyone's opportunity, and not to be confused with positional authority invested by a community in individuals as they are asked to fill certain functions the community sees as important. Certainly such individual leaders need to understand leadership, and they are not well equipped to serve if they fail in that understanding. But leadership is not about positional authority. Leadership is not about hierarchal structures or being placed over others.

LEADERSHIP THEOLOGY: A BIBLICAL ABSTRACT

A definition of leadership emerges from a theological understanding that is grounded in the revelation of God's nature. So it is within that revelation that we search for a definition of leadership. This abstract first examines the biblical record regarding God Himself, then moves to a practical definition we may apply in our experience. This chapter is not meant to be exhaustive in regard to the whole of the book or replace careful examination of the contributions to understanding from all its chapters. Let's begin with the nature of God.

God Is a God of Community

This remarkable revelation of God's nature is contained in the first narrative of Scripture. His desire to create is expressed in the words "Let us make" (Gen. 1:26).[1] The account may describe an invitation to collaboration with other realms of His creation or to the more intimate relationship of the Trinity, but in either scenario it is clear that the creative initiative is shared with community. His preference for community is seen in numerous aspects of the creation narrative: the distribution of authority to name the animals (Gen. 2:19), the assignment of care for the earth to humankind (Gen. 1:26), the capacity and responsibility to re-create and populate inherent in the created realm (Gen. 1:28). Even the formation of human life within family and society are evidences of His bias toward community.

The same regard for community is seen in the Abrahamic covenant (Gen. 12:1–3); God's people would be formed as a recognized community through whom salvation history would unfold. God approaches the redemption of His people from Egypt in collaboration with Moses, who, in turn, carries out his charge while working within the tribes and families descending from Abraham in Hebrew society. The incarnation narrative emphasizes the role of community in the birth and the ministry of Jesus (Luke 1:39–41). Jesus ministered with a community of close disciples, and He transformed them from a raw band of individuals into a Christian mission community that would expand the boundaries of Israel beyond its national identity (John 17:11). Marks of community are especially sharp in the shared life of the Early Church (Acts 2:42–47).

The emphasis for the Early Church is on a relational community rather than a hierarchal structure. Christian Scripture defines the church as a body of ministering members. Christ's followers are commanded to go and make disciples (Matt. 28:18–20) according to the priorities of God, adding converts to the church. The Greek word *ekklesia,* translated as "church," is translated in the Septuagint from the Hebrew *qahal,* meaning "a meeting of the people summoned together." In Acts 7:38 the congregation of Israel, led through the desert by Moses, is called ἐκκλησία. All believers are called, *klesis,* and they are gifted for ministry, so the Christian church is by nature a called-out relational community.

A biblical theology of leadership must consequently emphasize community. When God contemplates action He envisions community and engages with community rather than acting alone. He is a God of community. Leadership is a community process.

God Is Relational

The first tenet of a biblical theology of leadership is community, and relationship is implied by community. A biblical theology of leadership reveals the relational priorities of leadership. The Creator exclaimed "it is not good that man should live alone" (Gen. 2:18). Prior to the fall of humankind, God walks and talks with humans (Gen. 3:8). Abraham (Gen. 18:1) and Moses (Exod. 33:11, 18–23) are visited by God. Relationship is at the heart of the purpose for creation, and the Scriptures unfold a history replete with relational glimpses into the nature of God.

Further, Jesus is the Incarnate One, Immanuel, God with us (Matt. 1:23). He carries out His mission in intimate relationships. He lives with a band of disciples, sharing meals, walking and reflecting together, forming them for ministry through the relationships He has fostered. Jesus remarkably asserts a relational theology of leadership by His application of the term "friends" (John 15:12–17) to those He has personally mentored for missional leadership.

The relational nature of leadership is perhaps nowhere more clearly revealed than in the biblical tenet that we live not in our own power or strength but by the grace of God and with the presence of the Holy Spirit in our lives (Rom. 8:9–11). God dwells within us; we are filled with the Spirit. All believers live in connection with God through His Spirit, and need no intercessor but Christ. Thus the Christian lives in a most intimate and direct relationship with God, within His community, submissive to His guidance moment by moment.

Leadership, built on a biblical theology, is relational. God leads through relationships, and He generally does not initiate action by arbitrary authority or in isolation. He is a God of relationships. Leadership is a relational process undertaken within a community of servants and friends.

God Is Sovereign

A biblical theology of leadership establishes the sovereignty of God. While God moves within the framework of a relational community, He calls people to Himself and His holiness (1 Pet. 2:9). It is therefore evident that He is God; there is distinction between God and His creation (Ps. 8). His creation recognizes Him as sovereign, and He extends lordship over those who respond with faith to become disciples (Matt. 4:17–19).

A biblical theology of leadership calls for humility before a sovereign God. In the context of religious leadership, to believe Christ is the head of the church (1 Cor. 12; Eph. 5) means we seek His will, we wait on His will, we trust in His will. Biblical leadership takes on the shape of spiritual submission to His sovereign grace rather than independence of thought and action. As members of His body, we recognize Him as head, not ourselves. In the context of leadership, then, we do not replace His sovereignty by substituting humans in positions of religious headship who replace God by assuming authority over religious matters. We come together in relational community, and with prayer we listen for, and trust, God to lead us.

God Serves

Scripture transforms the dishonorable term for "slave" applied to the curse of Canaan (Gen. 9:25) into a term of honor. Moses adopts the role of servant (Exod. 4:10; 14:31). David speaks of himself as the Lord's servant (1 Sam. 23:10–11). Israel is spoken of as a servant community (Jer. 30:10). Isaiah speaks of the coming Messiah in the servant songs (Isa. 42:1–7; 49:1–7; 50:4–11; 52:13–53:12). And most revealing, Jesus demonstrates the character of God, the nature of a servant.

The Epistle to the Philippians (2:1–7) reveals that Jesus took on the role of servant:

> Therefore if there is any consolation in Christ, if any comfort of love, if any fellowship of the Spirit, if any affection and mercy, fulfill my joy by being like-minded, having the same love, being of one accord, of one mind. Let nothing be done through selfish ambition or conceit, but in lowliness of mind let each esteem others better than himself. Let each of you look out not only for his own interests, but also for the interests of others. Let this mind be in you which was also in Christ Jesus, who, being in the form of God, did not consider it robbery to be equal with God, but made Himself of no reputation, taking the form of a bondservant, and coming in the likeness of men.

The Christian Leadership Center of Andrews University comments on the impact of this Scripture passage as follows: "Some exegetes have suggested that the participle, *being*, in verse 6 should be understood as causal rather than concessive, so that it could read, '*precisely because* he was God, he became a servant.'"[2] Jesus thus would be demonstrating that it is the essential nature of God to be, among other characteristics, a servant. God is by nature a servant; it is not an exception to His nature.

Jesus offers a theology of servant leadership by His acts of service and His words. "Yet it shall not be so among you; but whoever desires to become great among you, let him be your servant. And whoever desires to be first among you, let him be your slave—just as the Son of Man did not come to be served, but to serve, and to give His life a ransom for many" (Matt. 20:26–28). "But he who is greatest among you shall be your servant. And whoever exalts himself will be humbled, and he who humbles himself will be exalted" (Matt. 23:11–12).

A biblical theology of leadership is one of servant leadership. Christ serves His creation, so much so that He lays down His life for them. He is by nature a servant, and He transforms the idea of serving to an honorable reflection of Godliness. We serve by leading, and we lead by serving.

God Is by Nature a Sharing God

He approaches creation with shared responsibility, and He models this essential nature within His creation in the formation of man and woman (Gen. 1:27; 2:18), who equally share their stewardship responsibilities. Humans are created in God's image, as sharing beings. God's intention for relational family networks (Gen. 5:1–4) reveals His intention that authority be shared in relational networks. Jesus sends the disciples out two-by-two in mission endeavor (Matt. 10), further illustrating God's intention for shared responsibility. He instructs His disciples to reject the authoritarian manner of the Gentiles (Matt. 20:25–28) in favor of the nature of a servant, implying sharing of responsibility and leadership. The law of leadership is love, and it is demonstrated by service. Service is sharing, and sharing is service.

Biblical leadership calls people to serve in the ways God has gifted them (Rom. 12:4–8) rather than as appointed by strategists. All are called and gifted for ministry, thus assigning the organization of the church to a spiritual process in which the Holy Spirit organizes and delegates ministry. Congregations were to choose from among themselves persons for distinct ministry according to their gifts (Acts 6) and confirm their ministry by the laying on of hands. Titus is encouraged to appoint elders in every city (Titus 1:5). At the same time, a ministry of some providing order through service within the larger body of believers is described. Peter refers to overseers (1 Pet. 5:2), the *episcopes,* who are from the congregation. Gifts that brought order to the church did not rule the church; instead, the gifts empowered the church through the shared ministry of its members.

A biblical theology of leadership is Kingdom oriented rather than organization driven. Throughout the kingdom of God He gifts all members for ministry and empowers them by His Spirit. Leadership is everyone's shared opportunity throughout the community, not an action limited to hierarchal position or authority.

God Takes the Initiative to Create

It is evident that God initiates; He is the Creator (Gen. 1:1). He imagines and takes action. The infinite variety of vegetation, of animal species, and of the land itself reveals His imaginative nature. Shape and color are the work of His creative art. He not only creates beauty, He also moves to establish the order and significance of things (Gen. 2:1–3). Thus, He is a God who takes the initiative to establish harmonious systems throughout nature and human relationships. He acts in the progression of history (Dan. 2:27–28, 44). He redeems (Matt. 18:11). He ordains ministry (John 1:33, 43; Acts 1:8). He establishes His church (Eph. 1:3–6). God is not a passive observer of the status quo. He changes things.

A biblical theology of leadership means initiating, creating, and acting together in a relational community. His community seeks purposeful change. God is a creative and transforming God, and He calls His community to share in that activity.

God Communicates

God communicates His purposes. When taking the initiative to create, He spoke: "In the beginning...God said" (Gen. 1:1–3). Scripture affirms the collaborative nature of God in a spoken delegation to Adam to name the animals and serve as steward (Gen. 2:19). God spoke in personal appearance with Abraham and Moses, through signs and wonders as in the Exodus (Exod. 40:34–38) and miracles (Matt. 4:23–24), through priests (Exod. 28:30) and prayer (Ps. 102:17). Most remarkably, God has communicated with us in Jesus, the Living Word (John 1). Jesus communicates the nature of the Father through His life (John 14:9–11).

Informed by the model of the way Jesus communicated, when the church needed to resolve issues in its life of mission, members came together to talk, collaborate, and counsel (Acts 15). The New Testament thus reveals a pattern for communication and collaboration in leadership modeled by Jesus. It is the nature of the pastoral Epistles to reason together as a church in matters of faith (1 Thess. 1:1–4).

A biblical theology of leadership suggests communication that is collaborative in nature. When God contemplates action He summons community and engages in communication rather than acting secretly. It follows, then, that leadership involves a process of collaborative communication within a relational community. Persons who are asked by the community to fill positions of authority likewise carry out those roles through communication and collaboration as members of the relational community they serve.

God Is Spirit

God is not of His creation. He is overall and above all. He is Alpha and Omega. He is the Lord of the universe. He alone is to be worshipped. The significance of that foundational truth for leadership is that it establishes a call to biblically faithful spiritual formation. Biblical leadership is an act of worship offered in relationship with God, God who is Spirit.

Perhaps unfortunately, Bible stories that have inspired us from childhood have often directed our perspective to the heroic nature of giants from ancient times. We tend to celebrate the courageous acts of David, the integrity of Joseph, the courage of Mary, the loyalty of Esther, the vision of Moses. But more to the point of understanding leadership, these legendary characters and the many more usual biblical personalities reveal that spiritual formation is required in the leadership challenge. The deeper interaction and worship of God through the life experience of these figures is what the Scriptures intend to convey to us. The biblical narratives themselves intend to reveal the nature of God, His relationship with His people, and our spiritual relationship with Him in a transforming community.

A biblical theology of leadership calls for ongoing, biblically faithful spiritual formation. God is Spirit, and He desires to be known.

Our appropriate response to Him is worship, which extends also to spiritual leadership. Biblical leadership is spiritual service; it is in that sense worship and not heroic individual action.

God Is Visionary

He envisions Israel in the land of promise (Deut. 34:1–4). He inspires vision of an earth restored (Dan. 2:44). He gives us vision adequate for our challenge (2 Kings 6:13–17). He cherishes a vision of peace and hope for us (Jer. 19:8–13). He acts on a vision for our redemption through Jesus (Matt. 17:1–9). In every age of the earth He communicates vision to His people (Rev. 1:1–3) both to reveal Himself and to generate hope. It is the nature of God to contemplate and cherish the future. He communicates that hope to us in vision, interpreted within divine intervention, symbol, physical revelation, and word.

A biblical theology of leadership is characterized by vision. God inspires vision, and He implants vision in those who worship Him. Leadership builds and promotes a God-given, passion-stirring shared vision within the spiritual community.

God Offers Himself

He is a God of sacrifice (John 3:16). The dominant theme of all scripture is the atoning sacrifice of Jesus for our salvation. Those God calls share that sacrifice as did Moses who interceded for Israel (Exod. 32:10–14). Jesus confronts those who would follow Him with the reality of what discipleship means in terms of sacrifice (Matt. 20:20–25). The apostles endured hardship, even to the sacrifice of their life, in witness to the gospel (Acts 12:1–2; 14:19–20). Jesus speaks of the sorrow that would accompany the life of the Christian (John 16:20–22). He is a God of sacrifice and seeks that level of commitment to mission in those who follow Him (Matt. 10:34–38).

A biblical theology of leadership calls servants of God to a sacrificial life. God has redeemed us by His sacrificial love, and He has called us to share in a willingness to forsake all for Christ. Spiritual leadership is a total and sacrificial commitment.

CHRISTIAN LEADERSHIP:
A BIBLICAL DEFINITION

The preceding abstract of a biblical theology of leadership leads to a biblically grounded definition of *leadership*. Theorists who characterize leadership as a phenomenon that defies definition would describe this attempt as presumptuous. However, scientific approaches applied to the effort to understand and define leadership have themselves produced not only leadership understanding, but also definitions of leadership. It is significant that current research has provided theories that are frequently congruent with the theological foundations we have noted in this work.

It is not our purpose to provide an exhaustive review of current leadership theory, nor to attempt to prioritize selected theories from the many alternatives. I have chosen to reference three theoretical approaches only to illustrate their congruence with a theological foundation. What these three leadership theories have in common is an approach to leadership as phenomena in a relational community as opposed to an individual action.

Joseph C. Rost, a scholar and researcher, articulates the first theoretical approach, which I would describe as *relational*. He affirms: "Leadership is an influence relationship among leaders and followers who intend real changes that reflect their mutual purposes."[3] Rost sees leading and following roles as fluid in a relational community. He states: "Leadership as an influence relationship has two characteristics: (1) it is multidirectional, in that influence flows in all directions and not just from the top down; and (2) it is non-coercive, meaning that it is not based on authority, power, or dictatorial actions but is based on persuasive behaviors."[4]

The second approach, *congruence,* is articulated by Robert Clinton, who writes from the Christian perspective of a seminary professor. Clinton notes: "Leadership is a dynamic process in which a man or woman with God-given capacity influences a specific group of God's people toward His purposes for the group. This is contrary to the popular notion that a leader must have a formal position, a formal title, or formal training."[5] Clinton sets forth a process of maturing stages in a person's life that each serve to bring leadership gifts into focus, or congruence. "Leaders must develop a ministry philosophy that simultaneously honors biblical leadership values, embraces the challenges of the times in which they live, and fits their unique gifts and personal development if they expect to be productive over a whole lifetime."[6]

The third approach, *adaptive,* is articulated by Ronald Heifetz, a business leader turned professor at the Harvard School of Business. Heifetz and others who develop current theoretical approaches to leadership understanding emphasize leadership as a relational activity among people committed together to a certain mission. The idea and nature of activity is given meaning. Activity is an expression of purpose, and it is a contribution in the process of leadership that calls for learning and growth. Heifetz writes: "Rather than define leadership either as a position of authority in a social structure or as a personal set of characteristics, we may find it a great deal more useful to define leadership as an *activity.* This allows for leadership from multiple positions in a social structure."[7] This theory describes leadership in terms of adaptive work, which consists of the learning required to form or reform values, beliefs, or behavior in a given community. Heifetz explains: "In this study, leadership is oriented by the task of doing adaptive work. As we shall see, influence and authority are primary factors in doing adaptive work, but they also bring constraints. They are instruments and not ends. Tackling tough problems—problems that often require an evolution of values—is the end of leadership; getting that work done is its essence."[8]

Academicians are not the only people offering leadership understanding. Business professionals, religious leaders, and even celebrities produce a barrage of publications that are likely to reach for a definition of leadership. Their appeal lies in their simplicity. Granted, inspiring narratives and prescriptive analysis are instructive at some level. But dismissing serious inquiry by offering catch phrases such as "Leadership is influence" or "You will know you are a leader when people follow" is no substitute for reflection, critical thinking, and solid truth. Such attempts will not work for the Christian because they promote understandings that are individual-centered and fall short of exploring the relational and community aspects of biblical leadership.

Theology lies at the heart of Christian leadership. It follows, then, that a biblical theology is the starting point for defining leadership. Our work has explored a biblical theology of leadership and enabled us to offer the following definition:

Christian leadership is the transforming relational process of a serving community sharing a common God-inspired vision and purpose. Empowered by the Holy Spirit and submissive to the Spirit's promptings, people freely associate for the transformation of society, church, family, and the individual. The community listens for the leadings of God, and it depends on divine guidance for community direction. Serving as gifted by the Holy Spirit characterizes the leading and helping actions undertaken throughout the community.

CONCLUSION: AN APPLIED THEOLOGY OF LEADERSHIP

How then should Christians go about the practice of leadership? The following is an applied theology of leadership for the church. For the purposes of this study, applied theology may be distinguished from practical or pastoral theology. Practical or pastoral theology forms in theological reflection emerging out of practice. They are in a sense a hermeneutic of action, moving from practice to theory to practice.

What follows is a theology of leadership applied to the activity of serving in the communities in which we live. Such a theology contributes to the purpose of the book in that the ground for practice begins with the understandings gained from Scripture. It does not reject the contributions of other streams of theological reflection, and, to be whole, it must take into account the understandings experience provides. But the starting point and normative influence is Scripture. A more expansive theological approach is engaged, but with a biblical starting point guiding the application. While this applied theology is illustrated in the context of the church, its principles are applicable across a broad range of human activity.

1. *Leadership is a community process.* God is a God of community. Just as Jesus was incarnate within human life, leadership occurs within a community. Leaders are participants in the leadership

process and are one with the community they serve. They are not distinct from, or positioned over or ahead of, that community. Their future is imagined within that community. Leadership has the building up of that community as its aim: to establish people in a spiritual community (Col. 1:28–29) in which intellectual, physical, and pastoral formation occurs.

Thus leadership is not considered the activity of authority or position in the community but is every community member's opportunity. Roles in leadership are fluid. A community member may at once lead in one context and follow in another. Community leadership is less hierarchal, though order and accountability are present. Leadership engages the service of all within the community in ways appropriate to their gifts, the context, and the time.

Leadership is initiated within a community. For a nation, village, denomination, or a congregation, its leadership emerges from within. Thus pastors are far more effective when their enduring commitment to a church and community is genuine. To approach leadership for a community with little regard for the community, with the attitude that the community is only a step on the way to one's personal ambition, falls short of the highest commitment of leadership.

2. *Leadership is a relational process.* God is a relational God. Leadership is given not only with the intention of pursuing the community's shared purposes, but also with the intention of being people in relationship with one another. Christian leadership knows nothing of superiority and dominance. Instead, leadership is measured in commitment and service among and to friends. Jesus expressed this eloquently in describing the disciples as friends (John 15:12–17). In leadership, relationships trump task. We prioritize people, and we see the end of leadership as the betterment of life for those people we serve.

People are at the same time leaders and followers in this relationship. If leadership is defined as a relationship, then both leaders and followers are doing leadership. All active players in a relationship practice influence. In relational leadership a good leader is a good follower, and the roles are fluid. If one loses the ability to follow, one at the same time loses her or his ability to lead.

3. *Leadership development begins with the spiritual transformation of the person.* It means transforming the life to servanthood. Humility, commitment, and willingness to sacrifice come from a converted heart. The primary relationship we experience in leadership is with our Lord. He provides not only community, but also Himself in the presence of the Holy Spirit. We go with the Holy Spirit, guided by His counsel, taught through His providential instruction, empowered by His presence and gifts, filled by His intimate indwelling presence. To lead without the presence of the Holy Spirit denies the biblical foundation of leadership.

4. *Leadership acknowledges the sovereignty of God.* God is sovereign. In the process of leadership, we should hold initiative and responsibility gently and humbly. We are stewards, and we share our vocations with one another. We are not called to be the answer for others, to determine the right course for others; instead, we are called to work with others in submission to the One who is head of the church. Leadership, regardless of the position that it might involve as a means to accomplish its role of service, requires humility.

Recognizing the sovereignty of God requires trust in Him. God is able. He can care for the church. The future of the church is not dependent on us. He is the Creator and Sustainer of the church. None of us need believe that we are of such importance that we are irreplaceable in God's plan for the future. We are servants together, and we humbly seek to do His will, trusting in His divine providence.

5. *Servant leadership is the appropriate model for applied biblical leadership.* Servant leadership is demonstrated by people who serve first, and then lead as a way of contributing to their community. Servant leaders may or may not hold formal leadership positions. Servant leadership exhibits trust, collaboration, foresight, listening, and the ethical use of power. Jesus modeled servant leadership. He might have chosen not to go through the pain and suffering of the cross, but at Gethsemane, Jesus prayed, "Father if you are willing, take this cup from me, yet not My will, but Yours, be done" (Luke 22:42). Jesus modeled servant leadership throughout His sacrificial ministry.

Servant leadership means we also set aside personal gain, make sacrifices, and put the needs of others above the direction we may prefer for ourselves. There are people in any community who are highly career-minded, people whose main motivation is to get themselves in a position where they will gain prestige, power, or personal reward. This motivation is the complete opposite of what inspires servant leadership.

6. *Leadership implies shared vision.* It is seeing things whole, seeing the entirety, understanding how things hold together, and forming synthesis. Vision is a capacity to see things in their relationship to other things. Created by God, called into unity by God, the church is a community that visions together. Individuals do not receive vision in isolation and press it on the church. We seek God-given vision as community. Our visioning engages our shared spirit, gives meaning and purpose to our efforts, and allows members to rise above self-interest and maintain motivation.

7. *We collectively exercise the courage to act.* We are a community that acts together. God takes initiative, is creative, and moves in the direction of the vision for His kingdom. We respond to His calling by applying our spiritual gifts and our talents to the transformation of society and building up of God's church. Acting together focuses collective energy and gives life to a shared vision. The action process requires teamwork and the shared organizing of a community's assets and resources. Commitment to action demonstrates leadership.

8. *We act creatively.* God envisions His preferred future, and He entrusts His community with the calling to move toward that idealness. Leadership connects with the desire to create a better future, which requires a willingness to change. The Spirit transforms our inner life and the life of the community. People will change because they are committed to the will of God, seek His kingdom, seek a better future for the next generation, and because they love. Leadership chooses progress toward God's will rather than the security of human tradition.

9. *Leadership means sacrifice.* A call to faith is a call to service. Service, or ministry, involves leadership in some way. Leadership is about change, and that means risk. It follows we are called to take risks. We are called to follow where we would sometimes prefer not to go. Only when others rise above our own self-interests do we know leadership.

Joy flowers from the root of sacrifice. Leadership, submitted to God and oriented toward others, is service. What greater joy may we experience? What higher purpose? We rejoice in Him; we are servants and friends!

FOR REFLECTION

Personal:

1. What are the challenges, both personal and cultural, you face in actualizing biblical leadership?
2. How would you describe the transformation required in your life to make biblical leadership a reality?

Organizational:

1. How is your organization supporting and encouraging spiritual transformation in its leadership development?
2. What would it take for your organization to embrace biblical ideas about leadership?

ENDNOTES

1. Scripture quotations in this chapter are taken from the New King James Version.

2. The Christian Leadership Center (CLC), Seventh-day Adventist Theological Seminary at Andrews University (Berrien Springs, MI).

3. Joseph C. Rost, *Leadership for the Twenty-First Century* (Westport, CT: Praeger, 1993), 102.

4. Rost, *Leadership,* 107.

5. J. Robert Clinton, *The Making of a Leader* (Oklahoma City: Navpress, 1988), 114.

6. Clinton, *Making of a Leader,* 203.

7. Ronald A. Heifetz, *Leadership without Easy Answers* (Cambridge, MA: Belknap Press of Harvard University Press, 1994), 120; emphasis in original.

8. Heifetz, *Leadership,* 26.

About the Authors

C. Adelina Alexe is a PhD student in religion at Andrews University. Prior to beginning her doctoral studies, she taught in Palau and China, and she completed a MDiv at Andrews University and a hospital chaplaincy residency in Delaware. She has presented several papers at professional meetings and has published a chapter in *Beyond Blessings*. She has a special interest in theodicy and narrative theology and is currently writing a book on stewardship.

Skip Bell, DMin is professor of Christian leadership and director of the Doctor of Ministry program at the Seventh-day Adventist Theological Seminary at Andrews University. He has a DMin from Fuller Theological Seminary. He is the author of numerous academic and professional articles and of one book, *A Time to Serve*. His primary focus has been leadership and administration, serving the church in pastoral, administrative, and academic roles.

P. Richard Choi, PhD is professor of New Testament studies at the Seventh-day Adventist Theological Seminary at Andrews University. He has a PhD from Fuller Theological Seminary. He has published numerous scholarly and professional articles, including "The Intra-Jewish Dialogue in 4 Ezra 3:1–9:25" and "The Problem of Translating ἐν τῷ αὐτοῦ αἵματι in Romans 3:25a."

Jo Ann Davidson, PhD is the first woman to teach in the Theology Department of the Seventh-day Adventist Theological Seminary at Andrews University. She has a PhD from Trinity Evangelical Divinity School, and her published works include *Jonah: The Inside Story, Toward a Theology of Beauty: A Biblical Perspective,* as well as a chapter in *Women in Ministry* (edited by Nancy Vyhmeister).

Richard M. Davidson, PhD is professor of Old Testament interpretation at the Seventh-day Adventist Theological Seminary at Andrews University. He has a PhD in religion from Andrews University. He is the author of numerous articles in theological journals and other publications. Some of his many books include *Flame of Yahweh: Sexuality in the Old Testament, Hermeneutică biblică,* and *In the Footsteps of Joshua.*

Jacques B. Doukhan, PhD is professor of Hebrew and Old Testament exegesis, director of the Institute of Jewish-Christian Studies, and editor of *Shabbat Shalom* at the Seventh-day Adventist Theological Seminary at Andrews University. He has a doctorate in Hebrew from the University of Strasbourg and a ThD degree from Andrews University. He has published numerous articles, reviews, and books, including *The Mystery of Israel* and *Ecclesiastes: All Is Vanity.*

Barry Gane, PhD is a researcher at Avondale College of Higher Education. He has been a church pastor, high school teacher, youth director, church consultant, and professor at the Seventh-day Adventist Theological Seminary at Andrews University. He has a DMin from Fuller Theological Seminary and a PhD in leadership from Andrews University. He is the author of numerous articles and a number of books, including *Youth Ministry and the Transmission of Beliefs and Values, Building Youth Ministry: A Foundational Guide,* and *Loving Them Back, Leading Them Home.*

Roy E. Gane, PhD is professor of Hebrew Bible and ancient Near Eastern languages at the Seventh-day Adventist Theological Seminary at Andrews University. He holds a PhD from the University of California and has authored several books, including *Cult and Character: Purification Offerings, Day of Atonement, and Theodicy,* as well as numerous scholarly articles.

Robert M. Johnston, PhD is professor emeritus of New Testament and Christian origins at Andrews University. He has also held teaching positions in Korea and the Philippines. He has a PhD in biblical studies from the Hartford Seminary. He is the author of three books, including *The Spiritual Life: Experiencing Jesus Christ as Lord* and *The Necessity and Utility of Antinomies,* and he has contributed numerous articles and chapters to various books and journals.

R. Clifford Jones, DMin, PhD is the associate dean at the Seventh-day Adventist Theological Seminary at Andrews University. He has a PhD from Western Michigan University, Kalamazoo, Michigan, and a DMin from New York Theological Seminary. He has published many scholarly and professional articles and one book, *Preaching with Power: Black Preachers Share Secrets for Effective Preaching.*

Jiří Moskala, PhD is professor of Old Testament exegesis and theology and dean of the Seventh-day Adventist Theological Seminary at Andrews University. He has a PhD from Andrews University and a ThD from Protestant Theological Faculty of Charles University. He has written many theological articles, and his books include *Evangelium pro dnešek* (Gospel for Today); *Evangelium podle Mojžíše* (The Gospel According to Moses); and *The Laws of Clean and Unclean Animals in Leviticus 11: Their Nature, Theology, and Rationale;* among others.

Stanley E. Patterson, PhD is associate professor of Christian ministry at the Seventh-day Adventist Theological Seminary at Andrews University. He has a PhD in leadership from Andrews University. His primary focus has been leadership and administration, serving the educational needs of ministry professionals engaged in graduate studies. Among his publications are the articles titled "Leading without Fear," "Pastoral Ministry: Management or Spiritual Leadership," and "The Three Tasks of Leadership: Worldly Wisdom for Pastoral Leaders."

Jon Paulien, PhD is professor of religion and dean of the School of Religion at Loma Linda University. He has a PhD in religion from Andrews University. He has published more than twenty books and one hundred scholarly and professional articles. Significant among his publications are his published dissertation, *Decoding Revelation's Trumpets;* fourteen articles in the *Anchor Bible Dictionary;* and scholarly articles in *Journal of Biblical Literature, Biblical Research,* and other journals.

Paul B. Petersen, PhD is professor of religion and biblical languages at Andrews University. He has a PhD in religion from Andrews University. He is the author of several books published in Danish, including *Jesus: Tillid Værdig* (Jesus: Worthy of Confidence), *Daniels Bog: Et Studium* (The Book of Daniel: A Study), and *Så Stor en Frelse* (Such a Great Salvation).

Leslie N. Pollard, PhD, DMin serves as president of Oakwood University in Huntsville, Alabama. He earned a doctor of ministry degree in preaching and worship from Claremont School of Theology. He also completed a PhD in New Testament language and literature from the Seventh-day Adventist Theological Seminary at Andrews University. His publications include titles such as *Embracing Diversity: How to Understand and Reach People of All Cultures* and "Ministerial Evaluation: Pitfalls and Opportunities."

Bernard J. Sauvagnat, PhD is a Seventh-day Adventist pastor and vice president of the French Bible Society. He has a High Diploma in biblical studies from the Institut Catholique in Paris, France, as well as a PhD in religious science. He is the author of *La Bible en couleurs* (The Vivid Bible), a manual for the inductive study of the Bible used for correspondence studies in the Franco-Belgian Union of the Seventh-day Adventist Church.

Thomas R. Shepherd, PhD is professor of New Testament interpretation at the Seventh-day Adventist Theological Seminary at Andrews University. His doctorate in public health is from Loma Linda University School of Public Health, and his PhD in religion is from Andrews University. He has published a variety of articles on New Testament topics and one book, *Inside Out, Upside Down: Surprising Lessons from 1–2 Peter.*

Douglas Tilstra, PhD is associate professor at Southern Adventist University and director of the Outdoor Education program. He has a PhD degree from Capella University. Two of his most prominent publications include "Leadership Formation in Ministerial Education—Part 3: A Comparison of Transformational Effects in

Three Selected Programs" and "The Way It Could Be: Leadership Development in Ministerial Education."

Sigve K. Tonstad, PhD is associate professor of religion at Loma Linda University. For a number of years he worked as a minister and physician in Oslo, Norway. He has a PhD in New Testament studies from the University of St. Andrews. He has written several books and many articles in Norwegian. His books in English include *The Scandals of the Bible, Saving God's Reputation: The Theological Function of Pistis Iesou in the Cosmic Narratives of Revelation,* and *The Lost Meaning of the Seventh Day.*

James R. Wibberding, DMin is pastor of the Cloverdale Seventh-day Adventist Church in Boise, Idaho. He also serves as chaplain of the Idaho Senate and adjunct professor to the Andrews University Doctor of Ministry program. He has a DMin from Andrews University. His other pursuits include advocating for the equality of women in ministry and helping to transmit the Christian faith to the next generation. His publications include the titles *Learn to Preach before Next Weekend* and "Training Lay Pastors in Your District."

Scripture Index

Subject Index

Note: Page references followed by n refer to endnotes.

Posidonius of Apameia, 236
"position, one who has a prominent," 128
positional leadership
  Acts of the Apostles and, 333
  in Creation narrative, 33
  in different cultures, 185
  in General Epistles, 212–220
  in Gospels, 153–55, 162n18
  in Historical Books, 65–67
  Nehemiah's rejection of, 250, 254
  in New Testament, 130
  Paul's rejection of, 189
  spiritual leadership and, 268
Posner, Barry, 66, 76, 78, 80, 84n26,
    84n36, 248, 346
"power," 122n13, 127, 129
power
  in Acts of the Apostles, 164
  allure of, in NT, 363
  demonic, 127–28, 130–31, 158
  in General Epistles, 216, 218, 220
  of influence. *See* influence of leadership
  in Nehemiah, 250–52
  in Old Testament, 12
  in Pauline Epistles, 188, 207n11
  in Prophets (books), 116
power-oriented leadership
  in Gospels
    Jesus's rejection of, 155–58, 160, 285
    Peter's transformation from, 295–96,
      300
  in Historical Books, 74
  in Old Testament, 17–18, 268
  Paul's rejection of, 190–91
  in Prophets (books), 111
Powers, Richard Gid, 239
prayer, leadership and
  in Acts of the Apostles, 170, 175, 180
  Deborah and, 266
  in Historical Books, 80
  in Jesus's leadership, 287
  in Nehemiah, 246–47
  in New Testament, 137
preaching, 180. *See also* proclamation of
    message
prejudice, 328
pride, 62, 111–13, 117–18, 158. *See also*
  arrogance

"priest," 12, 26n6, 128
priesthood
  of all believers, 55, 345, 372–73
  from firstborn to Levites, 344–355
  as gift of service, 20
  ministry versus, 54–55
priests
  in New Testament, 144n67, 234–35
  in Old Testament
    examples of, 82n8, 269, 350
    Nehemiah (book), 249–250, 253
    Pentateuch, 55–56, 60–61
    Prophets (books), 106–7, 109
    as "servants of God," 16, 27n13
    "service" of, 27–28n15, 54–55
    Wisdom Literature, 88
  See also specific priests
"prince"
  in Old Testament, 12, 26n6
  in Prophets (books), 107–8, 122n4
  translated from OT, 186
proclamation of message
  by apostles/NT prophets, 132–33
  by Jesus Christ, 158
  by OT prophets, 103, 107
  by Paul, 187–88
promises of God, dependence on, 68
"prophet," 12, 132–33, 161n5
prophetic ministry of Barnabas, 325–26
prophets
  in Acts of the Apostles, 168, 177
  apostles versus, 133, 144n51
  authority of, 104–5
  in Historical Books, 76–77
  as leaders, 82n8, 106–7
  in Old/New Testaments, 131, 214–15
  relational service of, 117–18
  rulers/leaders during time of, 107–13
  as "servants of God," 16, 27n13
  women as, 261, 264–65, 269–270
  See also specific prophets
Prophets (books) leadership principles
  Messianic Servant model in, 22–24,
    113–17
  overview/summary of, 103–4, 119–120
  personal/organizational reflections on,
    121
prosperity, leadership and, 79